Atoms for Peace

Atoms for Peace
A Future after Fifty Years?

Edited by
Joseph F. Pilat

Foreword by
Mohammed ElBaradei

Woodrow Wilson Center Press
Washington, D.C.

The Johns Hopkins University Press
Baltimore

EDITORIAL OFFICES
Woodrow Wilson Center Press
One Woodrow Wilson Plaza
1300 Pennsylvania Avenue, N.W.
Washington, D.C. 20004-3027
Telephone 202-691-4029
www.wilsoncenter.org

ORDER FROM
The Johns Hopkins University Press
Hampden Station
P.O. Box 50370
Baltimore, Maryland 21211
Telephone: 1-800-537-5487
www.press.jhu.edu/books/

©2007 by the Woodrow Wilson International Center for Scholars
All rights reserved
Printed in the United States of America on acid-free paper ∞

2 4 6 8 9 7 5 3 1

Library of Congress Cataloging-in-Publication Data

Pilat, Joseph F.
  Atoms for peace : a future after fifty years? / edited by Joseph F. Pilat.
     p. cm.
  Includes index.
  ISBN-13: 978-0-8018-8560-0 (hardcover : alk. paper)
  ISBN-10: 0-8018-8560-4 (hardcover : alk. paper)
  ISBN-13: 978-0-8018-8561-7 (pbk. : alk. paper)
  ISBN-10: 0-8018-8561-2 (pbk. alk. : paper)
  1. Nuclear industry. 2. Nuclear nonproliferation. 3. Nuclear terrorism. I. Title.
  HD9698.A2P54   2006
  327.1'747—dc22
                                                                    2006029064

 Woodrow Wilson International Center for Scholars

The Woodrow Wilson International Center for Scholars, established by Congress in 1968 and headquartered in Washington, D.C., is a living national memorial to President Wilson. The Center's mission is to commemorate the ideals and concerns of Woodrow Wilson by providing a link between the worlds of ideas and policy, while fostering research, study, discussion, and collaboration among a broad spectrum of individuals concerned with policy and scholarship in national and international affairs. Supported by public and private funds, the Center is a nonpartisan institution. It establishes and maintains a neutral forum for free, open, and informed dialogue. Conclusions or opinions expressed in Center publications and programs are those of the authors and speakers and do not necessarily reflect the views of the Center staff, fellows, trustees, advisory groups, or any individuals or organizations that provide financial support to the Center.

The Center is the publisher of *The Wilson Quarterly* and home of Woodrow Wilson Center Press, *dialogue* radio and television, and the monthly newsletter "Centerpoint." For more information about the Center's activities and publications, please visit us on the web at www.wilsoncenter.org.

Lee H. Hamilton, President and Director

Board of Trustees
Joseph B. Gildenhorn, Chair
David A. Metzner, Vice Chair

Public Members: James H. Billington, Librarian of Congress; Bruce Cole, Chairman, National Endowment for the Humanities; Michael O. Leavitt, Secretary of Health and Human Services; Condoleezza Rice, Secretary of State; Lawrence M. Small, Secretary of the Smithsonian Institution; Margaret Spellings, Secretary of Education; Allen Weinstein, Archivist of the United States; Tami Longaberger, designated appointee of the President from within the federal government

Private Citizen Members: Robin Cook, Donald E. Garcia, Bruce S. Gelb, Sander R. Gerber, Charles L. Glazer, Susan Hutchison, Ignacio E. Sanchez

*To the memory of
Warren H. Donnelly
mentor and friend to so many of us*

Contents

Foreword   xiii
  Mohamed ElBaradei

Preface and Acknowledgments   xv

Acronyms and Abbreviations   xvii

1 Introduction   1
  Joseph F. Pilat

Part I   The Enduring Legacy

2 Atoms for Peace at Fifty   15
  James Schlesinger

3 Atoms for Peace and the International Atomic Energy Agency   21
  David B. Waller

4 The Atoms-for-Peace Model and the Problem of Proliferation   33
   Stephen G. Rademaker

5 Strengthening Nonproliferation: The Path Ahead   39
   Mitchell B. Reiss

6 Atoms for Peace and the Future of Eisenhower's Vision   52
   Ambassador Jayantha Dhanapala

7 Toward Universal Nonproliferation and Disarmament   63
   Ambassador Mohamed I. Shaker

Part II Addressing Nuclear Proliferation and Terrorism

8 Atoms for Peace and the "Rogue States"   71
   Robert S. Litwak

9 The Current Proliferation Predicament   83
   Ariel Levite

10 Nonproliferation Efforts in Northeast Asia   91
    Ambassador Choi Young-jin

11 Toward Cooperative Security: Prospects for Nonproliferation and Arms Control   95
    Feroz Khan

12 Toward an Integrative Approach to Preventing Nuclear Terrorism   104
    Ambassador Linton F. Brooks

13 Preventing Nuclear Terrorism   111
    Laura S.H. Holgate

14 Second-Tier Suppliers and Their Threat to the Nuclear Nonproliferation Regime   117
    Christopher F. Chyba

Part III The Promise of Nuclear Energy

15 Atoms for Peace: Realizing the Vision   131
    Senator Pete V. Domenici

16 The Paradox of Nuclear Power   137
    Atsuyuki Suzuki

17 Nuclear Energy: New Challenges for the Future *Jacques Bouchard*	146
18 A Nuclear Future unlike the Past *Per F. Peterson*	156
19 The Future of Nuclear Power *Richard K. Lester*	165

Part IV Looking to the Future

20 A New Bargain *Daniel B. Poneman*	177
21 Atoms for Peace: Facing Emerging Challenges *Lawrence Scheinman*	183
22 Atoms for Peace and the Nuclear Fuel Cycle: Is It Time for a Multilateral Approach? *Tariq Rauf and Fiona Simpson*	194
23 A Nuclear Renaissance and the Future of the Atoms-for-Peace Bargain *Joseph F. Pilat and Kory W. Budlong Sylvester*	206
24 A Fissile Material Cutoff Treaty *Thomas E. Shea*	219
25 Conclusions *Joseph F. Pilat*	229
Appendix 1. Atomic Power for Peace	239
Appendix 2. Statute of the International Atomic Energy Agency	247
Appendix 3. Treaty on the Non-Proliferation of Nuclear Weapons	268
Appendix 4. Proliferation Security Initiative: Statement of Interdiction Principles	275
Appendix 5. Towards a Safer World	279
Appendix 6. President Announces New Measures to Counter the Threat of WMD	285
Appendix 7. Global Threat Reduction Initiative	294

Appendix 8. Multilateral Approaches to the Nuclear Fuel Cycle: Expert Group Report Submitted to the Director General of the International Atomic Energy Agency—Executive Summary   301

Appendix 9. Global Nuclear Energy Partnership   316

Select Bibliography   335

Contributors   339

Index   349

Foreword
Mohamed ElBaradei

President Eisenhower's "Atoms for Peace" proposal, and the subsequent establishment of the International Atomic Energy Agency (IAEA) as a practical manifestation of that vision, came at a time when the horrifying images of Hiroshima and Nagasaki were still fresh—and when fears of a widespread rush to acquire nuclear weapons were well founded. Atoms for Peace was an explicit recognition of the dual nature of atomic energy, and stemmed from the belief in its potential beyond that of the destructive capability of nuclear weapons as a means by which to benefit humanity. The speech invoked a solemn commitment to the ideal that nuclear science and technology should be used exclusively for peaceful purposes.

A half-century later, the course of nuclear nonproliferation, and the regime built to ensure this objective, appear to be at a crossroad. New threats such as those posed by the possibility of nuclear and radiological terrorism and the emergence of illicit nuclear supply networks have prompted questions regarding how, and indeed whether, the Atoms-for-Peace mandate can remain relevant as it is. Put simply, can the expanded use of nuclear energy coexist with the goal of ensuring the nonproliferation of nuclear weapons?

I believe it can. I believe that Eisenhower's vision is as relevant today as it was in 1953. I believe this is demonstrated when we examine thoughtfully the evolving relationship between the goals of the Atoms for Peace vision, and how these goals can be best pursued in the face of today's security concerns and tomorrow's security challenges. The contributors to this book provide their examinations of these ideas. They bring a wealth of experience and knowledge that enables this book to offer a substantial contribution to the debate, at a time when the future of the nuclear nonproliferation regime is at the forefront of world attention.

It is, however, particularly appropriate for the IAEA—as Eisenhower's "brainchild"—to continue to dedicate itself to turning this vision into reality. Eisenhower clearly understood the complexity of the task, noting that "in this quest, we must not lack patience." Fifty-two years since these words were spoken the Atoms for Peace vision remains an ongoing project, with patience still a virtue and the continuing debate and dialogue a prerequisite for its success.

Preface and Acknowledgments

Five decades after U.S. President Dwight Eisenhower's Atoms-for-Peace proposal was presented to the United Nations, it is at the heart of wide-ranging debates over nuclear energy, proliferation, and terrorism. Atoms for Peace is critical to understanding and addressing the nuclear programs of Iran and North Korea, the future of the Treaty on the Nonproliferation of Nuclear Weapons, and other elements of the international nuclear nonproliferation regime, the prospects for nuclear terrorism by al-Qaeda or others, and the benefits and risks posed by a nuclear energy renaissance. However, the origins, development, and future of Atoms for Peace have frequently been misunderstood or mischaracterized, with significant implications for policy.

To foster an understanding of the impact of the Atoms-for-Peace proposal and subsequent policy on the current and future nuclear environment, the Los Alamos National Laboratory, in cooperation with the Woodrow Wilson International Center for Scholars and the College of William and Mary, held on December 8–9, 2003, a conference to mark the fiftieth anniversary of the historic speech. Through the sessions of the conference, a forum was provided for an exchange of information and opinion among eminent nuclear scientists, statesmen, and scholars on the legacy and future of Atoms for Peace. The conference and other papers collected here reveal a conscious attempt to grapple with such vital questions as the role of the United States in international nuclear affairs, the nature of appropriate controls over nuclear cooperation and trade, the scope for and limitations of international cooperation in nuclear energy and nonproliferation matters, and the prospect for multinational and international institutional measures to achieve these ends.

The organization of the conference on "Atoms for Peace: A Future After Fifty Years?" and the preparation of the papers collected here for publication involved the work of many dedicated people. It is impossible to thank all of the individuals and contributors without whose help and assistance the conference and this volume would not have been possible.

I am grateful for the support and encouragement of John Browne and G. Peter Nanos of Los Alamos National Laboratory. I also benefited from the advice of John Immele, Paul White, Bryan Fearey, and Kory Budlong Sylvester of the Laboratory. Mildred Lujan, Sharon Hurdle, and Leslie Weaver provided invaluable and unstinting support for the production of this volume.

Timothy Sullivan, P. Geoffrey Feis, and Mitchell Reiss of the College of William and Mary provided support for the conference.

From the Woodrow Wilson International Center for Scholars, Lee Hamilton and Robert Litwak offered the benefit of their expertise. Tonya Boyce helped with the preparation of the conference, and Joseph Brinley and Yamile Kahn were critical in the publication of this volume.

Joseph F. Pilat

Acronyms and Abbreviations

ABM	Antiballistic missile
AEC	Atomic Energy Commission
ABWR	Advanced Boiling Water Reactor
ADA	Atomic Development Authority
AP	Additional Protocol
BWC	Biological and Toxin Weapons Convention
CAS	Committee on Assurances of Supply
CD	Conference on Disarmament
CEA	Commissariat à l'énergie atomique (France)
CISAC	Center for International Security and Cooperation
CPPNM	Convention on the Physical Protection of Nuclear Material
CTBT	Comprehensive Nuclear Test Ban Treaty
CTR	Cooperative Threat Reduction
CWC	Chemical Weapons Convention
DOE	Department of Energy
DPRK	Democratic People's Republic of Korea

EIS	Environmental Impact Statement
EPR	European pressurized water reactor
ESBWR	Economic simplified boiling water reactor
EU	European Union
FMCT	Fissile Material Cut-off Treaty
G-8	Group of Eight
Gen IV	Generation IV
GIF	Generation IV International Forum
GNEP	Global Nuclear Energy Partnership
GTMHR	Gas turbine modular helium reactor
GTRI	Global Threat Reduction Initiative
GWe	Gigawatts electric
HEU	Highly enriched uranium
IAEA	International Atomic Energy Agency
ICJ	International Court of Justice
INFCE	International Nuclear Fuel Cycle Evaluation
INFCIRC	Information Circular
INPRO	International Project on Innovative Nuclear Reactors and Fuel Cycles
IPS	International Plutonium Storage
JCAE	Joint Committee on Atomic Energy
KEDO	Korean Peninsula Energy Development Organization
LANL	Los Alamos National Laboratory
LEU	Low-enriched uranium
LWR	Light water reactor
MINATOM	Ministry of Atomic Energy
MIT	Massachusetts Institute of Technology
MNA	Multilateral nuclear approach
MOX	Mixed oxide
MPC&A	Material protection, control, and accounting
MWe	Megawatts elecric
NAM	Non-Aligned Movement
NASA	National Aeronautics and Space Administration
NGCC	Natural gas turbine combined cycle
NGNP	Next generation nuclear plant
NNSA	National Nuclear Security Administration
NPR	Nuclear Posture Review
NPT	Treaty on the Nonproliferation of Nuclear Weapons, or the Nuclear Nonproliferation Treaty

NRC	Nuclear Regulatory Commission
NSC	National Security Council
NSG	Nuclear Suppliers Group
NTI	Nuclear Threat Initiative
OPCW	Organization for Prohibition of Chemical Weapons
PSI	Proliferation Security Initiative
PTBT	Partial Test Ban Treaty
RFCC	Regional Nuclear Fuel Cycle Centers
SIT	Sterile Insect Technique
UNCPICPUNE	United Nations Conference for the Promotion of International Cooperation in the Peaceful Uses of Nuclear Energy
UNGA	United Nations General Assembly
UNSC	United Nations Security Council
WMD	Weapons of mass destruction
WWICS	Woodrow Wilson International Center for Scholars

Atoms for Peace

1

Introduction

Joseph F. Pilat

On December 8, 1953, President Dwight D. Eisenhower, in a historic speech to the United Nations General Assembly, announced an "Atoms-for-Peace proposal" that would redefine the principles of nuclear policy in the early years of the nuclear age. The president sought to expedite the development of the peaceful uses of nuclear energy. By offering the benefits of peaceful nuclear technology to those states that renounced nuclear weapons, he also sought to promote nonproliferation. The proposal was an arms control measure as well, as it foresaw the United States and other nuclear-weapon states providing excess nuclear material to an international authority that would use it for peaceful rather than military purposes.

President Eisenhower enunciated his bold proposal as follows:

> The governments principally involved, to the extent permitted by elementary prudence, to begin now and continue to make joint contributions from their stockpiles of normal uranium and fissionable materials

to an International Atomic Energy Agency. We would expect that such an agency would be set up under the aegis of the United Nations . . .

The United States is prepared to undertake these explorations in good faith. Any partner of the United States acting in the same good faith will find the United States a not unreasonable or ungenerous associate.

Undoubtedly, initial and early contributions to this plan would be small in quantity. However, the proposal has the great virtue that it can be undertaken without the irritations and mutual suspicions incident to any attempt to set up a completely acceptable system of worldwide inspection and control.

The Atomic Energy Agency could be made responsible for the impounding, storage and protection of the contributed fissionable and other materials. The ingenuity of our scientists will provide special safe conditions under which such a bank of fissionable material can be made essentially immune to surprise seizure.

The more important responsibility of this Atomic Energy Agency would be to devise methods whereby this fissionable material would be allocated to serve the peaceful pursuits of mankind. . . . A special purpose would be to provide abundant electrical energy in the power-starved areas of the world. Thus the contributing powers would be dedicating some of their strength to serve the needs rather than the fears of mankind.

The United States would be more than willing—it would be proud to take up with others principally involved the development of plans whereby such peaceful use of atomic energy would be expedited.[1]

President Eisenhower's Atoms-for-Peace proposal defines the contours of the nuclear landscape more than fifty years after it was developed and delivered to the United Nations in an atmosphere of grave danger and even greater hopes.[2] This vision of a regulated nuclear supply was less dramatic than the foundations of the failed Baruch Plan, but Eisenhower's proposal electrified the world. As a policy promoting wider nuclear cooperation under international verification of peaceful uses, Atoms for Peace marked the end of the postwar U.S. nuclear policy of secrecy and denial enshrined

---

1. "Atomic Power for Peace," an address by Dwight D. Eisenhower, president of the United States, before the General Assembly of the United Nations, December 8, 1953.

2. For a fuller discussion of the first three decades of Atoms for Peace, from which the following benefited, see Joseph F. Pilat, Robert E. Pendley, and Charles K. Ebinger, eds. *Atoms for Peace: An Analysis after Thirty Years* (Boulder, Colo.: Westview, 1985).

in the Atomic Energy Act of 1946, and provided the framework for future U.S. peaceful nuclear trade, cooperation and nonproliferation policies. Despite this propitious beginning, Atoms for Peace has been surrounded by controversy for five decades.

Since the mid-1950s, debate has raged around questions of the origins and development of the proposal. Was Atoms for Peace a propaganda ploy in the Cold War? Was Eisenhower misled by nuclear advocates, notably the scientists, the U.S. Atomic Energy Agency (AEC), and the congressional Joint Committee on Atomic Energy (JCAE), into supporting a misconceived and ill-timed effort to sell American nuclear material, equipment, and technology abroad? In embarking upon a new approach to U.S. nuclear policy, did the president and his advisors underemphasize the proliferation danger? Were the original objectives of Atoms for Peace, and in particular, the purpose of the international agency it envisioned, lost amid attempts to develop a practical program?

Over the years, these questions have been considered in the United States and abroad, in both governmental and academic fora. Nevertheless, after fifty years of debate, we do not yet have definitive, undisputed answers. Whether because the complexity of the issues or the controversies surrounding them left critical information unknown, or because Atoms for Peace has been enshrouded in myth, misunderstanding, and misinterpretation, the historical legacy of Atoms for Peace frequently bears little relation to the original proposal. But, as suggested, Atoms for Peace has been critical, and at times central, to thinking about nuclear issues for half a century.

In the nonproliferation realm, Atoms for Peace laid the framework for the International Atomic Energy Agency (IAEA) and the Treaty on the Nonproliferation of Nuclear Weapons (NPT)—the cornerstones of the international nuclear nonproliferation regime. The IAEA was created in 1958, and reflected in its statute the twin Atoms-for-Peace objectives of the prevention of proliferation and the promotion of the peaceful uses of atomic energy. The Agency was in all ways the institutional realization of the Atoms-for-Peace vision. Since its inception, it has been a critical advocate of nuclear nonproliferation and nuclear energy. And, its safeguards system pioneered on-site inspections.

When the NPT was concluded in 1968 and entered force into 1970, the IAEA became the verification agency for the treaty. However, IAEA safeguards were not designed to verify fully the no-weapon pledges of the treaty, but only the misuse of peaceful activities, especially diversion of declared materials to proscribed military uses. This limitation was desired by the parties at the time, and was largely not seen to be a problem until the early 1990s, when Iraqi and North Korean violations of the treaty highlighted the shortfalls of these inspections.

Noncompliance with safeguards since that time has also raised questions about the treaty itself. Embodying at its heart the Atoms-for-Peace bargain—that is, access to peaceful applications of atomic energy in exchange for verified pledges to forego proscribed military uses of the atom—the fate of the NPT regime and Atoms for Peace are inexorably intertwined. Accordingly, the regime is under serious pressure today, as is the treaty itself. In addition to the lack of consensus about dealing with noncompliance, structural problems with the treaty have been identified. The so-called Article IV "loophole" allows a state, in principle, to obtain the entire fuel cycle while in full compliance with the treaty. This opens up the possibility of using the treaty to develop a virtual weapon capability and then withdrawing from the treaty—all without violating its terms. Today, primarily because of concerns about the Iranian program, this prospect, which derives directly from Atoms for Peace, is seen as a critical problem for the treaty and the regime.

There are other problems with the regime, including three nuclear powers—India, Israel, and Pakistan—that have refused to join the NPT and cannot be expected to do so in the foreseeable future. These non-NPT states have been an issue for years. And although nuclear proliferation remains a serious threat, it is not spreading to the extent believed at the time of the Atoms-for-Peace proposal. The fear today is that if current problems are not dealt with, proliferation could spiral out of control as states seek nuclear weapons to protect themselves from newly armed nuclear neighbors.

Proposals to fix all of these problems by reforming the treaty and strengthening the regime are currently on the table. They include proposals for restricting access to sensitive nuclear technologies and for multinational/multilateral ownership of sensitive nuclear activities. To address vexing tensions with India, the United States has broken with a decades-old policy, and is pursuing a controversial plan to open cooperation on civilian nuclear arena in exchange for India's fuller integration into the regime.

The specter of nuclear terrorism was not contemplated in the proposal. But, the threat seems a greater concern today than at any time in the past due to the changing face of terrorism, the spread of technology relevant to nuclear-weapon production, and potential access to nuclear materials and weapons through transnational black market networks or supportive states, among other factors. This new reality raises questions about the relation of this emerging concern to Atoms-for-Peace activities and institutions. Atoms for Peace was put forward in a world in which states were the only major actors. That is no longer the case today, and the rising threat of nuclear terrorism cannot fully be addressed by Atoms-for-Peace institutions, although they are attempting to respond to this threat and one should not dismiss the beneficial supporting role that they can play in combating nuclear terrorism.

As for arms control, in its original expression, Eisenhower's Atoms-for-Peace proposal sought to reverse the trend toward ever-larger atomic military arsenals by promoting peaceful uses of atomic power. The president reasoned that nuclear material committed to peaceful uses would not be available for weapons, and believed that because weapon materials were so difficult to produce this would result in reductions in nuclear arms. With this end in mind, he called for the uranium producers and nuclear-weapon states to contribute fissile material to an international pool. To be administered by an international authority under the aegis of the United Nations, this pool would be used in the general interest—primarily to provide electrical power to regions of the world starved for energy.

The original proposal was modest in this regard. It did not require a global system of control and inspection. Nor did it demand extensive contributions of nuclear materials initially. In any event, it was not implemented in earnest and the premise on which it was based was overstated. Nuclear material production was not the chokepoint envisaged in the proposal, although it has been and remains a point of leverage in terms of stemming proliferation.

Arms control was pursued during the Cold War but saw little substantive progress until that great ideological conflict was nearing its end. Today, with the Cold War behind us, nuclear arms are being dramatically reduced. But, the very nature of nuclear arms control seems to be changing as well. The formal treaties and stringent verification regimes of the past are out of favor, and new approaches to realize old arms control goals are being put forward, especially in the United States. There are large questions about how arms control will develop in the future, but the issue of materials removed from weapon programs has, over the last decade, been a focus of attention.

Concerning nuclear power, reflecting the Atoms-for-Peace philosophy, the Atomic Energy Act of 1954 sought to provide an instrument for fostering the economic benefits of nuclear power while managing nuclear materials. It opened the prospect of extensive nuclear trade and cooperation through a network of bilateral agreements for nuclear cooperation that bound other states to certain nonproliferation commitments. In essence, the Atomic Energy Act of 1954 was founded on the idea of influence (or leverage) through responsible international cooperation under verification of peaceful uses (or safeguards).

For two decades, robust nuclear energy development in the United States and abroad occurred under the aegis of Atoms for Peace. Atoms for Peace provided the basis for a nuclear energy and nonproliferation policy in the United States that enjoyed broad, bipartisan support. Furthermore, during this period the United States dominated the international nuclear market and was the undisputed leader in nuclear technologies. Through the influence obtained by its nuclear mastery, the United States was instrumental in extending the sway of Atoms for Peace.

Fifty years after this historic speech, and undoubtedly in large part because of its influence, nuclear energy has become a significant element in the global generation of electricity. Yet the promise of energy too cheap to meter, as well as of atomic automobiles and airplanes, demonstrate the great, and wholly unrealistic, expectations surrounding the early years of civilian nuclear energy. The reality has been disappointing in comparison, although some believe we are now on the verge of a "nuclear renaissance" or a "second coming."

All of these developments remind us that it is extremely difficult, if not ultimately impossible, to foster the development of peaceful uses of nuclear energy while entirely preventing the risks of the further spread of nuclear weapons and nuclear terrorism from increasing. Atoms for Peace has been praised or pilloried, or both, as the cause of the situation that we now confront in these areas. And, as suggested, it has been highly controversial in the nuclear political arena. Assessments of Atoms for Peace are germane to, and could influence, present and future nuclear energy and nonproliferation policy debates.

These assessments have more than historical interest. Current nonproliferation policies continue to rely heavily on fuel cycle inducements and peaceful nuclear technology remains relevant today as a nonproliferation bargaining chip. The U.S. Global Nuclear Energy Partnership (GNEP) announced in 2006 seeks to further nuclear power while ensuring that the risks of proliferation and terrorism do not increase. In this respect, GNEP represents a modern attempt to extend the benefits of nuclear-generated electricity to those who would refrain from enrichment and reprocessing activities.

Ultimately, assessments of Atoms for Peace and associated policy recommendations vary with the political perspectives and agendas, as well as the historical sensibilities of the analysts. At one extreme are those who view Atoms for Peace as an unequivocal failure; at the other, it is seen as a resounding success.

Those who regard Atoms for Peace essentially as a failure tend to focus on the implementation of the Atoms-for-Peace idea as elaborated in President Eisenhower's original proposal. They ignore, or consider less significant, those elements of the Atoms-for-Peace policy that were inspired by the president's address to the United Nations, but only implemented during the course of the next two decades.

Those who are more supportive of the proposal have to deal with addressing the mounting pressures on the NPT regime, including IAEA safeguards. Of particular importance are the new proliferation threats and reality of states—as epitomized by Iran—misusing the Atoms-for-Peace bargain to move toward a virtual weapon capability as well as the growing concern about nuclear terrorism.

As the nuclear debate was being waged amid hopes for a dramatic rise in nuclear power globally, the fiftieth anniversary of the historic Atoms-for-Peace speech occurred. This looked to be an appropriate time to reassess the legacy of the proposal and the regime elements it underlies, and to look ahead to assess the relevance of Atoms for Peace for dealing with nuclear energy, nonproliferation, arms control, and terrorism issues over the next fifty years.

To undertake this assessment of Atoms for Peace's past and future, a two-day conference was convened at the Woodrow Wilson Center for International Scholars on December 8–9, 2003. This meeting, co-hosted by the Los Alamos National Laboratory, the Woodrow Wilson Center, and the College of William and Mary, sought to provide a balanced assessment of the future bounded in an analysis and appreciation of the past. Revised and updated conference papers, as well as some additional work, are collected in this volume.

James Schlesinger offers a sweeping assessment of the legacy and future of Atoms for Peace. He argues that the nonproliferation regime created under its auspices was successful during the Cold War era. However, since then, it has been eroded by absence of Cold War discipline and the emergence of new issues, including non-state actors. If we are to address the new threats, he argues, new instruments will be required. As for nuclear energy, Schlesinger argues that it has never offered what was promised in the 1950s. Nuclear energy has spread globally to the extent one might have expected, he argues, but significant growth depends on licensing and other reforms.

The papers by David B. Waller, Stephen G. Rademaker, Mitchell B. Reiss, Ambassador Jayantha Dhanapala, and Ambassador Mohamed Ibrahim Shaker also offer broad perspectives on the legacy of Atoms for Peace, including the IAEA and the NPT. Waller offers a view of the IAEA, the institution called for in the Atoms-for-Peace speech, and on its efforts to meet unprecedented nuclear challenges in the last two decades in particular. He argues that the IAEA is meeting the evolving challenges of its dual mandate of promoting nuclear power and preventing proliferation, as well as responding to new challenges of nuclear safety in the aftermath of Chernobyl and of nuclear terrorism, the dangers of which were highlighted by 9/11. Rademaker questions whether the Atoms-for-Peace idea of forgoing military for peaceful uses of nuclear energy remains relevant in today's world. He argued that it has been abused in the cases of Iran and North Korea, and that the NPT has structural problems that open it to misuse by others. He concludes that the NPT, based on the Atoms-for-Peace bargain, was challenged today but has contributed significantly to nonproliferation in the past and can do so in the future if parties recommit themselves to dealing with noncompliance. Reiss notes that the nonproliferation regime based on Atoms for Peace has served us well but is showing its age. The NPT and IAEA need to be strengthened, he argues, and augmented by new initiatives such as the Global Threat Reduction Initiative and Proliferation Security Initiative, if they are to meet the proliferation challenges of today and tomorrow.

Ambassador Shaker opines on the IAEA and the NPT, the principal institutional creations of the Atoms-for-Peace idea, outlining outstanding challenges and issues as well as opportunities. He warns that tightening nuclear export controls too greatly would be counterproductive. But, he argues that, with the political will, the international community can recommit to the vision of Atoms for Peace. He believes there is a real possibility to strengthen the IAEA and to expand its role in the area of disarmament. Ambassador Dhanapala notes that the multilateral disarmament agenda, including conclusion of a fissile material cut-off treaty (FMCT) and entry into force of the Comprehensive Test Ban Treaty (CTBT), is consistent not only with the NPT but also with the Atoms-for-Peace vision, although this agenda is in his view being blocked by the existing nuclear-weapon states. He called on states and nongovernmental organizations to develop the approaches needed to break this impasse.

Robert S. Litwak, Ariel Levite, Ambassador Choi Young-jin, and Brigadier General (Ret.) Feroz Khan focus on nonproliferation, including the need to address the difficult cases. Litwak suggests that the Atoms-for-Peace bargain has not been respected by the so-called "rogue states," notably Iran and North Korea, although they have used the bargain rhetorically to defend their pursuit of nuclear capabilities. He addresses efforts to deal with the rogue states and, in particular, the issue of whether regime change was an appropriate rogue state strategy. He argues that it results in calculated ambiguity on the part of these states while they accelerate their programs. He notes the successful effort to disarm Libya and the uncertain prospects of the North Korean agreement. He argues that regime assurance was key to any long-term solutions, as in Libya, but questions whether this could be achieved with Iran and North Korea.

Levite explores the current proliferation predicament, exemplified by threats posed by Iran and Libya, and argued that the problems with the nonproliferation regime, and the logic and legacy of Atoms for Peace, are in part responsible for this troubling situation. He held that the regime, by itself, cannot provide an answer to the current proliferation threat and advocated greater cooperative action among those who are committed to nonproliferation.

Ambassador Choi takes a philosophical look at the proliferation problem in Northeast Asia today. In a world where the proliferation danger is complicated by the rising terrorist threat, he asks whether we will choose "Atoms for Peace" or "nuclear proliferation." If we are to avoid disaster, in his view, the choice is clear in Northeast Asia and across the globe.

General Khan reflects on the legacy of Atoms for Peace in today's world, with special attention to South Asia. Arguing that the proposal has been abused for military purposes, and that current proliferation could lead to arms races and possibly war, he proposes a cooperative security framework designed to reduce nuclear dangers through, inter alia, use of best practices in nuclear safety and security.

Ambassador Linton F. Brooks, Laura S.H. Holgate, and Christopher Chyba assess issues that were not anticipated at the time of the Atoms-for-Peace proposal, namely, nuclear terrorism and second-tier suppliers. Ambassador Brooks argues that after the terrorist attacks on September 11,

2001, preventing nuclear terrorism has become central to ensuring U.S. and international security. He addresses efforts over the last four years to deal with nuclear terrorism, and argues that they cannot be separated from traditional nonproliferation efforts. As a consequence, the regime fashioned on Atoms-for-Peace principles is an important element of an integrative approach for dealing with a problem not contemplated when the speech was given or when key elements of the regime were created. Building on existing nonproliferation regime, and on important new U.S. and international initiatives, including the amendment of the Convention on the Physical Protection of Nuclear Material, he advocates a concerted, action-oriented approach to combating terrorism.

In similar fashion, Holgate notes that Atoms for Peace did not envisage the problems of the collapse of a nuclear power nor the rise of non-state actors committed to, and capable of, undertaking devastating acts of nuclear terrorism. She argues that the institutions created under Atoms-for-Peace auspices have played a role, but the urgency and levels of the responses by the United States and the world are not adequate. She puts forward a program for addressing the threat, which depends on moving urgently to secure nuclear weapons and materials globally.

Chyba delineates the challenges to the nuclear nonproliferation regime, including the NPT, posed by second-tier proliferation. He argues that we need to avoid the world of biotechnological proliferation—where we must cope with, and no longer shape, the reality. Warning that we may still encounter a nuclear future like the biological, he advocates strengthening supply-side measures while increasing attention to demand-side measures, from positive security assurances to deterrence to energy assistance.

Senator Pete Domenici, Atsuyuki Suzuki, Jacques Bouchard, Per F. Peterson, and Richard K. Lester address nuclear energy issues and prospects. Senator Domenici notes that President Eisenhower's vision remains unrealized today. He explains how the recently passed U.S. energy legislation contained provisions designed to spur nuclear energy development in the United States. He also noted that it was important to look beyond the United States and to work with the IAEA and other states to provide assistance in the peaceful uses of nuclear energy to developing states.

Suzuki looks at the paradoxes of nuclear power using Joseph Nye's concept of "soft power." Suzuki argues that the future of peaceful nuclear power for electricity generation depends fundamentally on deemphasizing its military origins and legacy and focusing on its soft power dimension, including its role in ensuring energy security, in order to attain public acceptance. Bouchard points to recent trends in nuclear power. He concludes that nuclear power is economically competitive with other sources of electricity and that it is safe and viable. He argues that a new generation of secure, proliferation-resistant reactors must rapidly be brought into operation as a high priority. Finally, he argues that a closed fuel cycle is the only option that meets the conditions of sustainable nuclear development.

Peterson looks at recent developments in the nuclear area, which have created new possibilities for the dramatic growth of nuclear-energy production. From improved licensing to advances in design and construction, there are advances that should make nuclear power cheaper, safer, and more efficient, he argues.

Lester recounts the conclusions of the 2003 seminal Massachusetts Institute of Technology study addressing the future prospects for nuclear energy. He argues that nuclear energy is not currently competitive with other methods of electricity generation, but that with changes in design and construction, along with a carbon tax or some other mechanism to capture the environment costs of fossil-fuel generated electricity, it could be. He advocates a once-through rather than a closed fuel cycle.

Daniel B. Poneman, Lawrence Scheinman, Tariq Rauf and Fiona Simpson, Joseph F. Pilat and Kory W. Budlong Sylvester, and Thomas E. Shea look to future problems and possible initiatives in reconciling the civil and the military atom. Poneman examines the history of Atoms for Peace and assesses that it has contributed positively to nuclear energy and nonproliferation and remains worthy. He argues, however, that to meet new challenges, a new bargain is necessary, one that harnesses the economic power of nuclear energy to achieve economic and security benefits in a "megatons to megawatts" deal modeled on the U.S.–Russian highly enriched uranium agreement. He holds that such a deal could be tested in Iran and North Korea.

Scheinman looked at the challenges confronting the world due to the Janus-faced nature of nuclear technology, challenges that were the inspiration of the visionary Atoms-for-Peace proposal, but which have become more difficult and complex in the last half-century. He argued that the IAEA, created as a result of Atoms for Peace, should remain central to nonproliferation efforts, but that it would require greater attention if it is to be effective in this endeavor, including increased resources, political support, and the like.

Rauf and Simpson argue that the recently renewed interest in multilateral approaches to the nuclear fuel cycle, especially the proposal by

IAEA Director General Mohamed ElBaradei, reflects the spirit of the original Atoms-for-Peace proposal. Such approaches, they argue, have a long history, but are needed today in response to new threats to the nonproliferation regime. Moreover, these approaches have a greater promise of success, they argue, than attempts to deny nuclear fuel-cycle technology to states.

Pilat and Budlong Sylvester explore the "proliferation resistance" debate and argue that misconceptions about nuclear energy dating to the Acheson–Lilienthal plan, and inherited by Atoms for Peace, pose challenges for the nonproliferation regime today and tomorrow. They note that these challenges to the regime, including structural problems like the Article IV "loophole" and the erosion of supplier constraints, are now receiving attention, and a series of initiatives have been proposed to address them. Pilat and Budlong Sylvester argue that the dramatic growth in nuclear power—a "nuclear renaissance—could worsen all existing regime problems. However, they suggest that an expansion of nuclear power could raise the stakes in a strong regime for key states and the international community. In the end, they argue, whatever the prospects for such a renaissance, states must commit to reforming the regime.

Shea advocates a fissile material cut-off treaty as a future step that would build on the Atoms-for-Peace concept and further its goals of nonproliferation and arms control and disarmament, as well as contribute to addressing the growing threat of nuclear terrorism. He outlines the scope and specific features of a possible FMCT.

In their totality, the papers collected here provide a diverse, rich, and comprehensive assessment of the current and future issues arising from the landmark Atoms-for-Peace proposal a half-century ago—one that defines current debates on nuclear energy and nonproliferation, and is germane to those involving nuclear arms control and disarmament as well as nuclear terrorism. If there is one overarching message embodied in all the papers, it is that Atoms for Peace and the regime that it engendered should not be replaced, but ways to ensure it will provide a basis for nuclear policy in the next fifty years should be sought.

Part I

The Enduring Legacy

2

Atoms for Peace at Fifty

James Schlesinger

Five decades ago, President Dwight Eisenhower delivered an address to the United Nations, which was immediately dubbed by the press "Atoms for Peace." To address the consequences of that speech, it is, I think, necessary to recall the psychological state of that time. It was a period of increasing dread. Hiroshima! Nagasaki! The first edition of *The Effects of Nuclear Weapons* had just been published—with all of the apprehension which that meticulous study generated.

In 1949, the Soviet Union had conducted, far earlier than expected, its first atomic test. In 1952, well before Ike's speech, Britain had its first test. Just a month after Britain's test, our first hydrogen bomb test vaporized the island on which it was tested. Within a year, the Soviet Union announced that it too had tested a hydrogen bomb. It appeared that the Cold War rivals were prepared to race each other in producing even more destructive weapons.

Yet, it was also a time of high expectations, now clearly exaggerated expectations, regarding the promised benefits of the peaceful atom. Those expectations were driven in part by a sense of guilt, associated with the previous use to which the atom had been placed. It was after all, the "Atomic Age"—later to be superseded by the "Age of Aquarius," the "Space Age," the "Computer Age," the "Information Age," and other ages.

Ike's principal goal had been to help quiet the anxieties that had developed in that period. Winston Churchill himself, reading the speech the day before Eisenhower delivered it at the United Nations, said that it would resound through "an anxious world" and might serve to channel efforts away from the creation of nuclear-weapon capabilities into constructive purposes. As Ike put it in the speech, "to find the way by which the miraculous inventiveness of man shall not be dedicated to his death, but consecrated to his life."[1]

What did that speech accomplish? First and foremost, it gave birth to the International Atomic Energy Agency (IAEA). Its responsibilities, later to be reinforced by the Nonproliferation Treaty, have expanded over the decades. The original notion that the United States and the Soviet Union together contribute nuclear materials to this international body for international use was something of a gesture and never came to fruition. What it did was to create an institution to carry the enterprise of the peaceful atom forward, to institutionalize both the goals and the process. It accepted as a reality that this was a world of sovereign nations and that others would have to be persuaded to join in the common enterprise. The "bargain" offered was to provide limited information on nuclear technology to non-weapon states, to permit them to participate in the knowledge and the benefits of the peaceful atom—but to stay away from nuclear weapons. Of course, the bargain represented a compromise. Like all compromises, it invited critics—including my colleagues at the RAND Corporation led by the late Albert Wohlstetter, who argued that stripped of its rhetoric, it would simply provide the knowledge to spread nuclear weapons.

Here is the upshot: Whether through foresight or lack of outside pressure, it worked for an extended period. Recall the pessimism of the 1950s and 1960s—President Kennedy who was "haunted by the feeling" that by 1975 there might be fifteen or twenty nuclear powers; Leo Szilard who rhetorically inquired, "What happens when Swaziland gets the bomb?"; and C.P. Snow who prophesized that within a decade, some of those weapons would

1. "Atomic Power for Peace," an address by Dwight D. Eisenhower, President of the United States, before the General Assembly of the United Nations, December 8, 1953.

be used. On the nonproliferation front, we have done far better than we anticipated at that time.

One of Ike's explicit goals was to create a degree of trust between the United States and the Soviet Union so that they would collaborate on these efforts to channel activities into peaceful pursuits. That has been a notable success even in the face of the antagonisms of the Cold War—in the face of the major power confrontation. The Soviet Union and the United States have generally collaborated in the IAEA, and they have acted to impose restraints on their allies and on others in seeking nuclear capabilities.

With the end of the Cold War and the end of the Cold War's discipline, however, that restraint has been breaking down. Knowledge of the fuel cycle has spread, and increasingly, nations have been tempted by and have sought nuclear-weapon capabilities. Some would blame the "bargain" on which the IAEA was founded but we must bear in mind that the 1953 proposals were not intended to last forever. As President Eisenhower's granddaughter, Susan Eisenhower, has observed, Atoms for Peace was "a vision not a blueprint"—and certainly not for all time. In the changed circumstances of today, we shall need more effectively to enforce existing safeguards—and to enhance those safeguards. Moreover, the presupposition that sovereign nations are free to do whatever they wish will have to be reexamined and will have to be modified. If need be, they will have to be modified through direct pressure (preferably, but not necessarily, multilateral) to bring deviant nations back into line.

What we have belatedly discovered is that the existing rules have provided a framework for the advancement of nuclear weapons under the guise of a peaceful program. Then, like North Korea, a nation can throw off the restraints by violation of or withdrawal from the Nonproliferation Treaty. It might be noted that, rather than through the long-feared power reactor route, the preferred route today appears to be through uranium enrichment. We have seen the rapid diffusion of the centrifuge to so-called rogue nations as the instrument for the acquisition of fissile material.

President Eisenhower hoped to hasten the day when fear of the atom would begin to disappear from the minds of people. But he could not have anticipated the threat of terrorism by non-state as well as state actors and the prospect that nuclear devices might reach the hands of those terrorists.

Supreme pragmatist that he was, Ike would have sought to strengthen institutions and to formulate policies that would prevent such nuclear spread through commerce or through theft.

Now let us turn to the other side of the bargain—to the enticement, the expected benefits of the peaceful atom, and most importantly, to nuclear power. Here we find a failure to live up to the high expectations of the middle 1950s. With the 1954 amendments to the Atomic Energy Act, nuclear power was launched in this country. That effort enjoyed enthusiastic support especially from the Congress and from the Joint Committee on Atomic Energy.

In retrospect, one can say we proceeded too fast. Some thirty years ago, when I was the chairman of the Atomic Energy Commission, I observed that it was as if the entire history of aviation, from Kitty Hawk to the 747, had been compressed into little more than a decade. Power reactors were and are a demanding technology. They were handed off, in a sense, all too casually to those not fully prepared to take care of them.

That reflected the presuppositions of the American free enterprise system. In this nation of countless utilities, it was assumed that all should have an equal opportunity under the modified Atomic Energy Act. The land rush was on! A small municipal utility in Piqua, Ohio, was an early winner—not disassociated from the fact that the ranking member of the Joint Committee just happened to hail from Piqua, Ohio. The utilities of all sizes crowded forward to get into the game. Nuclear power appeared to some as just another way of generating steam. All too frequently, reactor construction and operation were handed off to those who had run coal-fired plants. We wound up with all too many first-of-a-kind, one-of-a-kind, nuclear plants with a host of different operators. It was a formula for trouble.

It was also a formula for trouble in another respect. We had created special opportunities for obstruction. The nature of Anglo-Saxon law, in which statutory law expands through accretion and through case law, was part of the problem. First, the Atomic Energy Act itself, underscoring the concern for public safety, required public hearings before any facility could be licensed. Moreover, the practice came about to allow such hearings both for a construction license and for an operating license. Not surprisingly, those hearings became increasingly adversarial. How all of this would work out under the Administrative Procedures Act had not been thought through. Later, passage of the National Environmental Policy Act, under the Calvert Cliffs decision, resulted in the requirement to issue an environmental impact statement (EIS). That resulted in full public hearings on environmental as well as on safety issues and, if anything, those hearings became even more adversarial. By contrast, a coal-fired station could be built under state law and no EIS would be required.

Then came Three Mile Island—and the rush ended. A moratorium was imposed on plants under construction while the Nuclear Regulatory Commission (NRC) and the Kemeny Commission conducted their reviews. In the case of the NRC, the delays were stretched out through extraordinary congressional pressure. Inevitably, costs begin to mount. There were retrofits that were ordered by the NRC and, as a result of the extended delays, there was added interest to be paid. State commissions began so-called prudency hearings and imposed severe penalties. Utilities were thus not permitted to recover their costs. The whole unhappy experience was reinforced by the movement toward competition in generation and by the availability in later years of the combined-cycle gas-fired generator that had far lower capital costs, was quicker to construct and was far cheaper. The boom ended abruptly. Public support faded. The politics and the economics were no longer favorable for the use of nuclear power. The cheerleaders were and still are there, going through their routines—enthusiastically—but most of the fans have now gone from the stands, at least in the Western world.

The American experience was not necessarily replicated abroad. As the French will tell you (with a note of superiority), France is not burdened by the accretions of Anglo-Saxon law but is governed by the Code Napoleon. Thus, France's policy decisions could be carried out without repeated adversarial proceedings—and without numerous first-of-a-kind, one-of-a-kind plants. Germany, as a result of World War II, received the burden of an American-style constitution and thereby all the conflicting roles of the federal government and the Länder (or states).

Where does that leave us? If and when nuclear power is to be revived, it likely will reflect, as a recent Massachusetts Institute of Technology study indicates, growing concern about global warming and the consequences of the release of greenhouse gases that could lead to a willingness to compensate for the cost disadvantages of nuclear power—as well as concern regarding the cost, availability, and security of future supplies of fossil fuels. One should recognize that before the midpoint of this century, the world is likely to peak out in the terms of oil production and, shortly thereafter, it should begin to peak out in terms of natural gas. But a full revival of nuclear power will require far more. It will require a restructuring of the siting and licensing process. It will unquestionably require meticulous attention to the safe operation of plants. The director general of the IAEA has observed that an accident or even a significant safety incident would "cripple the nuclear industry." Senior officers of the World Association of Nuclear Operators recently warned that the industry is threatened by "the negligence and complacency" that has led in recent years to severe incidents in the United States, Europe, and Japan. Nuclear power remains a demanding technology.

What then are we to conclude a half-century after President Eisenhower's Atoms-for-Peace address? Clearly, there has been substantial success. Despite the setbacks, nuclear power has come a long way—perhaps as far as has might have realistically been expected. So much for the benefits. On the side of controlling the risk of nuclear spread, we have created institutions that can detect and can potentially punish those who would violate the existing rules—and thus limit the risk that the nuclear age has created. In this post–Cold War world of growing knowledge about nuclear matters, rising appetites for nuclear capabilities and now the added threat of terrorism, we still have a long way to go before we can be confident that the risks of the atom do not exceed the benefits.

Dwight Eisenhower was a supreme pragmatist. All in all, he would not be entirely satisfied with the results we have achieved, but also he would not be displeased.

3

Atoms for Peace and the International Atomic Energy Agency

David B. Waller

The International Atomic Energy Agency (IAEA) is, of course, an organization that owes its very existence to "Atoms for Peace." This heritage captures the essence of the IAEA's work—fostering nuclear technology, verifying its peaceful use, and enhancing nuclear safety and security.

Political controversies have frequently surrounded the Atoms-for-Peace initiative. As Lawrence Scheinman notes in his history of the Agency, international organizations often find themselves at the center of political debates, and "despite its uncommon record for dealing with subjects on their technical merits, the IAEA is no exception."[1] The Agency Secretariat, for its part, has consistently sought to avoid politics. As Mohamed ElBaradei reminded the Board of Governors at one point during the debate over Iran: "We [the Secretariat] intend, as always, to keep to technical matters and avoid any political coloring. We are—on this as on all other

---

1. Lawrence Scheinman, *The International Atomic Energy Agency and World Nuclear Order* (Washington, D.C.: Resources for the Future, 1987), 209.

issues—politically 'blind,' because political assessment is not the role of the Secretariat."[2]

In keeping with that tradition, this paper will not focus on the global political consequences of Atoms for Peace. Instead, it will concentrate first on the dual nature of the initiative, a point that is fundamental to the Agency's existence. It will then touch on some of the major challenges the Agency has faced and the significant changes that have resulted, especially during the last two decades, and conclude with a look at what may lie ahead. Throughout, it will offer a perspective from inside the Agency and from inside the debates of its Board of Governors. That is where the implementation of grand policy is repeatedly tested by the harsh practical realities of both resource constraints and the often sharply differing views and priorities among states—which, together, can generate heated exchanges regarding the proper "balance" among the Agency's areas of activity.

Duality

One aspect of the Agency has remained fundamental from the outset, namely the dual objective with which it was founded—the two sides of the atomic coin, or the quid pro quo: the commitment, on the one hand, to advancing the use of nuclear science and technology and, on the other hand, to containing the spread of nuclear weapons. This duality is clearly outlined in the Agency's Statute and was subsequently reinforced by the Treaty on the Nonproliferation of Nuclear Weapons (NPT), that other direct derivative of Atoms for Peace. Yet, questions have periodically arisen as to whether such a dual mandate is practicable. In fact, recent events have led some to argue that the two goals are fundamentally incompatible, and that the Agency should be split into two separate organizations.

The real contribution of the Agency in advancing Atoms for Peace can be measured in terms of its parallel progress on these mutually reinforcing, interdependent fronts, while maintaining, and when necessary, adjusting, the sometimes-precarious balance between them. It is the very dynamic of this delicate balance between the two mandates that holds the Agency together and results in the uniquely strong support it enjoys among its 139 member-states.

2. See www.iaea.org/NewsCenter/PressReleases/2003/DGIran9Sept03.pdf.

The solid majority of those member-states are from the developing world and, for them, the transfer of civilian nuclear technology is the clear priority. To reach consensus within the Board—a well-established tradition in keeping with the "spirit of Vienna"—that majority's acceptance of activities related to verification is carefully balanced by the support of the minority, the developed countries, for technology transfer. As stated by the late Munir Ahmad Khan, a former chair of the Board: "The Agency cannot live on safeguards alone. In the long run, it can survive only if it provides concrete and meaningful services for accelerating the socio-economic development of its member states."[3]

While the terminology used to express this duality has varied—"safeguards versus technical assistance," "promotional versus regulatory activities," or "verification versus technology transfer"—its nature remains essentially the same as that originally articulated by President Dwight D. Eisenhower. Fifty years later, while the political landscape has evolved and new challenges have arrived to replace the old, the dual nature of Atoms for Peace continues to dominate our program, the allocation of resources in our budget and much of our thinking.

Of course, it is essential to acknowledge straight away that certain peaceful applications can, in some instances, bring a peaceful nuclear program precariously close to a weapon capability. As ElBaradei put it recently, "the margin of security [between sensitive fuel cycle activities and weapon capability] under the current non-proliferation regime is becoming too slim for comfort."[4]

Let us first examine the Agency's technology transfer role.

Nuclear Technology Applications

Over the past five decades, nuclear applications have expanded to become a constant factor in daily life, at least in the developed world. The Agency's focus, however, has increasingly been the use of nuclear and isotopic techniques to address the daunting challenges in the developing world—disease, poverty, hunger, and a shortage of drinking water.

Consider the application of the radiation-induced "sterile insect technique" (SIT) to control insect pests. In 1997, Hans Blix, then the director

3. *Personal Reflections* (Vienna: International Atomic Energy Agency, 1997), 311.
4. *The Economist*, October 18, 2003, 44.

general, was presented with a small Lucite cube in which was encased what was claimed to be the "last tsetse fly from Zanzibar." The tsetse fly has long devastated sub-Saharan economies by killing livestock—including draft animals—and by spreading deadly sleeping sickness to humans. SIT worked to eliminate the tsetse fly in Zanzibar where other techniques, including the massive application of pesticides, had failed. The same technique has been used to eradicate the screwworm fly from Libya—as well as from all of North and Central America—and is being applied in Mexico and the United States against the Mediterranean fruit fly (or med fly), a major threat to fruit and vegetable crops.

An even greater socioeconomic benefit has resulted from radiation-induced mutations in crop plants. In particular, the development of new rice strains, or "cultivars" in Thailand, Japan, China, and Australia, has resulted in tens of billions of dollars of increased crop value at the farm gate. Similar results have also been obtained for other crops, such as cotton, bread wheat, chickpea, barley, and durum wheat. There is no doubt that these and more than 2000 other radiation-induced mutant cultivars represent a proven method in crop breeding, and have greatly contributed to an improved standard of living in Asia, as well as in other regions of the world.

The importance of this aspect of Atoms for Peace—using nuclear techniques to address socioeconomic needs—cannot be overstressed. There are many more examples. Isotope tracers are being used to monitor factors that affect nutrition—a huge problem in developing countries, where nearly 200 million children are chronically undernourished. The Agency is initiating an extensive campaign to raise funds to expand the availability of radiotherapy in the developing world, in response to projections of an impending crisis in cancer management in these countries. Isotope hydrology is being applied to understand the causes and effects of climate change, to monitor the integrity of dams and water reservoirs and to measure and manage the supply of drinking water in underground aquifers. In short, we are working to apply nuclear techniques where they will count the most, to enhance human development worldwide.

In 1953, however, the peaceful application of greatest interest and promise was, of course, nuclear power—which, according to the original vision in Atoms for Peace, would bring "abundant electrical energy in the power starved areas of the world."[5] This vision, needless to say, has not thus far

---

5. "Atomic Power for Peace," an address by Dwight D. Eisenhower, President of the United States, before the General Assembly of the United Nations, December 8, 1953.

been realized. Although the percentage of nuclear electricity in individual countries has reached as high as 75 to 80 percent, the global share has in fact never risen above 17 percent, where it has hovered ever since the Chernobyl accident in 1986. The only current growth market for nuclear power is in Asia, and most projections foresee a gradual global decline in the coming decades or, at most, only slight growth—despite projected enormous increases in electricity demand—due to the lack of political support for nuclear power and the economics of recently deregulated markets.

Many experts, however, believe that this situation could change. The increasing emphasis on preventing climate change, and the resultant need to minimize the impact of electricity generation, is leading to the more frequent mention by policymakers and others of the potential of nuclear power as a source of large-scale energy production that generates little or no greenhouse gases. A key factor in this opportunity for a revival of nuclear power will be the success of nuclear innovation—through efforts such as the Agency's International Project on Innovative Nuclear Reactors and Fuel Cycles (INPRO) and the U.S.-led Generation IV (Gen IV) initiative. These innovation efforts, if successful, INPRO and Gen IV efforts will address concerns related to safety, security, proliferation, waste disposal, and economics, paving the way for a new generation of reactors that benefit from five decades of design and operational experience.

Safety and Security

The past twenty years have witnessed dramatic changes in the area of nuclear safety—changes inaugurated, in large part, in reaction to the accident at Chernobyl and driven by an upsurge in international cooperation. The Agency's response to that disaster was rapid, facilitating an international review of the causes and progression of the accident. Indeed, by the time of the IAEA General Conference in September of 1986, the so-called Notification and Assistance Conventions had been both negotiated and opened for signature. The resulting momentum highlighted the need for significant safety improvements, provided the basis for the review of the Agency's safety standards and, in particular, underscored the importance of expanded international cooperation to ensure that safety performance would be raised in all facilities—in all countries.

The long-term result has been a complete international rethinking of the approach to safety, not only of nuclear power plants but also of other nuclear facilities and radioactive sources. The Agency has been at the forefront of this revolution, leading, as it has, to the development of international conventions (most recently those on nuclear safety, safety of spent fuel, and waste management) and widespread use of international peer reviews that use Agency standards as the baseline. Those standards have been strengthened with the support of many countries and are becoming accepted worldwide.

Turning now to security, I need hardly say that the events of September 11 dramatically called for the immediate consideration of terrorism in all its forms—including the threat of nuclear and radiological terrorism. It became rapidly apparent that "the lesson of Chernobyl" in the safety sphere should be applied to security as well: that is, that the international nuclear security regime should be urgently strengthened, without waiting for a "watershed" nuclear security incident to provide the impetus for security upgrades and expanded international cooperation.

The response of the Agency to the events of September 11 was swift—an action plan, building on an existing but modest nuclear security program, developed and approved by the Board within a very few months; the Nuclear Security Fund was established and received significant pledges. Member-states have been generous in providing both financial and in-kind resources to fund a broad range of actions, such as:

- New threat assessments
- Upgraded border monitoring
- Missions to locate and recover orphaned radiological sources
- Facility security upgrades
- Coordinated actions to reduce the threat of "dirty bombs" as terrorist weapons
- Increased coordination with relevant international law enforcement bodies

These efforts have been expanding in the last few years, and a major victory was achieved with agreements to expand the scope of the Convention on the Physical Protection of Nuclear Material to cover all civil nuclear activities.

Verification

Nuclear verification issues have been very much in the public spotlight over the past few years. The nuclear "watchdog," as the IAEA is called, has of late, been barking and rather loudly. Let us recall why.

The discovery in 1991, in the immediate wake of the Gulf War, of an extensive, well-financed clandestine nuclear-weapon program in Iraq was a watershed event—the first occasion on which it was concluded by the Agency that a state party to the NPT had violated its safeguards obligations. This revelation presented a profound challenge to the nonproliferation regime as a whole and to the Agency in particular. The IAEA's postwar role, pursuant to Security Council resolutions, was clear. It was to map out the program and destroy it, remove any nuclear materials that might be used for weapon production and establish a monitoring system to ensure that the program was not reconstituted. Security Council resolution 687 (1991) gave the Agency unprecedented powers, with access anywhere, to anyone, to any document, at any time.

However, it soon became clear that successfully addressing this challenge would have implications far beyond verification of Iraqi nuclear disarmament. Limitations affecting the ability of IAEA safeguards inspectors to fulfill their nonproliferation verification functions had earlier been acknowledged, and consideration had been given to strengthening the system, both at the NPT Review Conference in 1990 and by the Agency's Board and General Conference. However, it took a dramatic event, the discovery of Iraq's extensive clandestine program, to kick start an intensified process of reexamination and subsequent overhaul of the system. The objective was to overcome the reluctance of states to cede additional sovereignty and address the demonstrated need, now undeniable, for the capability to provide credible assurance, not only of the nondiversion of declared material, but also of the absence of any undeclared nuclear material or activities.

"Program 93 + 2," as it was known, first strengthened safeguards to the extent possible under the legal authority already conferred by existing safeguards agreements. The initial results of this process were soon put to the test by the noncompliance of the Democratic People's Republic of Korea (DPRK) with its NPT safeguards agreement. Using the lessons learned from Iraq, then Director General Hans Blix invoked the special inspection procedure in 1993. When that request was refused, the Board was asked to confirm that a special inspection was essential and urgent. Indeed, it was a particularly dramatic day in the Board Room when satellite imagery photographs, showing sequential construction and concealment at the locations in question over a period of weeks and months, were projected on the screen. That information, together with inspection data, environmental sampling, and record examinations, convinced the Board to conclude that a special inspection was necessary so that inspectors could verify the completeness and correctness of the DPRK's initial declaration and, in particular, determine what quantities of plutonium had been separated at Yongbyon before our NPT inspections began. Following the DPRK's denial of access, the Board found the DPRK to be in noncompliance and reported this to the Security Council.

This confrontation led ultimately in 1994 to the Agreed Framework between the United States and the DPRK, and thus, the Agency was never afforded the opportunity then or since, to verify the DPRK's initial declaration. Nonetheless, the Agency, for its part, demonstrated that it had already learned from the case of Iraq and was able to respond effectively to this new case of noncompliance, even coming so close on the heels of the first.

The international community appreciated the rapidity of the Agency's adaptation, as was reflected at the historic 1995 NPT Review and Extension Conference, in which state parties further indicated their willingness to accept more effective IAEA safeguards. This vote of confidence in the value of the Agency's role contributed to the momentum that culminated in 1997 with the adoption by the Board of the Model Additional Protocol.

The Additional Protocol (AP), of course, went beyond existing legal instruments and significantly expanded the Agency's capability to verify a state's compliance with its undertakings. It provides broader access to information and extended access to locations, whether declared or not. It has since become an integral, but unfortunately not yet universally applied, feature of the Agency's safeguards system. For countries with both a comprehensive safeguards agreement and an AP in force, the Agency can, indeed, now give credible assurance, not only of the nondiversion of declared material, but also of the absence of any undeclared nuclear material or activities.

Of course, in the middle of this chronology of challenges, came the nuclear tests by India and Pakistan in May 1998. However, these events—although a subject hotly debated and loudly condemned in the Agency's Board Room, and one that extended the last day of that year's General Conference until three o'clock in the morning—were a challenge to nonproliferation by states outside the NPT regime and, in that sense, beyond the Agency's oversight.

However, there were, of course, other challenges to come. Back in Iraq, in December 1998, on the eve of military action by the United States and the United Kingdom, the Agency's Iraq Action Team inspectors were obliged to leave and abandon their ongoing monitoring and verification program aimed at ensuring that the nuclear-weapon program, destroyed by the Agency in 1991–1992, was not being reconstituted.

Fast forwarding to November 2002, the Action Team—since renamed the Iraq Nuclear Verification Office—was tasked by the Security Council to return to Iraq to determine whether it had restarted its nuclear program during the four-year inspection hiatus since 1998. Although the three-and-a-half-month window before war was initiated was too short for the team to complete all aspects of its review, the director general was able to report to the Security Council in March 2003, that it had found no evidence of reconstitution in Iraq of a nuclear weapon program. The Iraq Survey Group reached the same conclusion.

As the director general has stated on numerous occasions, the Agency continues to have a verification mandate in Iraq, both under the various Security Council resolutions and under Iraq's NPT safeguards agreement. It should be allowed to return to Iraq as soon as possible to bring its credibility and experience to bear in completing its investigation interrupted in March, and to reinstate monitoring and verification activities, as mandated by the Security Council. He has also expressed the hope that a new, legally constituted government in Iraq would quickly conclude and bring into force an AP.

Of course, concerns also reemerged regarding the DPRK's nuclear program. Since 1994, the Agency's role under the Agreed Framework had been limited to maintaining inspectors at Yongbyon, continuously and under quite spartan conditions, to monitor and provide assurance of the "freeze" of the nuclear program at that location. In December 2002, however, the DPRK abruptly disabled the Agency's surveillance cameras, cut through Agency seals, and, on New Year's Eve, ordered the inspectors to leave the country. Very shortly thereafter, early in 2003, the DPRK announced its withdrawal from the NPT.

This situation has left the Agency sidelined, although we remain committed to continuing to work with the DPRK. We welcome the six-nation talks and hope that the September 2005 agreement is successful. In our view, any settlement should, at a minimum, provide for the full implementation of the DPRK's NPT safeguards agreement and an AP. The Agency also stands ready to verify the dismantlement of any nuclear-weapon-related infrastructure and components in the DPRK—drawing on its experience gained in the early 1990s in verifying both the voluntary dismantlement of South Africa's and the reluctant dismantlement of Iraq's nuclear-weapon programs.

The Agency's considerable experience and ever-improving techniques increase its capability to respond to subsequent challenges.[6] In the context of the most recent verification challenge, Iran, the environmental sampling techniques used in Iraq have, for example, been essential to the Agency's recent investigations. As a result of the numerous inspections, repeated dogged questioning from the Agency, and intense international pressure, today we have significantly greater knowledge and understanding of Iran's nuclear program—its history, nature, and extent—than at any time in the past. Iran, as the world knows, has finally admitted to having failed to adhere to many of its obligations under its NPT safeguards agreement. Agency inspectors have been on the ground in Iran, have been in the unique position of having seen and taken samples at all the facilities in question, have had direct interaction with the relevant people, and have brought their experience to bear in addressing this latest challenge. The resulting facts have been central to the comprehensive reports the director general has provided to the Board.

However, our work in Iran—as in other areas of verification mentioned here—remains a "work in progress." In his report to the November 2003 meeting of the Board, the director general reported that we had found no conclusive evidence by that time of a weapon program, but neither were we ready to conclude that the program is conclusively peaceful in nature. Extensive verification work remains, and full cooperation and transparency on the part of Iran, which we expect, will be essential. We have provided further reports, based on additional inspections and analysis since then. We are hopeful that the widely publicized attention given to the importance of the AP in the case of Iran will prompt others to take the necessary and responsible steps.

A recent initiative of the director general relates back, in a modified way, to Atoms for Peace, which called for nations "to make joint contributions from their stockpiles of normal uranium and fissionable materials to an international atomic energy agency."[7] The director general put forward his reassessment of that concept in an invited article in *The Economist*,[8] where

---

6. Libya asked the IAEA late in December 2003 to ensure through verification that all of its nuclear activities were under safeguards and used exclusively for peaceful purposes. Here again, the Agency's verification experience, particularly that acquired in Iraq and South Africa, is a major asset in providing the international community with such independent assurance.
7. "Atomic Power for Peace."
8. *The Economist,* 43.

he suggested studying multinational approaches to the proliferation sensitive front end of the fuel cycle (e.g., enrichment, reprocessing, and fuel fabrication) as well as the management and disposal of spent fuel.

At the United Nations General Assembly in November 2003, he suggested that these proposals would be an important step towards reassuring the international community that these portions of civilian nuclear fuel cycle programs are not vulnerable to misuse.

Conclusion

Have the dual objectives so fundamental to both Atoms for Peace and the Statute of the Agency been a success? The NPT Review Conference held in 2000 gave a resounding vote of confidence in the continuing relevance and value of the Agency's dual mission.

However, "money talks," and an even more basic vote of confidence in the Agency—and thereby in Atoms for Peace—was given by its memberstates in the form of a significant increase in the budget. To be fully appreciated, this increase—which came after fifteen years of constraining zero real growth and the risk of safeguards failure—should be viewed against the backdrop of the reduced, or at best flat, budgets of the vast majority of other United Nations' organizations.

Many have come to see the Agency's safeguards program, at just $100 million annually, as a bargain in the cause of nuclear diplomacy. However, we still do not have sufficient funds to perform independent particle analysis, nor to purchase satellite imagery to the extent we would like, nor to add certain other capabilities that would improve our independence and credibility.

The IAEA, the most significant institutional legacy of Atoms for Peace, has faced, dealt with, and learned and gained strength from this litany of challenges. Here, I must note how much it has benefited over the last two decades from the guidance and leadership of first Hans Blix and, since 1997, Mohamed ElBaradei.

Of course, there will be more challenges to come:

- The increasing fight for human development
- The campaign to ensure that, in the face of soaring electricity demand and the threat of climate change, innovative nuclear power technologies are available as a safe and economically viable solution
- The protection of nuclear facilities and materials against terrorism

- The task of rethinking and further strengthening elements of the nuclear nonproliferation regime

In meeting these challenges, the Agency will continue to rely on the strong support of its member-states, operating in the "spirit of Vienna," to maintain a balance between the two objectives—the dual promises—of Atoms for Peace.

4

The Atoms-for-Peace Model and the Problem of Proliferation

Stephen G. Rademaker

In President Dwight D. Eisenhower's Atoms-for-Peace speech is the kernel of the idea—the basic trade-off, if you will—of foregoing the military uses of the atom in exchange for receiving the benefits of the peaceful uses of the atom. This idea became a cornerstone of the Nuclear Nonproliferation Treaty (NPT). The same basic idea was subsequently incorporated into the Chemical Weapons Convention and the Biological Weapons Convention.

In evaluating the Atoms-for-Peace model, the question before us is whether this basic trade-off has fulfilled its promise. In particular, is it workable? That is, can we in fact draw an effective line between military and peaceful work on the atom, as well as on chemicals and biological agents? Further, is access to peaceful uses a necessary or effective incentive in the battle against weapons of mass destruction (WMD) proliferation?

The immediate threats to the NPT regime are well known and have been on public display for years now, first in North Korea, and more recently in Iran. In October 2002, North Korea admitted to a secret uranium enrichment program linked to its development of nuclear weapons. Obviously, this program compounded previous North Korean violations of the NPT—prior to withdrawing from the treaty—and other international agreements to which it had adhered.

More instructive from the perspective of the Atoms-for-Peace model, however, is the fact that this program was launched despite a nearly decade-long, multibillion dollar effort by the United States and other countries under the Agreed Framework to give North Korea civilian nuclear power plants for purposes of generating electricity. Certainly, no one would claim that North Korean behavior is the norm when it comes to nuclear trade-offs. However, if nothing else, this experience reminds us that the promise of peaceful nuclear technology—even when the market value of that promise can be measured in the billons of dollars—is not enough by itself to dissuade some countries from pursuing their nuclear-weapon ambitions.

Iran was never promised civilian nuclear power plants essentially free of charge, but Russia has relentlessly pursued the construction of such a reactor at Bushehr for much of the last decade, and Iran has been one of the largest beneficiaries of the International Atomic Energy Agency (IAEA) technical cooperation for peaceful purposes. Yet, to date, reports by the director general of the IAEA have established that Iran is in violation, in multiple instances, of its safeguards obligations under the NPT. While Iran has consistently denied any program to develop nuclear weapons, the IAEA has amassed an enormous amount of evidence to the contrary that makes this assertion increasingly implausible.

In what can only be an attempt to build a capacity to develop nuclear materials for nuclear weapons, Iran has clandestinely enriched uranium with centrifuges, pursued laser enrichment capability, and produced and reprocessed plutonium. Over many years, it attempted to cover its tracks by repeatedly neglecting to report its activities, and in many instances, providing false declarations to the IAEA.

The United States believes that the massive and covert Iranian effort to acquire sensitive nuclear capabilities makes sense only as part of a nuclear weapon program. The European Union (EU) and Russia, among others, have increasingly come to agree with the U.S. assessment of Iran's nuclear intentions. However, the international community as a whole must still come to a common position that Iran must forego fuel cycle elements that would help Iran bring those intentions to fruition.

The agreement between Iran and the foreign ministers of Britain, France, and Germany on Iran's nuclear facilities created some hope for a diplomatic resolution of the crisis. Under that agreement, Iran promised to disclose fully the history and extent of its nuclear program; to suspend, for some unspecified period of time, its uranium enrichment and reprocessing activities; and to sign the IAEA Additional Protocol (AP). Iran's decision to restart its suspended activities and the breakdown of Iranian–EU negotiations have been disappointing and resulted in this issue's being referred to the UN Security Council.

Any Security Council action on Iran must demand, inter alia, that Iran ratify the AP. The AP will oblige the Iranians to declare a wide variety of nuclear-related activities, including imports and research and development, and allow IAEA inspectors to inspect all aspects of these activities from the beginning. The AP will provide greater knowledge to the international community and, we can hope, protect us from another Natanz-like surprise. Without the AP, the IAEA has had insufficient authority to root out secret activities during their early stages, that is, before they involve nuclear material. At one time, this seemed adequate according to the theory that a country cannot build a bomb without nuclear material. However, the experience of the past twelve years in Iraq, North Korea, and Iran has conclusively demonstrated that the IAEA's authority to intervene needs to begin earlier and be broader in scope.

But the AP will not in itself be sufficient. We must never lose sight of the fundamental truth of all verification: the absence of evidence is not necessarily evidence of absence. Repeatedly, determined cheaters have proven capable of evading international arms inspectors. We must never forget the verdict pronounced on one such inspection effort, where the evasion was seen to be thoroughly organized. Using civilian camouflage, it was argued, an organization was set up to safeguard weapons and equipment. The ingenuity used to create machinery for future production of war material, and the success of the deception and denial effort, were regarded as amazing.

This assessment sounds like a description of the experience of international inspectors in Iraq or one of several other countries of concern. In fact, this was Winston Churchill's description of what happened when the Weimar government in Germany set out to evade arms inspections mandated under the Treaty of Versailles. Those inspections helped give rise to a false sense of complacency in Europe, with ultimately disastrous consequences. None of us should ever become complacent about this risk. We must recognize the limitations of verification systems against determined cheaters. Moreover, in the case of the NPT, we must understand that even when the system works, the most the IAEA can do is sound the alarm; it is up to governments to take effective action against WMD threats.

We also must not forget that the agreement reached by the three EU ministers with Iran reiterated Iran's right within the NPT regime to develop nuclear energy for peaceful purposes. This is the very "right" behind which Iran has concealed a nuclear-weapon program for almost two decades. Of course, neither the NPT nor the AP prohibits the construction of nuclear facilities that could be turned to nuclear-weapon–related activities at a later date if Iran abrogated or withdrew from the NPT. Before it broke down, the deal only required Iran to hit the pause button in its enrichment and reprocessing activities. Not surprisingly, the Iranians said at the time that this aspect of the agreement with the EU ministers would allow them to end their promised "suspension" of enrichment activities at an early date of their choosing—an action they have indeed taken.

It remains the case that under the NPT's basic trade-off, Iran can acquire all of the capabilities that it needs to produce nuclear-weapon materials, and then later withdraw from the treaty and use the material in weapons. As suggested, this risk will not be cured by Iran's acceptance of more rigorous inspections by the IAEA.

Let us turn for a moment to another trade-off embodied in the NPT—one that is constantly raised by non–nuclear-weapon states parties to the Treaty—Article VI and the commitment to disarmament. The United States continues to meet its obligations under this article. Over thirteen thousand nuclear weapons have been dismantled since the end of the Cold War. More than a dozen different types of warheads have been dismantled, and the number of nuclear weapons has been reduced by about 60 percent, including 80 percent of all tactical nuclear weapons. Now, with the entry into force in 2003 of the United States–Russian Treaty on Strategic Offensive Reductions, also known as the Moscow Treaty, we will cut the number of operationally deployed strategic nuclear warheads again, by about two-thirds, by the year 2012. This represents the largest reduction in nuclear forces ever mandated by an arms control treaty. In two decades, the United States will have eliminated or decommissioned three-quarters of its strategic nuclear arsenal.

In addition, the United States and Russia will dispose of more than 700 tons of excess fissile material so that it is no longer usable in nuclear weapons, contributing to the irreversibility of nuclear reductions. Some may debate whether this pace is fast enough, but it is not credible to argue that we are not on a steady, downward path consistent with Article VI.

Even as we significantly reduce our nuclear forces, the uncertainties of the post–Cold War security environment make it necessary for the United

States to consider ways to adapt its remaining, smaller nuclear forces to changing circumstances. We need to explore weapon concepts that can help ensure that we continue to have a credible deterrent to new and emerging threats.

We understand concerns about the possibility that any U.S. government move to develop, test, or build new or low-yield nuclear weapons would complicate nonproliferation efforts. However, even if the United States were to decide to move beyond merely exploring the feasibility of such weapons, concerns about the impact on proliferation, we believe, are overstated.

First, it is not at all clear that nuclear testing would be required in order to develop and build such weapons. Second, the NPT does not forbid us to modernize our nuclear forces and, in the past, deployments of new weapon designs—most recently the B-61 Mod 11 deployed in the latter years of the Clinton administration—have not elicited undue concern. Third, even if we were to deploy such weapons, they would never constitute a major portion of our deterrent force. Finally, it is fallacious to suggest that any American president would somehow be quicker to use a nuclear weapon because of a lower yield. The fact is that the United States has had low-yield nuclear weapons—tactical nuclear weapons—for many years, and the availability of such weapons has never lowered the threshold for the use of nuclear weapons. After more than fifty years of stewardship of nuclear weapons, the United States is fully aware of its responsibilities as a nuclear power. The political leadership of the United States, now and into the future, would have the utmost appreciation and respect for the consequences of any decision on use of a nuclear weapon. If such a decision would come to any president's desk as a last resort, it would be a matter of the highest concern to U.S. security.

The overall direction of U.S. policy in this regard is guided by the December 2001 Nuclear Posture Review (NPR), which calls for improving conventional precision strike capabilities and developing and deploying missile defenses, and by subsequent decisions. The effect of these policies is to reduce U.S. dependence on nuclear weapons for deterrence. The policies set forth in the NPR and our Moscow Treaty reductions are fully consistent with our obligation under Article VI of the NPT.

We should have no illusions, moreover, that faster progress on implementation of Article VI would curb the appetite of some countries for nuclear weapons. It is simplistic and misleading to suggest that countries pursue nuclear weapons primarily in reaction to the nuclear policies of the

United States and other legitimate nuclear weapon states. Countries bent on acquiring nuclear weapons have their own reasons.

The Iranian and North Korean nuclear weapon programs predated U.S. research programs on a robust nuclear earth penetrator and possible new low-yield nuclear weapons by many years. U.S. decisions to cancel these or other studies will not persuade Iran or North Korea to freeze and roll back their nuclear-weapon programs.

The fact is that the balance between the three pillars of the NPT—nonproliferation, peaceful nuclear cooperation, and disarmament—has become dangerously unbalanced due to the attitudes of too many NPT parties. The NPT's core purpose is preventing the spread of nuclear weapons. The very title of the treaty makes that abundantly clear. More NPT parties must begin to accord a much higher priority to Articles I, II, and III if the treaty is to continue to play a key role in global security.

In this context, the debate will continue over how to channel properly the "right" of NPT parties to peaceful nuclear cooperation. In all cases, but particularly with respect to countries that have established a record of seeking nuclear technology in violation of their safeguards agreements, we need to explore new ways of making sure that nuclear cooperation is provided in a manner that does not afford a shortcut to achieving the bomb.

A realistic, if grim picture, has been painted of the challenges posed to the NPT in light of the troubling North Korean and Iranian cases. Nevertheless, we have made some progress with North Korea. And, it must be recalled, the nuclear nonproliferation record over the past three decades has been far better than some forecast when the NPT entered into force in 1970.

The NPT and the international pressure that members exert through it unquestionably has established a strong norm against the spread of nuclear weapons, and helped prevent, slow, and redirect states from establishing nuclear-weapon programs. We need to understand that the effectiveness of the NPT is only as great as its members want it to be, and for that reason, there are weaknesses that some states can attempt to exploit.

5

Strengthening Nonproliferation: The Path Ahead

Mitchell B. Reiss

When President Dwight D. Eisenhower put forward his Atoms-for-Peace proposal fifty years ago, he presented a surprisingly optimistic worldview, characterized by the spread of peaceful nuclear technology, a means to control the arms race and a way to halt the spread of nuclear weapons. In 1963, President Kennedy famously predicted that fifteen to twenty countries would be armed with nuclear weapons within ten years. President Kennedy was proved wrong; unfortunately, so was President Eisenhower.

Fifty years after Eisenhower's famous Atoms-for-Peace speech, we find that less than ten countries have acknowledged producing nuclear weapons. On the plus side, one of these, South Africa, voluntarily dismantled its nuclear weapons. Also on the plus side, Belarus, Kazakhstan, and Ukraine voluntarily surrendered the nuclear-weapon systems they inherited at the breakup of the Soviet Union. In South America, Argentina and Brazil abandoned nuclear-weapon programs in the early 1990s and pioneered a regional confidence-building mechanism. Iraq has also been eliminated as a nuclear threat.

Notwithstanding these positive achievements, the negative side of the nuclear proliferation ledger is heavily weighted. India, Pakistan, and Israel have not signed the Treaty on the Nonproliferation of Nuclear Weapons (NPT). India was directly assisted in the development of its nuclear arsenal through the dissemination of civil nuclear technology, while Pakistan used pirated centrifuge technology to produce highly enriched uranium (HEU) for its weapon program, despite numerous pledges to the United States that it would not do so. North Korea has openly violated the NPT and its associated safeguards agreement, and in defiance of the international community, expelled International Atomic Energy Agency (IAEA) inspectors and withdrew from the treaty in 2003. Iran has taken a different approach, seeking to remain within the NPT regime while developing all the necessary components for a nuclear weapon program. Only when its perfidy was uncovered did it grudgingly acknowledge its violations. However, it has yet to acknowledge its nuclear-weapon aspirations and, of course, other countries have evidenced an interest in acquiring weapons of mass destruction (WMD).

As unsettling as this is, the proliferation balance is further skewed toward the negative side by the emergence of threats entirely unforeseen when the Atoms-for-Peace program was launched. When President Eisenhower proposed Atoms for Peace, the principal threat to international peace and security was the then-developing Cold War between the superpowers. The phrase "rogue states" was unheard of, and terrorists largely were limited to tossing hand grenades at police stations in Third World countries. Clearly, nothing like the chemical and biological weapons developed by Aum Shinrikyo, and sought by al-Qaeda, had been experienced.

Fifty years ago, the term "weapons of mass destruction" was not part of our everyday lexicon. Today, regrettably, it is a household word. Likewise, fifty years ago "ballistic missiles" belonged almost exclusively to two countries. Today, ballistic missiles are deployed worldwide and there is a flourishing, illicit market in ballistic missile—and now cruise missile— technology. Similarly, other countries have worked assiduously to acquire chemical and biological weapons and to make them even more deadly, even as the United States and its allies have taken steps to eliminate such weapons.

Adding to the problem of nuclear proliferation is the essentially dual-use nature of the facilities required for their fabrication. For example, facilities to enrich uranium for nuclear-reactor fuel also can enrich it for the production of weapons. Facilities for reprocessing highly radioactive spent fuel can extract plutonium for bombs. These dual-purpose facilities essentially permit would-be proliferators to maintain a stockpile of "virtual weapons" or to develop a nuclear infrastructure that could be the basis for a future "break-out" scenario.

The International Nuclear Nonproliferation Regime

As this threat has evolved over the past fifty years, so too has the U.S. approach to countering nuclear proliferation. The United States, along with other responsible members of the world community, has adopted a wide-ranging network to stigmatize the development and acquisition, beyond the five permanent members of the United Nations Security Council, of nuclear-weapon capabilities by any country, in any region, for any reason. Implementation of this strategy has been effected through a series of multilateral treaties and agreements, their accompanying international institutions and multilateral suppliers' groups to control exports of sensitive technologies. Multilateral alliances like the North Atlantic Treaty Organization and bilateral alliances between the United States and other countries such as Japan also have played a role in dissuading countries from seeing nuclear weapons as a means to enhance their national security. Collectively, these arrangements comprise the global nuclear nonproliferation regime.

Imperfect as it may be, this regime provides a legal ban on nuclear proliferation (beyond the five nuclear-weapon states recognized by the NPT) and establishes the important norm that nuclear proliferation is illegitimate. Even in cases where proliferation activity might not be technically "illegal"—such as when a proliferator is not a party to a particular WMD ban—the regime still stigmatizes proliferation activity.

It is widely understood that the web of treaties, agreements, and inspection mechanisms that comprise the nonproliferation regime is a necessary but not sufficient condition for international security. Individually, and even collectively, they cannot be relied upon to counter nuclear proliferation in all circumstances. Often, the existing regime can only delay determined proliferators; it cannot prevent them from eventual acquisition. Indeed, under the cover of existing nonproliferation arrangements, countries like North Korea and Iran have acquired the expertise and technology needed to develop nuclear weapons.

Reforming the NPT

The NPT was negotiated in the early 1960s, signed in 1968, and entered into force in 1970. In the three decades since, the nonproliferation regime constructed on the foundation of the NPT has served us well. However, like the Atoms-for-Peace proposal that fathered it, the NPT was crafted in a different era—and it is beginning to show its age. If it is going to continue in its usefulness, it needs to be continually reinvigorated to meet the proliferation challenges of the twenty-first century. What new thinking is needed to help preserve international peace and security in the twenty-first century? How do we address the new challenges?

The "National Strategy to Combat Weapons of Mass Destruction," which President Bush issued in 2002, outlines a comprehensive approach to counter nuclear and other WMD. The strategy has three principal pillars:

- Counterproliferation to combat WMD use—recognizing that the possession and increased likelihood of WMD use by hostile states and terrorists are realities of the contemporary security environment
- Strengthened nonproliferation to combat WMD proliferation—determining to undertake every effort to prevent states and terrorists from acquiring WMD and missiles
- Consequence management to respond to WMD use—committing to reduce, to the extent possible, the potentially horrific consequences of WMD use at home and abroad[1]

In this paper, some key elements of the second pillar, that is, strengthened nonproliferation, will be the focus.

Strengthening the IAEA

The direct result of Atoms for Peace was the International Atomic Energy Agency. The current administration strongly supports strengthening the IAEA as a critical element of our nonproliferation policy.

The IAEA safeguards system helps deter the diversion of nuclear materials from peaceful purposes and provides a means to detect diversions should they occur. Since 1999, the United States has significantly increased its voluntary contribution to the safeguards program, in addition to our annual assessed contribution of 25 percent of the IAEA's entire budget. In 2003, the forty-seventh General Conference of the IAEA approved a $25.1-million budget increase to be phased in over four years, breaking decades of

---

1. The White House, *National Strategy to Combat Weapons of Mass Destruction* (Washington, D.C.: U.S. Government Printing Office, December 2002).

zero-growth budgets. Over three-quarters of this increase were directed to safeguards. Appropriate increases in the safeguards budget, as required, should be supported.

Safeguards also should be strengthened through the universal adoption of the Model Additional Protocol negotiated in the mid-1990s. The Additional Protocol (AP) expands the information related to nuclear activities that states are required to declare to the IAEA. The AP also provides greater latitude to IAEA inspectors in investigating undeclared, suspect facilities.

Of special importance, better compliance with IAEA safeguards must also be pursued. Violations cannot be allowed to go unnoticed and willful violations cannot go unchallenged. Noncompliance must be the concern of all, not just a few. All of the parties to the NPT should join in condemning violations and in pressing for sanctions or other penalties in the absence of a return to compliance.

These efforts are necessary to strengthen the IAEA and NPT in the near term. However, strengthening these international nonproliferation instruments cannot take place divorced from efforts by member states to recommit themselves to their nonproliferation obligations and consider these obligations in light of current challenges. If the NPT is to remain a viable instrument in the struggle to counter proliferation into the twenty-first century, much more will be required.

The Article IV Grand Bargain

Article IV of the NPT codifies part of the so-called "grand bargain" envisioned in President Eisenhower's Atoms-for-Peace proposal. In exchange for the their commitment in Article II to forego the acquisition of nuclear weapons and in Article III to agree to IAEA safeguards and inspections, Article IV guarantees the "inalienable right" of the non–nuclear-weapon states party to the treaty to the peaceful development and use of nuclear energy. This bargain is the core of the agreement. Consequently, since Atoms for Peace was initiated, we have witnessed the spread of peaceful nuclear technology to provide energy throughout the globe. Today, some sixty countries possess small-scale nuclear research reactors, while over thirty operate nuclear power plants for the generation of electricity. The Atoms-for-Peace legacy to humanity also includes the use of nuclear research for science, medicine, and agricultural development.

Over the years, nuclear-supplier states have taken steps to ensure that their support for peaceful nuclear energy did not inadvertently lead to diversion for nuclear-weapon purposes. India's self-proclaimed peaceful nuclear explosion in 1974 made clear to all that nuclear-supplier states had to pay more attention to controls on fuel-cycle technologies with direct application to nuclear weapons, that is, enrichment and reprocessing. In response, nuclear suppliers agreed to exercise restraint in the transfer of "sensitive" facilities, technologies and weapon-usable materials. They also agreed, in the case of enrichment and reprocessing facilities, to encourage recipients to accept, as an alternative to national plants, supplier or multinational involvement in such projects.

More recently, North Korea and Iran have sought to develop these capabilities to produce the fissile materials necessary to build nuclear weapons. These countries have betrayed the promise of Atoms for Peace and subverted Article IV of the NPT. They have used Article IV as a cover for the development of infrastructure necessary for the production of nuclear weapons. If we are to sustain the NPT and the entire global nonproliferation regime well into the twenty-first century, we need to do a better job of detecting and deterring such activities.

We must seriously limit enrichment and reprocessing capabilities while allowing access to appropriate reactor fuels. The grand bargain of the NPT was never meant, and should never be used, to allow proliferators to develop and maintain a fissile material production capability under cover of an alleged "peaceful" program. The IAEA's director general, Mohamed ElBaradei, has highlighted this issue.[2]

The Other Half of the Bargain: Article VI

The five nuclear-weapon states recognized by the NPT also undertook nonproliferation obligations under the treaty. Article VI of the NPT commits the nuclear-weapon states, as it does all parties, to pursue negotiations in good faith leading to disarmament. In the thirty years since the NPT was signed, there have been significant accomplishments in reducing the nuclear arsenals of the United States and Russia.

The United States has reduced the overall number of weapons in our nuclear arsenal by 60 percent, and the number of tactical nuclear weapons by 80 percent. The United States–Russian Treaty on Strategic Offensive Reductions, known as the "Moscow Treaty," will reduce our operationally deployed strategic nuclear weapons even further. By December 31, 2012,

2. *The Economist,* October 18, 2003.

under the terms of this treaty, we will cut our strategic nuclear warheads by about two-thirds, to less than 2,200. It should be noted that the United States also long ago eliminated all biological weapons from its inventory, and is in the process of eliminating its chemical weapons.

These are not insignificant accomplishments, but should further reductions be expected? There has been a great deal of misunderstanding about the United States and Article VI. As a matter of law and policy, the United States remains committed to the eventual elimination of all nuclear weapons. Yet countries outside of the NPT regime are building up their nuclear-weapon capabilities and some non–nuclear-weapon states within the NPT regime are seeking to create nuclear arsenals anew. Nuclear proliferation has occurred in South Asia, North Korea threatens to unveil a "physical deterrent," Iran has been caught developing a nuclear-weapon infrastructure, and there may be others within the NPT regime seeking to create nuclear arsenals. Therefore, the United States is demonstrating its commitment, while others remain outside of this process.

Additionally, others are developing and proliferating chemical and biological weapons and sophisticated missile delivery systems. It is particularly disturbing to note that in excess of forty states that are parties to the NPT have not signed up to either the Biological and Toxin Weapons Convention (BWC) or the Chemical Weapons Convention (CWC). This would appear to be a direct violation of the spirit, if not the letter, of another obligation that Article VI imposes on all of its members, namely, that they pursue negotiations in good faith towards general and complete disarmament. While pursuing the goal of global security, stability, and peace through universal adherence to the NPT, we should not lose sight of the equally important necessity of obtaining universal adherence to and full compliance with the BWC and the CWC as well.

A final point: U.S. efforts to halt the spread of nuclear weapons are not only designed to enhance American security, they are designed to enhance the security of all countries. All members of the NPT have a fundamental self-interest in developing and implementing rigorous IAEA safeguards, adhering to the NPT, and sanctioning countries that violate their IAEA and NPT commitments. These actions are not a gift or a favor bestowed by the non–nuclear-weapon states upon the United States and the other nuclear powers. All countries have an interest in the strict enforcement of the NPT.

Indeed, with the new threats of a new century, security is more indivisible than ever before. The forces of globalization, clandestine networks of nuclear suppliers, new lethal technologies, failing and failed states, and the global threat of terrorism mean that no country is truly safe from the threat of nuclear proliferation. There is no sanctuary. The international nonproliferation regime benefits all or it benefits none.

Article X: "The Great Escape"

As with other arms control and nonproliferation agreements, the NPT contains a "supreme national interests" clause. This clause, contained in Article X of the NPT, permits state parties to withdraw from the treaty should "extraordinary events" related to the treaty negatively impact their security.

The intent of this "escape clause" is to provide nations with the flexibility to respond to events that are entirely unanticipated at the time they adhere to the treaty. There is an inherent logic to this, understood and generally accepted by all. No country wants to be indefinitely bound to an agreement that could be harmful to its national interests.

However, the withdrawal clause was never intended as a means for a state party to evade or undercut its treaty obligations and escape the consequences of noncompliance. Nothing in Article X suggests that the extraordinary events required to withdraw from the treaty can be one's own violations of the treaty. Likewise, nothing in Article X suggests that a state party can use the benefits of NPT membership to posture itself for the rapid development of a nuclear-weapon capability following withdrawal from the treaty. Indeed, such duplicitous actions directly violate the central obligations of the treaty. If the treaty is to remain a viable instrument of nonproliferation, attempts to subvert the NPT in this manner cannot be tolerated.

Although North Korea withdrew from the NPT earlier this year, the community of nations has continued to insist that it must come back into compliance with its treaty obligations. The international community also has made clear that North Korea must still answer for the violations it has committed as an NPT party. Would-be violators of the NPT should take note.

Other Initiatives

Careful consideration must be given to these central treaty articles as we seek to reinvigorate the NPT for the twenty-first century. At the same time, we cannot afford to wait to take action to bolster the global nonproliferation regime. The United States and other nations have launched a series of initiatives designed to promote that regime and foster international peace and security. Some of the new initiatives are outlined below.

Highly Enriched Uranium Minimization

In the decades following President Eisenhower's Atoms-for-Peace speech, large quantities of highly enriched uranium were exported to more than fifty countries by both the United States and the Soviet Union. Most of this material was used to fuel nuclear research reactors. Much of it remains stored at or near those reactors under security arrangements that vary widely. Since the late 1970s, the United States has sought to eliminate these stocks of weapon-usable material and, where this has not been immediately feasible, to enhance physical security at the storage sites.

In the last several years, we have sought to expand this effort in collaboration with Russia. Ongoing efforts include programs to:

- Develop new low-enriched uranium (LEU) fuels
- Assist in converting research reactors around the world to use LEU
- Return U.S.-origin HEU from reactors in some forty countries for permanent disposition in the United States

Russia also is pursuing a program to return Russian-origin HEU to Russia from as many as seventeen countries. Our goal is to reduce to an absolute minimum international commerce in an unsecure storage of weapon-usable uranium throughout the world.

Radioactive Source Initiative

Complementing the HEU minimization effort is the Group of Eight (G-8) Radioactive Source Initiative. At the time of President Eisenhower's Atoms-for-Peace speech, the threat of a radiological dispersion device, or "dirty bomb," was hardly a central concern. Today, it is an all-too-real possibility. Indeed, such a device may be particularly appealing to terrorist entities that may lack the technological sophistication to develop more sophisticated nuclear or biological weapons.

The G-8 initiative is intended to strengthen national controls on radioactive materials that, although not useable in the construction of a nuclear weapon, could readily be employed in creating a dirty bomb. In furtherance of this effort, in September 2003, the IAEA General Conference approved the Code of Conduct on the Safety and Security of Radioactive Sources to provide states with guidelines for the control of radioactive materials. The IAEA has encouraged its member-states to commit themselves to implement the code and to so inform the director general of the Agency. The United States has done so, and is encouraging other IAEA members to do so as well.

Follow-on activities by the G-8 countries will include the establishment of national registries for tracking radioactive sources; implementation of programs to recover abandoned, lost, or stolen radioactive sources; putting effective measures into place on the export of radioactive sources; and adoption of national measures to penalize the theft or misuse of radioactive sources.

In this regard, the United States has already moved to implement this initiative. Then Secretary of Energy Spencer Abraham announced in November 2003, the establishment within the Department of Energy of a special high-level task force that will focus its attention on reducing potential threats from high-risk radiological sources, including those that may be found at research and test reactors. The Task Force will identify, secure, and provide interim storage for high-risk radiological materials that could be used in radiological dispersion devices. In the short time since its creation, the new task force has initiated several cooperative efforts with the IAEA and its member-states to secure radiological materials worldwide.

Furthering this and other initiatives, the Global Threat Reduction Initiative, which is designed to secure, remove, and dispose of vulnerable radiological as well as nuclear materials, was announced by then-Secretary of Energy Spencer Abraham in May 2004.

G-8 Global Partnership

Another important G-8 nonproliferation initiative is the Global Partnership launched at the Kananaskis Summit in 2002. The goal of this initiative is to provide at least $20 billion over ten years for nonproliferation, threat-reduction, disarmament, and nuclear safety cooperation projects. The United States has committed to raising half of the $20 billion for the initiative. The initial focus of this initiative has been on projects in Russia.

The G-8 also welcomed the participation in the Global Partnership of six additional countries in the summer of 2003—Finland, the Netherlands,

Norway, Poland, Sweden, and Switzerland. At the Sea Island Summit in 2004, the G-8 called for expanding the program to include projects in additional states.

Proliferation Security Initiative

President Bush announced on May 31, 2003, in Krakow, Poland, a key initiative in the struggle to counter WMD proliferation—the Proliferation Security Initiative (PSI). This multilateral effort is intended to develop and implement a new, more robust approach to preventing the flow of WMD, missiles, and related technologies to and from state or non-state actors of proliferation concern. The United States initiated this effort with the help of ten other countries: Australia, France, Germany, Italy, Japan, the Netherlands, Poland, Portugal, Spain, and the United Kingdom. In September 2003, these eleven PSI participants agreed to and published the "Statement of Interdiction Principles." Since that time, more than fifty other countries from around the globe also have indicated their support for the PSI.

The PSI is specifically focused on disrupting the proliferation trade at sea, in the air, and on land. The interdiction of WMD components and critical technologies in transit to countries and non-state actors of proliferation concern can prevent such entities from acquiring these capabilities. At the very least, interception of such seaborne, airborne, and overland shipments can substantially lengthen the amount of time would-be proliferators will need to acquire WMD capabilities, as well as increase their acquisition costs. The PSI is now moving to establish the necessary mechanisms for interdiction cooperation. Our objective is to create a web of counterproliferation partnerships through which proliferators will have increasing difficulty in carrying out their trade in WMD and missile-related materials and technologies.

The PSI's interdiction principles envision cooperation among states on interdiction actions based on national legal authorities and international law and frameworks. A series of interdiction training exercises are being carried out throughout the globe to develop the capabilities that will further operationalize the initiative. Several of these exercises have already been successfully completed, including at-sea exercises in the Coral Sea and the Mediterranean. Planning for further development of PSI activities continues. The G-8, at Sea Island, called for expanding this effort.

The Terrorist Threat

All of these initiatives are intended to keep WMD and missile delivery systems out of the hands of would-be proliferators—both states and non-state entities. As noted, the idea of terrorists armed with nuclear weapons, or other WMD, was largely unheard of at the time of President Eisenhower's Atoms-for-Peace speech in 1953. Today, it is a real concern. Terrorist groups have increasingly evidenced their interest in obtaining—and using—weapons of mass destruction. For such groups, WMD is not a weapon of last resort, the ultimate guarantee of a nation's survival, but may be a weapon of first choice, designed to destroy societies and spread terror.

The proliferation of nuclear, chemical, and biological materials, knowledge, and technologies, as well as of legitimate facilities with inherent dual-use capabilities, increases the risk that a terrorist group will acquire the wherewithal to construct and use WMD. Indeed, the use of chemical and biological weapons by terrorist groups has already been demonstrated.

A number of state sponsors of terrorism, including Iran, North Korea, and Syria, are actively seeking to acquire WMD and missile delivery systems and, in some cases, to sell such technologies to other states. As President Bush stated when he appeared at the United Nations in September 2003: "Outlaw regimes that possess nuclear, chemical, and biological weapons—and the means to deliver them—would be able to use blackmail and create chaos in entire regions. These weapons could be used by terrorists to bring sudden disaster and suffering on a scale we can scarcely imagine. The deadly combination of outlaw regimes and terror networks and weapons of mass murder is a peril that cannot be ignored or wished away."[3] Our nonproliferation policy, and indeed, that of the entire international community, has an obligation to ensure that this doomsday scenario never takes place.

Conclusions

Fifty years ago, President Eisenhower presented a vision to the community of nations—a vision of a world simultaneously enjoying the benefits of nuclear energy without the threat of nuclear proliferation. It was a hopeful vision, full of optimism about the prospects for humankind. Fifty

---

3. Remarks by the President in an address to the United Nations General Assembly, New York, September 12, 2002.

years later, we must acknowledge that Eisenhower's vision has yet to be achieved. The world remains dependent on fossil fuels. Even more disturbing, not only has the threat of nuclear proliferation failed to decline, but it has assumed new shapes and forms that present new dangers.

We also should note that more than half a century after the invention of the atomic bomb, fewer than a dozen states actually have acquired nuclear weapons. Moreover, the community of nations has taken important steps to ensure the abolition of biological and chemical weapons. Other steps have been initiated to rein in the would-be proliferators of the world, and to keep WMD technology out of the hands of rogue states and terrorist groups alike. Much has been accomplished to ensure global security. More work needs to done. Fifty years after it was first presented to the world, Eisenhower's vision of Atoms for Peace remains a worthy, but still distant, goal.

6

Atoms for Peace and the Future of Eisenhower's Vision

Ambassador Jayantha Dhanapala

The fiftieth anniversary of President Dwight D. Eisenhower's Atoms-for-Peace speech to the United Nations General Assembly (UNGA) provides an opportunity to review the progress that we have achieved in the peaceful harnessing of the most powerful source of energy thus far discovered and to examine realistically the prospects for the future. Whether we discuss nonproliferation, arms control, or disarmament, there are clearly positive and negative factors that must be weighed in our common assessment of the situation today. They are not evenly balanced, but as we look to the immediate future, let alone to the next last fifty years, we can identify policies that will help to achieve the Eisenhower vision of sharing nuclear energy for peaceful purposes while, in his words, seeking the "reduction or elimination of atomic materials for military purposes."[1] The widespread tendency to engage in hand wringing and alarms over the state of the nuclear

1. "Atomic Power for Peace," an address by Dwight D. Eisenhower, President of the United States, before the General Assembly of the United Nations, December 8, 1953.

nonproliferation regime must be replaced by a collective endeavor to seek multilateral solutions.

This will not be possible without examining another major speech of President Eisenhower at the end of his term—the famous military-industrial complex speech. Both speeches will forever live in the book of history.

This paper will examine the main themes in the Atoms-for-Peace speech, briefly tracing their evolution over the last fifty years and describing their current status. It will next attempt to show how much of the disarmament dialogue in the multilateral domain of the United Nations bears striking similarities to the objectives Eisenhower had in mind. Finally, it will suggest some policy options that the international community must adopt if we are to ensure the health of the nuclear nonproliferation regime and proceed irreversibly through nuclear disarmament to the total elimination of nuclear weapons that Eisenhower wanted.

Three Significant Themes in the Eisenhower Speech

The Atoms-for-Peace speech was given at the United Nations General Assembly—supportive of the world body, imbued with a spirit of multilateralism and embracing a strong commitment to global agreements in the constructive pursuit of international peace and security. In the fifty years that have elapsed, support for the United Nations and multilateralism has waxed and waned. President Eisenhower's belief "that if a danger exists in the world, it is a danger shared by all"[2] is a belief in collective and cooperative security, which lies at the heart of the United Nations. It was also the period of the Cold War when only three nuclear-weapon states existed and the temptations to retain nuclear weapons and participate in a nuclear arms race must surely have been strong. Eisenhower's proposals led to the establishment of another multilateral institution—the International Atomic Energy Agency (IAEA).

The next U.S. president had to confront an expanded "nuclear club" and the Cuban crisis when the actual use of nuclear weapons was narrowly averted. President John F. Kennedy's concerns about nuclear-weapon proliferation led eventually to the Nuclear Nonproliferation Treaty (NPT) of 1968—another example of multilateralism in practice where the verifiable renunciation of the nuclear option by states was balanced by the promise of

2. Ibid.

nuclear disarmament by the nuclear-weapon states and the offer of the peaceful uses of nuclear energy, especially to developing countries. This is the "bargain" central to the NPT and the cause of the tension among its member-states.

Fifty years later, we have a world of five nuclear-weapon states with this status acknowledged in the NPT, four nuclear-weapon–capable states, some states suspected of harboring plans to acquire a nuclear-weapon capability and fear—aggravated by the tragic events of September 11, 2001—that terrorist groups or individuals might acquire nuclear weapons or weapon-useable materials. At the same time, the NPT includes as many as 187 states, ranking as the disarmament regime with the largest number of parties. The IAEA continues to face challenges in fulfilling its safeguards responsibilities, gaining from lessons learned from the clandestine development of nuclear weapons by Iraq, the Chernobyl disaster and more recently through the challenges posed by the Democratic People's Republic of Korea (DPRK) and Iran. The 1997 Model Additional Protocol has undoubtedly strengthened the verification of the obligations of the non–nuclear-weapon states, but as IAEA Director General ElBaradei acknowledges, more needs to be done.

Genuine multilateralism would require that the obligations of the nuclear-weapon states be met and monitored especially after the 1996 advisory opinion of the International Court of Justice (ICJ) and the final document of the 2000 NPT Review Conference. Although the total number of nuclear weapons remains lower than during the height of the Cold War, it remains alarmingly close to the number that reportedly existed when the NPT was signed.

The second noteworthy feature of the Eisenhower speech is the transparency advocated by the U.S. president who stated: "Clearly if the peoples of the world are to conduct an intelligent search for peace, they must be armed with the significant facts of today's existence."[3] In a spirit of openness, Eisenhower wanted to share the knowledge of nuclear fission with the rest of the world despite the perceived global reach of the "axis of evil" in 1953 in contrast to 2001. In a globalized world today, technological expertise can no longer be confined within national borders and the knowledge of nuclear energy may well have spread even without the IAEA and the international cooperation we have seen in the peaceful uses of nuclear

3. Ibid.

energy. However, the channeling of this assistance through the IAEA has regulated the dissemination of this knowledge with checks and balances leading to a growing awareness of the responsibilities that go with the use of nuclear energy. Nuclear safety measures such as the Convention on the Physical Protection of Nuclear Material together with nuclear export controls and the Cooperative Threat Reduction (CTR) program have had the cumulative effect of attempting to discriminate between responsible and unreliable users. This has often led to subjective judgments based on the political affiliations of individual states and the discriminatory reactions to the spread of nuclear-weapon technology.

Total consistency has therefore not been practiced and this may have been what Eisenhower meant by "elementary prudence." The practice of this elementary prudence should be undertaken by the IAEA in accordance with Agency procedures that are consistently applied in a nondiscriminatory manner with adequate safeguards. The emergence of states determined to flout global norms and non-state actors for whom such norms are irrelevant vastly complicate the tasks of the IAEA.

A further drawback is the continued lack of transparency on the numbers of nuclear warheads even within nuclear-weapon states that are democracies, the absence of democratic controls on the different stages of nuclear-weapon development, and the failure to encourage public discussion of nuclear-weapon policies. There is little evidence of a broad-based process that is both transparent and accountable in the decision making on nuclear policies, strategic doctrines, procurement, research, production, stockpiling, and deployment. Ideally, this should involve the executive, the military, the scientific community, parliament, the judiciary, and civil society in the interests of good governance and the fundamental right to participate in decisions on the very survival of nation-states and the global community.

Thirdly, Eisenhower was actually seeking nuclear disarmament and the elimination of nuclear weapons. He called for the "reduction or elimination of atomic materials for military purposes" and removing "this [nuclear] weapon out of the hands of the soldiers."[4] It is a theme that indisputably links this speech to his military-industrial complex speech. He saw the folly of relying on a nonproliferation strategy alone. In this speech, he also rejected the concept of deterrence, which prevailed long after his time. He opposed the use of nuclear weapons in the certain knowledge that it would

4. Ibid.

cause unmitigated disaster for the human race. "Surely no sane member of the human race could discover victory in such desolation,"[5] he noted.

Fifty years after those words were uttered, however, many countries are pursuing policies of nuclear deterrence while the actual use of nuclear weapons is now being contemplated in recently formulated nuclear doctrines. Eisenhower himself, faced with a growing Soviet conventional force in Europe, appears to have abandoned this stance when he announced the doctrine of massive retaliation in 1954. Needless to say, we are very far from achieving the total abolition of nuclear weapons despite successive consensus decisions within the NPT context and the Advisory Opinion of the ICJ in 1996.

The reduction of fissionable material stockpiles is another proposal that has not been implemented in the fifty years that has passed. The Fissile Material Control Treaty (FMCT) that has been proposed for negotiation in the Conference on Disarmament (CD) seeks the cessation of the actual production of fissile material for the manufacture of nuclear weapons. Although no mention of what is to be done with existing stockpiles has yet been made, this would strengthen the NPT. The Trilateral Initiative among the Russian Federation, United States, and IAEA would help as a confidence-building measure, and its completion and implementation are called for as one of the thirteen practical steps to implement Article VI of the NPT in the Final Document of the 2000 NPT Review Conference.

Eisenhower and the United Nations' Disarmament Dialogue

Eisenhower's thinking on nuclear weapons is in many ways part of the mainstream disarmament dialogue in the United Nations and in other multilateral fora—a dialogue with which I have been privileged to be associated for many years. In his farewell speech, he said, "Disarmament with mutual honor and confidence is a continuing imperative. Together we must learn how to compose differences, not with arms, but with intellect and decent purpose."[6] The very first resolution of the UNGA adopted on January 24, 1946, sought to establish a Commission to deal with the problems raised by the discovery of atomic energy. This Commission was the precursor of the IAEA, with authority to report and make recommendations to the UN

5. Ibid.
6. "Farewell Address," by President Dwight D. Eisenhower, January 17, 1961.

Security Council (UNSC) "in the interest of peace and security," the UNGA and the Economic and Social Council. The membership of the Commission was to be confined to the members of the UNSC and, interestingly, Canada, when that country was not on the UNSC. It is important to quote the terms of reference of the Commission. It was required to make the following specific proposals:

- For extending between all nations the exchange of basic scientific information for peaceful ends
- For control of atomic energy to the extent necessary to ensure its use only for peaceful purposes
- For the elimination from national armaments of atomic weapons and of all other major weapons adaptable to mass destruction
- For effective safeguards, by way of inspection and other means, to protect complying states against the hazards of violations and evasions

The famous Baruch Plan based on the Acheson–Lilienthal report (with the significant addition of sanctions as punishment for violators) was presented to this Commission in June 1946 by the United States. Seven years later, in responding to a resolution of the UNGA regarding the work of the Disarmament Commission, Eisenhower used many of these concepts in his speech. We see them reappear in the Statute of the IAEA and in the text of the NPT. Of special note is the use of the term "weapons of mass destruction" (WMD). Today nuclear, chemical, and biological weapons fall within this category. We have succeeded in establishing a Biological Weapons Convention in 1972, and a Chemical Weapons Convention (CWC) in 1993 banning these two categories of weapons of mass destruction.

The argument is persistently made that WMD cannot be "disinvented" mainly as a rejection of the feasibility of the elimination of nuclear weapons. Delegitimization and disinvention are two different concepts. The banning of nuclear weapons remains an unfulfilled task entirely because of the opposition of nuclear-weapon states. The distinctive feature of these weapons is not just the horrendous scale of death and destruction that they can cause but, more importantly, their impact on the continuity of the human race. Proven evidence of the effects of these weapons and especially nuclear weapons show that the impact on the human environment and the genetic structure of human beings imperils our continued existence. While evidence of these impacts in the United States has been revealed, it is not the only nuclear-weapon state to experience first hand the human and environmental effects of even the mere production and development of such weapons.

Equally untenable is the argument that nuclear weapons must not get into the "wrong hands." There can be no legitimate hands possessing these weapons of mass destruction and concepts like "managed proliferation" erode the moral basis of the NPT. They also distort the vision of Eisenhower whose appeal to remove these weapons "out of the hands of the soldiers" was a rejection of the military uses of nuclear energy for all countries and groups.

In recognition of this, the Partial Test Ban Treaty of 1963, the NPT of 1968, several nuclear weapon-free zone treaties, and the Comprehensive Nuclear Test Ban Treaty (CTBT) of 1996, refer to the objective of nuclear disarmament. Following the indefinite extension of the NPT in 1995, which was sought and obtained by the nuclear-weapon states, inter alia, as a reliable basis for further disarmament leading to the total elimination of nuclear weapons, the NPT Review Conference of 2000 elaborated an action plan of thirteen specific steps in its final document for the achievement of this.

Despite the failure of the 2005 Review Conference to reach consensus on these or other issues, it is important to review the implementation of these "Thirteen Steps" to which very little attention is paid within nuclear-weapon states themselves. An interim status report published by the Global Security Institute makes dismal reading. With the CTBT not in force, the current moratorium on nuclear-weapon testing is in a fragile state. Although there has been no progress in the CD on nuclear disarmament, the United States introduced a draft FMCT in the CD in 2006. We see new doctrines for new uses and types of nuclear weapons (including their pre-emptive use), the abrogation of the Anti-Ballistic Missile Treaty, the demise of the second Strategic Arms Reduction Treaty, and other developments. There is little encouragement for a success in these areas. However, the Cooperative Threat Reduction Program, the "10 plus 10 over 10" initiative, the Strategic Offensive Reductions Treaty of 2002, the Plutonium Management and Disposition Agreement between Russia and the United States, and the strong financial support given to the IAEA are some encouraging developments.

Given the debate between unilateralism and multilateralism, it is important to recall that Eisenhower stood for multilateral institutions and multilateral agreements, recognizing, no doubt, the invaluable legitimacy and universality they provide. Recent experience demonstrates that unilateral action is less desirable and durable than multilateral action and that eventually unilateral actions need to be multilateralized. This is especially true in the area of nuclear disarmament and nonproliferation. Diplomacy remains the best hope for a peaceful and successful resolution of the concrete problem of Iran's compliance with the NPT. Multilateral negotiations including the U.S. and Iran are a viable option while the Security Council remains seized on the matter. Likewise the broadening of the discussion with the DPRK in the six-nation conference format is more likely to be productive than a policy of unilateral coercion. Resolutions in the UNGA have again emphasized the importance of multilateralism in disarmament issues. The current problems of the CD can be traced to bilateral disputes, the solution of which will surely unblock the logjam on the adoption of a program of work, including on nuclear disarmament.

Verification is another common theme between Eisenhower and the United Nations as multilateral security and legitimate verification measures have to be built into multilateral agreements if they are to be credible and effective. Thus, the CWC, with its most intrusive inspections, the Model Additional Protocol of the IAEA, the technologically advanced International Monitoring System under the CTBT, and the widespread availability of commercial satellite imagery to civil society to publish information on nuclear issues all ensure that nations or groups that plan to cheat on global norms will not get very far. This is in addition to the national technical means available to the more powerful countries. Technology to enhance verification techniques is advancing all the time and there is every reason to be confident of this vital part of disarmament when we finally have a nuclear weapon convention to abolish nuclear weapons.

Another important issue is transparency, and reporting requirements at future NPT conferences by all states parties will help towards this end. We could indeed have global society better mobilized to support the NPT and the work of the IAEA:

- With verification accessible at a societal level
- With the growing consciousness of the need for a code of ethics among scientists in the defense sector
- With the interpretation and implementation of "whistle blowing" on violations of global norms and treaty obligations as a logical extension of the right to conscientious objection (buttressed by the Nuremberg Principles and the International Criminal Court's existence)

This presupposes that the international community is confident that global norms are being implemented fairly, without discrimination and within the framework of international law. The trivialization of the charge of WMD proliferation as a casus belli for unilateral action damages the nonproliferation regime and does not help to stop future violators or withdrawals.

Policy Options for the Future

With the á la carte multilateralists agreeing that the NPT is an indispensable multilateral agreement, the international community must work together to strengthen it further. The current trend towards aggressive counterproliferation is inherently flawed and counterproductive. Steps such as the Proliferation Security Initiative originally announced by eleven countries to interdict shipments of WMD delivery systems and related materials can only be effective if they conform to existing legal norms, including the Law of the Sea and the United Nations' Charter. Preemption must have the approval of the Security Council except in the most extreme cases of imminent attack, when the approval must be secured post-facto as soon as possible.

Another general principle that flows from the legitimate search for security by all non–nuclear-weapon states and the development needs of non–nuclear-weapon developing countries is the fact that security assurances to non–nuclear-weapon states against the use or threat of use of nuclear weapons have to be addressed. The spectacle of some states maintaining nuclear weapons as a means of defense while denying this same means to others is no longer sustainable.

While the logic of nuclear disarmament leading to the total elimination of nuclear weapons must be recognized and accepted, in the interim the need for security assurances to non–nuclear-weapon states is urgent. In every instance of either the nuclear threshold being crossed—or attempts being made to do so—this has happened in conflict-ridden neighborhoods or in situations of perceived risk to national security. Security guarantees may well have averted some situations, although the acquisition of nuclear weapons as a false status symbol can never be totally excluded until the possession of nuclear weapons is banned and/or delinked from great power status as in the case of Japan and Germany, two important global powers who are non–nuclear-weapon states. The persistent refusal to agree to negotiate a multilateral treaty providing security assurances to non–nuclear-weapon states within the NPT cannot be sustained. In the negotiations, conditions for receiving such guarantees could always be discussed requiring, for example, IAEA certification of good standing in terms of fulfilling NPT obligations such as by signing the Model Additional Protocol and being outside any alliances or pacts with any nuclear-weapon state.

The international economic situation is manifestly lopsided with approximately half the global population living on less than $2 per day. The Millennium Development goals endorsed by the leaders of all nation-states in 2000 are in danger of becoming a mirage. Linkages between economic deprivation, conflict, and violence are well known. For the culture of violence and terrorism to be replaced irreversibly by a culture of peace, we need to have economic development. Global military expenditure runs at more than $1 trillion per annum, according to the Stockholm Peace Research Institute, and the opportunity costs of that spending are enormous. More specifically, the potential of nuclear energy to help developing countries is significant. In medicine, in agriculture, and in many other nonpower areas, nuclear energy can assist developing countries without any risk of proliferation, and the IAEA needs to be funded to expand its excellent work in this field.

Other specific policy options open to the international community are, briefly:

- Expansion of the CTR program to include other countries with G-8 funding going beyond its current level
- The mandatory requirement of accession to the Additional Protocol of the IAEA as a prerequisite to receiving assistance, material, and technology for nuclear power for peaceful purposes
- The establishment of an Executive Council or Board elected by the state parties of the NPT at a future review conference meeting regularly, and serviced by the United Nations Department for Disarmament Affairs, to make recommendations on the NPT and to function as a "jury" of peers, if violations of the NPT are alleged
- The criminalization of violations of WMD treaties both at the national level and in the International Criminal Court, so that individuals will be put on notice that complicity with clandestine programs will meet with punishment

Conclusion

In a major article published in *The Economist* on October 16, 2003, IAEA Director General ElBaradei has argued cogently for a reappraisal of some of the premises of the NPT. With increasing difficulties in controlling access to nuclear-weapon technology and gaps like the nonproscription of enrichment or reprocessing technology, he has proposed a new approach. Limiting the processing of weapon-usable material, designing proliferation-proof nuclear energy systems that avoid using nuclear-weapon material, and multinational approaches to the management and disposal of spent fuel and radioactive waste are the main components of this approach. They require detailed and collective study to ensure that changed circumstances do not drive us to destroy a system of collective security when intelligent reform is possible.

United Nations Secretary General Kofi Annan has addressed the breakdown of the consensus on the collective security system that has prevailed for a greater part of the post–World War II period, the full efflorescence of which was heralded at the end of the Cold War. Pursuant to this, he appointed a sixteen-member panel of eminent persons, chaired by a former prime minister of Thailand to examine the major threats and challenges in international peace and security in its broadest interpretation and to recommend practical measures for effective collective action while assessing the available tools for this purpose. The report offers a viable path to the future; addressing WMD threats figured prominently in the panel's work. There is also the International Commission on WMD sponsored by the government of Sweden with Hans Blix as chair, which addressed the issue of WMD. It issued its report in June 2006.

We must contribute ideas and proposals to such efforts so that we can together design solutions to the urgent problems that Eisenhower addressed in his memorable speech. If we do so within the framework of collective security, recognizing that global security is indivisible, we cannot go wrong.

7

Toward Universal Nonproliferation and Disarmament

Ambassador Mohamed I. Shaker

In 1957, the International Atomic Energy Agency (IAEA) advocated in President Dwight D. Eisenhower's Atoms-for-Peace speech came into being. This was a significant event for world security and development. The philosophy behind Atoms for Peace was that the spread of nuclear technology around the world was bound to happen and, therefore, it should be encouraged, albeit under international control to guard against its misuse. This philosophy should prevail today because if the flow and spread of nuclear technology for peaceful purposes were further curtailed or restricted, we would be running the risk of further threats of proliferation of nuclear weapons.

Despite the export control regimes in existence today, certain countries have still managed to develop an advanced nuclear capability in undeclared facilities. This was partly due to the restrictions imposed on the export of certain technologies. Those states tried to get around extant restrictions and to develop nuclear technologies in secrecy. If these technologies had been exported under strict international control, the problems that we are facing today could have been different. This is not to say that these technologies should be exported to everyone, but that too many restrictions can be counterproductive. The emergence of export control regimes has in fact greatly affected the orderly and smooth cooperation anticipated by Article IV of the Treaty on the Nonproliferation of Nuclear Weapons (NPT). There was an attempt a few years ago by the Nuclear Suppliers Group to institute a dialogue, or a series of consultations, with recipients. This effort needs to be bolstered and widely institutionalized—to be "democratized"—in order to guarantee the unhindered development of nations in great need to diversify their technological capabilities. There is also need to reinstitute the Committee on Assurances of Supply of the IAEA.

When the IAEA was established, no one could have expected it to develop into a major world organization that we witness today. If we were to follow its growth and development, we would find out that as an arms control organization and as a promoter of peaceful uses of nuclear energy, it has gone through many stages and has faced many challenges. It rose up to these challenges. Regarding nonproliferation and arms control, the IAEA's success in developing several safeguard systems, including the Additional Protocol (AP) to the safeguards agreements concluded between the parties to the NPT and the IAEA, deserves recognition. The AP should allow the Agency to play a greater role as a verification agency in future arms control and disarmament agreements.

The then-director general of the IAEA, Hans Blix, in 1983, believed that the safeguards system of the NPT needed to be bolstered and was looking for new ideas on how to do that. Blix had a vision. As early as 1983, he felt the need for change. No progress was made at this time. However, ten years later, in the aftermath of the Second Gulf War and the revelations about the Iraqi nuclear program, the "93+2 program" was initiated, which led to the AP of 1997—two years later than had been anticipated.

The question of sovereignty has for a long time been perplexing for the IAEA and was responsible in a way for slowing progress in the development of an effective safeguards system. However, the times have changed. After the Iraqi invasion of Kuwait, the Agency had to face great challenges and had to adapt to the realities of the day. In this era, with discussions about humanitarian intervention or the right to preemption, which also infringe on the principle of sovereignty of states, it is now possible to make progress with regard to the AP. The protocol is a welcome step in the right direction. However, the protocol itself is insufficient to check proliferation. The ideas put forward by the present director general of the IAEA, Mohamed ElBaradei, are worthy of consideration. He advocated the following:

- Favoring the limiting of processing weapon-useable materials in civil nuclear programs exclusively to facilities under multinational control
- Development of nuclear energy systems avoiding the use of materials that may be applied directly to making nuclear weapons
- Adopting multinational approaches to the management and disposal of spent fuel and radioactive waste

These ideas could also be considered in the future establishment of nuclear-weapon–free zones; they could even be introduced to existing zones. The IAEA plays an important role in the application of safeguards in the countries that are parties to these zones. Future zones may have also their own control regimes that would be verified by the IAEA.

Nowadays, we are witnessing the violation by certain parties to the NPT of their undertakings in the treaty and in the safeguards agreements they signed with the IAEA. The breakthrough with regard to Iran and the ongoing attempts to find a diplomatic and peaceful solution to the North Korean problem are positive developments and ought to be pursued diligently in the coming years. Following the disarmament of Iraq, a settlement of these two cases should make the international community more determined to ensure full compliance of all parties to the NPT to their undertakings under the treaty and in their safeguards agreements. Unfortunately, a great number of parties to the NPT have not yet concluded those agreements. Moreover, adherence to the Additional Protocol has also been limited.

Compliance with the obligations and undertakings of the NPT is not the responsibility of the non–nuclear-weapon states alone, but of the nuclear-weapon states as well. Why should we expect North Korea, Iran, and Iraq to comply fully with their obligations, and not expect the same compliance on the part of nuclear-weapon states who have undertaken, in Article VI of the NPT, to move toward a world free of nuclear weapons—a world where general and complete disarmament would be the order of the day?

For the NPT to survive, the nuclear-weapon states parties to the treaty have to comply fully with Article VI of the NPT. The thirteen points agreed upon by the five nuclear-weapon states in the NPT Review Conference of 2000 have not been fulfilled. The 2005 NPT Review Conference could not agree on anything, including new disarmament steps. The United States introduced a draft treaty to cut off fissionable materials for weapon purposes in the Disarmament Conference in Geneva, but will such a treaty be negotiated and concluded? Where are we with regard to nuclear disarmament, where the failure in Geneva to dwell upon it is obvious? Lastly, where are we from the entry into force of the Comprehensive Nuclear Test Ban Treaty (CTBT) of 1996?

On the contrary, the U.S. Nuclear Posture Review indicates to us that we are not on the path of eliminating nuclear arsenals, but that we are on the path of retaining and operating strategic warheads for an indefinite period. Moreover, the prospective production of new small nukes is troubling. The possibility also of utilizing nuclear weapons in preemptive strikes against countries developing unconventional weapons is a deviation from the policy of deterrence.

If we were further to curtail proliferation, the nuclear-weapon states would have to embark on a serious process of disarmament and, more particularly, nuclear disarmament. In this respect, one can see a role for the Agency that has been expected by many; for instance, monitoring agreement on a cut-off of fissionable materials and ensuring that the released fissionable materials are devoted to peaceful purposes. This would be very much in the spirit of Atoms for Peace.

The founders of the IAEA had a vision, and the international community ought now to have its own vision as to the future role of the IAEA. This domain ought to be explored by referring the potential role of the Agency in the areas of verification, disarmament, and arms control to an expert group like the ones that were established within the IAEA to develop the safeguards systems of the Agency. Certainly, such an expert group cannot work in a vacuum. It would have to be assisted by the nuclear-weapon states, which could furnish it with ideas and information on how to proceed with its task. If the Agency were to be involved in such an enterprise, it would mean a second lease on life for the Agency. It could be a veritable Atoms for Peace II.

Those states outside the NPT, India, Pakistan, and Israel—the so-called "nuclear-weapon powers," to differentiate them from the nuclear-weapon states, as defined in the NPT itself—must be addressed. Shall we consider those states a lost cause for our nonproliferation efforts, or are there ways and means to bring them in concert with the efforts of the majority of the states of the world? For example, the idea of establishing a zone free of weapons of mass destruction in the Middle East, a proposal put forward by

President Hosni Mubarak of Egypt in 1990, is worth considering. If such a zone were realized, Israel would join all the states of the region, who all happen to be parties to the NPT. That is one way of overcoming the absence of Israel as a party to the NPT. The establishment of such a zone could be based on a number of basic elements, including:

- A regional control regime verified by the IAEA
- Coverage of all weapons of mass destruction despite the fact that each category of weapons has its own characteristics
- Security guarantees by the nuclear-weapon states
- A role for the neighboring states to the zone

It is hoped that once the roadmap of the Middle East is implemented, the Arms Control and Regional Security group established within the Madrid peace process would be reactivated and those issues could be discussed under its umbrella.

It would not reflect a lack of vision or ingenuity to involve India and Pakistan in any future arrangements that would bring them closer to the nonproliferation regime. Their commitment not to attack each other's facilities is a step in the right direction. They should be encouraged to follow the example of the Brazil-Argentina Agency for the Accounting and Control of Nuclear Materials.

The nonproliferation regime, with the NPT as its focal point, is a regime that can be adapted to changing circumstances. The Review Conference of the NPT is a valid and important instrument in this respect. The failed 2005 NPT Review Conference did not give a boost to the IAEA and encourage it to evolve and to be committed to the ideas, such as multinational controls on fuel cycle facilities as suggested by its director general. It did not request the IAEA to reconstitute its Committee on Assurances of Supply. It was and remains crucial that this Committee, which had failed in the past to find a formula to guarantee the supply of nuclear materials and equipment to all states, should be given a second chance to do so in the aftermath of the cases of Iran and North Korea. That is because the former, at one point, complained that it had difficulty in obtaining the ingredients for its nuclear power program. The Conference also did not espouse the idea of a United Nations conference on the spread of weapons of mass destruction. The proliferation problem, as all can realize, is the top item on the agenda of the foreign policy of leading nuclear- and non–nuclear-weapon states. The international community has failed, so far, to convene another United Nations Special Session on Disarmament. It has also failed to organize a United Nations Conference on Disarmament, similar to the United Nations conferences on environment, population, women, and so on, which captured the attention of world public opinion. In today's world, with the threat of terrorism with weapons of mass destruction, a conference on weapons of mass destruction is necessary. This is an issue that needs the concerted efforts of all states. In the 1980s, many observers thought nuclear terrorism sounded like science fiction, but not anymore. In such an endeavor, the IAEA as well as other bodies need to be more involved and they must possess the means to contribute to this agenda. This is already occurring, but more could be done. An analyst and leading observer of nuclear affairs has made the remark that the total figure of nuclear weapons in the world is equivalent to three tons of TNT for every human being and that, since 1957, not a single explosive device has been manufactured with material processed in a facility under IAEA safeguards.[1]

In the light of all the above, fifty years after the Atoms-for-Peace speech, is there any doubt that the international community can renew its commitment to this vision and go further beyond it in promoting nuclear peaceful cooperation under strict international control? Can the international community ensure a greater role for the IAEA in the future that would guarantee for it a peaceful world free of further proliferation of nuclear weapons, and even a world free completely of such weapons? If the political will exists, this is possible.

---

1. Georges Le Guelte, "Nuclear Proliferation: Current Trends and Prospects," paper presented at the Belgian Nuclear Society, Brussels, November 26, 2003.

Part II

Addressing Nuclear Proliferation and Terrorism

8

Atoms for Peace and the "Rogue States"
Robert S. Litwak

The Atoms-for-Peace bargain created incentives for states to forego nuclear weapons. The bargain and the institutional structure designed to implement it did envisage verification measures. However, these measures were designed primarily to provide confidence or reassurance of the behavior of participating states, which were expected to honor a solemn treaty obligation. As was demonstrated only in the early 1990s with Iraq and North Korea, and a decade later with Libya and Iran, states could readily deceive the verification system—International Atomic Energy Agency (IAEA) safeguards. The expectation of gentlemanly behavior built into IAEA safeguards proved to be naive. This has raised questions about the bargain as it has become clear that it is possible for states to use the premise of Atoms for Peace to develop a nuclear-weapon capability.

Does this demonstrate the bargain was unsound or, at least, that it should never have been expected to be seriously embraced by some states—those that are sometimes called "rogues"? To what extent can the incentive in the proposal be used to address the so-called rogue states today?

U.S. Rogue State Policy

To address these questions, a sense of what is meant by the term rogue states is in order. The term, in its current usage, dates back to 1980. It has been used by both the Clinton and Bush administrations to refer to states that were, inter alia, supporting or sponsoring terrorism and pursuing weapons of mass destruction (WMD). These two criteria are key to defining rogue state status.

The Clinton Administration

National Security Advisor Anthony Lake laid out the Clinton administration's rogue state policy in a controversial 1994 *Foreign Affairs* article, entitled "Confronting Backlash States." Although best known for its elaboration of the so-called "dual containment" policy toward Iran and Iraq, the article addressed the rogue state issue more generally, stating:

[O]ur policy must face the reality of recalcitrant and outlaw states that not only choose to remain outside the family [of nations] but also assault its basic values. There are few "backlash" states: Cuba, North Korea, Iran, Iraq and Libya. For now they lack the resources of a superpower, which would enable them to seriously threaten the democratic order being created around them. Nevertheless, their behavior is often aggressive and defiant. The ties between them are growing as they seek to thwart or quarantine themselves from a global trend to which they seem incapable of adapting.

These backlash states have some common characteristics. Ruled by cliques that control power though coercion, they suppress human rights and promote radical ideologies. While their political systems vary, their leaders share a common antipathy toward popular participation that might undermine the existing regimes. These nations exhibit a chronic inability to engage constructively with the outside world. . . . They are often on the defensive, increasingly criticized and targeted with sanctions in international forums. Finally, they share a siege mentality. Accordingly, they are embarked on ambitious and costly military programs—especially in weapons of mass destruction (WMD) and missile delivery systems—in a misguided quest for a great equalizer to protect their regimes or advance their purposes abroad.[1]

1. Anthony Lake, "Confronting Backlash States," *Foreign Affairs* vol. 73, no. 2 (March/April 1994): 45–46.

Lake concluded that "[a]s the sole superpower, the United States has a special responsibility for developing a strategy to neutralize, contain, and through selective pressure, perhaps eventually transform these backlash states into constructive members of the international community."[2] Strikingly, this policy enunciation underscored that "rogue" status derived from realist criteria relating to these states' external behavior, not their domestic policies (such as compliance with human rights norms). By contrast, the Clinton administration's overarching foreign policy strategy of "engagement and enlargement"—expanding the community of democratic states to achieve international peace—was grounded in the liberal Wilsonian tradition.

After the publication of Lake's *Foreign Affairs* article, the term "rogue state" gained wide currency within the Clinton administration. Secretary of State Madeleine Albright provided further elaboration when she told the Council on Foreign Relations in September 1997 that "dealing with the rogue states is one of the great challenges of our time . . . because they are there with the sole purpose of destroying the system."[3]

Once a country was branded a "rogue" or "outlaw" state and placed in that category, critics viewed any deviation from hard-line containment as tantamount to appeasement—a charge leveled at the Clinton administration when it negotiated a nuclear agreement with North Korea in October 1994. One observer called the rogue state strategy more an attitude than a coherent policy. In practice, however, the approach came up against hard political realities in North Korea and Iran that called its efficacy into question. As a consequence, in June 2000, the State Department announced its decision to use the infelicitous but more diplomatic sounding "states of concern" instead of "rogue states."[4] In explaining this shift, spokesman Richard Boucher said that "the [rogue state] category has outlived its usefulness. . . . It's not really a change in behavior or policy or what we're doing as much as it is finding a better description, or a better description because a single description, one size fits all, doesn't really fit any more."[5] The Clinton administration's foreign policy critics ridiculed the change as

2. Ibid., 55.
3. U.S. Department of State, Office of the Spokesman, "Secretary of State Madeleine K. Albright Address before the Council on Foreign Relations," September 30, 1997 (http://secretary.state.gov/www/statements/970930.html).
4. Steven Mufson, "A 'Rogue' Is a 'Rogue' Is a 'State of Concern'," *Washington Post,* June 20, 2000, p. A16.
5. For the transcript, see U.S. Department of State, Daily Press Briefing, Spokesman Richard Boucher, June 19, 2000 (http://secretary.state.gov/www/briefings/0006/000619db.html).

an Orwellian word game to rationalize a misguided policy of engaging outlaw regimes.

The Bush Administration

The Bush administration restored rogue state to the U.S. diplomatic lexicon in February 2001, but did so without specifying which particular states fell under that category.[6] In the Bush administration's pre-9/11 policies, two important underlying assumptions were evident. The first was a political prognosis concerning the states' future trajectory and long-term prospects for survival. Condoleezza Rice observed that, as the historical process of democratization and the extension of market economies has unfolded, "some states have been left by the side of the road." She argued that "[t]hese regimes are living on borrowed time, so there need be no sense of panic about them." The second was that, in addressing the threat posed by rogue states, "the first line of defense should be a clear and classical statement of deterrence—if they do acquire WMD, their weapons will be unusable because any attempt to use them will bring national obliteration."[7] After the September 11 terrorist attacks, these threshold assumptions about rogue states would be viewed differently—in Secretary Rumsfeld's view, through the prism of 9/11.

Reflecting this focus, the Bush administration denounced the "axis of evil"—Iraq, Iran, and North Korea—and declared that the greatest threat to international order arises from "the nexus of terrorism and proliferation." In the aftermath of "major combat operations" in Iraq in spring 2003, the administration faced escalating nuclear proliferation crises with the other two charter members of the axis—North Korea and Iran. Major constraints on the ability of the United States to bring about regime change in Pyongyang and Tehran, as well as the political fallout over the WMD intelligence debacle in Iraq, may have prompted the administration's pragmatic turn

---

6. For example, National Security Adviser Condoleezza Rice told CNN on February 4, 2001: "The President is committed to restructuring the nuclear relationship and making defenses against limited threats from rogue states or accidental launch a part of the new, restructured relationship [with Russia]" (www.cnn.com/2001/ALLPOLITICS/stories/02/04/missile.defense/index.html). When the White House press secretary, Ari Fleischer, was asked to specify the "rogue states" underpinning President Bush's advocacy of ballistic missile defense, Fleischer responded, "I am not going to go down and start delineating states. The President's concern is general." White House, Office of the Press Secretary, "Press Briefing by Ari Fleischer," February 5, 2001 (www.whitehouse.gov/news/briefings/20010205.html#NationalMissileDef).

7. Condoleezza Rice, "Promoting the National Interest," *Foreign Affairs* 79, no. 1 (January/February 2000): 60–61.

toward multilateral diplomacy. It has pursued this diplomatic course with North Korea, directly, through six-party negotiations (involving South Korea, Japan, China, and Russia), and with Iran, indirectly, through European Union foreign ministers and the International Atomic Energy Agency (IAEA). While these diplomatic efforts were being pursued, following secret diplomacy, Libya decided later in 2003 to disarm, showing to some in the administration a path ahead—one that appeared to have been, in part at least, influenced by military operations in Iraq.

With these considerations in mind, let us look at Libya, Iran and North Korea.

Libya

On December 19, 2003, Libya committed to eliminate its chemical- and nuclear-weapon programs. To this end, it stated it would:

- Declare all of its nuclear activities to the IAEA
- Accept international inspections to ensure Libya's complete adherence to the Nuclear Nonproliferation Treaty and sign the IAEA Additional Protocol
- Eliminate all chemical weapons stocks and munitions, and accede to the Chemical Weapons Convention
- Eliminate ballistic missiles with more than 300-km range when carrying a payload of 500 kg

To implement these commitments to dismantle its WMD and missile programs and eliminate all dangerous materials, Libya worked with the United States, the United Kingdom, the IAEA, and the Organization for the Prohibition of Chemical Weapons. On March 6, 2004, a total of 500 metric tons of equipment left Libya for the United States by ship. According to the White House, the shipment included:

- Centrifuge parts used to enrich uranium
- All equipment from Libya's former uranium conversion facility
- All of Libya's longer-range missiles, including five Scuds, and all associated equipment, including launchers

Since then, Libya has reportedly sent all of its nuclear-weapon–related equipment and material to the United States.

Of the Libyan disarmament effort, President Bush stated

Colonel Ghadafi made the right decision, and the world will be safer once his commitment is fulfilled. We expect other regimes to follow his example. Abandoning the pursuit of illegal weapons can lead to better relations with the United States, and other free nations. Continuing to seek those weapons will not bring security or international prestige, but only political isolation, economic hardship, and other unwelcome consequences.[8]

In pursuing this path, the Bush administration agreed to end Libya's diplomatic isolation and no longer block the state's reintegration into the international system. The Libyan WMD deal not only sets an important nonproliferation precedent, but also could serve as a model of rogue state rehabilitation. The breakthrough would not have occurred in the absence of an American assurance of nonintervention—explicitly dropping the U.S. objective of regime change in the face of a profound shift in Libyan behavior. But Ghadafi's shift relates only to his regime's objectionable external behavior with respect to proliferation and terrorism. That feature of the December 2003 agreement left the Bush administration open to criticism from human rights and democratization advocates, who argued that the United States should also press for internal change in Libya, just as it was doing elsewhere in the region through its Greater Middle East Initiative. The critics' underlying concern was that in the post-9/11 era the United States would not energetically pursue this political agenda. Washington would instead turn a blind eye to an authoritarian, secular leader who violated human rights norms at home, but eschewed WMD and destabilizing behavior beyond his borders, confronted al-Qaeda and Islamic extremism more generally, and provided a ready supply of oil to the world market.

To the extent that the Bush administration has articulated a broader concept of societal change in Libya, it is essentially regime change by evolution. The "process of rejoining the community of nations" is part of a long-term strategy in which the very process of outside engagement with Libya will promote a positive domestic political evolution. The underlying concept is that increased integration into the global economy (e.g., expanding trade relations with the European Union) will require modes of political transparency and accountability that over time will empower economic

---

8. Remarks by the President on Weapons of Mass Destruction Proliferation, National Defense University, Ft. Leslie J. McNair, Washington, D.C., February 11, 2004.

interest groups with increased political autonomy and thereby erode the Ghadafi regime's authoritarian grip on Libyan society. This concept of societal change in Libya is consistent with the Clinton administration's strategy of "engagement and enlargement." On the great power level, this liberal integrationist approach has been pursued toward China by U.S. presidents from Nixon onward. Facing the dilemmas of engagement, Ghadafi will likely seek to garner the tangible benefits of economic engagement while limiting its political consequences. Thus, the gritty near-term reality may reflect rather the critics' fears than the hopeful neo-Wilsonian vision.

Iran

The proliferation threat posed by Iran has appeared increasingly worrisome; its nuclear program has necessitated an IAEA response. The September 2003 resolution of the Board of Governors, inter alia, called on Iran:

- To suspend all further uranium enrichment-related activities, including the further introduction of nuclear material into Natanz, and, as a confidence-building measure, any reprocessing activities, pending provision by the director general of the assurances required by member-states and the satisfactory application of the provisions of the Additional Protocol
- To work with the Secretariat to promptly and unconditionally sign, ratify and fully implement the Additional Protocol, and, as a confidence-building measure, henceforth to act in accordance with the Additional Protocol.[9]

The demands on Iran and expectations about Iranian behavior in this and subsequent Board resolutions reflected the concerns of the Board. Although these concerns spurred the Board to action, the steps taken at the time did not go as far as some would have liked or perhaps as could have been expected given the nature and extent of violations. Iran was not referred to the UN Security Council at this time.

With a view to avoiding this fate, a European diplomatic initiative obtained Iraqi agreement to accept the Additional Protocol, which Tehran has

9. International Atomic Energy Agency, Board of Governors' Resolution, GOV/2003/69, September 12, 2003.

signed, and to suspend its enrichment activities. This was seen to provide the basis for a resolution of the issue. It was never clear that this agreement fully remedied the problem and new evidence of Iranian deception along with a statement of Iran's very limited commitment to suspending enrichment underscored this viewpoint. The Iranian decision to resume suspended activities resulted in referral to the United Nations Security Council.

If the Security Council does not act forcefully, Iran will in principle be able to finish the facilities it desires, and perhaps also a reprocessing capability, and then announce a withdrawal from the NPT. Here the scenario is rather a strategy of exploiting the NPT loophole. This form of regime abuse would not be affected at all by additional inspection rights. Accordingly, Iran presents a complex and difficult challenge to the regime. In the end, the case of Iran will not be dealt with successfully via inspections alone.

The nuclear crisis in Iran is playing out against the backdrop of this broader political struggle. The challenge for the administration is that the nonproliferation timeline, which is immediate because of the IAEA's revelations about Iran's undeclared uranium enrichment facilities, is at odds with the timeline for internal political change. Current views of political change in Iran divide into two competing schools—one positing a hard landing that leads to regime change, the other projecting a soft landing through regime evolution. The key determinant in these contending concepts of change is the new reality of Iranian politics—the rise of a politically energized civil society. Proponents of the hard landing school regard Iran as being in a pre-revolutionary situation, such as Eastern Europe was in 1989, or Iran itself was in 1979. Soft-landing adherents believe that regime evolution is possible either through the reformists' finally gaining political ascendancy or through pragmatic hard-liners' willingness to cut internal and external deals to ensure political survival.

The Bush administration has sent mixed signals on which the concept of political change is at the heart of its policy. It has not moved toward a Reagan doctrine–type policy of supporting external insurgents (although some outside the administration do favor support of the Iranian exile group Mujaheddin-e Khalq to pressure the Tehran regime). But in its support of Iranian civil society as the agent of change, the administration is conflicted on whether a politically energized population could bring down the theocratic regime or, alternatively, put pressure on the regime to implement the reformist agenda. Even among fervent proponents of the hard-landing school, few would argue that the theocratic regime is on the verge of being toppled through a civil society uprising. Indeed, the popular election of a hard-line conservative, President Mahmoud Ahmadinejad, on a nationalist and anticorruption platform called into question whether Iranian civil society would be an agent of positive change, from the U.S. perspective.

North Korea

The North Korean nuclear program poses a clear danger. North Korea has expelled IAEA inspectors, withdrawn from the NPT, reprocessed plutonium, proceeded with a uranium enrichment program, and threatened the testing, sale, and use of nuclear weapons. President Bush's objectives with respect to the DPRK are clear. All weapons and components, weapon-usable materials, and all related facilities and equipment must be removed from the country, and destroyed, disabled, dismantled, or otherwise rendered harmless. Meeting these objectives successfully will be daunting. The United States has considerable experience in dealing with some of the requisite tasks, but some are unprecedented in scope and difficulty. The environment will be different from postwar Iraq and Libya. It is not clear what is achievable.

As with Iran, the nuclear challenge with North Korea is embedded in the broader question of political change in that society. After the Pyongyang regime breached the 1994 Agreed Framework and began to reprocess plutonium from nuclear fuel rods at its Yongbyon facility, Secretary of Defense Rumsfeld reportedly sent President Bush a memo in April 2003 recommending that the United States enlist Chinese assistance to oust the Kim Jong Il regime.[10] The memorandum reflected one of the two contending concepts of political change driving policy options. In this hard-landing approach, the threshold assumption is that the North Korean regime is on the verge of collapse and that an economic strangulation policy, if supported by China, can push the regime over the edge. A variant of this regime change scenario is that the Chinese could be persuaded to engineer an internal coup that leads to the removal of Kim Jong Il and his immediate entourage, leaving a hard-line but more acceptable alternative in power.

10. David E. Sanger, "Administration Divided Over North Korea," *New York Times,* April 21, 2003, A15.

But the same factors that precluded a regime-change and preemption strategy in the 1990s still pertain. Preemptive military strikes on North Korea's nuclear facilities for counterproliferation purposes are likely to be indistinguishable to the Pyongyang regime from the initiation of general war, China and South Korea are opposed to a hard landing because they fear its political and economic consequences, and the Kim Jong Il regime has proved resilient and able to insulate itself from the consequences of economic collapse and famine.

Based on that pessimistic analysis of the Kim Jong Il regime's durability, adherents of the alternative "soft-landing" school regard the hard-landing regime-change scenario as a vain hope in any timeframe relevant to the proliferation issues at hand. This alternative soft-landing school—born of necessity, given the currently intractable conditions within North Korea—aims to achieve a near-term agreement on the nuclear issue within the context of a long-term process of political evolution. That strategy of change is reflected in the South Korean government's limited engagement of the North through its so-called "sunshine" policy. Proponents argue that an expanding web of economic relations (through economic joint ventures and trade relations) will promote an evolutionary process conducive to political reconciliation on the Korean peninsula. For soft-landing advocates, such instruments of economic engagement are "poison carrots" that could become agents of long-term societal change. Critics of this engagement strategy counter that these incentives are tantamount to appeasement—unreciprocated concessions propping up a hideous failed regime that otherwise would collapse.

Conclusions

So long as it remains the core of the nuclear nonproliferation regime, the Atoms-for-Peace bargain will be put forward as an incentive to nonproliferation, no matter what the behavior of the state or the prospects for success. The Atoms-for-Peace bargain was largely sound, and has posed little problem in states that respect international law. But the rogue states are a different matter. It is clear that the bargain has been and is being misused by these states. It has provided capability. It is also part of the rhetorical arsenal of the states that have misused it. Arguments based on the Atoms-for-Peace legacy have been ably used by Iran.

Iran has been unwilling to forego the curtailment of its nuclear program, which it claims is peaceful, and has argued that the program is allowed under the NPT on the basis of the underlying Atoms-for-Peace bargain. Moreover, the Iranians argued that the IAEA has not proven that Iran is seeking weapons. The North Korean case has been ineptly argued on these terms. The agreement reached in the six-party talks in September 2005 talks is challenged by North Korea's demand that it be provided with civil nuclear power along with other issues. As was the case in the Agreed Framework, it is expecting that the bargain be honored by the international community—and especially the United States—even though its avowed nuclear-weapon programs is a violation of its NPT, IAEA, and other obligations.

The prospect of nuclear incentives to bring these states back into the fold appears unlikely to be successful. The crux of the current impasse with Iran is the difficulty in determining with certainty whether nuclear technology obtained by Iran for civilian uses is now being diverted into a clandestine weapon program. Particularly thorny is nuclear fuel-cycle technology for the enrichment of uranium, which Iran asserts its right to possess under the NPT's Article IV. Centrifuges ostensibly producing low-enriched uranium for civilian reactors can easily be diverted to yield weapons grade highly enriched uranium. In Tehran, the perception that the United States is pursuing regime-change strategies is a motivation to continue its nuclear hedging and maintain a degree of ambiguity about its intentions and capabilities. North Korea, which is demanding a nuclear power reactor in exchange for giving up its nuclear arms, has been taking a similar approach and, if the six-party agreement collapses, may continue to do so in the future.

In addressing the nuclear crises with North Korea and Iran, where regime change and preemption were not practical options, the alternative has been deterrence and reassurance. Utilizing a structured negotiating approach, the North Korean regime was presented with a clear choice between the tangible benefits of behavior change and the penalties for noncompliance. This approach led to the September 2005 agreement, but its long-term success remains to be seen. In Iran, offering a similar choice is needed. The military components of American power should be used to induce Iran to choose the option of behavior change. Red lines setting "a clear boundary for acceptable behavior can prove a successful deterrent, but only if backed by the credible threat to escalate, including the use of force."[11] As in the case of Libya—and possibly also in North Korea if the

11. Joel S. Wit, Daniel B. Poneman, and Robert L. Gallucci, *Going Critical: The First North Korean Nuclear Crisis* (Washington, D.C.: Brookings Institution Press, 2004), 406–407.

terms of the agreement are fully realized—leaving these regimes a political exit by being prepared to provide a security guarantee of nonaggression and noninterference is a central aspect of reassurance. The challenge for the Bush administration is that its rhetoric and policies—the "axis of evil" speech, the preemption doctrine, and President Bush's April 2003 speech "redefining war" to permit targeting regimes rather than civilian populations[12]—undercut its ability to offer a credible security assurance to Iran and North Korea. Indeed, as negotiations with Iran and North Korea seek to curtail their nuclear programs, both countries may seek to cultivate ambiguity about the status of their capabilities in order to deter what they perceive as a regime-changing threat from the United States.

12. Remarks by the President to Staff of Boeing F-18 Production Facility, Boeing Integrated Defense Systems Headquarters, Boeing F-18 Production Facility, St. Louis, Missouri, April 16, 2003.

9

The Current Proliferation Predicament

Ariel Levite

The norm enunciated by President Dwight D. Eisenhower fifty years ago is as relevant and important today as it ever was. Yet in terms of its practice, it is currently subject to the most acute challenge of the last thirty-five years and perhaps the greatest it has ever faced. And this challenge lies first and foremost in the nonproliferation domain.

While the traditional tools of arms control and nonproliferation remain relevant today, as they currently stand, they are woefully insufficient to meet the acute and rapidly escalating proliferation challenges that we face. A vigorous new effort to confront these challenges is urgently needed, which must be multilateral in nature, led by the United States, and sophisticated enough to incorporate as key allies not only the Europeans but also Russia, China, and leading countries in Africa, Asia, and Latin America (from South Africa to Brazil).

The Atoms-for-Peace legacy remains an important source of inspiration for dealing with these new challenges, because it has so poignantly recognized the tension between proliferation and energy requirements inherent in the dual nature of nuclear fuel-cycle technology. But the specific formula that it has advanced for balancing energy requirements and nonproliferation, a formula whose spirit has later been embodied in the Treaty on the Nonproliferation of Nuclear Weapons (NPT) and in the classical safeguards of the International Atomic Energy Agency (IAEA), is dated. It will need to be fundamentally revisited in order to address the new realities presented by both the renewed appetite for nuclear power and the novel nuclear proliferation challenges presented by the likes of Iran, the Democratic People's Republic of Korea (DPRK), and, in a different form, by Pakistan as well. The growing global demand for energy, especially for clean alternatives to fossil fuels, inevitably enhances the role of nuclear power in meeting some of those energy requirements. When one looks realistically at the estimates of energy consumption in the decades ahead, it is clear that nuclear power will have to play a significant role in addressing them, particularly in the developing world and among both NPT and non-NPT members alike. The cumulative experience since the original Atoms-for-Peace formula was advanced, coupled with the extremely likely prospect that nuclear power will not only see a revival but also dissemination in the developing world, must give a special sense of urgency to the need to come up with an innovative package that is not only economically viable and meets ever more exacting environmental and safety standards, but also meets new and different nonproliferation standards. As the role of nuclear power inevitably grows in the future, it is thus important to revisit the original formula for balancing among these various requirements.

At least some of the problems we presently face in the proliferation domain—and also part of the solution for today's predicament—lie in the original Eisenhower bargain of promoting peaceful nuclear applications as a means for stemming nuclear proliferation. This bargain thus merits some reconsideration.

Article IV of the NPT, originally designed to win over countries of Western Europe, Australia, Japan, and the like, has been severely abused by several key countries that have used the treaty not only to adopt a hedging posture but also to obtain nuclear technology (or for that matter as a guise to supply others with such technology) under the false pretense of developing or promoting peaceful nuclear applications. And these states have proceeded to divert this nuclear knowledge and technology, as well as to use the reassuring cover of NPT membership (and safeguards applications) to far less benign purposes clearly proscribed under Article I and II of the treaty.

Moreover, the treaty as it currently stands does not explicitly ban nations from first acquiring nuclear knowledge and technology under the guise of peaceful application (Article IV) and subsequently exercising their right to withdraw from the NPT while keeping all of these previously acquired benefits. Nor does it require them to assume any new safeguards or other obligation in the process of doing so. While this loophole in the treaty has attracted a long legal debate, its significance has been made clear by the actions of the DPRK, which had opted out of the treaty after acquiring the technology, leaving it with a nuclear-weapon capability. But things may get even worse. Some nations may follow this path and, once discovered, manage to actually fend off punitive action against them by threatening to pull out of the NPT if they are actually sanctioned for noncompliance with the treaty. Remarkably enough, such behavior gives them a fair amount of political leverage over all those who fear the repercussions of such a withdrawal. And lest anyone think that this is merely a theoretical prospect, recall that much of the Iranian story in recent years has revolved exactly around this possibility.

So what started out as a pretty reasonable gamble, to use Atoms for Peace as an incentive for nations to desist from developing nuclear weapons, has come back full circle to haunt us at present. But arguably the original bargain did yield some success, and what may have been flawed is not the concept itself but rather its precise formulation and imperfect implementation. And perhaps we can presently harness the growing demand for nuclear energy, coupled with the small club presently possessing commercially viable peaceful nuclear technology, to craft a more nonproliferation-robust and still legitimate bargain. Such a bargain would be based on a distinction between access to nuclear power technology and services and access to fuel cycle technology. Access to the former could in turn be made contingent on overall nonproliferation conduct and, in particular, their exercise of restraint. Furthermore, this offer could also be extended to non-NPT parties whose overall nonproliferation credentials are nevertheless sound, as a way of drawing them closer to the nonproliferation regime in return for allowing them access to modern peaceful nuclear technology.

For such an approach to prove viable, another weakness of the current nonproliferation regime—enforcement—would also need to be addressed. Presently the nonproliferation regime is greatly weakened by a woefully inadequate enforcement capacity that gravely affects its deterrent capacity against cheating. Once again, the DPRK is a case in point. The DPRK first cheated and subsequently reneged on its NPT obligations as well as on other nuclear agreements to which it voluntarily subscribed. Yet to this day the United Nations Security Council has consistently found itself unable to deal with this challenge. Iran clearly presents a similar challenge. The Security Council's paralysis could not be overcome in both cases despite the IAEA's eventual documentation of noncompliance with their safeguards obligations. And the Iranian case is especially grave because it has taken a few years to bring to the attention of the Council almost two decades of gross Iranian violations of its IAEA safeguards obligations, and to date enforcement capacity of the Security Council has been wanting. Worse still, the two failures of the DPRK and Iran may even be feeding off each other, serving as a source of inspiration for some and catalyst for others to contemplate nuclear ambitions. Now that the message has begun to sink in that the difficulty of detection coupled with the shortfalls of enforcement make it possible to violate nuclear treaties and get away with it, the challenge both to the integrity of the whole nonproliferation regime, and even more broadly to international security, is grave indeed.

This brings us to the third problem plaguing the nonproliferation regime, which did not exist at the time that the Atoms for Peace was originally conceived. Its origins lie with the spread of nuclear knowledge and technology since that time, and the emergence of new sources of supply, particularly for the more sensitive nuclear fuel-cycle technologies. New state and non-state suppliers have emerged that are willing and able to undercut the nuclear export control regime. Some of these suppliers still reside within the Nuclear Suppliers Group. But alarmingly, a growing number of problems come from new suppliers in possession of such sensitive technology. These new state and non-state suppliers (such as the network run by A.Q. Khan of Pakistan) have done especially grave harm by disseminating (as was the case with Libya and Iran) uranium enrichment technology, and particularly centrifuge (and to a lesser extent also laser) enrichment technology (both products and production know-how), as well as heavy-water research reactor technology. In some cases, these new suppliers even provide long-range ballistic-missile technology exports.

Tragically, the traditional nonproliferation tools of arms control and supplier regimes do not have much to offer in the way of addressing these novel nonproliferation challenges. The decade-old deadlock in concluding (and even negotiating) any effective new global and universal arms control treaties at the Conference on Disarmament—or for that matter anywhere else—seems unbreakable. Prospects for the IAEA Additional Protocol to become a universal norm and condition of supply (especially for the most critical cases) hardly appear any more encouraging. In fact, even the track record associated with the application of existing IAEA safeguards is uninspiring. The IAEA has been struggling to confront these and other emerging challenges to the safeguards system. The Agency has made remarkable gains in upgrading its expertise (human and technical alike) to detect diversion. Yet it is hung up on completing other critical improvements necessary to make it into a truly reliable verification mechanism. It is manifesting both a limited ability (at the bureaucratic level) and even less will (at the political level) to undergo the profound cultural and structural changes necessary to transform it into a truly reliable nuclear watchdog. The Agency has proven appallingly slow and weak in detecting clandestine efforts (e.g., in Libya), and even more reluctant to share its suspicions (when arising) even with its own Board of Governors, let alone with the broader international community. The IAEA has been aware of some problems with Iran's compliance with its safeguards obligations for almost two decades before it has made these concerns public, and even that development had only occurred after the Agency had been subjected to a huge international pressure to do so.

In order to wrap up this assessment of the current predicament of the nonproliferation regime, I will touch on, however briefly, one additional issue, namely the depressing prospect for enhancing the effectiveness of cooperative verification mechanisms. It would seem that we have reached the upward limit of intrusiveness that sovereign nation states are willing to accept. This currently holds true well beyond the nuclear realm per se, reflecting a deep-rooted resistance on both political and practical grounds (rather than on legal grounds). That this is the case may be easily observed when we examine the unwillingness to employ intrusive inspections even in those cases where suspicions of noncompliance arise and no dearth of legal authority to exercise such inspections exists. One case in point is the unwillingness of the Organization for the Prohibition of Chemical Weapons to press ahead (even once) with challenge inspections under the Chemical Weapons Convention. Another case in point is the profound reluctance of the IAEA to employ (against the will of an inspected state party) its special inspections authority under its Statute. This reluctance seems to be grounded in the combined fear of compromising intelligence to facilitate such inspections, stigmatization of the inspected party as a result of the inspection, and retaliation by that party in its aftermath. Even more ominously, however, it would seem that the unwillingness to seek such involuntary inspections without the explicit consent (or even initiative) of the inspected party is further reinforced by concern about triggering an acute crisis if evidence for noncompliance indeed surfaces in the course of such inspection, or unleashing a far broader crisis (one affecting the viability of the regime as a whole) if such inspections fail to uncover anything of concern. But the problem we face here also has a cultural dimension, especially pronounced in the case of the IAEA. Because of its schizophrenic mandate (of promoting peaceful uses of atomic energy while also applying safeguards) rooted in its Atoms-for-Peace origins, the Agency's institutional culture assigns a high premium to cooperation with member-states, greatly diminishing its willingness to act as a reliable watchdog and confront them when necessary.

Finally, we need to acknowledge a related distinct possibility that safeguards or for that matter any other form of routine multilateral monitoring and inspection regime would create or sustain a false sense of confidence about compliance with nonproliferation and arms control obligations. The significance of such a possibility is greatly heightened when it turns out that successive IAEA director generals have either failed to articulate their nonproliferation concerns or refused to take serious action to look into their own concerns or serious compliance concerns raised by others, and have further aggravated the problem by repeatedly making statements implying that the Agency has not found any proof that a certain nation is pursuing a nuclear-weapons program. Even under the best of circumstances, the IAEA would be operating on somewhat shaky grounds when making such statements given its limited mandate for inspections (especially when the Additional Protocol is not in force). But how could such statements be justified when concerns do exist and the Agency nevertheless fails to (or even does not even seek to) exercise some of the inspection rights (such as special inspections) that it does possess? Furthermore, given that the IAEA derives its inspiration from the Atoms-for-Peace scheme, it is oriented toward detecting diversion of nuclear materials from safeguarded facilities, but not to looking for evidence of weaponization, which lies completely outside its mandate. And this constitutes one more gap between the obligations inherent in the NPT and the IAEA safeguards system that is the sole existing monitoring mechanism for verifying compliance with them.

These grave concerns concerning the viability of the early-warning mechanisms in place are not merely theoretical possibilities. They have all been evident in one form or another in the recent crises with Iran, the DPRK, and Libya, and previously with Iraq as well. And given how deeply rooted they are, we must worry that these cases may only be the tip of the iceberg. Nor are these concerns any longer predominantly those of knowledge. As a result of the recent Iraq war, the legitimacy of action on the basis of (national) intelligence has been largely tarnished. So the findings of the IAEA and similar bodies currently constitute the difference between legitimacy and lack thereof, and consequently also between the ability to act to confront an emerging threat and the inability to do so.

So where do we go from here? We need to think increasingly about undertaking multilateral like-minded nonproliferation initiatives, rather than about negotiating universal new treaties. This should be the way to go not because this necessarily is the preferred way to proceed, but rather because it may be the only realistic way to make headway at present, and because in some cases at least, it could make a huge difference. As a matter of priority, such an initiative should aim to lock in a re-interpretation of Article IV that would prohibit the proliferation of new national fuel-cycle facilities, whether as part of a formal process or merely (if the former proves elusive) as a practical interpretation adopted by a like-minded coalition.

We need to acknowledge that variants of this idea have already been suggested by, among others, the director general of the IAEA, who sees multinational ownership of fuel-cycle facilities as a key complement to the Agency's verification activities. But we must also emphasize that it is not absolutely necessary to adopt such a universal and global arrangement in order to stem the tide of proliferation. Progress in securing new nations' commitment to forego construction of fuel-cycle facilities could be made by offering them a new bargain based on access to nuclear power reactors, and if necessary, to assurances about nuclear fuel supplies as well. Such a package would not only be designed to entice countries to abandon indigenous nuclear fuel-cycle facilities, but also, and just as importantly, to shift the burden of proof for sound nonproliferation conduct from the suppliers to the recipients of nuclear technology. Once recipients assume the responsibility of reassuring suppliers of their good faith as a condition of supply, the ominous challenge to prove noncompliance in a convincing and legitimate fashion would be greatly eased for the Agency, thereby paving the way for much more safe and reliable dissemination of nuclear technology. Under these circumstances, a structural and cultural reform of the IAEA would still be necessary in order to enhance its performance in the nonproliferation domain, but the difficulty of implementing such a reform could be somewhat reduced.

Regardless of how one feels about any or all of the specific ideas suggested here, there is an overriding message that should have come across from the above analysis. The message is that the prevention of proliferation has to become once again a top foreign policy priority. This is not presently the case, nor has it been in recent years (essentially, not since the heyday of Atoms for Peace). Thus, if we are to stem the tide and spare ourselves truly agonizing dilemmas and potentially catastrophic outcomes, urgent high-level attention must be directed to this effort, notwithstanding its lackluster political appeal.

While coercive measures of various types may well have a role to play in the nonproliferation domain—ranging from those included in the Proliferation Security Initiative (PSI) to preventive action—they hardly provide comprehensive and enduring solutions to the key problems at hand. What we need to understand is that these may influence supply while we must simultaneously work on squelching demand for nuclear proliferation. The challenge lies in working the issue with a coalition of the willing that is as broad as possible, which would include at least some nontraditional allies. Both Iran and the DPRK constitute contemporary cases in point.

Thanks in no small degree to the multinational dimension, the Iran episode playing out in front of our eyes has been, at least thus far, a partial success in this regard, having attracted a huge amount of high-level political attention, and ultimately also coalition partners ranging from the European Union, Canada, Australia, and Japan, to Brazil, China, and Russia. While such a broad-based coalition may not suffice at the end of the day to stop the nuclearization of Iran and the demise of the entire nuclear nonproliferation regime, it most probably is a necessary condition for success. We stand only a slim chance of meeting this grave challenge in the absence of such a broad-based coalition.

10

Nonproliferation Efforts in Northeast Asia
Ambassador Choi Young-jin

As we ponder what the future holds for humankind as the twenty-first century unfolds, we find ourselves transfixed by the "war on terror" zeitgeist. International terrorism has magnified the specter of nuclear proliferation in a way that clearly distinguishes the concerns we have today from those of the past. In this context, fifty years after the Atoms-for-Peace speech by President Eisenhower, this paper will approach the issue of nonproliferation from an angle that takes into account the problems facing northeast Asia.

Nuclear proliferation arguably constitutes—along with climate change—the most serious threat facing humanity in the twenty-first century. The current configuration of the nuclear proliferation issue includes five permanent members of the United Nations Security Council, who are permitted to possess nuclear weapons within the Nuclear Nonproliferation Treaty (NPT) regime. Three countries—India, Pakistan, and Israel—either have or are believed to have developed nuclear weapons outside the NPT regime. There are two countries, Iran and North Korea, who have, or are suspected to have, nuclear-weapon programs. Finally, Japan, South Korea, and Taiwan, as well as a large number of other advanced industrial states, are endowed with both the technological and financial resources that would allow them to rapidly and easily develop nuclear weapons.

The most critical link in this configuration is between the last two segments, especially between North Korea on the one hand and Japan, South Korea, and Taiwan on the other. These states are all located in northeast Asia, which, along with North America and Europe, constitutes one of three global economic epicenters that together account for roughly three-quarters of global economic output. With infinite potential in terms of dynamism and population size—double the population of Europe and North America combined—northeast Asia is poised to become a global economic engine as the twenty-first century unfolds. However, this otherwise peaceful and prosperous region is now threatened by the specter of nuclear proliferation.

Pyongyang has claimed that it possesses nuclear weapons and is increasing its arsenal. If it is proven that it has gone nuclear, this would trigger a very strong international reaction, especially from South Korea, Japan, the United States, China, Russia, and the European Union. The upshot would be further isolation of, and increased pressure on, North Korea from the international community, rather than encouraging the economic assistance it desperately needs.

Calculations in Pyongyang must have judged the crux of the matter to be whether the international community would, in the end, acquiesce to this *fait accompli*. In other words, would the international community allow Pyongyang to have it both ways, that is, to become a de facto nuclear-weapon state and still gain the acceptance of the international community?

The five neighboring countries now involved in six-party talks have made it very clear to Pyongyang that a nuclear North Korea will not be tolerated. It is highly unlikely that these are empty threats, because northeast Asia cannot run the risk of a nuclear domino effect.

Not only would the extraordinary economic prosperity brought by peace and stability in the region be put at serious risk, but a nuclear arms race in northeast Asia would also be the beginning of the end for the NPT regime as we know it. The international community cannot afford to allow the NPT regime to unravel, especially because the war on terrorism has only just begun and the prospect of nuclear terrorism is too horrible to contemplate.

From the North Korean perspective, there may be more problems than can be seen from outside. North Korea is currently torn between political survival and economic revival. This dilemma may lie at the heart of the riddle surrounding the North Korean nuclear question.

The international community must stand firm in its principled position, namely, "Pyongyang cannot have it both ways." Let us hope, meanwhile, that Pyongyang finds wisdom in the old saying: "Can the medicine be worse than the disease?" The prospects for the six-party talks in Beijing, in the final analysis, depend solely on how Pyongyang responds to this crucial question. Even if we now have renewed hope for a resolution of the North Korean nuclear issue, the problems we have already encountered remind us that, fifty years after the Atoms-for-Peace speech, we are now unquestionably at a critical juncture. We stand at a crossroads between "Atoms for Peace" or "nuclear proliferation." For humankind, one of the most critical questions of the twenty-first century will be whether Atoms for Peace or the specter of nuclear proliferation prevails. If we can accept what reason dictates, the choice is clear and simple. Nuclear proliferation is completely unreasonable. The peaceful use of nuclear energy has to be the answer. Then why is it so difficult for Atoms for Peace to prevail over nuclear proliferation? How is our reasoning flawed? Should our future be trusted to the powers of human reasoning?

Ultimately, we are dealing with a question of evolutionary dimensions. Austrian scientist Konrad Lorenz noted the paradox that humanity's greatest gifts and strengths—its unique faculties of conceptual thought and verbal speech—were not only blessings, but direct causes of all of the great dangers threatening humanity with extinction. Humankind has changed little biologically since emerging as *Homo sapiens* some fifty thousand years ago; it is expected to remain much the same for the next one or two million years. It has been endowed with a uniquely human tool, namely, its mental capabilities. Yet, these distinctive capacities cut both ways: they give us both unprecedented prosperity and the potential to extinguish our species by, for example, environmental degradation and nuclear proliferation.

Human beings are, after all, the first species in history to threaten its own existence. If, in all our wisdom, we prove incapable of resolving a problem that we ourselves created, humanity may never fulfill its potential as endowed by biological evolution. We may instead bring about our own extinction along with those of countless other species with whom we share the planet. The question—one asked by Lorenz—is whether humankind will prove to be only an aggressive primate with a megalomaniac perception of its mental capacity.

We need to make a critical and collective decision about nuclear energy. History shows that humankind does not make important decisions by reason alone. Historically, catastrophe and tragedy motivated the wise men of the past to forego momentary parochial self-interests in order to make epic decisions for the common good of generations to come.

There is the rub. Now that humankind has nearly conquered most forms of natural catastrophe, self-interest and parochial interests seem to have become the prevailing dynamic of the human psyche. Potential twenty-first century catastrophes such as environmental degradation and nuclear proliferation, however, cannot and will not be resolved by the pursuit of naked national interests. They threaten our very existence, which makes the burning question of the twenty-first century: "How do we escape our own trap?"

How shall we rally the troops to overcome the governing dynamic of our time, namely parochial and national interests? The answer to this seems elusive. As we continue to search for it, we seem to have nothing but reason to depend on for making the most critical choice of our time: Atoms for Peace.

As expressed in the Eisenhower's "Atoms-for-Peace" proposal, we have to find the way by which "the miraculous inventiveness of man shall not be dedicated to his death, but consecrated to his life."[1] We owe it to our children.

---

1. "Atomic Power for Peace," an address by Dwight D. Eisenhower, President of the United States, before the General Assembly of the United Nations, December 8, 1953.

11

Toward Cooperative Security: Prospects for Nonproliferation and Arms Control

Feroz Khan

In thinking about the future, a world living in a cooperative security paradigm is better than a world living under a confrontational model. Further, a multilateral approach is better than a unilateral one, although there are differences over whether universalism should be achieved in multilateral institutions or by cooperation only with like-minded states. In addition, as we look to the future, we must recognize that emerging nuclear nations will emulate what the superpowers did during the Cold War.

With these considerations, let us turn to the legacy of President Eisenhower. He said, in his Atoms-for-Peace speech fifty years ago:

> I know that the American people share my deep belief that if danger exists in the world it is a danger shared by all and equally if hope exists in the mind of one nation, then that hope should be shared by all.[1]

---

1. "Atomic Power for Peace," an address by Dwight D. Eisenhower, President of the United States, before the General Assembly of the United Nations, December 8, 1953.

This sense of shared danger and hope is critical. Few people today would argue that the 20th century invention of nuclear energy has left humankind with tremendous potential for peace and prosperity as well as destruction. Whereas President Eisenhower saw the atom as a source of hope for the future, today the atom is viewed as a matter of concern. Worries about "proliferation" then were not quite as profound as they became subsequently with the maturation of the nuclear age. Nuclear energy, per se, is not a cause of concern unless other technologies are combined with it, making it either peaceful or dangerous. Today, the future of nonproliferation and arms control looks bleak, but with a leap of imagination and the spirit of cooperation, we can still reach the objectives of enhancing world peace and security.

History bears out two clear lessons. First, the march of human invention and technology continues, whether it was from transistors to microchips or from nuclear energy fission to nuclear bombs. Consequently, the international nuclear nonproliferation regime must take into account the continuous advance and diffusion of human knowledge and technology. Second, and related to the first, technology sharing must be done very carefully. There is the potential for the "promiscuous spread" of such technology once it gets into wrong hands.[2]

Fifty years ago, this fear permeated the world just when the United States was on the verge of sharing nuclear technology around the world. Today, we stand at the brink of introducing exotic missile defense technology into regions of tension. Fifty years from now, will we regret that we shared such technology irresponsibly?

Motives for Proliferation and Nonproliferation

Why do states go nuclear? There is general agreement that nations pursue nuclear weapons in an attempt to improve their security situation. Nuclear weapons can deter key adversaries from nefarious designs. Other factors come into play as well. Some nations view nuclear weapons as a source of pride and prestige. For them, nuclear weapons are the currency of power. This is the word coming from India. Technological determinism, favored as an explanation in the past, does not seem a plausible causal factor. Many countries today have the capacity to develop nuclear weapons but have not

---

2. This phrase is from John Foster Dulles. See William B Bader, *The United States and the Spread of Nuclear Weapons* (New York: Pegasus, 1968), 9–35.

pursued that path. Some have had security guarantees that others do not (Japan, Taiwan, South Korea, etc.). In other cases, domestic factors can play a role. Sweden and Australia, for instance, had the capacity to go nuclear, but decided not to exercise it because of their own internal compulsions. Such domestic restraint did not take place in South Asia, however. In fact, myths about nuclear weapons were exploited to gain domestic approval in both India and Pakistan.[3] Lastly, global norms play a key role in determining the costs of proliferation activity. Norms in the 1960s encouraged France to go nuclear, but global norms persuaded Ukraine in the 1990s to give up their nuclear inheritance.[4]

What are the motives for arms control? States enter into arms control because it is in their national interests. If arms control is a global norm, states will seek benefits in exchange for accepting those norms. The second and overriding motive is national security. If states determine that arms control enhances their national security by tying down a key adversary, they will pursue this instrument. To restate this point, national security concerns override global norms. As Michael Mandelbaum put it: "Individuals will eat forbidden foods, even one another, if the alternative is starvation; nations will acquire and use forbidden weapons if they deem it necessary for survival."[5]

States will refrain from the pursuit of nuclear weapons if they feel that proliferation increases their vulnerability and decreases their political influence. They will challenge the nonproliferation or arms control regime if they perceive that there exist double standards and if they think that nuclear possession will increase their power and prestige, reduce their security concerns, or provide economic spin-offs.

There are three categories of proliferators. The first one involves privileged countries, such as Israel, that quietly snuck into the club with few or no questions asked. Their status will not be questioned so long as they keep quiet. Others, such as India, aim to make a loud bang when crashing through the club's gate. Then, there are countries like Pakistan that react to their surroundings. Nothing would stop Pakistan from acquiring nuclear

---

3. Peter R. Lavoy, "Nuclear Myths and the Causes of Proliferation," in Zachary Davis and Benjamin Frankel, eds., *The Proliferation Puzzle,* Security Studies, vol. 2, nos. 3/4 (Spring/Summer 1993): 202.

4. Scott D Sagan, "Why Do States Build Nuclear Weapons? Three Models in Search of a Bomb," *International Security,* vol. 21, no. 1 (Winter 1996/1997): 54–86.

5. Michael Mandelbaum, "Lessons of the Next Nuclear War," *Foreign Affairs* 74, no. 2 (March/April 1995): 25–30.

capability after it was clear India was on such a path. Israel and Pakistan both represent what Mandelbaum has referred to as "international orphans." They "feared for their lives, having neighbors that they felt did not accept the legitimacy of their existence as sovereign states."[6] States facing such threats turn to nuclear weapons—viewed as the ultimate victory-denying instruments, not war-winning weapons.

Interestingly, all three countries—India, Israel, and Pakistan—while defying other global norms, have preserved one norm. Nuclear weapons have never been used in anger since 1945.

Ike in Perspective

When President Eisenhower sought to promote nonproliferation through Atoms for Peace, the world then was, of course, very different from today's. Eisenhower had earlier led the battle for freedom in Europe against fascism, the first genie of the twentieth century stuffed back into its bottle, and, as president, he was fighting to put the second genie—communism—back into the bottle. However, this fight was occurring in a new world—a nuclear world. The president knew that he could not go it alone. He chose the United Nations for his forum and not a domestic audience, a fact that he even mentioned during his epochal speech. Eisenhower recognized the significance of multilateralism and chose that policy tool over unilateral options. The first atomic age was barely a decade old then; the character of the nuclear age and the connotation of proliferation and arms control were still evolving. The ethos of the nuclear age has since changed profoundly, as the first nuclear age has paved way for the second. However, the principles that governed the first age stand equally applicable today in several ways.

The need for multilateralism, through strengthening the United Nations forum, was one clear legacy of the nuclear age. At the time when President Eisenhower was leading the United States, nuclear weapons formed part of integral munitions; his policies helped convert them into deterrent weapons.[7] The precedent of nonuse eventually became formalized during the Reagan–Gorbachev era. It was recognized that nuclear wars cannot be

---

6. Ibid.
7. Nuclear weapons were considered to be available for use as other munitions. See U.S. National Security Council (NSC), Basic National Security Policy, NSC 162/2, October 29, 1953, in U.S. Department of State, *Foreign Relations of the United States* (hereafter FRUS), 1952–1954, vol. 2:578–597.

won, and must never be fought. This golden axiom must extend to conventional war between nuclear adversaries. When nuclear weapons are on the chessboard, even moving a pawn could draw the queen out.[8] States locked in conventional conflict face the potential for the inadvertent use of nuclear weapons while navigating through the "fog of war."[9]

Inevitability of Spread

President Eisenhower correctly identified the danger of proliferation. He said in his speech:

Atomic realities of today comprehend two facts of great significance. . . . First, the knowledge now possessed by several nations will eventually be shared by others—possibly all others. Second, even a vast superiority of weapons and a consequent capability of devastating retaliation, is no preventive, of itself, against the fearful material damage and toll of humans lives that would be inflicted by surprise aggression . . . but let no one think that vast sums for weapons and systems of defense can guarantee absolute safety. . . .[10]

These two important messages are still important: Proliferation is ordained and there is no convincing defense against a nuclear attack.

Because Eisenhower understood that the spread of technology was inevitable, he appealed to the multinational system and to the conscience of the international community. He underscored the illogical nature of a maddening arms race that had already begun. This faith in multilateral institutions, combined with a belief in the multilateral approach, formed the foundation of Atoms for Peace. After all, if the United States did not

---

8. This analogy is from a well-known and respected Indian scholar, Lt. Gen. (ret.) V.R. Raghavan, who heads the Delhi Policy Group, a major think tank in New Delhi. Raghavan asserts that nuclear weapons are like a "queen on the chess board [influencing] every move of bishop or a pawn," and hence cannot be ignored even when "contemplating small (conventional) operations." V.R. Raghavan, "Nuclear Doublespeak—Allowing Pakistan to Make Nuclear Threats Helps Its Conflict Plans," *The Telegraph* (Calcutta), January 29, 2003 (available at http://www.telegraphindia.com/archives/archive.html).

9. For views on the consequences of "fog of war" and nuclear weapons by this author, see Martin Schram, *Avoiding Armageddon: Our Future, Our Choice* (New York: Basic Books, 2003), 52–60.

10. "Atomic Power for Peace."

provide the technology, the Soviet Union likely would. The United States was aware of the risks of horizontal proliferation. For instance, in September 1955, Isador Rabi, chair of the Atomic Energy Commission General Advisory Committee, warned in explicit terms to U.S. State Department nuclear affairs advisor, Gerard Smith, that without effective controls to prevent the diversion of commercial nuclear facilities to military uses, "even a country like India, when it had some plutonium production, would go into the weapons business."[11]

Harold Stassen, Eisenhower's ambassador to the United Nations, talked about the inevitability of proliferation two years later. He stated, "It would be perfectly possible, even under the most effective control of some . . . future governments . . . to take away and divert without the knowledge of the inspectors, a quantity of fissionable material from which twenty, forty, or even fifty multimegaton bombs could be fabricated. . . ." In his view, "100 percent perfection of inspections or of accountability" in order to prevent such diversions was not possible or necessary.[12] Controlling proliferation was not necessary because of a faith at the time in deterrence.

There are two types of proliferation: tangible and intangible. Tangible proliferation is easier to control. Examples include hardware such as fissile material, key components, weapons-processing facilities, and so on. Intangible transfers consist of the "software" that can be transmitted by faxes, mail, and e-mail attachments. These technologies did not exist during Eisenhower's days, but he recognized that proliferation of knowledge could be as dangerous and was just as important as the proliferation of hardware.

Ambiguity

Among the legacies of Eisenhower is one involving ambiguity and nuclear signaling. This aspect was not covered in his Atoms for Peace speech. McGeorge Bundy had noted of Eisenhower: "He was very careful indeed not to lose his control, either by unconditional public threat or by delegation of authority. The nuclear reply remained a possibility, not a policy. As he told Vice President Nixon in 1958, 'You should never let the enemy know

---

11. Gerard Smith, September 14, 1955, *FRUS,* 1955–1957, vol. 20:198 (memorandum for the file).

12. Cited by Henry D. Sokolski, *Best of Intentions: America's Campaign against Strategic Weapons Proliferation* (Westport, Conn.: Praeger, 2001): 32.

what you will not do.'"[13] Eisenhower and Nixon believed that such ambiguity provided deterrence. Emerging nuclear nations such as Pakistan have imitated this ambiguity as a conscious policy. As Sir Michael Quinlan has noted, "Pakistan's rejection of no-first-use seems a natural refusal to lighten or simplify a stronger adversary's assessment of risk; it implies retention of an option, not a positive policy of first-use as a preferred course."[14]

Yet another legacy of the nuclear age, although one that President Eisenhower did not contribute to, is the concept of preventive war. There was great fear at the time about surprise knockout blows, part of a larger cult of the nuclear offensive. The belief in the 1950s was that after a certain number of nuclear weapons were acquired, a nation willing to strike first would have an unbelievable advantage. As Henry Sokolski has observed, a driving motivator for establishing the International Atomic Energy Agency was to act as a repository for fissile material, impairing the ability of any state to achieve such an offensive capability. It is ironic that in the 1950s, the United States hoped the international community would stop preventive wars and, today, the United States hopes the international community will condone them.

Such talk about preventive war is dangerous because regional countries aspiring to dominance mimic the United States. Word for word, policy pronouncements coming from Washington are echoed from regional capitals. When the United States talks about preemption, New Delhi does as well. United Nations Secretary General Kofi Annan was prompted to note that this shift towards unilateralism might have untoward consequences. He stated, "If . . . nations discount the legitimacy provided by the UN, and feel they can and must use force unilaterally and pre-emptively, the world will become even more dangerous. . . ." Such an approach could lead to "a proliferation of the unilateral and lawless use of force, with or without credible justification."[15]

Today, the prospects of missile defense technology cooperation are somewhat analogous to what Atoms for Peace was in 1955. Nuclear energy technology was transferred with good intentions and for good reasons, but

---

13. This was in reference to the crisis with the People's Republic of China over the Quemoy and Matsu Islands in the Taiwan Strait. See McGeorge Bundy, "The Unimpressive Record of Atomic Diplomacy," in Robert J. Art and Kenneth Waltz, eds., *The Use of Force: Military Power and International Politics,* 6th ed. (Lanham, Md.: Rowman and Littlefield Publishers, Inc., 2004), 89.

14. Michael Quinlan, "How Robust Is India–Pakistan Deterrence," *Survival* 42 (Winter 2000–2001): 149–150.

15. Cited in "Binding the Colossus," *The Economist,* November 20, 2003, p. 25.

it was exploited by some states for other ends. Similarly, missile defense technology also has the potential to be shared and exploited. Proliferation would encourage unilateral actions by states seeking regional hegemony and would prompt arms races and aggravate regional situations—something President Eisenhower cautioned against in the nuclear context.

Cooperative Security

It is equally important to underscore and remember that President Eisenhower spoke of hope, not just of dangers. Hope must be for all people. Hope for just one country is danger for another. Absolute security for one country generates absolute dangers for all others. The only way forward is through the creation of a climate of cooperative security, where hopes and dangers are shared and the collective goals and concerns of humankind are paramount. Such a cooperative security regime reflects the true spirit of the legacy of President Eisenhower.

A future cooperative security regime must integrate three key elements:

- Expanding the Proliferation Security Initiative (PSI) to include all states
- Creating global security and safety norms
- Sharing technology that enhances stability

First, in the context of the PSI, an information-sharing network needs to be created in which efforts by all states, both internal and external, can be coordinated. The PSI must be expanded into an international regime, rather than a loose conglomeration of countries, and conform to international law.

Second, global security and safety norms must be created which address three key areas:

- Loose control of sensitive materials
- Inadequate security arrangements at sensitive facilities
- Insufficient material accountancy

Knowledge of security, safety, and organizational best practices must be shared.

Third, only technology that enhances stability should be shared. Distinguishing between such stability-enhancing technology and instability-creating technology is a difficult task, but technology that has the potential to cause regional instability must not be transferred.

Finally, the legacy of President Eisenhower, which began sharing nuclear technology and material, will only culminate with global and complete disarmament as promised in Article VI of the Nonproliferation Treaty. Since that might take a while, meaningful discussions on the Fissile Material Cutoff Treaty (FMCT) need to commence. The FMCT ought to be the landmark global arms control treaty of the twenty-first century. President Eisenhower would be pleased with the successful culmination of such a treaty.

12

Toward an Integrative Approach to Preventing Nuclear Terrorism

Ambassador Linton F. Brooks

At the time the Atoms-for-Peace speech was delivered, President Dwight D. Eisenhower was aware of the grave dangers of nuclear proliferation. But the proliferators were seen to be states. Today, we are concerned about nonstate actors getting access to nuclear weapons or weapon-useable materials.

The threat of nuclear terrorism is now in the center of the U.S. and international security agenda. After the September 11 terrorist attacks and subsequent attacks around the world, the international community has mobilized to confront the specter of terrorists armed with nuclear and other weapons of mass destruction (WMD).

Since September 11, important work has been undertaken to address nuclear terrorism. Efforts are underway to improve security of nuclear and radioactive materials, to update antiterror norms and controls over nuclear technologies, and to heighten awareness of dangers arising from nuclear terrorism.

As impressive as these gains may be, far more remains to be done to keep nuclear and radiological weapons out of the hands of terrorists and states that sponsor them. A useful step forward would be to move towards an integrated strategy that joins more conventional antinuclear terror activities—that is, securing nuclear and radioactive assets against theft and sabotage—with efforts to strengthen the core of the nonproliferation regime—that is, safeguards, physical protection, export controls, and strengthened treaty regimes—to prevent terrorist acquisition or brokering in WMD technologies. Prevention of nuclear terrorism and traditional nonproliferation programs form two halves of the same walnut; we cannot treat them as separate enterprises.

Sovereign Responsibility: A Starting Point

The fight against nuclear terrorism must involve all states. Opportunities for terrorists and their supporters to access weapon capabilities are expanding beyond national borders, as illustrated by the A.Q. Khan network and its ability to manufacture components off-shore and move weapon-related technology to clandestine end users.

If we look to lessons for the future, the first one is that as a matter of principle, unless all states accept sovereign responsibility over activities under their jurisdiction and control—whether that is trade and border controls or regulation of nuclear materials or nuclear facilities that are in conformance with international regimes—we risk some future, catastrophic act of nuclear terror. This is a future that we have a collective responsibility to avoid.

President Bush's Nonproliferation Initiatives

An approach that rests on the principle of sovereign responsibility will work best when nonproliferation regimes are strong. Regrettably, the patchwork of treaties, arrangements, and state obligations that form the nonproliferation regime is facing serious challenges.

On February 11, 2004, President Bush highlighted nuclear proliferation dangers and called on the international community to "translate into action" the consensus that proliferation cannot be tolerated and must be stopped. The president's proposals involve four imperatives.

First, efforts to secure high-risk materials must be expanded. This is an important area of work for the United States and our Group of Eight (G-8) and other partners. Cooperation with Russia, given its vast stores of weapon-suitable material, is a first-order priority. Our strategy to ensure the security of weapon material has five core elements:

- Stopping the further production of fissile material usable in weapons
- Consolidating high-risk material and repatriating fresh and spent highly enriched uranium (HEU) from research reactors
- Protecting vulnerable nuclear and radioactive materials by accelerating security upgrades and deploying radiation detection systems at strategic transit points worldwide
- Eliminating excess weapon-grade plutonium, continuing to downblend excess HEU for commercial power and, to the extent possible, ending the use of HEU in civil nuclear applications
- Ensuring that sustainable national nuclear regulatory programs are in place to keep nuclear materials and facilities under proper control

This cooperation has yielded tremendous progress in recent years, protecting or eliminating fissile material equivalent to many hundreds of nuclear weapons.

Newer initiatives like the U.S. Global Threat Reduction Initiative (GTRI) are moving forward to build international support for national efforts to identify, secure, recover, and facilitate the disposition of nuclear and radioactive materials of possible interest to terrorists. Since September 2004, GTRI has repatriated fresh HEU fuel from Uzbekistan and the Czech Republic to Russia, initiated regional training programs and more than ten other joint projects.

As the two largest nuclear states, a special burden falls on the United States and Russia to keep nuclear and radioactive materials out of the hands of terrorists. Cooperation with Russia on nuclear security will remain a priority for the United States. Cooperative programs have wide support, are well funded, and are a regular discussion item between the U.S. and Russian governments, as was indicated by the Joint Statement on Nuclear Security Cooperation at the Bush-Putin meeting in Bratislava in 2005. An important and growing element of our cooperation is to exchange best practices, first with one another and subsequently with all states and with the International Atomic Energy Agency (IAEA). No matter how good a security system is, there is always something to learn in exchanges with other professionals.

The United States is not advocating measures for others that it is unwilling to accept for itself. We are tightening regulatory controls and have dramatically improved our internal security posture. We have installed additional protective barriers external to facilities, and upgraded existing barriers for increased strengthening. Our perimeter alarm systems have been enhanced to counter the increased threat, and we have strengthened security to protect sensitive shipments. Facility access controls for employees and visitors to our facilities have been upgraded, and we have enhanced our protective forces training to focus on tactical training to oppose terrorists. We take this threat very seriously.

Second, states must scrupulously comply with international nonproliferation undertakings, whether under the Nuclear Nonproliferation Treaty (NPT), IAEA safeguards, international nuclear and radiological conventions, or the new UN Security Council Resolution 1540.

The NPT requires that all states complete a safeguards agreement with the IAEA; yet more than thirty treaty states have yet to do so. Many fewer states have signed, much less ratified, the Additional Protocol (AP) to IAEA safeguards or have the infrastructure to control exports or monitor borders for illicit, WMD-related trade. This lucrative opportunity to potential proliferators must be eliminated. The United States has shown leadership in signing and ratifying the AP, which, as President Bush has recommended, must become a new universal standard for nonproliferation.

Knowing what we now know about the sophistication of the nuclear black market, if trade controls fail then countering proliferation through the interdiction of trade is clearly needed. This is the purpose of the Proliferation Security Initiative (PSI), launched by the United States and others in 2003 to promote interdiction principles, share information, and conduct operational exercises. Resolution 1540 and PSI come together in an important respect: in order for interdiction to succeed, states must have the legal basis and means both to identify and hold seized trade.

The global reach of the A.Q. Khan network was telling in this regard. Consider the report of the Malaysian inspector-general of police concerning the involvement of a Malaysian company in the Libyan nuclear procurement ring. According to this report, nuclear specialists in Malaysia were unable to identify controlled components as those that might contribute to Libya's uranium enrichment program. This experience was repeated in other countries, and suggests that unless states take seriously their domestic responsibilities to control activities under their jurisdiction, the gaps exploited by the Khan network will continue to be open to tomorrow's proliferators and terrorists.

In addition to greater vigilance by states, targeted and coordinated programs of assistance are also needed. The United States promotes cooperative exchange programs on export control, border security, and physical protection to redress these implementation gaps. The programs have expanded in recent years to include more than fifty countries in every major region of the world.

The international community must also consider how it can respond to states that take the responsible course of abandoning weapons of mass destruction. The United States recently expanded efforts to redirect former Soviet weapon scientists towards peaceful commercial employment to include Libyan and Iraqi scientists. These efforts are needed to prevent leakage of WMD know-how, but they also aid states that have turned away from the pursuit of weapons of mass destruction to build their economies and science and technology base.

More could be done to improve coordination of international outreach programs, including use of the IAEA and Organization for the Prohibition of Chemical Weapons to inform members of 1540 requirements and facilitate training activities or elaborate "codes of conduct" and "best practices" for industry and nuclear users.

Third, the integrity of the NPT and IAEA safeguards must be preserved, especially in regions linked to terrorism, religious extremism and long histories of armed conflict. Although the articles of the NPT and the original IAEA safeguards agreement were drawn up years ago, they remain relevant in today's world. Our goal must be to ensure that these arrangements are strengthened, complied with, and fully enforced.

Some argue that proliferation in North Korea, Iran, and, before it recanted, Libya, tell the troubling story of an NPT too outdated or weakened to blunt nuclear proliferation. The United States believes this critique is misplaced. Nonproliferation institutions express the will of their members. If we are dissatisfied with regime performance, then the burden falls on us—the peaceful, cooperative governments—to correct deficiencies and demand redress, including earlier intervention by the United Nations Security Council, from those who violate their treaty and international safeguards obligations.

To brace IAEA safeguards, President Bush called for the creation of a special IAEA verification committee to monitor and enforce compliance with nuclear nonproliferation obligations. The IAEA's Board of Governors created this committee in 2005. We look forward to examining in the committee ways in which IAEA verification authorities can be improved or even expanded. Equally encouraging is the creation of new units within the IAEA to review commercial satellite imagery and monitor foreign procurements. To the extent these new capabilities provide the IAEA with earlier warning of evasive activities, they should be a welcome addition to IAEA safeguards and our common nonproliferation and antinuclear terror goals.

For safeguards and global security measures to be fully effective, we need full implementation of new instruments that address nuclear terror. The United States was a strong proponent of efforts in 2004 to complete new export/import guidance for the IAEA Code of Conduct on the Safety and Security of Radioactive Sources.

Implementation of this guidance is essential for controlling beneficial civilian devices when exported from one country to another and for preventing their theft or use in malicious acts, such as detonation of a dirty bomb. President Bush and the other G-8 leaders urged all states to implement the revised code of conduct and recognize it as a global standard at the Sea Island Summit in 2004. We call upon all member-states to apply the revised code of conduct to prevent diversion of sources and acts of radiological terrorism.

In the same vein, the Convention on the Physical Protection of Nuclear Material (CPPNM) has been expanded to cover physical protection not only during international transport but also during all phases of civilian nuclear energy use. The code and the CPPNM are integral parts in the prevention of nuclear and radiological terrorism, and we will work with others to ensure that these instruments are universally applied.

Fourth, the proliferation of enrichment and reprocessing technology must be stopped. While terrorist acquisition of an enrichment plant is a low risk, the continuing spread of sensitive nuclear technologies can only create greater opportunities for substate actors to acquire weapons materials. Libya, Iran, and North Korea all to one degree or another benefited from the illicit acquisition of enrichment or reprocessing technologies. Unfortunately, the NPT's right to peaceful nuclear cooperation (Article IV) makes no distinction between sensitive fuel cycle and other nuclear technologies.

Recognizing this risk, President Bush in 2004 proposed that supplier nations refrain from transferring enrichment and reprocessing technologies to states that did not already possess full-scale, functioning enrichment and reprocessing plants. The Nuclear Suppliers Group and G-8 nations continue to examine this proposal, as well as others that would establish solid eligibility criteria for receipt of such transfers and make the AP a new condition of peaceful nuclear trade.

Conclusions

At the opening of the nuclear age, Albert Einstein warned that the advent of nuclear fission had changed everything except the way we think, and thus we drift towards disaster. In Einstein's world—the world that President Eisenhower faced at the time of his historic Atoms-for-Peace speech— there were one or two masters of nuclear technology. That world was far different from the one we live in today, in which nuclear science and materials are widespread, but the risk of disaster remains. Nuclear security in today's age of terrorism requires global participation, not just by national governments, but also by police forces, border guards, cities, communities, harbors, research institutes, and factories.

With a concerted and action-oriented approach to combat nuclear proliferation threats, one that involves the cooperation and input of nations and respect for international agreements, norms and standards, the United States is convinced that the consensus against proliferation will, as President Bush suggested, be "translated into action."

13

Preventing Nuclear Terrorism

Laura S.H. Holgate

Fifty years ago, President Dwight D. Eisenhower recognized the dangers to the United States posed by the spread of the most destructive force known to humankind in the form of nuclear weapons. He sought to limit these dangers through a grand bargain. He offered the world access to the beneficial aspects of nuclear technology in exchange for limits on access to its destructive power. Fifty years later, it is hard to argue with the effectiveness of the nonproliferation regime based on this premise; instead of the feared dozens of nuclear powers, we have at most four additional entrants to the original club of five. At the same time, the foundations of that regime have been fundamentally shaken by two forces completely unimagined fifty years ago—first, the collapse of the world's largest nuclear power and, second, the rise of sophisticated, well-funded non-state actors.

The Nuclear Nonproliferation Treaty (NPT) and related norms and structures have helped moderate these new threats in many important respects. Its principles were key to the nuclear renunciations of post-Soviet Belarus, Kazakhstan, and Ukraine. NPT-based nuclear smuggling and physical protection programs have thwarted terrorist plots. However, we have not seen the degree of urgent action necessary to prevent nuclear terrorism, either from the multilateral nuclear nonproliferation regime or from national governments.

Let us recall that before the terrorist attacks on September 11, 2001, many experts—especially those familiar with the inadequate security surrounding nuclear materials—had been harboring the hope that we had time to attend to these deficiencies and that, even if hostile groups could acquire nuclear weapons and launch a nuclear attack, no one would. We had the hope that there was an element of human decency in even the most hate-filled human beings, and that this would hold them back from the massive killing of innocents.

September 11 shattered that hope. We understood on that day that if we are to prevent nuclear terrorism, we have to block the terrorists aggressively in their efforts to acquire nuclear weapons and materials. The most stunning fact of September 11 is not that the attack happened, as horrid and wicked as it was. What is most alarming today is that September 11, after it happened, did not give rise to new and urgent worldwide actions to physically secure weapons and nuclear materials at their source to preclude the possibility that terrorists could get their hands on them. Unsecured weapons and materials anywhere are a threat to everyone, everywhere. We also understand that, in recent years, our efforts to prevent nuclear terrorism have not come close to matching the threat.

Osama bin Laden has been frank to tell the world that he sees it as a "religious duty" to acquire weapons of mass destruction. Reportedly, the terrorist who took hostages in the Moscow Theater in October 2002 had similar ambitions for nuclear weaponry. However, the danger that bin Laden or other terrorists might succeed in getting nuclear weapons, while deadly serious, is a wholly containable threat if we have the will to act. We know what to do. We know how to do it. We simply need to get on with it. As U.S. Senator Richard Lugar has observed, we need to dedicate ourselves to a global cooperative effort to make sure that every nation with nuclear-weapon capacity gives a full accounting of and secures what it possesses, and pledges to prevent access to other states and terrorists.

It must be recognized that we are making some progress. Thousands of deactivated weapons, hundreds of tons of nuclear materials secured and hundreds more destroyed, and thousands of weaponeers reemployed is progress. The International Atomic Energy Agency (IAEA) Board of Governors agreement to increase the Agency's safeguards budget is progress.

The Group of Eight (G-8) commitment to a global partnership to stem proliferation is progress. However, we cannot afford to think that as long as we are doing something, we are doing enough. Cooperative programs are trapped in bureaucratic stand-offs, the G-8 pledges have yet to materialize into concrete action, and there is not an apparent sense of urgency to either of these actions.

We need to face facts and acknowledge painful truths. First, we must acknowledge that the very broad distribution of know-how and technical expertise in the world makes it possible for an only moderately sophisticated or well-funded terrorist organization to acquire the means to make a nuclear weapon, if it first succeeds in acquiring nuclear material. This is clearly so for highly enriched uranium (HEU), and a number of experts fear that it is also true of plutonium.

Second, we must acknowledge that plutonium produced in civilian nuclear power programs yields plutonium suitable for making nuclear weapons and that highly enriched uranium at research reactors throughout the world is at risk. The world does not yet universally admit the first fact about reactor-grade plutonium, and is entirely too casual about addressing the second fact about HEU at research facilities.

Third, we must acknowledge that current physical security arrangements for nuclear materials at many facilities around the world are inadequate in the post–September 11 world.

Fourth, we must acknowledge that current safeguards designed to keep material from being diverted by a state to military use are inadequate to the task, and this inadequacy is particularly evident when it comes to safeguarding fuel-cycle facilities.

Fifth, we must acknowledge that three non-NPT states—India, Israel, and Pakistan—have nuclear weapons and materials inventories, and that the world has a strong interest in seeing to it that these capacities are safely secured and controlled.

And lastly, we must acknowledge that the international community has yet to develop a plan to roll back North Korea's nuclear-weapon program.

If we can make these acknowledgments, we will be speaking in a straightforward manner about the extent of the threat. Then, we will be forced to confront the fact that our current efforts aim at something far short of full security.

How many officials from around the world would sign a document guaranteeing that nuclear materials are secure against a well-organized and well-funded attempt by terrorists willing to sacrifice lives to acquire or divert those materials? Who would assert the adequacy of global efforts to prevent unauthorized acquisition or use of nuclear weapons? Who has confidence in a nuclear future that contemplates the unbounded distribution of both civilian nuclear power and fuel-cycle facilities in the developing world? Who has a plan for bringing India, Pakistan, and Israel under the NPT, or creating some transparent arrangement for giving the world confidence over the security and control of their nuclear stockpiles?

Yet, who can deny that these are the challenges we must face and solve if we are to give any assurance of safety to the people of the world? In this context, where should we concentrate our efforts? The United States and Russia are the owners of the vast majority of the world's nuclear weapons and materials; therefore, they have a special responsibility to reduce the threats posed by their own Cold War hangovers and, together, assist others in nuclear security as well as reductions and prevention of nuclear terrorism.

Standing with President Putin at the White House, President Bush said that the highest priority is to keep terrorists from acquiring weapons of mass destruction. President Putin has made similar statements and it is clear that he believes Russia faces similar threats. These statements are welcome, but words alone are not enough. President Bush must make it known in the Congress, the White House, and throughout his administration that his top priority is keeping weapons of mass destruction out of terrorist hands, and he must give this matter his sustained personal attention. He must make it the central element in our security relationship with President Putin and the Russian Federation. Hopefully, the agreement at the Bratislava Summit will do just that.

The United States and Russia must work together to provide high-level leadership and build a global partnership against catastrophic terrorism. Our allies and friends must take the necessary steps and do their part as participating and contributing partners.

This partnership is essential as it could reduce the risk rapidly and dramatically. This means working with President Putin to remove obstacles in Russia to our cooperative work. It means making Russia a full partner with global responsibilities. It means requesting and fighting for the budget resources necessary to get it done. It means coordinating the effort among the agencies of the U.S. government and the nations of the world to develop a global partnership to keep nuclear weapons out of terrorist hands.

The dangerous reality is that over half of the potentially vulnerable nuclear material in Russia lacks security upgrades. Tens of thousands of weapon scientists lack adequate pay or productive peaceful work. Scores of research reactors fueled with highly enriched uranium around the world remain dangerously insecure. India, Israel, and Pakistan are isolated from international cooperation on nuclear security. And, despite budget increases, the IAEA remains dangerously underfunded and inadequately staffed.

A serious, effective plan to improve security for nuclear materials and weapons around the world would, among other things:

- Focus intensive, sustained leadership from the highest levels of the U.S. government on an integrated, prioritized plan for blocking the terrorist pathway to the bomb. This includes a single senior leader in the White House with full-time responsibility and accountability for leading the effort.
- Build the G-8 "Global Partnership Against the Spread of Weapons and Materials of Destruction," announced in June 2002, into a broad and effective working partnership that will take rapid action to keep nuclear weapons and weapon-usable materials from being stolen and falling into the hands of terrorists or hostile states. The United States and Russia would both play leading roles in the effort, shifting from a donor–recipient relationship to a genuine nuclear security partnership.
- Ensure that the Global Threat Reduction Initiative is a truly focused program with the authority, resources, and expertise needed to remove all nuclear material from the world's most vulnerable sites as rapidly as possible, negotiating tailored incentives to facilities to convince them to give up their material.
- Follow up the Bratislava Summit by working with Russia to complete rapidly security upgrades for all Russian nuclear warheads and materials, followed by comprehensive upgrades, using a partnership-based approach integrating Russian experts throughout.
- Forge security partnerships with other key states, such as Pakistan, whose nuclear weapons or materials might be threatened by terrorists.
- Provide for expanded safeguards and security capabilities of the IAEA through budgets, training, and authorities.
- Build effective global standards for nuclear security for each nation with nuclear weapons and materials to meet, combined with an offer of assistance to any state willing to commit to these standards but unable to do so alone.

These actions are achievable and affordable.

Those who have experience with nuclear matters must face facts and acknowledge painful truths about the inadequacies of our actions. It is critical to draw attention to the gap between the threat and our response, and to generate discussion about how to close the gap. A number of creative and serious ideas have emerged to address the perils we face. Yet we know that even the best ideas will not protect us if they are merely subjects of discussion.

We need to do more to exhort our governments to act. There is a worrisome disconnect between the rising danger, stagnant government responses, and a falling sense of public urgency. In a serarch of major world newspapers for news stories concerning nuclear matters in the month before the attacks of September 11, a total of 57 stories were identified. In the month following, there were 1,106 stories. Two years later, there were only 348 stories—a 66 percent plunge.

We have a great challenge. As Ted Turner has noted, media attention to nuclear terrorism has begun to fade, resulting in weak public pressure for action. We have to find a way to get the leaders of our governments to act with the same urgency that they would after an attack, but to do so before an attack—because that's the only way to prevent an attack. This confers a great responsibility on us all.

14

Second-Tier Suppliers and Their Threat to the Nuclear Nonproliferation Regime

Christopher F. Chyba

In this paper, I will discuss second-tier proliferation and the threat that it poses to the nuclear nonproliferation regime.[1] I will then step back to compare the outcome of a possible collapsed nuclear nonproliferation regime and the situation that we will soon face with respect to biological weapons. The comparison emphasizes that we want to avoid a nuclear-

---

1. Second-tier proliferation may be distinguished from first-tier proliferation as follows. First-tier proliferation is the spread of nuclear weapons–relevant material or know-how from states or private entities within states that are members of the formal nuclear exporter groups, such as the Nuclear Exporters Committee (or Zangger Committee) or the Nuclear Suppliers Group. Second-tier proliferation derives from activities by other states (or private entities within them) that may be supplying nuclear weapon–relevant material or know-how on the international market. This definition is taken from Chaim Braun and Christopher F. Chyba, "Proliferation Rings: New Challenges to the Nuclear Nonproliferation Regime," *International Security* 29, no. 2 (Fall 2004): 5–49. The nuclear nonproliferation regime may be defined as "international agreements and cooperative national actions to prevent the spread of nuclear weapons to additional countries or to terrorists." This definition, and a history of the nonproliferation regime

weapon future that looks anything like our biological-weapon future, which is a particularly disturbing future. In the case of exponentiating biotechnology, for the most part, we simply have to cope with what that future holds. We may no longer be in a strong position to shape it, although we need to make wise choices where we can.[2] We want to continue to be able to shape our nuclear future.

The goal of the international nuclear nonproliferation regime is to defer for as long as we can the proliferation of nuclear-weapon technologies and know-how. But these technologies are sixty years old, and there is a kind of inevitability to their eventual spread around the world. If so, it is the responsibility of those working to preserve the nonproliferation regime also to address the international and regional security calculations made by countries when deciding whether to pursue a nuclear-weapon program. If second-tier proliferation continues to progress, and nuclear weapon–relevant know-how and technology continue to spread around the world, the future success of the regime will increasingly depend on addressing these demand-side issues.

Challenges to the Nonproliferation Treaty

The nuclear nonproliferation regime is much broader than the Nuclear Nonproliferation Treaty (NPT), and we are going to need all of the tools of the full regime. However, because the NPT anchors the nonproliferation regime, and is a kind of concrete expression of Atoms for Peace, it is appropriate to begin by summarizing and analyzing the challenges to the NPT.

First, consider the NPT's Article I—the pledge of the nuclear-weapon states not to transfer nuclear weapons "to any recipient whatsoever," and

---

beginning with President Eisenhower's Atoms-for-Peace speech, may be found in George Bunn, "The Nuclear Nonproliferation Regime and Its History," in George Bunn and Christopher F. Chyba, eds., *U.S. Nuclear Weapons Policy: Confronting the New Challenges* (Washington, D.C.: Brookings Institution Press, 2006).

2. For a discussion of these points, see Christopher F. Chyba and Alex L. Greninger, "Biotechnology and Bioterrorism: An Unprecedented World," *Survival* 46, no. 2 (Summer 2004): 143–162; and Institute of Medicine and National Research Council, *Globalization, Biosecurity, and the Future of the Life Sciences* (Washington, D.C.: National Academies Press, 2006).

not to assist non–nuclear-weapon states to manufacture or acquire them.[3] The enforcement of Article I, from the point of view of the nuclear-weapon states, is in the form of export controls, both with respect to nuclear export controls and with respect to missile technology. The Missile Technology Control Regime specifically discusses the importance of missile proliferation from the point of view of so-called weapons of mass destruction (WMD) proliferation.[4] It is clear that there have been many failures with respect to Article I.

Article II of the NPT is the pledge of the non–nuclear-weapon states not to receive any transfer of nuclear weapons or assistance "from any transferor whatsoever" in making such weapons.[5] That commitment is under considerable pressure due to second-tier proliferation. We may be moving toward a world—we are not there yet—where certain states in the developing world have sufficient nuclear and missile technological know-how spread among them that they can barter among themselves to obtain the additional assistance that their nuclear-weapon and missile technology programs need, with fewer and fewer requirements for technology transfer from first-tier suppliers. The A.Q. Khan nuclear smuggling network provides the most powerful examples of these kind of second-tier relationships.[6] We may be moving into a realm where proliferators—including sub-state actors acting on the black market—are able to violate Article II of the NPT while cutting themselves loose of the mechanisms that have been put in place under Articles I and III.

3. "Treaty on the Non-Proliferation of Nuclear Weapons between the United States and Other Governments," signed at Washington, London, and Moscow, July 1, 1968, entered into force, March 5, 1970. See Appendix 3 in this volume.
4. "Weapons of mass destruction" was a term frequently used by the Bush administration, the press, and many scholars during the lead-up to the war in Iraq. I prefer not to use the term because (1) radiological and chemical weapons are poorly described as "weapons of mass destruction," given that they are unlikely to achieve casualties greater than those achieved by conventional explosives; and (2) the term "WMD" lends itself to intellectual confusion as it tends to blur important differences among nuclear, biological, and other weapons. For a discussion of these points, see Christopher F. Chyba, "Toward Biological Security," *Foreign Affairs* 81 (May/June 2002): 122–136.
5. NPT, Article II.
6. For a detailed account of the A.Q. Khan network and its implications for the nuclear nonproliferation regime, see Braun and Chyba, "Proliferation Rings." For a more skeptical view of the effectiveness and long-term significance of the Khan network, see Alexander H. Montgomery, "Ringing in Proliferation: How to Dismantle an Atomic Bomb Network," *International Security* 30 (Fall 2005): 153–187.

In that kind of world, we are increasingly going to have to emphasize demand-side measures. A critical question is whether we are dealing with more than a small number of hard cases. Is our concern with the last few countries that somehow have not been brought into the nuclear nonproliferation regime or, rather, should we view the nuclear and missile trade relationships among North Korea, Pakistan, and Iran as harbingers of what is to come rather than as a final set of issues that have to be addressed? To the extent that we may be looking at harbingers of what is to come, then even as we work for a robust response to those particular instances of concern, we have to think more broadly about the mix of incentives and disincentives that face potential proliferators within the nonproliferation regime.

Article III of the NPT requires safeguards for non–nuclear-weapon state nuclear programs.[7] In this respect, and especially the idea that the Additional Protocol (AP) will make safeguard agreements more robust, there is some tension between Article III and addressing demand-side motivations.[8] I will address this shortly. It should first be noted that, even with the AP, there are substantial challenges to monitoring and verification. But we want to be wary of the "silver bullet fallacy"—a silver bullet being a magic bullet that always hits its target. We want to avoid the fallacy that if a particular measure does not solve the problem in itself, then it is somehow unworthy of support. There are no silver bullets in this arena. We are going to have to rely on a web of measures, each of which is imperfect.

Articles IV and VI present the explicit bargains present in the nonproliferation regime. Under Article IV, non–nuclear-weapon states have an "inalienable right . . . to develop research, production and use of nuclear

---

7. NPT, Article III.
8. The Additional Protocol is a more robust set of safeguards requirements under Article III of the NPT than had previously been in place, and represents a significantly greater intrusion into a country's sovereignty than the previous monitoring and inspection regime. Adherents to the AP must divulge ten-year fuel-cycle research and development plans to the IAEA, the activities and identities of persons or entities carrying out these plans, export/import information, and descriptions of many facilities. Adherents may also be subject to far more intrusive inspections. See International Atomic Energy Agency, "Model Protocol Additional to the Agreement(s) between State(s) and the International Atomic Energy Agency for the Application of Safeguards," Information Circular 540 (Corrected) (September 1997). For a thorough discussion, see Christopher F. Chyba, Chaim Braun, and George Bunn, "Strategies for Tackling Proliferation Challenges," in Bunn and Chyba, eds., *U.S. Nuclear Weapons Policy*.

energy for peaceful purposes."[9] In effect, this is the quid pro quo for these states' relinquishment of nuclear weapons in Article II and their acceptance of safeguards in Article III.

Two issues with respect to Article IV should be noted. The first, which has received the most attention, is latent proliferation—that is, the pursuit of nuclear-weapon programs under the guise of Article IV–sanctioned activity, despite a state's ultimate intention of violating its obligations under Article II.[10]

The second Article IV issue is that nuclear power as envisioned under Atoms for Peace has turned out to be not quite as great a bargain as was originally believed. That is to say, nuclear power has not been the low-cost energy option initially envisioned, but rather is a very demanding technology. Moreover, peaceful nuclear explosions, embodied in Article V of the NPT, are no longer in the mix of quid pro quos in this bargain of the benefits of nuclear power for nuclear-weapon restraint.

Therefore, the Atoms-for-Peace bargain envisioned in Articles IV and V no longer carries with it the same apparent incentives for non–nuclear-weapon states that it did five decades ago. Moreover, the non–nuclear-weapon states that are pursuing nuclear power are facing increasingly onerous inspections required under Article III—especially as we move into the era of the AP. It is natural to ask whether states will make an evaluation that the downsides of adhering to their obligations are no longer equaled by the benefits of Article IV or other aspects of the treaty.

There are other important benefits of the peaceful atom that do not often attract as much attention, such as benefits to health (e.g., the IAEA eliminated the sleeping sickness–carrying tsetse fly from Zanzibar through the release of radiation-sterilized male flies).[11] At a minimum, as we move to increasingly onerous requirements under Article III, we have to think about what the bargain continues to look like for those countries that we are hoping will continue to turn away from nuclear-weapon programs and remain within the NPT.[12]

9. NPT, Article IV.
10. For further discussion of this challenge, see Christopher F. Chyba, Chaim Braun, and George Bunn, "New Challenges to the Nonproliferation Regime," in Bunn and Chyba, eds., *U.S. Nuclear Weapons Policy.*
11. See IAEA, "Campaign Launched to Eliminate Tsetse Fly," WorldAtom Press Release (PR2002/0219, February 2002).
12. For an elaboration of these points, see Chyba et al., "Strategies for Tackling Proliferation Challenges."

Finally, the second explicit bargain within the NPT is Article VI, in which each of the parties to the treaty pledges to negotiate toward nuclear disarmament.[13] The Bush administration argues that the United States has a continuing commitment to its obligations under Article VI. U.S. Secretary of State Colin Powell, in remarks sent to the 2003 Nonproliferation and Preparatory Meeting, said that U.S. actions are based on a "desire and an intention" to reduce U.S. reliance on nuclear weapons.[14] Obviously, there is some tension between that statement and other statements from the administration as well as funding from Congress to investigate new nuclear warheads and to move to shorten the time towards nuclear testing.[15] An important question is whether international perceptions of those decisions may lead, in the future, to a kind of train wreck in the NPT, with the worst case being the treaty's collapse.

One might be skeptical of claims from some in the international or arms control communities that the sky may be about to fall. After all, as the Bush administration called into question a number of multilateral regimes, and as it withdrew from some, it was told repeatedly by some in the arms control community that the sky might fall.[16] Yet the sky remains aloft. That might suggest that the concerns are overblown. This history makes it an uphill

---

13. The actual language on NPT Article IV follows: "Each of the Parties to the Treaty undertakes to pursue negotiations in good faith on effective measures to cessation of the nuclear arms race at an early date and to nuclear disarmament, and on a Treaty on general and complete disarmament under strict and effective international control." For a discussion of the kind of international inspection and monitoring regime that would be required for the verifiable build-down to low numbers of nuclear warheads, see Committee on International Security and Arms Control, National Academy of Science, *Monitoring Nuclear Weapons and Nuclear-Explosive Materials: An Assessment of Methods and Capabilities* (Washington, D.C.: National Academies Press, 2005).

14. Secretary of State Powell affirmed that "the United States remains firmly committed to its obligations under the NPT. We are pursuing a number of avenues that promote the goal of nuclear disarmament. The Moscow Treaty and other U.S. actions are based on a desire and an intention to reduce our reliance on nuclear weapons and eliminate surplus stocks of weapons-grade material." Message from U.S. Secretary of State Colin Powell to the 2003 Preparatory Committee Meeting for the 2005 NPT Review Conference, quoted by Assistant Secretary of State J.S. Wolf, "Remarks to the Second Meeting of the Preparatory Committee," April 28, 2003.

15. For a discussion of these points, see Roger Speed and Michael May, "Assessing the United States' Nuclear Posture," in Bunn and Chyba, eds., *U.S. Nuclear Weapons Policy.*

16. For a discussion of what did not happen after U.S. withdrawal from the Anti-Ballistic Missile (ABM) treaty, despite some predictions, see Wade Boese, "Missile Defense Post-ABM Treaty: No System, No Arms Race," *Arms Control Today* (June 2003) (http://www.armscontrol.org/act/2003_06/mdanalysis_june03.asp).

argument for those who suggest that movement by the United States toward research into a new class of nuclear warhead may cause the sky to fall at an upcoming NPT Review Conference.

But that is only one side of the ledger. The other side is to ask how confident we are with the inductive extrapolation that the sky will continue not to fall in the future. We may be in the position of the National Aeronautics and Space Administration (NASA) with respect to foam strikes on the space shuttle during liftoff. NASA kept launching the space shuttle in the face of foam strikes, the foam strikes kept not destroying the shuttle, and the extrapolation was made that it therefore must be safe to continue to launch the space shuttle despite ongoing foam strikes. But the Columbia disaster occurred due to a foam strike.[17] In retrospect, shuttle flights with ongoing foam strikes were like driving back and forth to the store in a car whose gas gauge is on empty, and arguing that because in one trip after another the car does not run out of gas, it must be possible to keep driving back and forth forever without the gas ever running out.

In the NPT context, getting a sense of the balance of those two perspectives—the "sky may fall" and "it's safe to drive on empty"—is extremely important. It may be even more important to understand the extent to which U.S. actions with respect to disparaging multilateral regimes may cause foot-dragging or hedging on the part of other countries in the nonproliferation regime that do not cause the sky to fall in a dramatic way but which accumulate, drop by drop, into an ongoing undermining of the regime and U.S. national security interests.

A Future Like That of Biological Weapons?

What if the NPT were to collapse? With or without the NPT—although the danger would be far greater without it—we want to avoid a nuclear weapons future that resembles our biological-weapon future. In the case of biological weapons, biotechnology is developing exponentially within the developed world, but it is also spreading rapidly throughout the developing

17. See, for example, William Langewiesche, "Columbia's Last Flight," *The Atlantic Monthly* (November 2003) (http://www.theatlantic.com/doc/200311/langewiesche). His points include the following: "[S]imply put, it had become a matter of faith within NASA that foam strikes—which were a known problem—could not cause mortal damage to the shuttle. Sean O'Keefe, who was badly advised by his NASA lieutenants, made unwise public statements deriding the 'foamologists'; and even Ron Dittemore, NASA's technically expert shuttle program manager, joined in with categorical denials."

world.[18] Singapore has now made biotech one of the four pillars of its economy, and China has tens of thousands of people working in hundreds of biotech labs. There is a kind of inexorable spread of biotechnology around the world for the very good reasons of public health, food security, and economics. What that is going to mean, though, is that the same techniques of genetic engineering that allow one to modify organisms for good outcomes will be broadly available to those seeking to modify organisms to make pathogens far deadlier.[19] That technology is going to become broadly available to small groups of the merely technically competent. That means, in the biological case, that what we are going to have to do is to learn how to cope with the world that we are inevitably going to face. We are not currently in a strong position, except with respect to some particular specific issues, to shape that world.

For as long as possible, we want to be able to continue to shape our nuclear future, not just to try to figure out how to cope with it. That means finding a way to preserve for as long as possible the nuclear nonproliferation regime.

In the nuclear realm, the A.Q. Khan network made use of a broad range of suppliers and contacts in both first- and second-tier nuclear supplier countries. But these included Scomi Precision Engineering in Malaysia, a company that manufactured centrifuge parts in a country that has not been thought of as a nuclear supplier state.[20] Here, too, there is the impression of an inexorable spread of these technologies, although at a much slower pace than is the case in the biological realm. In the meantime, even as we seek to restrict the further spread of nuclear-weapon technology, we had better be adopting approaches, including regional security efforts, that will speak to the demand-side requirements of countries that are would-be proliferators.

Nuclear Supply and Demand

I close with a few remarks on supply-side and demand-side steps that could be taken, particularly with respect to the challenge posed by second-tier proliferation networks.

18. See, for example, Institute of Medicine and National Reseach Council, *An International Perspective on Advancing Technologies and Strategies for Managing Dual-Use Risks* (Washington, D.C.: National Academies Press, 2005).
19. For a survey of the landscape of the relevant biotechnological techniques, see Institute of Medicine and National Research Council, *Globalization, Biosecurity and the Future of the Life Sciences*.
20. For details, see Braun and Chyba, "Proliferation Rings."

The first critical supply-side step is to prevent any direct route for warheads or nuclear materials to reach terrorists. This means that Cooperative Threat Reduction needs to be upheld and expanded. We also need to maintain export controls even though they are not a silver bullet and they may become less effective as time goes on. This waning efficacy certainly does not mean that we should provide any simple routes into nonproliferation by letting down our guard. Moreover, countries that are not currently captured within the Nuclear Suppliers Group (NSG) need to continue to be encouraged to mirror those arrangements unilaterally, such as in those measures declared by China before it joined the NSG.[21]

There are several new supply-side measures that speak to the proliferation network challenge. The first concerns the attempt to universalize export controls under UN Security Council Resolution 1540. Under this Resolution, in a remarkable experiment in Security Council lawmaking, in 2004 the United States and the United Kingdom gained unanimous UN Security Council approval for global nonproliferation standards for national action. These included a requirement that nations adopt national export controls to prevent terrorists from gaining access to nuclear, chemical, or biological weapons, or the missiles that might carry them. Resolution 1540 also added global requirements for the protection of nuclear material against theft by terrorists or thieves, complementing the NPT's provisions for detecting the diversion of nuclear material to nonpeaceful purposes.[22]

The Bush administration's Proliferation Security Initiative (PSI) is a second example of a new supply-side measure. The PSI, announced in 2003, provides a way to inspect ships, aircraft, and land vehicles for "contraband" related to nuclear, chemical, or biological weapons.[23] It is hardly foolproof, but recall the silver bullet fallacy. However, the PSI obviously brings with it substantial intelligence requirements.

In addition to supply-side measures, we need to think about demand-side measures. The goal is to influence the calculations of potential proliferators. There is obviously a broad range of levers, many of which go well beyond the NPT.

21. "White Paper on Nonproliferation," State Council, China, December 3, 2003.
22. See UN Security Council Resolution 1540 of April 28, 2004, available at www.un.org/Docs/sc/unsc_resolutions04.html.
23. White House, "Remarks by the President to the People of Poland," Krakow, Poland, May 31, 2003 (www.whitehouse.gov/news/releases/2003/05/20030531-3.html).

The first is deterrence. Deterrence in this case is the threat of political, economic, and military punishment if one is caught trying to violate Article II obligations. The AP, in this context, is a demand-side tool of deterrence. Under the AP, catching a signatory nation if it tries to violate its obligations is more likely, so the protocol makes deterrence more credible. On the other hand, it comes with the irony that it makes the regime more onerous, so in this sense the AP increases the costs of the regime to non–nuclear-weapon states.

So the next question has to be, what is the benefit of the AP to the non–nuclear-weapon states? One benefit is enhancing regional security. If it is the case that by working for a broad application of the AP, a state perceives that it helps maintain a world where it can be more confident that other states in its region are not trying to violate the NPT, it may be a bargain that is worth pursuing. But if a state finds itself near a state or states that appear to be, or in fact have been, developing nuclear capabilities despite being members of the NPT, that bargain may seem a lot less compelling.

We may need to look at other ways of reassuring countries that in fact signing on to these additional obligations are in their interest. That can include positive security guarantees in some cases, and it could include increased cooperation under Article IV. It is worth remembering that the budget for the technical cooperation program at the IAEA is a substantial fraction of the monitoring budget of the IAEA. There are other incentives that we need to consider. Many, for example, are now raising nuclear reactor fuel leasing issues.[24] Other non–nuclear energy incentives can also be considered.

Incentives may also be married with sanctions or other forms of pressure. The war in Iraq reminds us of the intelligence requirements, high costs, and potential unintended consequences of preventive war as a nonproliferation tool. This does not mean that coercive diplomacy, accompanied by the threat of military force, should never be employed, and it does not alleviate concern over the difficulty of achieving UN Security Council action for the enforcement of the nonproliferation regime. But it emphasizes the importance of employing all other tools before choosing military action.

---

24. For example, see the IAEA Expert Group, "Multilateral Approaches to the Nuclear Fuel Cycle," Report to the Director General, Information Circular 640 (February 22, 2005), chapter 2, paragraph 18.

Conclusions

The imperfection of all of these measures—both existing measures and new initiatives—is frustrating. The best that we can hope for is a self-reinforcing web of approaches to nonproliferation. The world has changed in the fifty years since President Dwight D. Eisenhower's Atoms-for-Peace speech, so the relative strengths of the different strands in this web of approaches need to change. In particular, in light of progress in second-tier proliferation, we need to place greater emphasis on demand-side measures, even as we preserve the importance of the supply-side measures. This will continue to require an approach to the proliferation challenge that weighs the long-term consequences of short-term actions, and has the patience to make strategic choices that are in the long-term national interest.

Part III

The Promise of Nuclear Energy

15

Atoms for Peace: Realizing the Vision

Senator Pete V. Domenici

President Dwight D. Eisenhower demonstrated remarkable vision in presenting his remarks on the peaceful atom to the United Nations fifty years ago. At that time, the framework of the challenge confronting the world with nuclear technologies was only dimly visible. With that speech, he launched this nation and the world on a quest to harness the atom solely for purposes of peace—a quest that remains unmet today.

At the time of his speech, the United States had conducted forty-two nuclear test explosions and used two weapons to end World War II. The Soviet Union had demonstrated its nuclear-weapon capability. However, the dimensions of the Cold War, which President Eisenhower hoped to avoid, were only vaguely defined. Nevertheless, his words ring true today:

> Let no one think that the expenditure of vast sums for weapons and systems of defense can guarantee absolute safety for the cities and the

citizens of any nation. The awful arithmetic of the atomic bomb does not permit any such an easy solution.[1]

The president further noted that the ability of the United States to lay waste to an aggressor would be a hollow victory indeed—hardly befitting the founding principles and ideals of this nation. He noted that such reasoning would be:

> to accept helplessly the probability of civilization destroyed—the annihilation of the irreplaceable heritage of mankind handed down to us generation from generation—and the condemnation of mankind to begin all over again the age old struggle upward from savagery toward decency and right and justice.[2]

In some ways, we have come a long ways from Ike's words. Yet in other ways, we still have a long way to go.

Frustration over our slow progress forty-four years after the Atoms-for-Peace speech led me to speak at Harvard in 1997, and issue a challenge to the nation's leaders to work toward realizing the promise of nuclear technologies to benefit all of mankind. Indeed, much of my energy over the last decade has been devoted to more effectively realizing the vision of Atoms for Peace, from both military and civilian perspectives. I have frequently noted that the citizens of the world will fully realize the benefits of the atom only when all nations of the world have fully controlled and mitigated the military threats of this technology.

I have championed many initiatives on the military side of this equation, from the Nunn–Lugar Cooperative Threat Reduction to the Material Protection, Control and Accounting Program, the U.S.–Russia Highly Enriched Uranium (HEU) Purchase Agreement, and the Plutonium Disposition Program.

We have seen good progress in some of these initiatives. Certainly, the Nunn–Lugar program has accomplished a great deal. Significant quantities of fissile materials are better controlled today. There is less HEU in Russia's stockpile. Plans to reduce further the nuclear arsenals of the United States and Russia are positive.

However, we still face immense challenges, including the following:

---

1. "Atomic Power for Peace," an address by Dwight D. Eisenhower, President of the United States, before the General Assembly of the United Nations, December 8, 1953.
2. Ibid.

- We have made little headway in addressing the longstanding need for vastly improved controls over, and reductions in, tactical nuclear weapons.
- The amount of Russian fissile materials not under adequate control is far too large.
- Promising programs for diverting the skills of Russian weapon scientists to commercial endeavors have been stymied by limited access to the closed cities.
- Far too many radioactive sources are poorly controlled, posing significant risks for use in so-called "dirty bombs" by terrorist groups.
- Too many reactors around the world remain fueled with HEU.
- Too many of our programs still focus solely on the Russian Federation, instead of recognizing that we should be working as co-leaders with the Russians in a global partnership for nonproliferation programs that encompasses all willing nations.

The absolutely vital Plutonium Disposition Program, which for so long had been stalled by wrangling over the legal issue of liability indemnification, is now on a path to implementation. This program is not just in U.S. interests, and it is not just in Russian interests. It is a concrete step toward a safer world. It was incredibly frustrating to watch the endless negotiations on this point. Negotiators seemed to forget the importance of the underlying program.

In 2003, I became chair of the Senate Energy and Natural Resources Committee. In that role, I have invested an immense amount of time in crafting a national energy policy. As a nation, we face an immense challenge in meeting our growing energy needs while preserving the environment that we cherish.

In the course of this challenge, I have noted how simple my task would be if I only needed to satisfy one region of our nation. However, the challenge is not that simple. We need a policy that meets the needs of the entire country, and it cannot be done in a piecemeal fashion.

We have succeeded with this new energy policy.[3] The nation now has a comprehensive approach to our diverse needs—an approach that balances conservation, improved efficiencies, and new production.

Achieving increased production while meeting our environmental mandates is far from simple. There is no simple or single silver bullet that will

3. Energy Policy Act of 2005 (Public Law 109–58).

solve this dilemma. We must harness all the clean energy sources we have to meet our citizens' needs. Nuclear energy must be a part of that equation.

No other energy source offers the clean, reliable, baseload power that we derive from nuclear energy. Yet for many reasons, development of nuclear energy has been on hold in this nation for over a quarter-century. Either we reverse that trend now or we will watch developing nations like China and India one day overtake us in the employment of advanced nuclear power plants that provide what I consider to be the cleanest, safest, and most environmentally friendly energy in the world.

The true words of President Eisenhower echo over the years to remind us of the importance of nuclear power:

> The United States knows that peaceful power from atomic energy is no dream of the future. That capability, already proved, is here—now—today. Who can doubt . . . that this capability would rapidly be transformed into universal, efficient, and economic usage[?][4]

In the energy bill, I set out to chart a course over the next decades toward a strong role for nuclear power, both here and around the world, both in developed and in developing nations. I can best summarize my efforts here with a discussion of six key goals now embodied in law.

A first priority was that I had to ensure that the liability foundation for our nuclear programs since 1957 remains intact. For that reason, the law incorporates a twenty-year extension of the Price–Anderson statute.

Then I had to reverse that quarter-century dearth of new plant construction. We simply must see new domestic plants constructed. It does us little good to compliment ourselves on our foresight in developing and licensing advanced reactor designs—designs which are providing reliable power around the world today—when we have none of these reactor designs in operation here.

Thus, my second priority was to provide production tax-credit incentives for electricity produced by the first half-dozen new nuclear power plants. In addition, we offer federal loan guarantees for innovative technologies—including new advanced nuclear reactors—that will diversify and increase energy supply while protecting the environment. With those few plants, we can show the public that nuclear power plants can be built in this country, and that they can be built with economic and safety considerations consistent with the public's demands.

4. "Atomic Power for Peace."

My third priority offers a standby support framework against regulatory or judicial delays during construction and up to commercial operation caused by factors beyond the private sector's control. With these first few plants, we can convince the investment community that new plant construction is a solid investment opportunity, not one to be shunned.

My fourth and fifth priorities are essentially tied in importance. They are to reestablish our technology base to meet new needs with new reactors, and to develop better waste management solutions.

The law authorizes a major new research and development reactor program to demonstrate a new generation of ultrasafe, ultraefficient reactors that minimize waste production and proliferation concerns. It further demands that the project enable research and development for advanced approaches to both electricity and hydrogen production.

As an aside, let me note that progress toward a hydrogen economy is another major emphasis in the law. The opportunity to convert our transportation system to hydrogen fuel offers immense benefits, but only if we can produce that hydrogen cleanly and economically.

We cannot mine or drill for hydrogen. We have to produce it. That requires energy. The law supports alternative production approaches, from solar to nuclear to biological.

In the area of nuclear-waste policy, I am convinced that our citizens demand better solutions to nuclear waste than we have today. Now we plan to simply bury and forget about our spent fuel—never mind that it retains an immense store of energy or that its constituents are highly toxic.

There are better solutions, and I have championed their study over the last few years. With the energy law, we authorize expanded programs to develop better strategies for spent-fuel management. These strategies will go far beyond Yucca Mountain and will result in better use of, and far less toxicity from, any future repository.

Finally, my sixth priority in the bill was my recognition that we do not have human resources in the pipeline to support an expansion of nuclear energy, much less to appropriately control and mitigate the military challenges of the nuclear genie. We need stronger university programs, with more students challenged and motivated to master these technologies to contribute to the future workforce. For that reason, there are strong educational programs in the law.

I am confident that we will use the new law to work towards fulfillment of more of Ike's vision. The law will enable our nation to proceed with development of nuclear power here at home. However, my vision, like

Ike's, does not stop at our own borders. We must help provide developing nations with the energy resources they need so that they too can grow and prosper. The seeds of unrest and terrorism will be far less fertile as the standards of living of all peoples are raised towards our own.

As we assist these nations, we should suggest that they focus their attention on clean energy sources, to avoid the environmental problems that many developed nations like the United States are experiencing with past energy sources. Nuclear power should be one of the clean technologies we offer to them.

Now, obviously, many of those developing nations do not have the necessary infrastructure to produce and safeguard nuclear materials or to design new reactors. We can and should help them in specific ways, such as providing small, sealed reactors, along with full assurances from the developed nations to guarantee to provide all their life-cycle fuel services. Those same life-cycle fuel services should be offered to many other nations for large reactors as well.

We should work through international organizations, like the International Atomic Energy Agency that Ike's vision created, to craft global approaches to fuel production and waste handling in ways that minimize proliferation concerns. We just require the will to work through and with the international community to make them a reality.

President Eisenhower offered an immense challenge to the world and, while parts of his vision have been realized, many parts of it remain unfulfilled. Susan Eisenhower emphasized this view in a speech in 2003, when she noted that: "Atoms for Peace is a vision—not a blueprint."[5]

Today we need to redouble our efforts to realize that vision, which Ike summarized so well when he closed his speech with these words:

> [T]he United States pledges before you—and therefore before the world— . . . to devote its entire heart and mind to find the way by which the miraculous inventiveness of man shall not be dedicated to his death, but consecrated to his life.[6]

---

5. Susan Eisenhower, remarks at "Nuclear Energy and Science for the 21st Century: Atoms for Peace Plus 50," Washington, D.C., October 22, 2003.
6. "Atomic Power for Peace."

16

The Paradox of Nuclear Power
Atsuyuki Suzuki

Joseph Nye of Harvard University wrote *The Paradox of American Power*, which was published after the tragedy of September 11, 2001. The book is laid out under the following headings:

- "The American Colossus"
- "The Information Revolution"
- "Globalization"
- "The Home Front"
- "Redefining the National Interest"

This paper draws a comparison between the logical structure of Nye's volume and the architecture for a successful nuclear future.

The first point of the analogy would replace the American colossus with the nuclear colossus. Nye wrote, "Not since Rome has one nation loomed so large above the others."[1] No other nation has had the great economic,

1. Joseph S. Nye, Jr., *The Paradox of American Power: Why the World's Only Superpower Can't Go It Alone* (Oxford and New York: Oxford University Press, 2002), 1.

cultural, and military power that the United States now possesses. But, Nye argued, even with that preponderance of power,

> many transnational issues—whether financial flows, the spread of AIDS or terrorism—cannot be resolved without cooperation of others. Where collective action is a necessary part of obtaining the outcomes we want, our power is by definition limited and the United States is bound to share.[2]

In similar fashion, as Albert Einstein noted, the discovery of nuclear energy is an unparalleled human discovery comparable to Peking man's discovery of fire. However, history shows that this awesome discovery has not brought about easy solutions for global problems, such as the economic divide between North and South or global climate change. Rather, it has given rise to nuclear proliferation concerns.

Obviously, American power exists and it seems to be in the interest of the global community for the United States to maintain its power for the foreseeable future unless it creates another world order system. Similarly, nuclear energy exists, and there seems no doubt that the global community needs to maintain the use of nuclear energy for sustainable development, and for moving towards higher standards of living, better health, and a cleaner environment. The reality, however, is that the global future of nuclear energy looks very vague at present. The news that Germany's second-oldest nuclear power plant at Stade was switched off shows that reality symbolically. A majority of people throughout the world think Germany is launching the world's fastest withdrawal from nuclear energy, although the closure of that plant's operation was actually and primarily taken on economic grounds without government pressure. Nevertheless, the fact is that nuclear power is used as a political tool in such a way that promising to phase it out is often a condition for forming coalition governments. The fragile or vulnerable nature of nuclear energy ironically stems from the inherent characteristics of the nuclear colossus—innovative, powerful, and advanced. As suggested, it seems something similar to what Joseph Nye called the "paradox of American power."

The main thesis of Nye's book is that in a world marked by rapid technological advances and the increasing power of nongovernmental organizations, including transnational corporations and terrorists, the United States must understand the limits of its power and reach out to the interna-

2. Ibid., 140.

tional community. This logic applies not only to military but to economic power as well. As Nye argued,

> On many of the key issues today, such as internal financial stability, drug smuggling, or global climate change, military power simply cannot produce success, and its use can sometimes be counterproductive.[3]

This logic applies not only to military but to economic power as well. In the new century, according to Nye, the United States will rely less on traditional measures of power and more on the power that derives from the appeal of U.S. culture, values, and institutions—what he calls "soft power."[4] This message may suggest a viable basis for creating a roadmap for maintaining nuclear power's standing while reducing its vulnerability in the years to come.

To follow Nye's idea, the first thing to consider is the relationships of nuclear power to the information revolution. Without trying to go through the details of all of these relationships, there is one thing that is markedly noticeable—the necessity of openness or transparency in connection with the use of nuclear power. Unfortunately, major reasons for the eroding confidence in the nuclear industry have been closely linked with the lack of transparency. In Japan, for instance, a series of nuclear scandals and troubles observed over the last several years were clearly due to the insufficiency and inappropriateness of information management.

We have two types of nuclear safety issues. One is how to install and manage the technical measures for radiological protection based on a defense-in-depth philosophy together with multiple physical barriers. Apart from some exceptional events like the Chernobyl accident, we have not had any serious incidents or accidents with this to date. However, the other issue of nuclear safety cannot be ignored and actually seems of greater moment than the first, that is, the procedural aspect of safety such as regulatory frameworks and accountability to society. What has been revealed in the recent nuclear-related events in Japan is that this second type of safety issue is a real concern. Japan is now taking every effort to improve the situation, particularly with respect to the regulatory framework, but what is equally or even more important is each company's autonomous efforts to ensure accountability whether required by law or not.

3. Ibid., xv.
4. Ibid., 8–12, and passim.

The Tokyo Electric Power Company, for instance, has started providing live television views via website of the actual circumstances of an airtight inspection test of a reactor container—an inspection that was once badly managed to cover up statutorily unsatisfactory data. Providing a live view through the Internet is enormously effective in preventing the recurrence of such an unacceptable event. It demonstrates accountability to the public. Usually, this type of information disclosure costs a great deal and is difficult to implement. Because of the economic advantages prevailing in existing nuclear power plants relative to non-nuclear electricity, however, the nuclear industry could afford such transparency measures. Nuclear power companies must maximize the benefit expected from information technology for improving transparency, which would significantly help to obtain public support for nuclear energy. Such improvements seem to be representative of the soft power aspects that Nye believes can often be the most effective ones.

The next dimension that Nye presents is "globalization." This dimension should be considered in formulating the roadmap for nuclear energy as well. The greenhouse gas emission issue, for example, could not be solved by nuclear energy alone, but neither could it be solved without nuclear energy. This is a very typical example that shows the global dimension of nuclear energy. Another example is, of course, the proliferation risks that stem from the use of nuclear power. Clearly, U.S. leadership and global partnership are indispensable to reduce this risk and to draw benefits from nuclear power globally, and a new international regime seems necessary to strengthen security measures. In designing such a regime, we should keep in mind Eisenhower's words: "Nuclear technology is to serve the hopes rather than the fears of mankind."[5]

No simple answer exists but, rather, humankind still faces the challenge Eisenhower already identified fifty years ago, that is, "gaining the benefits of nuclear technology in a way that limits the risks to security."[6] A number of proposals have been made, ranging from controlling nuclear technology on the one hand to changing the institutional requirements for the nations that could access this technology on the other. Again, whatever it may ultimately look like, the necessary new architecture should be built with the maximum use of soft power. In this regard, it seems that we need to be

---

5. "Atomic Power for Peace," an address by Dwight D. Eisenhower, President of the United States, before the General Assembly of the United Nations, December 8, 1953.
6. Ibid.

patient. While soft power usually takes time to be effective, once it is in effect it is often longer lasting than traditional power alone.

One of the possibilities open to us is to establish a global network for nuclear spent-fuel management. U.S. policy has been focused on pursuing only the rapid direct disposal of spent fuel and to urge other nations to follow that policy, which sometimes conflicts with these nations' sovereignty. That appears to be a kind of traditional power approach and does not well fit the realities and requirements of the age of globalization. On the contrary, other nations are unlikely to follow the U.S. program, especially the Yucca Mountain project, because it is too costly and politically too sophisticated in spite of remarkable progress made in recent years. The United States is the only country that can undertake such an incredibly huge project. People around the globe may think that U.S. nuclear policy is based on a sort of isolationism. Fortunately, it has shifted gradually, becoming internationalized to a certain extent over the last couple of years.

What would be more acceptable globally would be the establishment of a multinational system where spent nuclear fuel is managed with more centralized and intensive international safeguards. It is true that this does not much help resolve the situation in North Korea, for instance. Nevertheless, it would generate a tremendous amount of benefit for many nations that intend to use nuclear energy for peaceful purposes only. It would provide the most economical and flexible option for managing spent fuel—not merely in terms of direct costs but also taking into account indirect costs associated with such externalities as security and environmental concerns.

In this context, an interim spent-fuel storage option for decades might be more practical for the time being than an international repository. That is because, internationally, there are a variety of views on the value of spent fuel for recycling. Sociopolitically, an extremely big decision is inevitably required of any hosting state if it is to be a final disposal repository, which entails an indefinite international commitment on its part. In the case of interim storage, another set of challenging issues would be raised if there were efforts to reach an international agreement concerning how to manage spent fuel after the storage period, which might have to be fixed in a prescribed manner, as well as to agree on how to minimize the ensuing nonproliferation concerns. Such an agreement would not be easy to reach. Nevertheless, pursuing an interim storage option first, in a kind of staging approach such as was recommended in the 2003 U.S. National Academy of Sciences study on high-level radioactive waste management, offers the best solution. What is desirable for most states is not to dispute the merits and demerits of reprocessing and recycling, but to provide an institutionally more comfortable scheme that facilitates the broad use of nuclear energy in many nations. This approach is consistent with the soft-power approach recommended in Nye's book.

What is the importance of the home front? To some extent, each state is faced with a cumbersome domestic political situation regarding the public acceptance of nuclear energy. Needless to say, any solution would not come to pass without public support, and the issue of how to encourage it, especially on a global scale, is critical. Building broader international confidence in nuclear power might be a remarkable help to each country's domestic acceptance of nuclear energy. Looking at the global trend in which nongovernmental organizations and transnational corporations are increasing their power, we can perhaps glean some insights on what must be done to ensure the future of nuclear power.

Many lessons have been learned from the past in the area of public perception and risk communication, inter alia, in connection with the use of nuclear power. One of the lessons is the importance of identifying and meeting public demands rather than attempting to convince the public of a decision after it has already been taken. From this, the first thing we should do is to try to understand the global public's primary concerns regarding the use of nuclear energy. Many of these concerns stem from the legacy of the military nuclear programs of the past fifty years. If this is the case, then the highest priority should be placed on how to manage and dismantle this legacy, not only from a domestic view, but internationally as well. Addressing both domestic and international concerns is crucial to building and sustaining the global support for nuclear power in the century to come.

What Nye emphasizes in the chapter titled "The Home Front" is the capability of providing the power that derives from the appeal of culture, values, and institutions.

> How well will Americans respond to the challenges of this global information age? A nation can lose power as a result of being overtaken by rising nations, but . . . this is not the most likely challenge. The barbarians did not defeat Rome; rather, it rotted from within. People lost confidence in their culture and institutions, elites battled for control, corruption increased, and the economy failed to grow adequately. Today

terrorist barbarians cannot destroy American power unless we also rot from within.[7]

This observation, as well, suggests a good analogy for the future development of nuclear energy. That is because the nuclear future rests similarly on the capacity to utilize its soft power derived from the appeal of its culture, values, and institutions rather than from its hard, physical power, which is a potential source for mass destruction as well as for producing electricity. Some people might think nuclear energy would lose ground through such an effort, as a result of being overtaken by other energy alternatives like wind power and solar energy. However, that is not likely to be the case. Nuclear power rotting from within would be more likely than its being surpassed by alternative energy options. The fragile and vulnerable nature surrounding current nuclear energy prospects are connected, largely, with the origin of nuclear technology, that is, its military application.

The fact is that a multitude of nuclear legacies have accumulated over the past fifty years during the Cold War period, and as classified information has been disclosed, many concerns have surfaced with respect to safety, security, and environmental issues. These issues were largely a result of military activities that were managed with little attention to public safety and environmental concerns. The long shadows of these legacies loom over current global views on nuclear technology. Without the elimination of those legacies, it will not be possible to obtain worldwide support for extended use of nuclear energy in the future.

Then, what about redefining the nuclear interest, analogously to the national interest as presented in the Nye volume? Can we explore successful avenues for the future uses of nuclear energy? In order to respond to this challenge, one has to know the changing nature of the nuclear interest. The most attractive feature of nuclear energy used to be its tremendously high fuel economy, that is, two million times more energy produced from the same amount of mass consumed as fossil fuel. This is the hard-power aspect of nuclear energy. However, we have realized that nuclear energy has another remarkable attractiveness, that is, its robustness in light of the uncertainties of the global fuel markets for oil and natural gas. The greatest incentive in Japan for the use of nuclear energy is that very robustness, that is, so-called energy security in a broad sense. This is an aspect of the soft rather than the hard power of nuclear energy. Its potential role in alleviating

---

7. Nye, *Paradox of American Power,* 111.

global warming concerns is also an aspect of its soft power that was not widely identified at the time of President Eisenhower's speech. These views should be shared and form the foundation of a kind of global consensus.

The way to manage spent fuel recommended during Eisenhower's age was very solid and hard. In other words, the United States used to suggest to other nations that they ship their spent fuel back to the United States after burning it at their reactors in order to utilize plutonium in the United States for some particular purposes. Apparently, the United States realized that this was too narrow a view and altered its policy. Noteworthy is why other nations actually were able to adapt to such a drastic U.S. policy change. The answer is again related to soft power. Relative to other types of ordinary waste, like garbage, the amount of spent fuel is so miniscule in volume and thus more easily managed technically, that other nations can store it mostly at reactor sites, albeit reluctantly. This inherent element of the nature of nuclear power provides the advantage of flexibility, while, ironically, it often leads a paradoxical situation with high-level radioactive waste management. In other words, the schedule of disposing the waste is apt to be delayed because the prolonged storage of spent fuel is, in most cases, the most practical option and provides a sociopolitical refuge from making a big, controversial decision. However, the nature of nuclear energy allows this and other such issues to be managed through soft power. Yet, there remains the security issue potentially associated with such prolonged storage.

Finally, it has been suggested that transparency is a key element related to the soft power of nuclear energy. What is proven from the past fifty years of the peaceful use of nuclear energy is that transparency or openness is a kind of prerequisite for building confidence nationally and internationally. The meaning is twofold. First, transparency is the most effective measure for nuclear material safeguards if it is appropriately managed for security. Second, it also is the most effective method for maintaining a sound safety culture as well as obtaining acceptance of nuclear energy from the public at large. Transparency is a cultural product of democracy and, conceivably, sovereign nations employing nuclear power through transparent mechanisms would achieve a greatest outcome in terms of culture, values, and institutions.

In concluding, the prospects for nuclear energy over the next fifty years significantly rest upon the architecture we will build. That architecture should be designed to focus more on the soft power aspects of nuclear energy than the hard. For example, nuclear nations have a responsibility to convince the global public that the use of nuclear energy is certainly beneficial not merely in terms of fuel production efficiency, but also in terms of robustness of fuel supply or energy security. An internationally more cooperative approach to management of spent fuel would increase these benefits, heightening levels of transparency, and ensuring accountability. In the century to come, every state will be unavoidably faced with global challenges that could not be resolved without involving other nations, and the recent global situation has indicated the overriding need for the reorientation of each nation's policy towards the creation of more intensive and extensive global partnerships. The next fifty years of Atoms for Peace should be one of the drivers of such global movement.

17

Nuclear Energy: New Challenges for the Future

Jacques Bouchard

The expected increase in energy demand makes it necessary for us to seriously and urgently study the questions of global warming due to greenhouse gas emissions and the eventual depletion of fossil fuel resources. This clearly means that as we produce more energy, we must produce a minimum amount of carbon dioxide and keep the costs under control and acceptable for the user. A growing number of prospective studies envision that nuclear energy, because it is carbon-free, will play an important—an essential—role in the world energy mix of the twenty-first century.

Among the challenges that must be taken up for this vision of a large expansion of nuclear power to materialize, it is sometimes argued that economics is the major one, ahead of waste management and natural resources management. This argument is based on the perception that, today, nuclear power would not be an economically competitive choice in deregulated markets compared to natural gas.

On the basis of our experience with nuclear production of electricity, it is interesting to have a look on some price figures. The curves in Figure 1 show

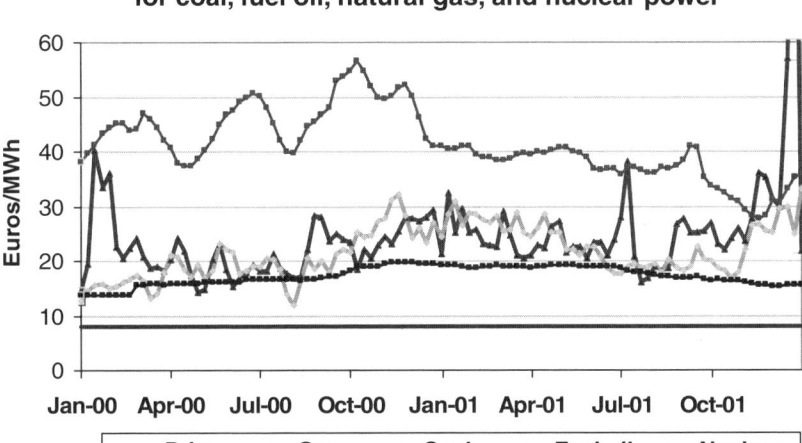

Figure 1. Nuclear Today: An Affordable Energy

the evolution of the market prices in Europe in recent years. The line marked price in Figure 1 corresponds to actual spot market prices. The others show the cost of electricity production with various fuels. It is easy to see that nuclear is the only one with a cost always much lower than the market price.

Several European economic studies published in recent years on the comparative costs of electricity production, including studies by the French government and the Organization for Economic Cooperation and Development/ Nuclear Energy Agency report in 1998, highlight this trend. Although the studies were carried out for different purposes by different actors, and were based on different methods, these studies converge to show that the total generation cost for new nuclear plants built in Europe is projected to be in the range of 22 to 32 euros per megawatt-hour (See Table 1). The total production cost may be 20 percent lower than the cost for combined-cycle gas turbine units. These studies demonstrate the competitiveness of nuclear energy compared to other sources of energy, in particular combined cycle gas turbine (CCGT) plants.

Moreover, prospects for internalization of the greenhouse gas emission cost in the total production cost will boost even further the competitiveness of nuclear compared to gas-fired plants in Europe.

Table 1
Cost of Nuclear Megawatt-hour Compared to Natural Gas Turbine Combined Cycle Technology

MWh*	Nuclear	Gas Turbine
Total cost of generation	22 to 32	26 to 57
Cost of impact on environment (including climate change: ExternE 99 study)	2 to 7	5 to 35
Total	**24 to 39**	**31 to 92**

*Real discount rates from 5% to 10% for power generation and 3% for external costs.

In late February 2003, selected provisional results of a study performed by the French Ministry of Industry to update its 1997 assessment were published. The most recent information, including updates of some studies from the late 1990s, show nuclear results at less than 30 euros per megawatt-hour, which is less costly than CCGT technology, assuming an 8-percent discount rate and a series of ten European pressurized water reactors (EPRs). Both technologies exhibit comparable production costs at an 11-percent discount rate. For an EPR, overnight construction costs have been estimated to be close to 1,050 euros per kilowatt of electricity.

These figures suggest that the cost reductions of new nuclear plants are greater than gas cost reductions resulting from technological improvements. The CCGT technology cost per kilowatt-hour is still penalized by the high share of gas in the cost and risk of price variability.

Concerning generation-IV (Gen IV) systems, the clear objective is also to keep nuclear energy as competitive as possible by reducing operation costs as well as construction costs. In the economic scale used to assess the proposed systems in the selection phase, ultimate values such as $20 per megawatt-hour and $1,000 per kilowatt of electricity for overnight construction costs have been considered.

With economy comes safety. Generation II reactors have gained considerable maturity and competitiveness, and have a long operating experience (Figure 2). We have capitalized more than ten thousand reactor years of experience with the second generation, and thus may consider them as safe and reliable.

The very good record achieved with light-water reactor (LWR) technology has logically led manufacturers to design a new generation of reactors based on the same technology. However, regulatory constraints govern-

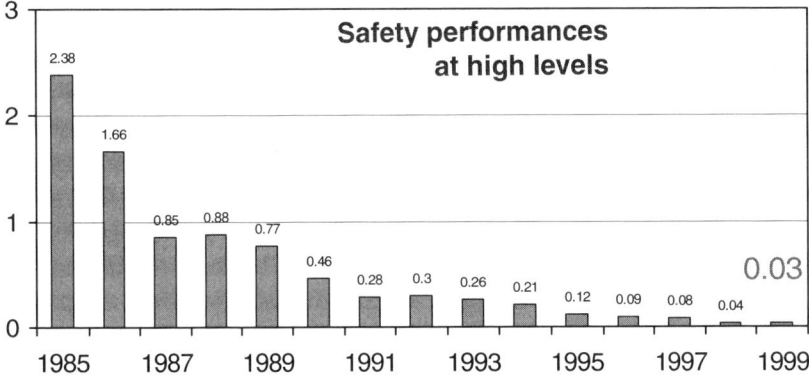

Figure 2. Safety of Generation II Reactors: Satisfactory Data Over 15 Years

ing their construction and operation increased after the accident at the Three Mile Island power station in the United States in 1979 and the Chernobyl accident in 1986. These accidents were the reasons for increased safety measures in existing reactors. They helped us better understand the human factor, allowing regulatory a more sophisticated concept of reactor operation that progressively has taken account of probabilistic safety studies.

In 1993, French and German authorities adopted new safety policies in Europe for future pressurized water reactors, including "European utilities requirements" as defined by European electricity producers. New safety guidelines were written on the basis of these requirements. They apply to risk prevention and a limitation of risk consequences, so that in the case of a major accident, radioactivity would not have any effect outside the power station site, thus limiting pressures to evacuate populations outside the immediate vicinity of the power station.

In the so-called generation-III reactors, such as EPRs, the main development focus was on safety. In particular, design features include improvements to mitigate the consequences of very-low-probability severe accidents likely to lead to core meltdown. As a result, the already very small probability of a major accident with core meltdown has been reduced by another factor of 10, from 1 in 100,000 years to 1 in 1,000,000 years, and the impact of this type of accident outside the containment structure has been reduced.

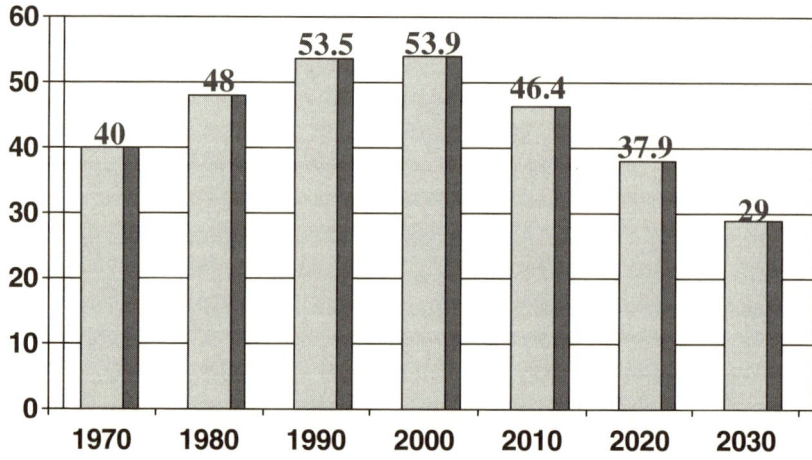

Figure 3. European Energy Independence Rate

Concerning the security of energy supply (Figure 3), the European energy-dependence rate will increase steadily in subsequent decades, as regional energy production decreases, and energy consumption increases in the same timeframe. A situation comparable to that of the 1970s during the first oil shock, which triggered the launch of nuclear energy as well as substantial energy savings, is likely.

Considering future nuclear energy systems, experts participating in the Generation IV International Forum (GIF) considered the relationship between energy production and consumption, and very quickly concluded that the fourth-generation system should be used for energy applications other than electricity. This could be achieved by using an energy carrier such as hydrogen and using nuclear power for district heating or desalinating seawater in countries lacking adequate freshwater sources.

Although industry has already made great efforts to reduce its carbon dioxide emissions, solutions for resolving carbon dioxide emissions in the transportation sector have not yet emerged. Around two million cars were sold in China in 2002, and this figure is expected to increase tremendously in coming decades. We foresee nuclear production of hydrogen as an important alternative to avoid risks of major climate disorders. Of course, technical and economic challenges need to be resolved before making a full demonstration, but we do not see any major obstacle to reaching that goal.

Considering nuclear energy prospects for the next fifty years, let me now turn to proliferation resistance concerns. The risk of proliferation should not be underestimated, and the French government fully supports various measures and external controls, taken on an international basis, to avoid this risk. We have very strict domestic and European controls, and we are fully convinced that they are suitable for avoiding any significant diversion.

Concerning the question of "closed cycles" versus "open cycles," both past and current experience tells us that, in most cases, proliferation activities were not in direct relation to civilian use of nuclear energy and, in particular, we have not yet been faced with attempts to misuse nuclear materials coming from commercial reprocessing and recycling under international control. Furthermore, studies of the relative proliferation risk of fissile material as well as past experience show that enriched uranium—not plutonium—is undoubtedly the most attractive material for proliferators.

For Gen IV systems, the aim is to design systems that are as intrinsically unattractive to proliferators as possible. This is now under consideration at an early stage of the international work performed within the GIF framework.

Finally, external controls and safeguard systems should be improved or reinforced and adapted to current geopolitical situations while meeting international consensus. However, one can raise the question of whether all the countries are or will be ready to accept these reinforced measures.

In the same vein, public opinion is raising questions and revealing concerns about security and physical protection issues. We do not yet have the answers to all of these questions, and we absolutely need to think about and work on these issues.

To the present, economics, safety, and security challenges have been considered in the design of nuclear power plants. What is new is that so-called sustainable development criteria are becoming important in the design of next-generation systems. The main sustainable development criteria are to minimize environmental consequences, particularly waste, and to save resources.

For a long time, from the perspective of its contribution to long-term radiotoxicity, removing plutonium from spent fuel has been considered the top priority. On this basis, it is essential to recycle plutonium. This is the reason why we have developed a plutonium recycling strategy, which is now being implemented in France, with more than 1,200 tons of mixed oxide fuel recycled in pressurized water reactors.

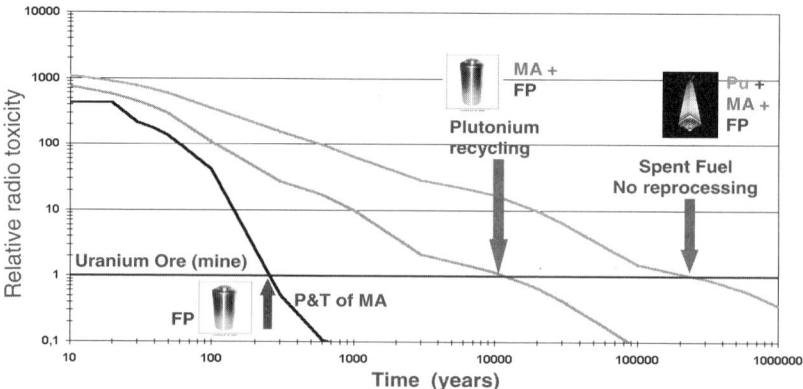

Figure 4. Benefits of Advanced Fuel Cycles in Terms of Waste Management
FP = fusion products; MA = minor actinides; P&T = partioning and transmutation; Pu = plutonium

As Figure 4 shows, the benefits of "advanced fuel cycle" approaches in terms of waste management should not be underestimated. Benefits of these approaches follow:

- Long-term safe conditioning of high-level, long-lived radioactive waste by vitrification
- Reduction of geological repository capacity needs by cutting waste to be disposed of
- Reduction of long-term risk of repository through decrease of its long-term radiotoxic inventory
- Drastic reduction in the challenge of demonstrating the long-term safety of the repository by reducing the toxic waste lifetime with partitioning and transmutation of all actinides

The second priority is removing minor actinides, as this brings an additional and significant reduction to the potential impact of waste on the environment. Considerable progress on partitioning and transmutation—one of the high-level waste management strategies under investigation within the framework of the French radioactive waste management Research and Development Act of 1991—has been made.

The key role of public and political attitudes towards the feasibility and acceptability of high-level waste disposal should not be underestimated. One interest in spent-fuel is to reduce reprocessing waste volume.

Early values of waste volumes generated by the La Hague reprocessing plant were expected to be of the same order of magnitude as those encountered with the direct disposal option. After improvements, the industrial experience demonstrates that waste production is now reduced by a factor of approximately four, thus reducing geological repository capacity needs as well as intermediate pool storage at reactor sites (Figure 5).

Another criterion for sustainability is the preservation of natural resources (Figure 6). According to a study of the future of nuclear energy by the Massachusetts Institute of Technology, which assumed that the number of reactors throughout the world will grow by a factor of three by the year 2050, uranium ore prices will undoubtedly increase significantly over current levels. Closed cycles and fast reactors are notable means of extending uranium resource capacity from a time scale of around one century to several thousand years.

Gen IV systems will be designed to manage all the actinides with advanced, integrated fuel cycles. As fast neutrons are also well suited for the transmutation of all actinides, this combination (illustrated in Figure 7) should make a great contribution to the minimization of nuclear waste as well as to the preservation of uranium resources.

This leads us to view the closed cycle as the only option that meets the conditions of sustainable nuclear development. Furthermore, meeting these conditions requires us to set challenging technological innovation goals for

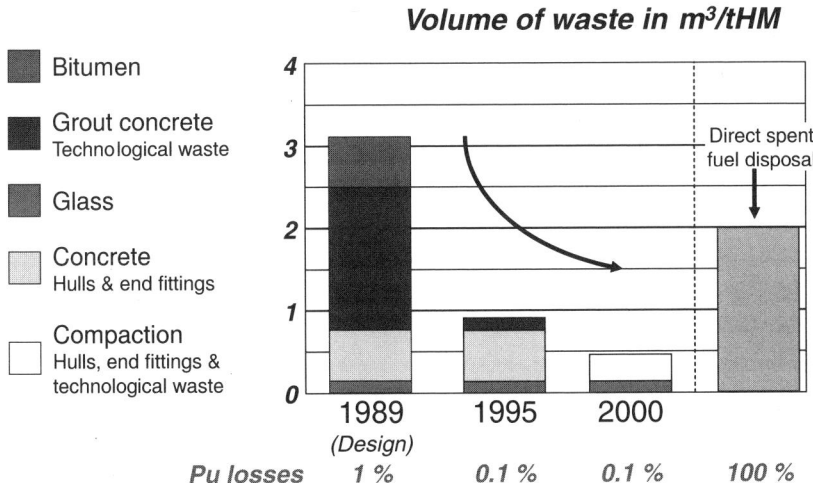

Figure 5. Closed Cycles: Minimize Wastes

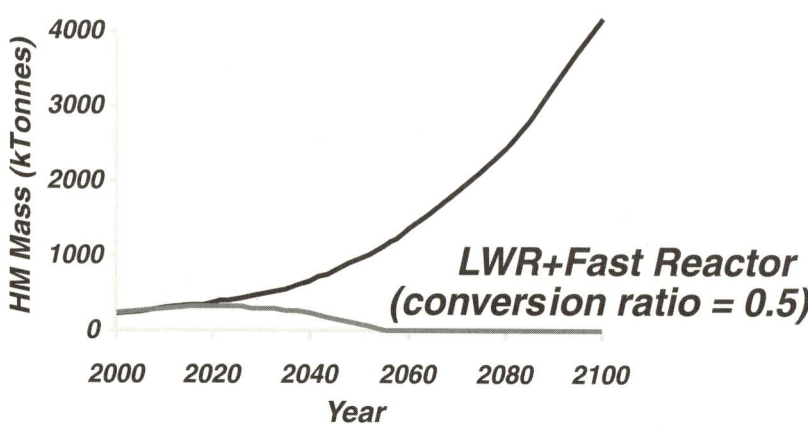

Figure 6. Preservation of Uranium Resources

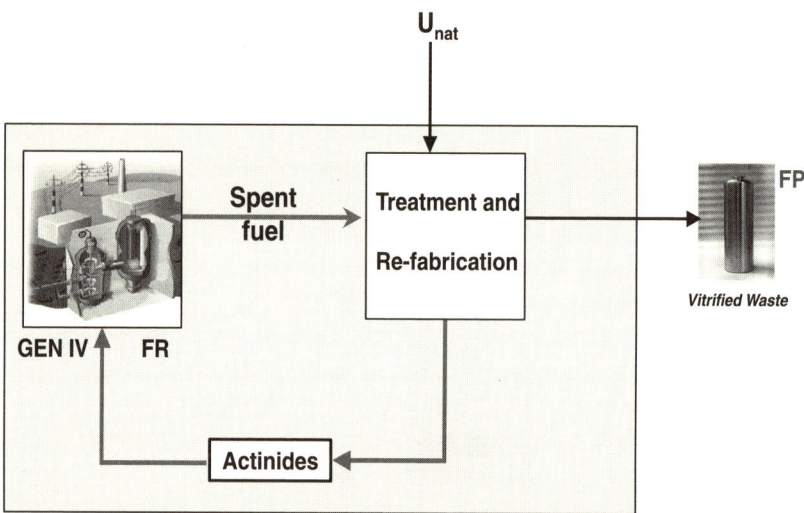

Figure 7. Closed Fuel Cycles: A Path towards Sustainability

Gen IV nuclear systems. We must engage immediately so that these Gen IV systems can be brought to industrial maturity in the next half-century and, thereby, enable the realization of ambitious global nuclear growth scenarios.

In conclusion, a few principles should be highlighted:

- Nuclear energy is already competitive and will remain so in the next decades in comparison to other sources of energy, especially gas.
- Nuclear energy is safe and reliable today. Relying on an industrial maturity and long operations experience, new generations of nuclear power plants will be safer still.
- Resistance to proliferation risks and security against external aggression are important matters that have to be accorded high-level attention.

Our understanding of public attitudes towards nuclear energy makes us place the minimization of both the quantities and radiotoxicity of ultimate waste as one of the essential features of sustainable nuclear energy development. Optimizing the use of natural resources is another essential feature of sustainability. This leads us to view the closed cycle as the only option that meets conditions of a sustainable nuclear development.

If we make the right choices, nuclear energy will meet sustainable development and play a key role in the twenty-first century.

18

A Nuclear Future unlike the Past

Per F. Peterson

What is going to be different in the nuclear power arena in the future? In the early part of the 1990s, the Chernobyl accident of 1986 still had a significant negative effect on the level of interest in nuclear energy in the United States, as well as globally. Moreover, the State of the Union Address by President Clinton in January 1993 announced that the United States was going to discontinue unnecessary research; the single example given was nuclear energy research and development. This announcement, and the public policy position it embodied, had an enormous negative impact as well. In the United States, reactors with persistently low capacity factors were being decommissioned at a steady rate of about one per year. From the perspective of the universities, the nuclear industry and the utilities had completely stopped hiring young people because they did not want to bring them in for just ten to fifteen years, which they estimated would probably be the time period in which all the plants would be shutting down.

In the mid-1990s, the situation changed. It was discovered that nuclear power plants could actually be sold as opposed to just decommissioning them. These earliest plants were sold for prices around $25 per kilowatt, compared to the $2000 per kilowatt that might have been required to build a new nuclear plant. The capacity factors for these plants rose rapidly under the new and more capable management, and it was very rapidly understood that all plants could actually run at a high capacity and produce very inexpensive electricity. This led to the present situation, in which there has been a resurgence of interest in nuclear energy and, indeed, the potential to build new plants in the not-too-distant future in the United States.

Both the problems with nuclear energy in the early 1990s and developments since then have affected the universities. Some of the most recent information on student enrollment at a few universities with nuclear engineering departments, such as the Massachusetts Institute of Technology, the University of California at Berkeley, the University of Michigan, Texas A&M, and the University of Illinois at Urbana-Champaign, is very interesting in this regard. As noted, plants were being decommissioned, and students were not being hired out of nuclear engineering programs. This led to plummeting student enrollment in all university nuclear engineering programs. Even during the Clinton presidency, though, a change occurred. The changes actually can be readily ascribed to what was starting to happen with license renewals and plant sales, which led to a rebound in utility hiring. Companies and utilities suddenly realized that not hiring anyone over a five-year period meant that they were not well positioned to argue that a twenty-year license renewal meant anything at all. It was recognized that people who can competently run nuclear plants were needed. Looking to the near future, new plant orders and the clear articulation of national policy in favor of nuclear energy will have a substantial effect on student interest in the field of nuclear engineering.

As we think about the future promise of nuclear power, we must begin with the fact that uranium is extraordinarily abundant in the environment, much of which can be used for fuel. In fact, detailed measurements of uranium in U.S. soils show that, on the average, there are about six tons per square mile in just the top yard. If one plans to use uranium as an energy source, it is not going to run out, particularly if one uses it efficiently. This point is important because radioactive material is ubiquitous, and is encountered on a daily basis, including every time one gardens in the backyard.

The availability of uranium is only one factor—and perhaps not the most important one—in a renewed discussion of the economics of nuclear energy. More fundamentally, it is necessary to look at how much material it takes to build infrastructure. These numbers are much harder to massage, or essentially, to argue about. In the 1970s, to build a nuclear power plant an average of about forty metric tons of steel and about 190 cubic meters of concrete were required for every megawatt of installed average capacity in a nuclear reactor. Design changes resulting from the Three Mile Island accident caused these numbers to increase by 20 to 30 percent, as is the case for the Advanced Boiling Water Reactors built over the last decade in Japan and Taiwan. The new passive light water reactor designs have reversed this trend, and actually use less steel than those of the 1970s. Furthermore, the U.S. Department of Energy's Generation-IV (Gen IV) program may be able to cut resource usage—steel and concrete inputs—by as much as a factor of two from 1970s values. This should have a significant effect on capital costs because concrete and steel comprise 95 percent of nuclear plant construction.

How do the inputs for nuclear plants compare to alternative energy sources? Regarding wind, accounting for typical capacity factors of 25 to 30 percent—and not taking into account the lifetime of the machines—typical current technology consumes about 460 metric tons of steel per megawatt of average power output. This does not include inputs for electricity storage or backup power generation, which are required to address the intermittency of the power generation. Interestingly enough, coal plants with steam Rankine cycles actually take more material to build than 1970s-era nuclear plants, almost double the steel inputs. Moreover, the use of coal as fuel for these plants has environmental and other costs, albeit there is no full accounting for them. There is no fundamental reason that capital costs for building nuclear plants could not be lower than those for coal plants.

Next, I discuss natural gas and why this energy source dominates the current market. Combined cycle gas turbine (CCGT) plants have an extraordinarily high power density. Nuclear plants simply will never compete with them in terms of capital costs. The main question is whether natural gas prices will remain sufficiently high that it will not be affordable as the fuel for CCGT plants. The capital costs associated with natural gas plants are never going to be matched in nuclear power plants. Much of the steel for gas turbines is highly specialized, but there is a large difference in the amounts required.

What elements of the current situation are different from the time when the United States was actively building plants thirty years ago? In the early 1980s, for example, building a plastic model for any nuclear facility might require an entire floor of a large office building; large numbers of people were needed to busily work on the model. When design changes were required, it was literally necessary to cut out sections of the models and to rebuild them. Today, design changes can be made with a click of a mouse. Additional design changes were then required at the plant site. There is absolutely no need to have the same number of engineers at a plant site now, because it is no longer necessary to worry about problems that were not caught during the design process. The situation is vastly different now in terms of the design tools we possess. Students in the engineering field are coming out of college able to work with three-dimensional and computer-assisted design tools.

The same applies to the processes for construction. For example, ABWRs were built in the 1990s on a time scale of fifty-two months—from looking at the excavated bedrock to producing commercial power. There are interesting features in the evolution of construction. It is becoming highly modular. At Diablo Canyon, for example, there is an overlook where one can see a piece of two-inch diameter rebar. This is supposed to teach one about the strength of these nuclear plants. The interesting thing about the rebar is that it is all tied together with big sleeves into which molten metal is poured. This approach is not necessary today.

The situation has evolved dramatically in terms of manufacturing and fabrication. This affects both cost and the ability to construct various items rapidly, such as cruise ships. Everything is designed on computers today. In the case of a cruise ship, for example, each of the modules is individually fabricated because all of the cutting of materials and welding is performed with automated machinery. Using this approach, where the modules are assembled like Legos, cruise ships can be built in less than a year. There is an effort to bring the same techniques to the construction of nuclear plants as well. All of these advances drive the cost down. The steel and concrete, and not nearly as much labor, are the principal cost drivers in this case.

The regulatory environment is another key aspect of the picture of nuclear power's future, which is entirely different now. An important point in this regard is that every plant now has a testing laboratory. Commercial parts, such as valves and other components, are bought and certified, as opposed to buying nuclear-grade parts. This approach is utilized because nuclear-grade items are difficult to find, but also because it is much cheaper to proceed in this fashion.

License renewals must also be considered. This is not just an example of why existing plants are valuable, but also provides some clues as to how flexible the licensing system has become and how rapidly it can respond to changes that can increase safety and improve economic performance. License renewals are coming in at 18 months.

What is especially notable is the flexibility to make changes in plant design. There have been large numbers of power upgrades in the United States, and additional upgrades are expected. Some plants are implementing multiple upgrades. These upgrades can now be completed in as little as 12 months' time.

Design certification is also occurring. By recertifying the plant design, additional savings can be realized from power upgrades. One of the notable changes is that the regulatory system no longer generates an impediment to rapid evolution of the technology.

If there are actions that can be taken to reduce capital costs or to take advantage of experience, it should be anticipated that this will happen. This is contrary to the way the issue appeared in the 1980s, when experts were thinking in terms of building large numbers of identical plants as the solution. It is worthwhile to consider some of the lessons that were learned in the 1980s and assess whether they are applicable today—given modern tools and modern technology. It may be useful to look at further rapid evolution to try to capture economic and safety benefits.

The Economic Simplified Boiling Water Reactor (ESBWR) is likely to have a very easy time going through design certification. In part, this is because the safety basis for this plant is vastly simpler than that for existing plants. In particular, if one looks at a large break-loss cooling accident—because of natural circulation and the enormous inventory of water in the reactor vessel even during a large break—the closest one gets to uncovering the core is two meters. In most existing plants, the procedure is to completely uncover the core and then try to re-flood it. One of the major issues that has preoccupied experts in the field of thermohydraulics is predicting the very complex sequence of events that occur in a very brief period of time and in a very highly coupled way. For the ESBWR, predicting the peak temperature and peak containment pressure are things that can literally be done on the back of the envelope. It is easier for the Nuclear Regulatory Commission to license a plant where individuals can calculate the most important safety-related parameters on the back of an envelope and then compare the results to detailed calculations.

Another important development to note is that it is possible, using passive safety systems, to cut the quantities of material used in a reactor in half. If simple scaling alone is done, the conclusion is that a nuclear island costs half as much for an ESBWR that puts out as much power as an ABWR. This should translate to about a 30-percent reduction in capital cost.

There will be potential advances in safety and economics. The major areas that contribute to safety also provide important economic opportunities. Could concrete and steel use be cut by a factor of two from what was used in the reactors of the 1970s? One of the first places to look for opportunities is actually in containments and structures, particularly in terms of trying to get away from high pressure and large amounts of stored energy that can be released rapidly. This means that for gas-cooled reactors, it is important to make sure that one can license confinements instead of containments based on the argument that they are actually safer. Other very interesting types of reactors use very low volatility coolants—liquid metals and molten salts.

It is also useful to look at much longer time constants for core heating. In this context, it is desirable to have large thermal inertia and large temperature margins so that a very long period is necessary for core materials to heat up. Peak temperature is reached within two to three minutes in a large break-loss coolant accident in a current pressurized-water reactor. In a pool-type reactor, peak fuel temperature is reached within about fifty hours after an accident would disable the normal cooling of the reactor. It is vastly simpler to understand and predict the maximum fuel temperatures, when they are reached very long after the initial transient occurred.

If possible, we should get rid of expensive and complex safety equipment. There should be no need for anything except emergency power supplies, and there probably is not even a need for those.

Finally, it is desirable to get to highly efficient and particularly high-power density systems in order to compete against combined-cycle natural gas plants. Achieving this will require higher temperatures, advanced materials, compact closed gas-power cycles instead of steam, and looking at the direct thermal chemical hydrogen as the most efficient way to make that commodity. Moving towards a capability to rapidly evolve—a part of which comes from the reformed licensing framework—should be a goal. It is possible to reach the point where the full recycling of actinides is achievable. It is important to proceed by taking manageable steps, but to attempt to rapidly build new infrastructures, if possible.

One approach is to utilize direct-cycle electricity conversion with about fifty megawatts in thermal (from a 600-megawatt reactor) going to hydrogen generation. Work on this approach has begun as part of the Next

Generation Nuclear Plant (NGNP) program. One way to achieve this goal, in principle, is by using high-temperature ceramic fuels. There is enormous experience with these coated particle fuels. They make use of nuclear-grade graphite with high-temperature capabilities and oxidation resistance similar to what is used on the space shuttle. This material is capable of going to very high temperatures without damage. Very high temperature capability in fuel allows a large amount of heat-up under accident conditions, which can provide very large thermal inertia.

Another area for examination is advanced materials. For example, interesting materials have recently been developed for disk brakes, telescopes, drive shafts, and rocket nozzles, and carbon–carbon composites have been developed that can literally be machine glued together. Once all the complex parts have been produced, they are placed in the vacuum furnace and exposed to liquid silicon. It glues itself together and becomes a silicon carbide reinforced carbon–carbon composite.

We may anticipate that it will be possible to make compact heat exchangers, such as a fifty-megawatt heat exchanger for the NGNP. There is interest in molten salts as the intermediate coolant for that plant, given their very high thermal capacity and excellent heat-transfer capabilities. There is interest in the potential to build reactors that would use molten salts as the primary coolant to cool graphite fuels. It is known that the most inert material in the world for molten salts is carbon; they are transparent as well and capable of going to very high temperatures without boiling.

If one takes the same fuel that is currently being used in a gas-cooled reactor, which relies on conduction to remove heat from the core and, instead, immerses it in a deep pool of molten salt, the effect of thermal capacity of the fuel and coolant can be increased by a factor of four. That suggests that a vessel exactly the same size as the gas turbine modular helium reactor (GTMHR) could potentially generate four times as much thermal output and then allow much better economies of scale in terms of power output from plants.

One can consider these new directions as possible goals in the development of Gen IV reactors. One can also look at approaches to achieve a very high power density and efficient power conversion cycle, such as ideas that could take advantage of the thermodynamic efficiency gain that comes from multiple reheat stages. One such concept utilizes a GTMHR power conversion unit together with molten salt as the heat transfer media to provide heat for the flow going into each one of the turbines. Overall, one can achieve up above 50-percent thermodynamic efficiency quite easily. At

2,400-megawatt scale, a compact arrangement like this would generate 1,300-megawatts electric. The power density goes up substantially from what is achieved from gas-cooled reactors because of the higher thermodynamic efficiency and because the power conversion unit is separated from the primary plant by an intermediate salt tube, it could be put in a non–nuclear grade turbine building.

It is important to pay more attention to addressing the issues related to waste management. As noted, one of the most important things to realize in terms of thinking about closed fuel cycles is the fact that decisions on closed fuel cycles are not going to be driven in the near term by a scarcity of uranium. One can easily argue that the repository capacity is currently the scarcest commodity in the world, as there is none except for a small amount available for defense transuranic waste at the Waste Isolation Power Plant site in New Mexico. The efficient use of repository capacity is going to be one of the key factors that will drive any effort to move to closed fuel cycles.

Yucca Mountain has a unique characteristic: it is a nonsaturated site. It is ventilated. That means that in terms of decay heat removal, there are going to be substantial differences between reprocessed waste and spent fuel in terms of capacity and thermal performance.

With respect to the economics of closed fuel cycles, in the United States, the policy is to internalize the cost of waste management by charging consumers an appropriate fee, currently set at 0.1 cent per kilowatt-hour. This translates roughly into $310 per kilogram of fuel, depending on burn-up. The actual cost for Yucca Mountain on a sliding scale is about $540 per kilogram. A substantial amount of interest can be collected on that $310 per kilogram, so the $540-per-kilogram cost does not pose a problem. If one takes into account the effects of collecting interest, a relatively small initial fee can grow substantially. This is important in terms of U.S. recycle policy. If the recycle policy is based on the need to recycle in order to minimize waste and load on repositories, there is no real need to rush. If there is a rush, recycling will be more expensive. It is similar to what we witnessed with decommissioning. If one can postpone activities, the total cost will be less. Furthermore, if one does postpone activities, the opportunity to develop technology is further enhanced.

A key issue is policy for waste management. Site selection has occurred. Litigation will have to be completed, and its outcome assessed. Completion of construction is set for 2010, but it is important to consider that, because we have a national policy to charge consumers an appropriate amount for the federal government to provide for the disposition of their waste, it will be necessary to have some idea as to where that waste will go in order to predict the cost. Calculations of this kind were last done in 2001 in the Department of Energy Waste Fund Fee Adequacy Report. Another such report is unlikely until the policy question of what to do beyond the current 70,000–metric ton statutory limit for the Yucca Site is resolved. Because that limit will be reached in 2014, there is clearly a need for a viable policy but, again, technically there is no need to rush. The capacity of the Yucca Site is somewhere between 150,000 to 300,000 metric tons based on the way it is going to be licensed and how aggressively license amendments are pursued. This capacity is not going to be reached until 2030.

If a decision to move to advanced fuel cycles were taken, the capacity of the site becomes essentially infinite. There is technology that can be used. As noted, molten salts have tremendous promise, as does fusion. In the coming decade, the scientific viability of fusion should be demonstrated with actual power production.

To conclude, the promise of President Eisenhower's Atoms-for-Peace speech clearly remains. It will be imperative to shape the major events, which are now occurring, in order to realize the enormous potential of nuclear energy. With that comes responsibility to do the right thing with the technology.

19

The Future of Nuclear Power

Richard K. Lester

The business of making fifty-year predictions, including predictions about the field of nuclear power, is not for the fainthearted. One that seems relatively safe is that the most important commercial product of nuclear technology for the next fifty years is going to be an ordinary household commodity, which is to say electricity. In the longer run other applications of nuclear technology may become more important. We are still at a very early stage in the world of nuclear applications. We are less than seventy years removed from the discovery of nuclear fission but, just as a point of comparison, we are more than 170 years removed from the discovery of electromagnetism. It is interesting to contemplate all that has happened in the field of electromagnetism over the last one hundred years and then to consider where we might be one hundred years from now with respect to the applications of nuclear energy.

For the next fifty years, though, the most important commercial product, as noted, is almost certainly going to be electricity. Of course, there is nothing unique about this product. It is produced in many different ways.

One of the characteristics of electricity service is that the customer does not usually know how the kilowatt-hours he or she uses were generated. From the customer's perspective, a nuclear kilowatt-hour is indistinguishable from a solar or coal kilowatt-hour. This means that nuclear power cannot stand out from the other ways used to generate electricity. It must be competitive economically, or else customers will not be interested.

The discipline of the marketplace therefore imposes on nuclear energy a requirement to conform. In other respects, however, nuclear energy is exceptional. Because of the circumstances of its birth and because of the special characteristics of the technology and the materials involved, nuclear energy has always required special treatment. Separate institutions and laws have been created to manage and regulate it, with a more prominent role for government than in other areas of electrical power production. The degree of separation of the nuclear energy enterprise from the rest of the electric power industry varies from one country to another. But the separation exists everywhere. As an industrial enterprise, nuclear is unlike any other. This paradoxical merger of the exceptional and the mundane, and the tensions inherent in it, have been present throughout the first fifty years of the nuclear industry.

These tensions have been exploited by nuclear opponents and advocates alike. Opponents have criticized the nuclear enterprise for, in effect, not being special enough. They have accused the nuclear industry of being insufficiently careful in its stewardship of its technology. They have pushed for more stringent oversight and have sought to prevent the development of the industry along certain trajectories. Many of these actions have no doubt been well intentioned, but some have been motivated by the recognition that, in the final analysis, nuclear must be cost competitive and that by forcing cost increases, regardless of whether they are justified, they can achieve their ultimate goal of shutting down the industry.

Supporters of nuclear power have also found opportunities in the paradox. They have sometimes used the special character of nuclear to argue that, in effect, it should not have to compete with other sources. Perhaps because of the long years spent behind the cloak of government protection, one sometimes finds an odd disconnection from the real world. Nuclear people sometimes forget that nuclear technology is producing an indistinguishable commodity for which the only criterion in the marketplace is price.

These tensions have been managed reasonably well to date. However, during the next fifty years, the inherent contradictions will become even more acute because of two major developments:

- The worldwide trend towards the introduction of competitive markets for wholesale electricity generation
- The changed international security environment

Because of these two factors, nuclear power will increasingly be subject to the forces of market competition, while simultaneously requiring even more meticulous stewardship and vigilant protection against those who wish to use it to acquire nuclear weapons. Squaring this circle will require leadership and statesmanship on the part of the nuclear community and, it should be said, a willingness to reconsider and perhaps forego previous strongly held positions.

The third major factor that will affect the environment for nuclear power over the next half-century is the prospect for global climate change. This prospect was the starting point of the recent Massachusetts Institute of Technology (MIT) study on the future of nuclear power.[1] The members of this interdisciplinary group at MIT, which began its work late 2001 and completed it during the summer of 2003, shared the increasingly broad consensus among the scientific community that greenhouse gas emissions must be reduced if the world is to avoid serious ecological and economic harm.

When it comes to electricity generation, at least for the next few decades, there are only a few realistic options for reducing carbon dioxide emissions:

- Increased efficiency in electricity generation and use
- Expanded use of renewables
- Continued use of fossil fuels, coupled with carbon capture and sequestration
- More nuclear power

The purpose of the MIT study was not to predict which of these options will ultimately prevail or to argue for their comparative advantages. In fact, the study took the view that all of these options will be required and that it would be a serious mistake to eliminate any of them from an overall strategy for reducing carbon emissions.

The question the study addressed was narrower and more specific: What action must be taken to make nuclear power a significant option for meeting increased global electricity demands while, at the same time, reducing greenhouse gas emissions?

1. John Deutch, et al., *The Future of Nuclear Power: An Interdisciplinary MIT Study* (Cambridge: Massachusetts Institute of Technology, 2003). The author was a member of the interdisciplinary study team.

At the present time, the prospects for nuclear power to play such a role are not promising. Official forecasts call for a rapid increase in world electricity use in the coming decade, perhaps as much as 75 percent by the year 2020. But those same official forecasts call for a mere 5-percent increase in nuclear-generating capacity over that same period. Unless significant additional investments are made, nuclear power supply is likely to decline after that point as existing reactors are retired. While some countries such as South Korea, Finland, China, and India are on a path to construct new reactors, other important nuclear countries seem committed or resigned to phasing out nuclear power gradually.

If the current situation is to be reversed, four major challenges will have to overcome:

- The problem of economic competitiveness
- Concerns over nuclear safety
- Concerns over the disposal of nuclear waste
- Concerns over proliferation risks

The focus of the study was to examine these issues and to identify what will be needed to overcome them. To make things more concrete, the study postulated a global growth scenario: by the year 2050 about 1,000 GWe (gigawatts electric) of installed capacity (or a thousand 1,000-MWe (megawatts electric) reactors) would be deployed worldwide, which is a little less than three times current levels. There is nothing magic about this number and it certainly is not a prediction. But if nuclear plants were deployed on that scale, they would make a significant contribution to greenhouse gas reduction. If, for example, they were displacing coal-fired generation, about 1.8 gigatons (1.8 billion tons) of carbon emissions would be avoided per year, which is roughly 25 percent of the expected increase in global greenhouse gas emissions in what is effectively the "business as usual" scenario. Just for comparison, global emission of greenhouse gases today total about six gigatons per year of carbon equivalent.

Another way to think about that 1,000-GWe figure is that it would mean that nuclear generation would roughly maintain or slightly increase its current share of the world electricity market in the mid-century timeframe. Under some scenarios, for example, the nuclear share would increase from today's 17 percent to about 19 percent by mid-century.

In the broad picture, if you take into account trends in population growth and economic growth, it is not possible to achieve a level of deployment of nuclear power like this without a combination of:

- Continued commitment to nuclear power growth by Japan, Korea, and Taiwan
- Renewal of activity in Europe
- Large deployment in the most populous emerging economies
- Major expansion in the United States

We need all of those things to happen in order to achieve an overall level of nuclear deployment large enough to make a significant contribution to reducing greenhouse gas emissions.

Again, the report does not say that this should happen. Nor does it say that it will happen. But it does indicate what would have to happen if nuclear power were to have a significant impact on global warming. In other words, what the scenario allows us to do is analyze the major challenges scaled to the level at which nuclear power would actually make a meaningful contribution to solving the global warming problem.

Let us now look, selectively, at some of the key findings and recommendations of this study.

In the crucial area of economic competitiveness, the study found that, first, nuclear power is not now cost competitive with either coal or natural gas in the regulated market. Second, that plausible, although so far unproven, reductions in capital cost, operations, and maintenance costs and construction lead time could significantly reduce that gap, although they would not eliminate it. Third, such improvements, if combined with policies that internalize the social cost of carbon emissions, for example through a carbon tax or an equivalent cap and trade system, could very well make nuclear power cost competitive.

To reach those conclusions, the team built an economic model to evaluate the real cost of electricity from alternative sources. What the model does is to simulate the economic conditions that commercial investors investing in merchant plants in competitive markets in the United States would realistically face. For example, the model assumes that construction and operating costs and performance risks would be held by the private investors, which implies a higher cost of capital than what would generally be available to either government-owned utilities or to investor-owned utilities subject to cost-of-service economic regulation.

Under economic conditions typical of the United States, and using parameters based on the most recent actual experience rather than engineering estimates of what might be achieved in the future under ideal conditions, the study estimated that nuclear is today as much as 50 percent more expensive than conventional pulverized coal or natural gas.

This assumes an average capacity factor of 85 percent over a forty-year lifetime.

Cost improvements in nuclear technology and construction practices would bring the cost down very significantly. Those improvements are plausible, although they are not yet proven and, in light of past experience, one has to be an optimist to believe them. There is nothing wrong with optimism, but actual investment decisions will of course be made on the basis of hard-nosed appraisals of costs and risks.

On the issue of safety, the study assumed that the expected number of accidents involving a serious release of radioactivity would have to remain at one or less over the next fifty years if the global growth scenario is to be viable. Given the magnitude of the deployment being discussed, this, in turn, implies the need for a ten-fold reduction in the expected frequency of serious reactor core accidents. The study judged that this is achievable with advanced light-water reactor plants, and that other designs, such as the high-temperature gas reactor, offer the prospect of even better safety performance. However, achieving this safety standard will also require the development of the necessary workforce, highly competent managers, and effective management processes. This has been an area of vulnerability even in advanced economies and it is likely to be a major challenge in the developing economies that will need to participate in the global growth scenario. It will also require more attention to the safety of fuel-cycle facilities.

Waste management is clearly one of the main obstacles to this global nuclear growth scenario. The report concurred with the many independent expert assessments that have concluded that mined geological repositories will in fact be capable of safely isolating the high-level waste for the long period required. The study analyzed both once-through and closed-fuel cycles from a waste management point of view. It concluded that a convincing case for closed fuel cycles has not been made on the basis of waste management considerations alone, and that the benefits of advanced fuel cycles featuring partitioning and transmutation would not outweigh the associated safety, environmental, and security risks, and the increased economic costs.

It is possible that future technological advances would change that assessment. Moreover, we can expect that the trade-offs involved would be evaluated differently in different societies, which may have different preferences and which certainly confront different constraints, whether geological, demographic, political, or economic. For the fundamental conclusion to change, however, not only would the long-term risks from geologic repositories have to be considerably higher than the performance assessments currently indicate, but the incremental costs and short-term safety and environmental risks associated with partitioning and transmutation would also have to be significantly lower than current analyses suggest.

One final conclusion in this area is that waste management strategies are potentially available in the once-through cycle that could offer benefits at least as great as those claimed for advanced versions of the closed fuel cycle, and with fewer short-term risks and lower costs. One example of the possibilities here is the deep borehole variant of the geologic disposal approach.

With regard to proliferation, three issues are of particular concern in the global growth scenario:

- Stocks of separated plutonium that are directly usable for weapons
- Nuclear fuel-cycle facilities with inadequate controls
- The transfer of technology, especially enrichment and reprocessing technology, that brings nations closer to nuclear-weapon capability

The risks in the global growth scenario are underlined by the fact that in this scenario, nuclear power will have to be introduced and developed in many countries with a broad range of security circumstances.

The principal finding in this area is that nuclear power can expand as envisioned in the global growth scenario with acceptable incremental proliferation risks, if built primarily on the once-through thermal reactor fuel cycle and if combined with strong safeguards and security measures.

The study judged, however, that international safeguards and the broader nuclear nonproliferation regime are not adequate to meet the security challenges posed by the global growth scenario. Among the features of this regime that are in need of serious reconsideration is the historical presumption that everything that is not explicitly prohibited is permitted. The viability of the global growth scenario will depend in part on a reevaluation of this fundamental point, especially as it relates to the spread of enrichment, reprocessing, and plutonium recycling technology.

These findings in the areas of economic competitiveness, waste, safety, and proliferation lead to an important general conclusion: over the next fifty years, the best choice to meet these challenges is the open, once-through fuel cycle. The study recommends that priority be given to the open fuel-cycle architecture until at least mid-century, with advanced closed fuel cycles possibly deployed later, but only if significant improvements are realized through research. It judged that there are adequate uranium resources available at reasonable costs to support this choice under a global growth scenario.

Let us turn to recommendations. On the issue of economic competitiveness, the study's main recommendation is that the U.S. government should provide a modest financial incentive to push first movers to demonstrate the cost and regulatory feasibility of new nuclear power plants.

The study proposed a production tax credit of up to $200 per kilowatt for up to ten nuclear power plants. This benefit could be paid out at about 1.7 cents per kilowatt-hour for the first year and a half of full power operation. The production tax–credit mechanism was preferred because it offered the greatest incentive for projects to be completed—there is no subsidy if the plant is not completed and operated—and because it can be extended to other carbon-free technologies. In fact, wind projects already enjoy a 1.7 cent per kilowatt-hour tax credit for the first ten years of life. A 1.7-cent credit is equivalent to a credit of about $70 per ton of avoided carbon emissions if the electricity would have otherwise come from coal plants. While the public subsidy would cease after a year and a half under this scheme, the carbon-emission reduction benefit would continue for the rest of the life of the nuclear plant, perhaps fifty years or more. Of course, this measure will be effective in stimulating additional nuclear investments if and only if the industry can live up to its own expectations of being able to reduce the capital cost of new nuclear plants considerably.

On the issue of waste, there were two important recommendations. First, the study called, as others have done, for an explicit strategy to store spent fuel for a period of several decades before further processing or disposal. Building long-term storage into the waste-management system architecture, by creating a network of centralized storage facilities in the United States and internationally, will create additional flexibility and provide nonproliferation benefits.

Second, to prepare the way for a major expansion of nuclear power, the U.S. waste management program should look beyond Yucca Mountain, where it has been exclusively focused for fifteen years, and should be broadened to address both improvements to the current mined repository approach, as well as alternatives to it. As an example of the latter, it was noted above that the study recommended an aggressive program of research on deep borehole disposal.

On the issue of proliferation, the report calls for a number of actions to strengthen the International Atomic Energy Agency (IAEA) safeguards system, including:

- General adoption of the Additional Protocol
- Move to a worldwide system of continuous real-time materials protection, control, and accounting, using containment and surveillance techniques, which goes well beyond the current system of accounting, reporting, and periodic inspections
- Allocation of safeguard resources using a risk-based framework
- Refocusing of the IAEA so as to deal overwhelmingly with safeguards and safety functions for which it is uniquely positioned by virtue of its bilateral agreements and United Nations affiliation

More broadly, the report calls for a reexamination of the Nuclear Nonproliferation Treaty, Atoms for Peace, and the IAEA safeguards framework as it pertains to nuclear fuel-cycle development. As the then-U.S. Secretary of Energy Spencer Abraham suggested in his speech at the United Nations in November 2003:

We also may need to think about new approaches to the fuel cycle that strictly limit the use of enrichment and reprocessing and access to nuclear weapons technology[,] . . . while ensuring that nuclear medicine, agriculture, energy supplies, and other critical benefits can be enjoyed in all responsible nations.[2]

Finally, with respect to research, the most important recommendation is that the U.S. government should establish a nuclear systems modeling project to carry out the analyses, research, simulation, and collection of engineering data that are needed to evaluate all fuel cycles from the viewpoint of cost, safety, waste management, and proliferation resistance.

These recommendations, and there are others in the report, have been criticized by some for going too far and by others for not going far enough. Many people find something to disagree with. On the other hand, the report has already begun to have an impact in certain areas. For example, the Department of Energy seems to have abandoned a proposal that would have

2. Remarks by Secretary of Energy Spencer Abraham to the United Nations, New York, November 5, 2003.

led to a 2000-ton-per-year commercial scale reprocessing plant by the year 2015. It seems to be preparing to ramp up its support for fuel-cycle analysis, modeling, and simulation along the lines that the report suggested.

The report is more than a shopping list of individual items, however. It is an attempt to chart out a coherent way forward for nuclear power. The authors believe that the development pathway sketched out in the report is more likely than any other path to lead to the exercise of the nuclear option on a large scale in the future. Not everyone will be persuaded of the merits of this approach. But if the report stimulates constructive discussion about these issues and how to move forward, it will have succeeded in its fundamental objective.

Part IV

Looking to the Future

20

A New Bargain

Daniel B. Poneman

Amid the historical swings of the balance between nuclear energy and nonproliferation, how did we get to where we are? All of the institutions and approaches that have constituted the international nuclear nonproliferation regime remain worthy, but we really need to go beyond them and attempt some new initiatives. This paper discusses the history of Atoms for Peace, and then describes the new initiatives that should be considered.

The Atoms-for-Peace era can be divided into generations. The first generation extends from December 1953 to May 1974, a period of great enthusiasm for nuclear energy. You might say that the entire Atoms-for-Peace story was accepted more or less uncritically by the governments of the world in that era. This is a period during which we saw the widespread dispersion of research reactors—at a time when we did not worry too much about a state taking 99 steps out of 100 towards nuclear weapons under the cover of Atoms for Peace and then bolting from the regime. The Indian test, the so-called "peaceful-nuclear explosion" of May 1974, put an end to that notion.

When it became clear to all that not only had a Canadian-supplied research reactor—CIRUS—been responsible for the production of plutonium, but also that the United States had supplied the heavy water that moderated that reactor, it led to a very strong reaction in the U.S. Congress. Senator John Glenn and others were very involved in moving to a new phase in which the United States and walked away from some of those earlier assumptions and took a much tougher approach to the proliferation threat. So did President Carter, in his nonproliferation policy statement of April 7, 1977. Both the President and Congress moved to an approach that was, to use a current phrase, much more unilateralist than multilateralist. This policy sought, for example, to impose sanctions on countries that did not walk the line that the United States thought was appropriate.

This restrictive approach lasted about a generation, until May 1998 At that time, both India and Pakistan—notwithstanding the domestic legislation that the United States had promulgated, threatening a multitude of unilateral sanctions—went ahead and tested nuclear weapons, for reasons that apparently their leaders considered good and sufficient. The fact that they tested nuclear weapons in the face of these sanctions simply demonstrates that the sanctions that the United States had threatened obviously did not stop them. We could not easily impose those sanctions on India because we found that we had become dependent upon things such as Indian software to keep U.S. satellites orbiting. As for Pakistan, if there was anything that we could imagine that would be worse than a Pakistan with nuclear weapons, it was a Pakistan with nuclear weapons falling into an abyss of political or economic instability. Thus, concerns about the political stability in, and the economic viability of, Pakistan, sanctions there became implausible. We realized that the sanctions, which had been so vigorously proposed, had to be waived. That left us thinking about what to do next.

While we were still thinking about that problem, we were confronted by the September 11 terrorist attacks. September 11 obviously underlined the need for a real rethinking of our approach to the threats we all face. The safety that we had felt from the oceans surrounding the U.S. territory had suddenly vanished.

In the context of this history, let us turn to the institutions of Atoms for Peace, which formed the predicate to what followed. The International Atomic Energy Agency (IAEA) was created in 1957. Strong support for the Agency remained critical to global nonproliferation efforts. Indeed, the greater role that the IAEA took on after the Gulf War, culminating in the promulgation of the Additional Protocol, really started a new era for the Agency.

The IAEA remains a critical part of our arsenal for nonproliferation. But it does not purport to do more than provide timely warning and it does not possess enforcement mechanisms. Moreover, monitoring or safeguarding weapons lie outside its mandate. Therefore, whenever you get into these types of safeguard issues—namely the expansion of the IAEA mandate from inspecting civil nuclear facilities to inspecting nuclear-weapon facilities—you face concerns that the IAEA, if used for weapon inspections, could become a source of, rather than a bar against, proliferation. In brief, safeguards inspectors become conduits of information related to nuclear weapons.

Second, we have the Treaty on the Nonproliferation of Nuclear Weapons, which is absolutely critical. Again, it does not provide, as we have seen time and again, a physical bar to cheating. Its normative value is absolutely essential to our continuing nonproliferation efforts, but we cannot put all of our eggs in that basket. We have continuing export control efforts through the Nuclear Suppliers Group and the Zangger Committee. Using export controls to stop supplies from reaching the wrong hands is a critical but, ultimately, a wasting asset, as we are now dealing with a technology that is sixty years old and weapons that can be designed more easily than anyone would like, although not as easily as some might think. Finally, with respect to institutions, we have the United Nations Security Council which, when roused, focused, and coherent, is potentially very important and useful, but is not always able to exhibit all of these qualities, at least not at the same time. All of these existing institutional approaches have done much good.

Arms control, including the Moscow Treaty, has also been valuable, but we all know that treaties are difficult and arduous to negotiate and often fail. They also may be more fervently embraced by some and often are vulnerable to the possibility of cheating. Another mechanism that has served us well for decades is nuclear deterrence. Nuclear deterrence has clear limits of utility, which were demonstrated by September 11. Obviously, deterrence depends on having a return address which one can target and send an opponent a response to that which has just been received. However, terrorists do not often leave return addresses. Moreover, deterrence depends on a particular view of human nature. If you read Hobbes's *Leviathan,* you understand that, at the least, you need a minimal sense of self-preservation to rely upon if you expect notions of deterrence to obtain. In a terrorist context—in which, if not the leaders, then certainly the cannon fodder they send in to do the suicide bombings and therefore are not driven by the desire for self-preservation—you can no longer count on deterrence.

As a consequence, we need a new approach. This is because all of the measures that we have employed to date are necessary but not sufficient. We need to go back to the Atoms-for-Peace premise. We need to acknowledge that the duality of the atom is inherent, but we need a more integrated approach than in the past. Specifically, what we need to do is to enlist the political power of nuclear energy and to enlist the assets that the marketplace for energy makes available in support of, and as a driving force toward, improved national security. That may sound a bit theoretical but, actually, it is not. It is quite practical and, indeed, it is exactly what the highly enriched uranium (HEU) deal between the United States and Russia entails. The genius behind that deal is that it aligned commercial motives with security objectives to achieve very practical results. As a result of this deal, the Russians have now down-blended the equivalent of thousands of warheads of HEU that have been converted to low-enriched uranium fuel for use in nuclear reactors to generate electricity. That, in turn, is equivalent to approximately 10 percent of the electricity in the United States. It is amazing to think that, in effect, one in ten of our homes are lit by former Soviet nuclear weapons, but in fact they are.

The point here is not to balance peaceful versus military applications, but rather to conjoin the energy potential and security risks of the atom—to treat these two sides of the same coin as one. That is appropriate. A "proliferation Chernobyl"—that is, a significant and unexpected nuclear proliferation incident somewhere in the world—would be as devastating to the nuclear energy industry as the Chernobyl accident. Consequently, we need to understand that interrelationship in order to find ways to have energy and security policies work together.

The attractiveness of such an integrative approach increases if we take into account the increased recognition of the role that nuclear energy plays in our energy future, by way of providing a carbon-free energy source at a time when we are finding it increasingly difficult to meet the targets of the Kyoto Treaty. We are now looking toward an energy future that includes the generation-IV nuclear reactors and the Global Nuclear Energy Partnership. If we are committed to moving in that direction, let us try to put that in the context of programs that can limit the risk of nuclear proliferation. Specifically, the fuel-leasing concepts that are being studied in the Bush administration are worthwhile. Why? The law passed by the Duma allows Russia to take back spent fuel from outside Russia. If you provide the back-end solution that many utility operators, especially in Asia, have been desperately searching for, and combine that with a private company able to provide reactor fuel, you can offer countries around the world a package nuclear-fuel leasing deal. That would include countries with which the United States may have proliferation concerns.

The deal begins with the provision of fresh fuel, which you fabricate to the specifications of the reactor operators of participating states. The lessees then irradiate the fuel in their reactors. After the irradiated spent fuel is removed from the reactors and cools down on site, the lessor comes back to take it away. When you take away the spent fuel, you obviously take away the plutonium within the spent fuel. The leasing company would provide essentially a cradle-to-grave fuel service that would be very attractive to a number of utilities, especially for countries that have small nuclear programs that could not economically, on the basis of any kind of rational analysis, justify building a full fuel-cycle indigenously.

If you find a country that is unwilling to accept that kind of a proposal, it does call into question the motivation for its nuclear energy activities. This is not intended to be framed as a punitive approach to proliferation, but a contractually based one, which has the benefit of bringing genuine energy benefits to those who are genuinely interested in energy. It also provides a way to remove plutonium-laden spent fuel from commercial reactors.

If you were to say, for example, that you would fuel the nuclear reactor with fuel derived from former weapon materials themselves, you get an additional nonproliferation benefit and an additional mechanism by which you can absorb fissile materials from, in particular, the former Soviet nuclear arsenal. Obviously, this already works in the case of HEU, but the profits that would be available in this kind of scheme could be sufficiently robust to take on some of the plutonium disposition tasks while also providing enough of a subsidy for using plutonium to offset its commercial disadvantages. If you embed plutonium-based fuel in enough uranium-based fuel, the leasing company could still be profitable.

Why would a utility want to burn former warhead material? According to public polling data that has been gathered in Europe and elsewhere, if you show the public that the nuclear energy activities in which you are engaged have the benefit of disposing of legacy materials from the Cold War and former nuclear weapons, you would find a significant increase in support of nuclear power.

Without belaboring this point, it appeared that we have an early opportunity to test out this kind of proposal in the case of Iran. We should all look at the disclosure of the Natanz enrichment facility and recognize that it has brought Europe and Russia to an appreciation of the genuine proliferation threat posed by Iran. We also need to look at the willingness of the Europeans to take a more active role in blocking the proliferation threat from Iran while holding their own Trade and Cooperation Agreement hostage, and Russia's expressed willingness to insist on the return of the spent fuel as a condition for concluding the Bushehr deal. Iran had agreed with the Europeans to suspend uranium-enrichment activities and signed the Additional Protocol. Although the Iranian decision to resume suspended activities dims the prospects for implementation of this deal, the situation is still open and offers an opportunity to take all of the mechanisms embedded in this commercial engine and perhaps end up with a world that is much safer than we now have.

At the same time as both kinds of mechanisms are set up, some of the spent fuel, if it can still be found in North Korea, can be removed as a proliferation threat from that country and taken into Russia on a potentially commercial basis. That could be a winning solution for nonproliferation, for nuclear energy, and for the safety of us all.

21

Atoms for Peace: Facing Emerging Challenges

Lawrence Scheinman

The International Atomic Energy Agency (IAEA), the institutional expression of Atoms for Peace, stands at the center, or perhaps more appropriately given the turbulent times in which we find ourselves, at the epicenter of the international nuclear nonproliferation regime, and at the nexus of nuclear energy and nuclear proliferation. While the Nonproliferation Treaty (NPT) and the IAEA safeguards system are arguably stronger today than before—the former having been indefinitely extended in 1995, the latter having been upgraded to deal with undeclared nuclear activities as were detected in Iraq after the first Gulf War—the challenges they face are serious and complex.

The challenges to the regime are serious and complex because three states—Israel, India, and Pakistan—remain outside the NPT, and two of them—India and Pakistan—have since tested and declared themselves to be nuclear-weapon states. In addition, North Korea has terminated safeguards, withdrawn from the NPT, and stated that it has developed a nuclear deterrent. Meanwhile, the attempt by Iran to acquire the capability to enrich uranium, reprocess spent fuel, and produce heavy water, places it on a path to develop a full national nuclear fuel cycle, and has produced a controversy of near-crisis proportions.[1] Although activities such as those undertaken by Iran are nominally consistent with Article IV of the NPT, the clandestine manner in which those activities have been pursued and their tenuous relationship to Iran's professed goal of generating nuclear power raise troubling questions about whether—as some contend—the real intent of these efforts is to acquire a nuclear-weapon capability and eventually withdraw from the NPT on the grounds provided in Article X of the treaty, that is, that "extraordinary events related to the subject matter of this Treaty have jeopardized the supreme interests of its country."[2]

Added to these concerns are the uncertainties generated by terrorist group interest in gaining access to weapons of mass destruction (WMD) and the continued concern about the safety and security of weapon-usable materials, especially in the case of Russia. This raises the question of what role the nonproliferation regime in general, and the IAEA safeguards system in particular, should, and can, play in reducing the risk that such groups might acquire nuclear and other weapons of mass destruction.[3]

The IAEA is charged with the responsibility of verifying compliance by states with nonproliferation undertakings and of doing so by the application of comprehensive safeguards as outlined in Information Circular 153 (INFCIRC/153) that was negotiated by IAEA member states upon the entry into force of the NPT. The objective of NPT safeguards is deterrence by risk of early detection and it is the obligation of the state to report to the IAEA all nuclear material in peaceful nuclear activity. The expectation is that no undeclared nuclear material should be present on the territory or under the jurisdiction of the state. Although the traditional system focuses on declared nuclear material and inspections normally are limited to nuclear material reported to the Agency by the government, there are added provisions for situations in which the Agency has reason to believe that informa-

---

1. Coverage and analysis on Iran are extensive. A useful starting point is Arms Control Association, "The Iran Nuclear Crisis: A Chronology" in *Arms Control Today* (June 2005). See also Jean du Preez and Melissa Kessler, *Iran's Game of Nuclear Poker: Knowing When to Fold,* Monterey, Calif.: Monterey Institute of International Studies, Center for Nonproliferation Studies, August 26, 2005 (cns.miis.edu/pubs).

2. For a discussion on withdrawal, see George Bunn and Roland Timerbaev, "The Right to Withdraw from the NPT: The Views of Two NPT Negotiators," *Arms Control and Security Letters,* no. 5 (September 2005).

3. See Charles D. Ferguson, William C. Potter, et al., *The Four Faces of Nuclear Terrorism* (London: Routledge, 2005), and Graham Allison, *Nuclear Terrorism: The Ultimate Preventable Catastrophe* (New York: Henry Holt, 2004).

tion provided by the state would not enable it to meet its safeguards obligation, in which event access could be anywhere in the state the Agency asked to go. These are the special inspection provisions of INFCIRC/153. The Agency has a reciprocal responsibility and right to ensure that the state fulfills its obligations. The effectiveness of the system depends on the quality of the safeguards staff, the cooperation of the state in enabling the IAEA to fulfill its responsibilities, and the political resolve of the Agency's sovereign state members to support the Secretariat in achieving full compliance with safeguards obligations.[4]

In the aftermath of the 1991 Gulf War and the discovery of significant unreported nuclear activity in Iraq, steps were taken to reinforce safeguards. The traditional safeguards system was strengthened in several ways, beginning with implementation of existing, unused authority, and ending with the granting of new authority to be applied in the form of an Additional Protocol (AP) to existing safeguards agreements. One example of enhancing existing authority relates to the question of when a state is to provide the Agency with design information regarding construction of a facility that would eventually contain nuclear material, or the modification of an existing facility. The practice had been for the state to provide information at least 180 days before nuclear material was to be introduced into the facility, but in 1992 the Board of Governors determined that the Agency should be notified as soon as a state makes the decision to construct a facility.[5] All non–nuclear-weapon states party to the NPT safeguards system took steps to meet this criterion with the exception of Iran, which did so in February 2003 only after the revelation of the existence of the Natanz enrichment facility. Iran had failed to notify the Agency at the appropriate time and was the last state to comply with the 1993 Board decision.

The strengthened safeguards system focuses not only on correctness but also on the completeness of state declarations, that is, the AP is a mandate to provide credible assurance of the absence of undeclared nuclear activities. Its provisions regarding information include a full accounting of past and present nuclear activities and an indication of future nuclear plans.

---

4. For a discussion of safeguards, see David Fischer, "Safeguards: Past, Present and Future," Bruno Pellaud, "Experience and Challenges," and Richard Hooper, "Strengthened Safeguards," in *IAEA Bulletin* 39, no. 4 (December 1997). See also Lawrence Scheinman, *Cooperative Oversight of Dangerous Technologies: Lessons from the IAEA Safeguards System,* prepared for the Project on Advanced Methods of Cooperative Security (www.cissm.umd.edu/documents/Scheinmanarticle.pdf).

5. See Hooper, "Strengthened Safeguards."

It takes a statewide approach to verification. It broadens the access rights of inspectors at declared nuclear sites, enabling access to any place or installation on the site, even if it does not contain nuclear material or does not involve activities specific to the nuclear fuel cycle. It covers plants that manufacture components, components of components (e.g., of centrifuges), or non-nuclear materials (e.g., heavy water) that could end up in nuclear use. It bears emphasis that the full-scope safeguards system developed to fulfill IAEA responsibilities under the NPT intended that states submit comprehensive declarations and included provisions to deal with the possibility that this might not be the case. In this sense, the strengthened system was a reaffirmation and reinforcement of existing rights and obligations at least as much as a creation of new rights.

Whether strengthened safeguards are sufficient as well as necessary, needs to be determined. If they are not, how we need to think about the future is another question. A particular challenge is that of centrifuge-enrichment activities. That raises the question of Article IV of the NPT and consideration of alternative means to national development to make good the commitment on access to peaceful uses of nuclear energy, such as institutional approaches, which include regional or multinational fuel-cycle arrangements. Those ideas are mentioned in a 2003 invited opinion piece in *The Economist* by IAEA Director General Mohamed ElBaradei.[6] Concepts along these lines reach back to the Acheson–Lilienthal Report and the Baruch Plan, which put forward a rationale and a plan for denationalizing nuclear activity. Some experts have been writing on this theme and offering less draconian alternatives for organizing the nuclear age since the late 1970s.[7]

As we go forward, what steps need to be considered? Strengthening the IAEA safeguards system is a priority concern, and acknowledged as such by the decision of the Board of Governors in 2005 to establish a Special Committee on Safeguards and Verification to explore ways and means to further strengthen the safeguards system. Surely a first step is to bring the 36 states party to the NPT that have yet to conclude a comprehensive

6. Mohamed ElBaradei, "Towards a Safer World," *The Economist,* October 18, 2003; *Multilateral Nuclear Approaches to the Nuclear Fuel Cycle: Expert Group Report to the Director General of the International Atomic Energy Agency* (INFCIRC/640, February 22, 2005).

7. See, for instance, Lawrence Scheinman, "Multinational Alternatives and Nuclear Non-Proliferation," *International Organization* (1981). Republished with a new introduction as "The Nuclear Fuel Cycle: A Challenge for Non-Proliferation," *Disarmament Diplomacy,* 76 (March–April 2004).

safeguards agreement with the IAEA despite the obligation under the NPT to do so within eighteen months of acceding to the treaty. In some cases more than 10 years have passed without an agreement being concluded. While it is the case that in virtually all of these instances the state has no significant nuclear activity to verify, quite aside of the legal obligation to do so their non-participation undermines the principle of universality that lends credibility and strength to the safeguards principle. The endorsement of an AP by the Board of Governors in 1997, both as a reaffirmation and augmentation of safeguards was a significant step forward. The problem is that since then, the implementation process has been slow. Nine years after adoption, out of 187 parties to the NPT (including the five nuclear-weapon states which have all signed AP consistent with their safeguards undertakings), 114 agreements had been approved by the Board of Governors. Of these, 107 were signed but only 75 were in force.

Even in the event of a tide of new ratifications, the safeguards system will still have limitations. Not even ardent supporters regard a strengthened safeguards system as a panacea or as a final solution to the challenge of detecting undeclared nuclear activities. In particular, centrifuge enrichment activity poses two verification challenges for the Agency:

- Detecting undeclared production of highly enriched uranium (HEU) or excess low-enriched uranium (LEU) at declared LEU plants
- Detecting clandestine plants for the production of HEU, possibly fed with LEU (which significantly reduces the enrichment capacity required to produce a given amount of HEU)

The safeguards-specific measures below may help to reduce the risk of undetected enrichment activity:

- More comprehensive information
- Greater access through complementary access
- Wider use of technologies such as environmental sampling
- Where called for, use of special inspection rights that have been available since the comprehensive safeguards system was negotiated in 1970.

However, measures beyond safeguards may be necessary.

One such measure is tightening up the export control regime. This first became a necessity in the aftermath of the Indian nuclear test in 1974; the advent of growing interest in access to plutonium, which was stimulated in part by the energy crisis of 1973 and the U.S. decision to close the order books on enrichment in the early 1970s, and by the strong promotion of breeder reactor concepts. Other than the asserted requirement that a non–nuclear-weapon state party to the NPT be acting in conformity with the nonproliferation purposes of the treaty as expressed in Articles I and II, Article IV of the NPT does not put any particular constraints on nuclear development for exclusively peaceful purposes under safeguards. Thus, a state can, consistent with the provisions of the NPT, establish a uranium enrichment capability and a plutonium reprocessing capability. It can put itself in a position to move rapidly to nuclear weapons should it invoke the provision in Article X of the NPT, allowing the right to withdraw. Export control has become increasingly important and difficult in the face of the emergence of second- and third-tier suppliers, and of the evident existence of a subnational nuclear equipment, technology, and material marketplace that can service nuclear-weapon development for interested parties. This speaks to the need for increased legal and administrative measures of control in all states, a greater willingness to share intelligence information, and increased coordination in applying police measures to thwart an underground nuclear bazaar. United Nations Security Council Resolution 1540 of April 2004 is an important first step toward achieving this objective.[8]

These considerations underscore two issues that need to be addressed. The first is whether the provision in Article IV of the NPT asserting "the inalienable right of all the parties to the treaty to develop research, production and use of nuclear energy for peaceful purposes without discrimination"—in conformity with Articles I and II of the treaty, that is, in conformity with the principles and purpose of the treaty, namely nonproliferation—needs to be revisited. It would not be with a view to amending the provision, but rather to seek creative ways of delivering on the objective of assuring full access to the benefits of civil nuclear activity that avoids the proliferation of national nuclear fuel cycles. This is particularly important, given the fact that not all weapon-relevant activities would necessarily come within the purview of even strengthened international safeguards and that, even if all activities were being monitored, a state may still invoke the withdrawal clause and rapidly close on producing nuclear weapons. The same considerations apply to NPT Article IV.2 regarding the

8. For a discussion and analysis of Resolution 1540, see Merav Datan, "Security Council Resolution 1540: WMD and Non-State Trafficking," *Disarmament Diplomacy* 79 (April–May 2005).

term "fullest possible exchange." Here is a key word and a link to the "in conformity" language of IV.1.

Obviously related issues are whether the commitment to nonproliferation, pursuant to the NPT, should be considered irreversible, unless under extreme conditions, and whether the standard to be applied for legitimately invoking the withdrawal provision should, therefore, be set sufficiently high as to be attainable under only the most exceptional circumstances. At the very least, a state in breach of its obligations under the treaty should not be (and would not be under the Vienna law of treaties) free to withdraw from it before mending its breach and coming back into compliance.

This raises another question about the IAEA safeguards regime; namely, what measures are necessary to ensure that noncompliant behavior that undermines nonproliferation undertakings and commitments will be met and rebuffed by a solid front of states, preferably acting under the auspices of the Security Council pursuant to the United Nations Charter? This relates specifically to the statement in 1992 made on behalf of the Security Council by its then-president, British Prime Minister John Major, that the Council would regard the proliferation of weapons of mass destruction as a threat to international peace and security and that

> noting the importance of the decision of many countries to adhere to the NPT and the integral role in the implementation of that treaty of fully effective IAEA safeguards[,] . . . the members of the council would take appropriate measures in the case of any violations notified to them by the IAEA.[9]

These observations lead to some important conclusions. First, the IAEA is important to nonproliferation and, therefore, there is a need to ensure that it is vested with all of the authority, human and financial resources, and political support needed to effectively carry out its responsibilities at a level calculated to earn the confidence of states in the system. While uniformity is not necessarily the answer to all challenges, anything less than uniform standards insofar as safeguards are concerned will surely sap confidence and reliance in a world of sovereign states inevitably laced with conflicting interests, agendas, and demands. This is not to say that ancillary verification arrangements might not be required to overcome uncertainty in particular bilateral or regional situations—for example, an eventual Middle East zone free of nuclear weapons or of WMD—but they should preferably be seen

9. UN Security Council, S/PV. 3046 (1992).

as additives to global arrangements, not as alternatives. This point is also relevant to the North Korean situation that we face today.

Second, there is a need to take steps to make the AP to comprehensive safeguards agreements an obligation of states and not, as it stands today, a voluntary act that may or may not be exercised. If not made obligatory by decision of the Board of Governors, at a minimum adherence to the AP should be made a condition, agreed by all supplier states, for entering into any new transfer agreements with states. Arguably, an effort should be made to recast existing agreements to include a commitment to the AP as a condition for continuation of supply under preexisting arrangements.

Third, there is a need to focus consideration on the ways and means to formulate institutional arrangements. Those could include regional fuel cycle centers or multinational ventures or consortia that have the effect of limiting enrichment and reprocessing activities to a few secure locations but, at the same time, meet the demands for assured nuclear supply for civil nuclear activity. Institutional is not synonymous with an organization, although the two may and often do go together. Contractual arrangements such as leasing and take-back agreements also could be considered.[10] The reciprocal obligation of a benefiting state not to develop a national capability is central to this approach and this raises the question of safeguards and transparency. In pursuing this line of reasoning, attention would have to be given to the need to avoid adding new layers of discrimination or differentiation to those that already exist in the NPT—that is to say, it would be important to avoid creating approaches that can be interpreted by developing states as a new form of colonialism. One step in that direction would be for all states to place themselves within the framework of a common regime. However, just as strengthened safeguards are not panaceas, neither are institutional arrangements. Both are additive strategies for nonproliferation and access to peaceful benefits of nuclear energy. They can work synergistically to achieve both purposes and need to be seen in that light. It bears comment that, in the case of reprocessing, many nonproliferators would oppose breathing new life into what they hope is a moribund enterprise, even in a multinational context.[11]

10. See John Deutch, Arnold Kantor, Ernest Moniz, and Daniel Poneman, "Making the World Safe for Nuclear Energy," *Survival* 46, no. 4 (Winter 2004–2005): 65–80.

11. The current discussion of plutonium reprocessing includes a new method known as uranium extraction plus, or UREX+, that does not produce separated plutonium. See, for instance, Robert Shane Johnson, Acting Director, Nuclear Energy, Science and Technology, U.S. Department of Energy, Statement to the Subcommittee on Energy of

Finally, the reaffirmation and strengthening of the declaration of the Security Council that WMD proliferation will be regarded as a threat to international peace and security, and dealt with accordingly with no political space between the permanent members on this matter, is critical. Reports to the Council by the IAEA of breach of compliance with safeguards must be acted on collectively and resolutely. In the final analysis, compliance is a singularly important matter and the most significant challenge confronting the regime and its components. The emphasis on an active and involved Security Council does not foreclose the possibility for national or multinational measures to counter proliferation such as the Proliferation Security Initiative promoted by the United States and supported by a number of other states.[12] However, the legitimacy of such measures is enhanced to the extent that they enjoy support by, and operate under the authority of, the UN Security Council and the effort should be made to pursue a diplomacy that brings that result about.

In closing, a few general observations might be offered. First, we should not forget that the IAEA is an international organization, not a sovereign entity with all the attributes that implies. Its constituents are sovereign states and the success or failure of the organization is dependent on the support it receives from its constituents.

Second, expectations that we have of the IAEA should be commensurate with the political, economic, technical, and human resource support provided to it. You cannot authorize a police officer to stop cars traveling in excess of fifty miles an hour, give him a vehicle capable of traveling no more than forty miles an hour, and yet expect results; the same applies in the case of international organizations. The IAEA has, until recently, suffered chronic shortfalls in the budgetary realm dating back to initiation of a policy of zero real growth in the early 1980s, despite the fact that the amount of nuclear material to be safeguarded increased significantly in the years following. Insufficient resources pose a threat to the ability of the

---

the Committee on Science, U.S. House of Representatives, June 16, 2005; and *Advanced Fuel Cycle Initiative: Objectives, Approach and Technological Summary*, Report to Congress, prepared by U.S. Department of Energy, Office of Nuclear Energy, Science and Technology (Washington, D.C., May 2005).

12. See U.S. Department of State, *The Proliferation Security Initiative: What Is the Proliferation Security Initiative?*" (June 2004) (usinfo.state.gov/products.pubs/proliferation). See also *CRS Report for Congress: Proliferation Security Initiative* (Washington, D.C.: Congressional Research Service, January 14, 2005) (www.fas.org/spp/starwars/crs/RS21881.pdf).

Agency to implement its mandate and ultimately to its real and perceived effectiveness.

Third, U.S. leadership in the Agency goes a long way toward achieving positive outcomes. An example of this is the leadership in breaking zero real growth. Another would be to empower and show confidence in the IAEA to address the challenges to the safeguards regime posed by North Korea and Iran. Working with, and largely through, the IAEA to dismantle the Libyan nuclear-weapon program that the Libyan government voluntarily acknowledged was a significant step in this direction.

Fourth, safeguards can be effective tools of detection and deterrence if ample information, along with technical and political support, is provided by member-states. Technology and motivations change—and with them levels of reinforcement of Agency resources should change commensurately—which is to say, a failure or a limitation revealed by behavior should be seen as a reason to seek to strengthen the system, not to abandon it to other approaches.

Fifth, effectiveness of IAEA and safeguards could be enhanced if members of the Nuclear Suppliers Group would take the responsibility to inform each other and the IAEA whenever a license application for a nuclear or dual-use item is denied. Exports and imports are supposed to be reported, but decisions not to export are under no such obligation. Information enhancing transparency is a critically important factor in regime effectiveness and Agency awareness of the fact that a state or its agent is seeking certain kinds of dual-use equipment could go a long way toward filling in gaps in understanding the full scope and measure of state's activity in the nuclear field.

Atoms for Peace was a daring idea intended to address a number of problems ranging from containing a nuclear arms race to reckoning with the reality that the nuclear genie was no longer containable and that, over time, more states would acquire the knowledge, know-how, and resources to develop a national nuclear capability. It put into play a national policy of controlled nuclear cooperation. It instigated the establishment of the IAEA, both to promote access to nuclear energy for peaceful purposes and to ensure that the assistance it provided was used only for its declared peaceful purpose. It laid the foundation for the principle of verification through safeguards. It was a progenitor of the NPT. It accelerated the pace of nuclear development around the world. However, spread was inevitable, and the challenges we face today cannot be attributed simply to Atoms for Peace but to a much broader set of political-security factors and considerations. Even if it accelerated the pace of nuclear spread, Atoms for Peace also provided a framework and structure for the expansion of nuclear energy worldwide where otherwise largely anarchic development might have prevailed.

Atoms for Peace, warts and all, may better be seen as an example of initiative and daring in the face of seemingly intractable problems. Drawing upon the experience of nuclear sharing and nuclear cooperation—lessons of the strengths and weaknesses of the rules of the game, policies, binding and voluntary agreements, and resulting institutions established over time to manage this technology—should stimulate and inform creative thinking about managing the atom in the more diverse and problematic political and security environment in which we live, compared even to a mere decade ago.

Nuclear energy is Janus-faced, a consideration that has led some to argue against its continued use and development, but others to strive to find ways and means to mitigate its dark-side risks in order to exploit its potential for serving the economic and social development goals of mankind. The prospect of global abandonment is not plausible. At the same time, the perils of the peaceful atom cannot be disregarded. The challenge of harnessing the benefits of atomic energy entails the continuing challenge of containing the risk of proliferation that can be ignored only at our peril.

22

Atoms for Peace and the Nuclear Fuel Cycle: Is It Time for a Multilateral Approach?

Tariq Rauf and Fiona Simpson

When President Dwight D. Eisenhower unveiled his Atoms-for-Peace plan before the United Nations General Assembly, it is unlikely that anyone listening at the time appreciated that the ideas it put forward would ultimately become the common ancestor for all subsequent forms of international nuclear cooperation. Soon after the nuclear age began, the United States—which at the time still maintained a monopoly on nuclear weapons—had unsuccessfully advanced a proposal for multinational control of the nuclear fuel cycle. The 1946 Baruch Plan, named for U.S. diplomat Bernard Baruch, called for states to transfer ownership and control over civil nuclear activities and materials to an international development agency. Ultimately, however, it was left to the 1953 Atoms-for-Peace plan to stand as the catalyst for, and provide the principles underlying, eventual international cooperation in the field of nuclear technology.

A version of this paper was originally published in the December 2004 issue of *Arms Control Today* magazine (www.armscontrol.org). Reprinted with permission.

Atoms for Peace differed from previous proposals not only by explicitly highlighting the dual nature of nuclear energy, but in putting forward a grand, global vision beyond the narrow context of superpower rivalry: the capacity of nuclear energy to transcend its military applications in order to provide, as Eisenhower put it "a great boon, for the benefit of all mankind."[1] The military-peaceful duality of atomic energy, addressed in the speech, in turn laid the groundwork for the establishment of both the International Atomic Energy Agency (IAEA) and, later, the Nuclear Nonproliferation Treaty (NPT). In so doing, it became the forbearer not only of international nuclear cooperation and nonproliferation efforts in an overarching sense, but also of recent efforts and explorations of possible multilateral approaches to the nuclear fuel cycle.

The interest in such approaches has waxed and waned over the years. However, the continuing spread of nuclear technology, along with the emergence of clandestine nuclear supply networks, has led to discussion on revisiting multinational approaches to the nuclear fuel cycle. The idea had been explored in the 1970s and 1980s, but failed to win approval. However, it has gained a new relevance recently amid several new and serious challenges to the nuclear nonproliferation regime: the discovery of Iran's uranium-enrichment program, which is now subject to IAEA safeguards; Libya's December 2003 admission and renunciation of its clandestine nuclear-weapon development program; and the admission by Abdul Qadeer Khan, the "father" of Pakistan's nuclear-weapon program, that he had organized a clandestine network to supply Iran and Libya, as well as North Korea, with uranium-enrichment technology.

These events have led to a rethinking of how the 1968 NPT and the related nuclear nonproliferation regime might be reinforced. The NPT remains the world's most adhered-to multilateral arms control treaty, currently with 189 states parties, the only holdouts being India, Israel, and Pakistan.[2] It is based on an inherent, intricate, and interlinked three-part bargain: all states parties that did not have nuclear weapons prior to January 1967 are required to renounce any ambitions for developing or possessing nuclear weapons. Furthermore, although these states parties may use nu-

---

1. "Atomic Power for Peace," an address by Dwight D. Eisenhower, President of the United States, before the General Assembly of the United Nations, December 8, 1953.
2. According to the February 12, 2003 resolution adopted by the IAEA Board of Governors, North Korea's NPT safeguards agreement remains in force and is binding. Neither the UN Security Council nor the NPT depository states, as far as is known, have rendered any definitive opinion regarding North Korea's withdrawal from the treaty.

clear material and technology exclusively for peaceful purposes, they are required to subject their nuclear material and activities to IAEA verification. Finally, nuclear-weapon states are required to pursue measures to achieve nuclear disarmament at an early date. In addition, several NPT states parties that are the principal suppliers or trans-shippers of nuclear material and technology are administering export controls as required under the NPT regime (the Zangger Committee) or to supplement the regime (the Nuclear Suppliers Group, or NSG).

Two basic approaches have been put forward; both seek to ensure that the nuclear nonproliferation regime maintains its authority and credibility in the face of these very real challenges. One calls for the further denial of technology to non–nuclear-weapon states and the reinterpretation of the NPT's provisions governing the transfer of nuclear technologies. It is unlikely to succeed in light of lowered technical barriers to the development of sensitive technology and the increasing unwillingness of many non–nuclear-weapon states to accept additional restrictions to their right to peaceful nuclear technology under the NPT. The other approach would use multinational alternatives to national operations of uranium-enrichment and plutonium-separation technologies, and to storage of spent nuclear fuel.

The Long History of Multinational Approaches to the Nuclear Fuel Cycle

As noted above, the idea of international nuclear cooperation, or the sort necessary for multilateral approaches to the nuclear fuel cycle, is not new, having been foreseen in Atoms for Peace. However, the real heyday for these types of explorations was twenty years after Eisenhower's speech, during the second half of the 1970s and the early 1980s. After India conducted a "peaceful" nuclear test in 1974, concerns grew that other countries could follow India's example and use their civilian nuclear program and plutonium reprocessing technologies to build nuclear weapons. Yet, at the same time, countries wished to solve this problem within the context of the newly minted NPT, which sought to assure all states that they would be permitted to use nuclear energy for peaceful purposes under IAEA safeguards.

Out of such concerns, the first feasibility study on multilateral approaches to the nuclear fuel cycle was undertaken. The Regional Nuclear Fuel Cycle Centers (RFCC) study of 1975–1977 was created to provide a forum for countries to examine the possibility of joining together to set up fuel cycle centers at selected sites. In keeping with contemporary concerns, the emphasis in this and other studies of the time was on the back end of the cycle, specifically reprocessing and plutonium containment. Although the RFCC study drew some favorable conclusions regarding the technical viability of such an endeavor, it also highlighted some potential problems, among them the risks of technology transfer and the interrelated difficulties of providing assurances of supply to all stakeholders, including making provisions for the possibility of host-country withdrawal or interference.

The International Nuclear Fuel Cycle Evaluation (INFCE) study of 1977–1980, which, among other things, touched upon the possibility of regional fuel-cycle facilities and prospects for multilateral cooperation on plutonium storage, came to similarly positive technical conclusions. However, due in large part to diminishing concerns over the likelihood of a "plutonium economy," the disinclination of some countries to give up national control over reprocessing, and the general lack of political will, neither the RFCC or INFCE studies resulted in any further pursuit of multilateral approaches.

The IAEA Expert Group on International Plutonium Storage, the next initiative in the field, moved away from the discussion of regional fuel-cycle centers to examine instead the prospects for IAEA-supervised management, storage, and disposition of spent nuclear fuel. Once again, no consensus was reached on IPS, as states were unwilling to renounce sovereign control over nuclear technology and fuel. The same fate met the studies undertaken by the IAEA Committee on Assurances of Supply (CAS) in 1980. After seven years, twenty-one sessions, and little or no agreement among the participants, CAS went into formal abeyance, where it remains.

The efforts that began in the 1970s in the area of multilateral approaches finally ended with the UN Conference for the Promotion of International Cooperation in the Peaceful Uses of Nuclear Energy (UNCPICPUNE) in 1987, but like its predecessors, UNCPICPUNE yielded little in the way of concrete results in this regard.

The first to propose a fresh look at multilateral approaches was IAEA Director-General Mohamed ElBaradei. Addressing IAEA member-states at the September 2003 General Conference, ElBaradei said that such approaches, based on improved nuclear technology control, greater operational transparency, and nuclear fuel and power plant supply assurances, could serve to strengthen the nuclear nonproliferation regime while not impeding the development of nuclear energy for states wishing to choose that option.

ElBaradei's proposal put forward the possibility of supplementing and thereby strengthening the nonproliferation regime by reexamining the need for each state party to control all aspects of the nuclear fuel cycle, particularly with respect to the uranium enrichment and plutonium separation and the storage and disposal of spent nuclear fuel. Thus, the regime could be strengthened by placing these technologies under some form of multilateral or multinational control.[3] To explore this idea, an independent expert group was set up at the IAEA to consider possible multilateral approaches to the nuclear fuel cycle. This group submitted its report in February 2005.[4]

Old Regime, New Challenges

When the NPT entered into force in 1970, sensitive nuclear technology was widely considered out of the reach of most countries. This is clearly no longer the case. Access to such technologies has increased particularly over the last few years. As many as forty countries may now have the technical know-how required to produce nuclear weapons, and the legal regime has not kept pace with these technological developments.

In the absence of an enhanced legal regime, the sole remaining and somewhat fragile barrier to development of nuclear weapons may be a state party's assessment of its security situation and requirements. Such considerations are rarely fixed but change over time. In the face of external events, a country that now has no interest in incorporating nuclear weapons into its security doctrine may one day decide otherwise. One of the fallacies of the so-called "good guys/bad guys" distinction is that occupants of these categories may move from one to the other. Betting on future nonproliferation solely on the basis of the current benign intentions of states parties dangerously narrows the margin of security.

Can the NPT Be Altered?

One straightforward option for strengthening the nonproliferation regime involves altering the NPT itself, whether de facto or de jure. In particular,

---

3. The terms "multilateral" and "multinational" are used in a broad sense to refer to arrangements beyond solely national control.

4. See *Multilateral Approaches to the Nuclear Fuel Cycle,* Expert Group Report Submitted to the Director General of the International Atomic Energy Agency, issued as INFCIRC/640 (www.iaea.org).

some have suggested reinterpreting existing NPT language that guarantees non–nuclear-weapon states the right to pursue nuclear technology exclusively for peaceful purposes if they forego nuclear weapons (Article II) and submit to IAEA safeguards (Article III). Such an approach, however, is unrealistic.

Article IV of the NPT has two interconnected elements. The first reaffirms the inalienable right of all NPT parties "to develop research, production, and use of nuclear energy for peaceful purposes, without discrimination and in conformity with Articles I and II of this Treaty." The second is a reaffirmation that "[a]ll the Parties to the Treaty undertake to facilitate and have the right to participate in the fullest possible exchange of equipment, materials and scientific and technological information for the peaceful uses of nuclear energy," and places an obligation on the parties to "cooperate in the development of nuclear energy for peaceful purposes," especially in the territories of non–nuclear-weapon states parties, with due consideration for the needs of the developing areas of the world.

Article IV was specifically crafted to preclude any attempt to reinterpret the NPT so as to inhibit a country's right to peaceful nuclear technologies as long as the technology is not used to produce nuclear weapons. Moreover, there is no formal mechanism for reinterpretation of the NPT. Any reinterpretation would probably have to occur through a consensually agreed decision at a review conference, which takes place every five years. This is how some past decisions and documents, which have not sought to alter any of the articles of the treaty but to provide benchmarks for implementation, were approved, such as at the 2000 Review Conference, where the states parties agreed to take thirteen practical steps to demonstrate their progress in implementing Article VI of the NPT.

Past experience, however, does not bode well for using such an approach. Some non–nuclear-weapon states have expressed frustration, for example, that some nuclear-weapon states such as the United States and Russia have backed away from the thirteen steps. Given this history, it is unlikely that a reinterpretation of Article IV would hold or that an agreement on reinterpreting the NPT could be reached in the first place.

More broadly, the non–nuclear-weapon states would be disinclined to contribute to what many of them increasingly view as the growing imbalance in the NPT. They believe the nuclear-weapon states have backed away from their original guarantee that the non–nuclear-weapon states would enjoy "the right to participate in the fullest possible exchange of equipment, materials and scientific and technological information for the peaceful uses of nuclear energy," as well as the right to receive assistance in this arena from "parties to the Treaty in a position to do so." The increasing concerns that the states parties "in a position to do so" are not only no longer doing so but are placing still more restrictions on supply have fostered a belief among many non–nuclear-weapon states that the NPT bargain is being corroded.

The Limitations of a Denial Approach

Cognizant of these difficulties, a related but somewhat narrower approach has been advanced by President George W. Bush and British Foreign Secretary Jack Straw. In February 2004, President Bush told an audience at the National Defense University that "enrichment and reprocessing are not necessary for nations seeking to harness nuclear energy for peaceful purposes."[5] In view of this, he proposed that the forty-four–nation NSG "should refuse to sell enrichment and reprocessing equipment and technologies to any state that does not already possess full-scale, functioning enrichment and reprocessing plants."[6]

This approach also found voice in a proposal the same month by Straw, who questioned whether states that fail to comply with their safeguards obligations "should not forfeit the right to develop the nuclear fuel cycle, particularly the enrichment and reprocessing capabilities which are of such proliferation sensitivity."[7] The Straw proposal went on to suggest that "this does not mean that they would be deprived of the possibility of constructing and running civil nuclear power stations. These could still operate with fuel supplied by countries honouring their safeguards obligations."[8]

Even though the Straw proposal is closer to the multilateral approach suggested by ElBaradei, both the Straw and Bush proposals proceed from the basis of a denial of certain nuclear technologies. Yet at the same time, the demand for nuclear energy and related technologies has continued and even risen as countries seek to add nuclear power to their energy mix to reduce their reliance on fossil fuels and in the future to meet their Kyoto Protocol carbon emission reduction quotas.

In this world, export controls, such as those of the NSG, serve as a useful but only temporary barrier to further proliferation. They are inadequate to

5. Remarks by the President on Weapons of Mass Destruction Proliferation, National Defense University, Ft. Leslie J. McNair, Washington, D.C., February 11, 2004.
6. Ibid.
7. Statement by UK Foreign Secretary Jack Straw in the House of Commons, February 25, 2004.
8. Ibid.

address the most severe proliferation challenges as they rely on informal, nonbinding arrangements that are far from universal. Moreover, in recent years the spread of nuclear technology has been facilitated by clandestine nuclear supply networks ostensibly out of the control of governments.

These networks are easily established in response to the continuing and rising demand for nuclear technology. Current media attention has focused on A.Q. Khan and his international associates, but it should not be forgotten that similar networks also supplied Iraq prior to 1991. These networks appear to have encompassed companies and entities in more than thirty countries, ostensibly without the knowledge of their governments, including members of nuclear export control bodies such as the Zangger Committee and the NSG.

Indeed, the attempt to place ever more restrictions on supply may well have contributed indirectly to the emergence of clandestine nuclear supply networks. Iran, for example, has claimed that it was forced to turn to clandestine sources to meet its needs for civil nuclear technology when more open sources were shut off.

The concerns evoked by these clandestine networks, the availability of and increasing access to nuclear technology, and the possibility that some countries may be tempted to use such technology for nonpeaceful purposes cannot be ignored, particularly given past evidence of some countries not complying with their safeguards obligations. Consequently, it seems the time has come for new thinking or, to be more accurate, for a reexploration of some old thinking in the light of new challenges.

Pros and Cons of a Multilateral Approach

ElBaradei's initiative in the fall of 2003 attempted to jump-start this debate.[9] He did not set out a detailed plan but suggested a few guidelines. He said that any such venture would require proper rules of transparency and, crucially, assurance that legitimate users could obtain access to nuclear fuel for peaceful uses.

The potential benefits of such an approach for the nonproliferation regime are symbolic and practical. As a confidence-building measure, multilateral approaches have the potential to provide enhanced assurance to the international community that the sensitive portions of the civilian nuclear fuel cycle are less vulnerable to weapon proliferation, without singling out

9. For an outline of these proposals, see "Curbing Nuclear Proliferation: An Interview with Mohamed ElBaradei," *Arms Control Today,* November 2003, 3–6.

"good" and "bad" countries. If implemented, these measures may also have the potential to facilitate the continued use of nuclear energy for peaceful purposes and enhance the prospects for the safe and environmentally sound storage and disposal of spent fuel and radioactive waste.

The inherent proliferation risks of enrichment and reprocessing technologies could be reduced by having more than one country involved in their operation, because any country that sought to break out of its NPT commitments would not only be choosing to violate the will of the international community but potentially forcing a confrontation with another state or states that might not want to choose such a course.

In addition, such approaches could strengthen nonproliferation norms by requiring nuclear verification and security and safety measures that go beyond existing international agreements and conventions. The partners in such endeavors could conceivably allow IAEA inspectors "any time, anywhere" access rights, in addition to the use of any verification technologies deemed necessary by the agency, as well as other agreed confidence-building measures.

Multilateral approaches would provide benefits of cost-effectiveness and economies of scale for smaller countries or those with limited resources while providing the benefits of the products of nuclear technology, that is, nuclear fuel for power plants and subsequent storage of spent fuel. Similar benefits have accrued in other high-technology and high-security sectors, such as aerospace and high-speed computing.

The argument, however, is not straightforward. Opponents of multilateral approaches point to loss or limitation of state sovereignty and independence of ownership or control over a key technology sector. Countries with differing levels of technology, institutionalization, political relationships, economic development, resources, or requirements might find multilateral approaches inconvenient, unfeasible, restrictive, or simply not beneficial. Others might argue that multilateral approaches could lead to further dissemination or loss of control over sensitive nuclear technologies and to weaker nuclear security and safety standards.

To be sure, if all sensitive technology is available to all participants in a multilateral arrangement, then there is no benefit to be gained. To guard against this, multilateral efforts must come with some restrictions in order to avoid the risks of sensitive technology transfer. Within a multilateral context, however, this can be done at a larger stage than unilateral denial policies, allowing countries greater access to truly peaceful nuclear technology while discouraging them from developing independent national programs either overtly or covertly that can lead to weapon development. To meet the twin objectives of nonproliferation and "multilateralization," nuclear facilities can be provided to partners in a "black box" mode, that is, the technology holders construct and operate facilities that are managed and operated multilaterally, without technical know-how being disseminated.

Any viable future multilateral approach will require states parties with nuclear weapons to set an example by using their enrichment and reprocessing plants to provide nuclear fuel to other states that have eschewed these technologies. Assurances of supply will need to be devised in a manner that is commercially competitive, avoids monopolistic situations, and provides for backup supply in the event that some suppliers might be unable to provide the required services for whatever reason.

Conclusions

Most observers agree that the new challenges to the nuclear nonproliferation regime require a fresh response. Any attempt to strengthen the regime by further denial of technology, however, holds little likelihood of success. A new look at multinational approaches to the nuclear fuel cycle is clearly in its infancy, and its progress dependent mainly on political will.

Still, despite the disappointments of past initiatives of this kind, such ideas merit serious consideration. More than fifty years ago, the Atoms-for-Peace proposal established a legacy of innovation in the nuclear area, and recognition of the need to view such issues in a global context. Eisenhower's speech also established a tradition in this area of transforming grand visions into reality and turning words into deeds.

In the continuing spirit of Atoms-for-Peace, the IAEA's Director General set up an independent international Expert Group on Multilateral Approaches to the Nuclear Fuel Cycle in August 2004. This expert group included participants from 26 countries, who examined the nuclear fuel cycle and multinational approaches at four meetings convened during a seven month period and, as noted previously, released their Report in February 2005. The report was then distributed at the May 2005 Review Conference of the 189 States party to the Treaty on the Non-Proliferation of Nuclear Weapons.

The report of the Expert Group outlined five approaches to strengthen controls over fuel enrichment, reprocessing, spent fuel repositories, and spent fuel storage. These approaches follow. First, reinforce existing commercial market mechanisms on a case-by-case basis through long-term contracts and transparent suppliers' arrangements with government backing. Second, develop and implement international supply guarantees with IAEA participation. Different models should be investigated, notably with the IAEA as guarantor of service supplies, for example, as administrator of a fuel bank. Third, promote voluntary conversion of existing facilities to multilateral facilities, and pursue them as confidence-building measures, with the participation of NPT non–nuclear-weapon states and nuclear-weapon states, and non-NPT states. Fourth, create, through voluntary agreements and contracts, multinational, and in particular regional, multilateral approaches for new facilities based on joint ownership, drawing rights, or co-management for front-end and back-end nuclear facilities, such as uranium enrichment, fuel reprocessing, disposal and storage of spent fuel, and combinations of these. Integrated nuclear power parks would also serve this objective. Fifth, the scenario of a further expansion of nuclear energy around the world might call for the development of a nuclear fuel cycle with stronger multilateral arrangements—by region or by continent—and for broader cooperation, involving the IAEA and the international community.

The report concluded, inter alia, that the potential benefits of multilateral approaches for the nonproliferation regime are both symbolic and practical. As a confidence-building measure, multilateral approaches can provide enhanced assurance to the partners and to the international community that the most sensitive parts of the civilian nuclear fuel cycle are less vulnerable to misuse for weapon purposes. Joint facilities with multinational staff put all participants in the endeavor under a greater degree of scrutiny from peers and partners and may also constitute an obstacle against a breakout by the host partner. They also reduce the number of sites where sensitive facilities are operated, thereby curbing proliferation risks and diminishing the number of locations subject to potential thefts of sensitive material. Moreover, these approaches can even help in creating a better acceptance for the continued use of nuclear power and for nuclear applications, and enhance the prospects for the safe and environmentally sound storage and disposal of spent fuel and radioactive waste.

In the wake of this report and its recommendations, activities have been undertaken by several IAEA member states in order to explore these recommendations more thoroughly. An "International Conference on Multilateral Approaches for the Nuclear Fuel Cycle" was held in Moscow in July 2005, and discussions and papers by various states since then have focused on proposals for establishing a mechanism for reliable access to nuclear fuel, in the hopes that countries would therefore have no need of developing indigenous fuel cycle capabilities. In September 2006, the IAEA held a special meeting titled "New Frameworks for the Utilization of Nuclear Energy in the 21st Century: Assurances of Supply and Non-Proliferation" to discuss the various proposals with a view to seeking general agreement on the way forward.

Thus, it may be that new thinking on an old idea holds out the promise of a strengthened and relevant regime, one that is able to cope with contemporary and future challenges. It is clear, however, that the emphasis on cooperation, development, and nonproliferation that are an integral part of such an approach would be in keeping with its lineage, as begun in 1953.

23

A Nuclear Renaissance and the Future of the Atoms-for-Peace Bargain

Joseph F. Pilat and Kory W. Budlong Sylvester

Fifty years after the Atoms-for-Peace speech, nuclear power is heavily utilized around the world, although its role in the global economy anticipated in the 1950s has not been achieved. Despite this, the Atoms-for-Peace bargain—access to peaceful nuclear technology in exchange for pledges not to develop nuclear weapons and some level of inspections to verify these pledges—became the basis of international nuclear commerce and the nonproliferation regime. Does the bargain hold today? What will occur if we witness a nuclear renaissance, a "second coming" of nuclear energy?

If nuclear power's future is to be different from its past, the following issues will have to be addressed effectively: economics, safety, waste management, proliferation, and terrorism.

All of these issues have presented challenges in the past and are manageable to some extent. Technology has and will continue to play an important role in dealing with them. In the case of proliferation and terrorism, there is a prospect for fuel-cycle, safeguards, and physical protection technologies to reduce—but not eliminate—risks. In the debate over "proliferation resistance," all of these possibilities have come into play. However, there is no "silver bullet" here. But there is promise, particularly if new technologies are mated to appropriate institutional measures.

This essay looks anew at the Atoms-for-Peace bargain, its place within the current nonproliferation regime, and its possible role in the future.

The Origins of Proliferation Resistance

It was the prescient Acheson-Lilienthal report that first speculated on the role of nuclear technology in the future. The authors noted that the contribution of this new technology may be most strongly felt in medical and research areas. Quoting from an unpublished scientific study, the report states: "We should not be astonished if the greatest benefit of this program were in fact to lie in therapy for some of the neoplastic diseases, such as cancer, or in the increased understanding of biological systems or of the realities of the physical world, which will in turn open up new fields of human endeavor."[1] With the wide-ranging nuclear medicine applications in use today, some have argued that this has proven to be true.

The Acheson-Lilienthal report also made the first attempt to draw distinctions between various steps in the nuclear fuel cycle in terms of their proliferation risks. The issues raised mirror much of today's debate on "proliferation resistant" fuel cycles. In both cases there is an attempt to clearly identify intrinsic fuel-cycle measures that can be used to reduce proliferation dangers.

While recognizing the inherent dual-use nature of the nuclear fuel cycle, the report found shades of gray. It proposed that "dangerous" nuclear activities be reserved for an international "Atomic Development Authority" (ADA) that would own and license the use of all fissile material. While clearly preferring that even safe activities be executed internationally, "safe" activities carried out by individual nations would be allowed.

In its reasoning, a nuclear activity is dangerous if it offers a solution to any of three major problems of proliferation: obtaining raw material, producing fissionable materials, and fabricating a weapon. Dangerous activities were identified as uranium and thorium mining, operation of plutonium production reactors and reprocessing facilities, and of course, weaponi-

1. *A Report on the International Control of Atomic Energy, Prepared for the Secretary of State's Committee on Atomic Energy* (Washington, D.C.: U.S. Government Printing Office, March 16, 1946), 19.

zation. Safe activities were those involving relatively small amounts of fissile material, fissile material production facilities of low capacity, and certain types of power reactors.

A number of assumptions, inter alia, underpinned their analysis including:

- Uranium is scarce, making its control an effective nonproliferation lever.
- Both fissile ^{235}U and plutonium can be isotopically denatured, that is, be made "unusable" for weapons.
- Research reactors will only be deployed with denatured ^{235}U and plutonium and at such low power that production would be infeasible.
- Power reactors will be "suitably designed" such that only "a minimum of supervision" will be necessary to preclude plutonium production using uranium targets.
- Diversion of material at a power reactor to weapons use would require actions of a "spectacular character and difficulty."[2]

These assumptions shaped the Acheson-Lilienthal ADA proposal, and were largely reflected in the Atoms-for-Peace proposal. Today each of these assumptions can be regarded as questionable. Uranium is a relatively plentiful natural resource with significant deposits found around the globe. Denaturing plutonium has proven to be more difficult than initially thought. It is now understood that, while less attractive, plutonium produced in commercial power reactors is usable in a nuclear explosive.

The history of reactor development has deviated from the Acheson-Lilienthal vision. Many research reactors were fueled with highly enriched uranium, sometimes in significant amounts. Some reactors where also built with sufficient thermal power to enable plutonium production. Power reactors were not designed to be incapable of undeclared irradiation and plutonium production. Some designs have even utilized on-line refueling. Technology diffusion, both in terms of reprocessing, enrichment, and even weaponization, have somewhat lowered the bar for proliferators making the technical achievement in some regards less than "spectacular."

Another change is that today's threat includes radiological dispersal devices. While of dramatically lower consequence, these weapons mean that even small mass quantities of material are of concern. Today they may properly be labeled as "dangerous."

2. Ibid., chapter V, 25–30.

Proliferation Resistance Today

Given how much has changed since 1946, what are we to make of the nuclear enterprise today? What does "proliferation resistance" mean in today's world?

Of course, a single answer does not exist. The term means different things to different people. While perhaps there is greater agreement on what constitutes a dangerous activity, there is less consensus on the degree of risk posed and the necessary countermeasures.

Although concerns over reprocessing remain, the availability of uranium enrichment technology as a result of the A.Q. Khan network and globalization has made even "safe" low-enriched uranium a concern. Given the difficulty of detecting clandestine gas centrifuge facilities, some have questioned the proliferation resistance of once-through fuel cycles that require enrichment, thereby further dispersing enrichment technology worldwide.

The adoption of a "spent-fuel standard" in the mid-1990s has generated a certain amount of confusion. Created to provide practical guidance in U.S. efforts to dispose of surplus plutonium stockpiles arising from disarmament activities, it has found its way into proliferation resistance debates leading some to equate "resistance" with a "radiation barrier." This has led to renewed consideration of "partial decontamination" reprocessing schemes.[3] These flow-sheets were previously examined in the 1970s for the same purpose. Even though they are relevant for theft scenarios, the utility of this material storage standard for state-level proliferation is less clear, as they present little technical barriers and can complicate safeguards.

Safeguards play a dramatically different role in the current proliferation resistance debate today. Inspections were soundly dismissed in Acheson-Lilienthal, where it was unanimously concluded that "there is no prospect of security . . . [for a system] which relies on inspection and similar police-like methods."[4] Far from adopting this view, safeguards have been increasingly relied upon to address proliferation concerns even for "dangerous" activities. There remain widely varying views as to their efficacy.

A novel approach in today's proliferation resistance efforts is an attempt to make nuclear facilities more "safeguardable." The objective of this strategy is to make facilities easier to safeguard by eliminating certain diversion and concealment scenarios through clever design choices while

---

3. Such approaches leave various radioactive elements commingled with plutonium. The fuel is fabricated remotely for recycle in a nuclear reactor.

4. *A Report on the International Control of Atomic Energy,* 4.

enabling the application of more advanced safeguards approaches. While promising, the impact of such approaches is yet to be seen.

International control has again emerged as a potential fix to the proliferation problem. The ADA proposal had as one of its objectives organizing fuel cycle activities to make the application of safeguards more "manageable."[5] This is consistent with recent proposals put forward by the director general of the International Atomic Energy Agency (IAEA) and others for multilateral ownership and operation. The Bush administration's Global Nuclear Energy Partnership (GNEP) would limit enrichment and reprocessing activities to states which currently possess those capabilities. In exchange, these states would provide fuel for, and take back spent fuel from, states with only reactors, potentially for ultimate disposal. In each case, the inherent difficulty of dealing with latent proliferation scenarios is recognized and addressed though the elimination of national facilities.

In light of current notions of proliferation resistance, along with the technical realities underlying them, it is clear that both so-called "intrinsic" and "extrinsic" measures must be a part of any future efforts to reduce proliferation. Will these measures build on the Atoms-for-Peace legacy or undo it? Will the international nuclear nonproliferation regime based on the Atoms-for-Peace bargain, be capable of being the foundation for combating proliferation during the next fifty years? Will it be a viable component of future nonproliferation thinking? A review of the regime is warranted.

Status of the Regime

What is the status of the international nuclear nonproliferation regime? In 1997 or early 1998, one would have had a very different impression of the nuclear proliferation threat and of the future prospects of the regime. At that time, the worst fears about the breakup of the Soviet Union—the prospect of four nuclear-weapon states emerging from the ashes—were not realized. An unprecedented problem had been managed via unprecedented efforts to deal with loose nukes, the brain drain, and so on. The list of "usual suspects" was decreasing—Argentina, Brazil, and South Africa gave up programs or weapons. The Treaty on the

5. Ibid., 8.

Nonproliferation of Nuclear Weapons (NPT) was extended indefinitely. Efforts to strengthen IAEA safeguards resulted in the Additional Protocol (AP), which was designed to fix the problems that Iraq's illicit program revealed in the early 1990s. Other positive trends could be noted. Serious problems remained, but to many they appeared manageable.

Following the 1998 nuclear tests in South Asia and later reinforced by September 11, there has been growing concern about proliferation. Increasing proliferation dangers appeared in South Asia, Saddam's Iraq, North Korea, and Iran. Lateral proliferation, as exemplified by the A.Q. Khan network that supplied Libya, Iran, and North Korea with Pakistani nuclear technology, was recognized to pose a real threat. Technology diffusion through the Internet as well as through the prospect of loose nukes, materials leakage, and brain drain in the former Soviet Union, Pakistan, and other states was seen as worsening. Both trends worsened and were exacerbated by problems with eroding export controls. A growing concern was attached to hedging strategies (virtual proliferation) as states confronted an uncertain world. In the same vein, the prospects of radiological and nuclear terrorism have been seen to be rising.

For the last decade—and especially since 1998—while threats seemed to worsen, pressures on and problems with the regime have become clearer. The regime is no longer decisive in determining nonproliferation successes or failures, it could be argued.

The regime has not appeared central to nonproliferation activities or able to address new post–Cold War, post–September 11 threats. We have only to think of the United Nations Special Commission on Iraq after the Gulf War and then the United Nations Monitoring, Verification, and Inspection Commission and the coalition war in Iraq; Cooperative Threat Reduction (CTR) and Materials Protection, Control and Accounting programs, and so on, after the breakup of the Soviet Union; the counterproliferation initiative, preemption doctrine, and the Proliferation Security Initiative (PSI); the Agreed Framework for North Korea; and the limited, short-lived "responses" to the 1998 nuclear tests by India and Pakistan. No doubt, these activities largely were seen to support nonproliferation and some were the result of efforts to work through the regime, but in large part, they were external to the regime and not, as in regime theory, designed first and foremost to buttress the regime. To a significant degree, their potential impact on the regime was not considered when these approaches were being formulated.

Regime Challenges

The regime was and remains under challenge. Let us look at key regime elements.

Nonproliferation Treaty

The NPT, the centerpiece of the regime, is challenged by new weapon states, which cannot be accommodated within the treaty and affect the views of key non-nuclear states such as Japan and Brazil. The NPT is challenged by North Korean withdrawal from the treaty and, more generally, by Article X, which allows states to withdraw. It is challenged by Iranian programs, which are not compliant with the treaty's provisions and beyond that—a point that is directly related to the Atoms-for-Peace bargain—are creating a virtual weapon capability. The reemerging Article IV debate exemplified by Iran is a problem, as is the increasingly bitter Article VI debate,[6] involving the Comprehensive Test Ban Treaty (CTBT), a fissile material cut-off treaty (FMCT), concerns about progress in arms control efforts, and perceptions of the U.S. Nuclear Posture Review (NPR).

There remains limited consensus on enforcement of compliance and how to deal with noncompliance. In the latter case, there are concerns about the U.S. preemption doctrine with the perception that the United States will act as judge and jury in dealing with noncompliance. In this context, setting aside debates regarding the decision to go to war in Iraq, the removal of Saddam Hussein ended more than a decade of open defiance of nonproliferation norms. International focus shifted to flawed intelligence and away from criticism of a divided UN Security Council incapable of enforcing compliance, which was undermining the credibility of the nonproliferation regime.

The U.S.-Indian Civil Nuclear Cooperation Initiative of 2005 could have both positive and negative affects on the regime. If the deal is finalized, it would be the first of its kind with one of only three non-signatories to the NPT. Some fear that offering the benefits of Article IV to India makes the NPT "bargain" less valuable, and may lead states to rethink their commitments. The ultimate impact on the regime and on arms control more broadly will be determined by its details and by future Indian, and other

---

6. *A More Secure World: Our Shared Responsibility,* Report of the Secretary-General's High-Level Panel on Threats, Challenges and Change (New York: United Nations, 2004).

states', actions. If fuel supply provisions in the agreement lead to an expansion of India's nuclear arsenal, history will judge the agreement harshly. If, on the other hand, the agreement leads to a vested Indian interest in the regime, perhaps actively supporting an FMCT or drawing China and Pakistan into regional arms control talks, it could produce valuable benefits to the regime.

International Atomic Energy Agency

The IAEA is also challenged. Expectations have been high, perhaps unduly high, for the effort to strengthen safeguards that culminated in the AP. The Protocol breaks new ground in inspections, but the effectiveness of new measures, as well as of integrated safeguards, remains to be fully demonstrated in the field. More fundamentally, the number of states ratifying the AP has been disappointing, a situation that the Agency and member-states are trying to remedy. A key issue is how IAEA actions taken to date on Iran will play out. Resolutions of the Agency's Board of Governors have been important, as has the decision to refer Iran to the UN Security Council. But action by the Council remains uncertain, and diplomatic efforts have broken down.

In terms of addressing terrorism concerns, the IAEA has made some progress. Amendments have been made to strengthen the Convention on the Physical Protection of Nuclear Material. During its July 2005 conference, the states party to the treaty made the protection of nuclear facilities and material a legally binding obligation. Previously the Convention only applied to material in international transit. There is also agreement to improve cooperation between states in areas such as radiological source recovery. The Agency is continuing to expand its assistance to states in order to improve their physical protection at facilities. However, such actions remain voluntary. The Agency does not have the authority or responsibility to perform inspections or otherwise certify the adequacy of such protection systems.

Nuclear Suppliers Group

The Nuclear Suppliers Group (NSG) faces erosion. NSG rules need to be reinforced and strengthened. There is reason to be concerned about Russian and other countries' exports to proliferant States. The U.S.-Indian agreement of 2005 could require fundamental changes in the way that the NSG does business. Concerns have been raised that the arrangement will weaken the NSG's requirement of full-scope safeguards and open the door to similar trade with Pakistan. Whether the NSG will make a one-time exception for India or enact broad changes in its guidelines remains to be seen. Technology diffusion, black markets, and lateral proliferation also raise questions about the long-term relevance of the NSG as these developments show that nuclear supply is no longer the preserve of a few advanced industrial states.

United Nations Security Council

The United Nations Security Council was seen as the last great hope in addressing proliferation problems, including the North Korean crisis of the early 1990s. However, there was and is limited consensus within the Council on enforcement and none on the use of force. This had led to paralysis on Iraq. The Security Council may be heading to a stalemate on Iran, as no basis for a resolution of differences between key states is apparent.

There have been proposals for reform of the Security Council. The Secretary General's High Level Panel on Threats, Challenges and Change[7] developed proposals for expanded membership under varying conditions to make the council more inclusive and reflect emerging geopolitical realities. While making the Security Council more representative, such moves would likely further divide its membership making the possibility of decisive action even more remote.

The panel also examined the sensitive issue of "prevention" as a nonproliferation strategy. This issue had received great attention in the wake of the Iraq war. While noting that in some cases preventive military action may indeed be necessary to maintain international peace, the panel concluded that the Security Council was the proper entity for taking preventive actions under international law.[8] Issues remain, however, concerning differing threat perceptions between states and the ability or the inability of the Council to act when necessary.

The Council has sent a clear message on states' responsibilities regarding prevention of terrorism involving weapons of mass destruction (WMD). United Nations Security Council Resolution 1540 directs states to refrain from assisting subnational organizations in their pursuit of WMD

7. Ibid., 55.
8. The Commitment of the United States of America to Article VI of the Treaty on the Nonproliferation of Nuclear Weapons, 2005.

and to criminalize such activities. It also requires states to establish domestic controls to prevent WMD-related proliferation. If acted upon, this decisive action should help eliminate inconsistencies between states with regard to prosecution of proliferation-related crimes.

Impacts of U.S. Policies

Beyond regime problems, it has been argued by critics that U.S. policies embodied in the Department of Defense's 2001 Nuclear Posture Review and national security strategy documents will undermine the regime. In the case of the NPR, there is a perception of increasing U.S. emphasis on nuclear weapons, including a desire for new weapons and new testing. This will make weapons more attractive to proliferators, it is argued.

There is the perception of an end to United States interest in arms control as well. The Moscow Treaty is viewed by critics as a farce. It is held that the responsive force negates reductions in any event. The CTBT stalemate and other problems with formal arms control affect the Article VI debate. There is a perception that the U.S. strategy demonstrates that the U.S. commitment to multilateral nonproliferation is eroding, and that the United States is unduly focused on unilateral solutions, including preemption, that will undermine such regime elements as negative security assurances and the like.

These criticisms do not reflect the reality of either U.S. nuclear policy or its arms control effects. The U.S. policies have been misunderstood and often mischaracterized; while setting a strategic course in changing times, they are fully consistent with the U.S. commitment to Article VI of the NPT. In contrast to the views of critics, the Nuclear Posture Review, the Moscow Treaty, and CTR activities all make a compelling contribution to Article VI.

The Nuclear Posture Review, which calls for dramatic reductions in the numbers of nuclear weapons and removes nuclear weapons from the center of U.S. deterrence and defense, put forward a revolutionary U.S. nuclear policy. The NPR recognized that the strengthening of deterrence could be achieved by the growing ability to achieve certain nuclear missions with conventional capabilities. Defenses and a responsive defense infrastructure are given increased status. U.S. emphasis on nuclear weapons has been reduced in this NPR.

If the NPR outlines a vision fully consistent with the spirit and obligations of the NPT, the record of action is also considerable. The Moscow

Treaty reflects the reasoning of the NPR. It reduces the number of operationally deployed strategic nuclear forces to between 1700 and 2200 by 2012. The total stockpile will be reduced by nearly a half by that year. U.S.-Russian cooperative threat reduction efforts to reduce dangers also constitute a real success story. With this effort, the United States has helped Russia eliminate large numbers of ballistic missiles, strategic bombers, and ballistic missile submarines. As well, it has led to greater security for, and even partial elimination of, Russian weapon-origin material.

Despite this record, the criticism has continued. This is not surprising as it reflects, at least in part, the belief that U.S. policies and actions in the nuclear realm will determine, to some extent, the threat of proliferation. However, the proliferation threat today is not due to failures of U.S. leadership, and it is too simplistic to ascribe the problem to the United States not setting a good example.

The leadership of the United States, however, is critical in global nonproliferation efforts. And U.S. leadership has been demonstrated in efforts to reform and strengthen the regime. In President Bush's landmark February 11 nonproliferation speech,[9] there were initiatives to, inter alia:

- Reinterpret Article IV of the NPT to close the so-called "loophole" that allows proliferants to develop the means for weapons legally
- Take practical steps to limit fuel cycle risks by a ban on new states from developing reprocessing and enrichment technologies
- Strengthen export controls, especially for sensitive technologies
- Require the AP as a condition of supply
- Deal with noncompliance in part through reforming the IAEA's Board of Governors
- Build on successful CTR and PSI actions

"Shocks" to the Regime

Even with reforms to the regime, it may be subjected to "shocks," which may or may not appear likely today. These may include:

- Nuclear use in South Asia—only a few years ago this was a grave concern

9. Remarks by the President on Weapons of Mass Destruction Proliferation, National Defense University, Ft. Leslie J. McNair, Washington, D.C., February 11, 2004.

- Pakistani loose nukes, leaked materials, and brain drain
- An Islamist regime in Pakistan
- Nuclear-weapon tests in South Asia or North Korea
- The sale of fissile material or nuclear weapons by North Korea or Iran

Other possibilities could be raised, including a dramatic rise in nuclear power growth—a so-called second coming of nuclear power that stresses key elements of the regime, from safeguards to export controls. Let us examine the potential impacts of this scenario.

A Nuclear Renaissance?

A second coming of nuclear energy, if there is one, will highlight and increase pressures on arguably the regime's weakest point, the heart of the Atoms-for-Peace bargain, Article IV of the NPT.

There is concern growing in some circles, particularly post-September 11, about the misuse of nuclear technology and whether the civilian nuclear power enterprise is worth the risk. The case of Iran's program in pursuit of a virtual-weapon capability highlights the issue of the acceptability of risks associated with ostensibly peaceful nuclear programs. Export controls will come under increasing pressure if the nuclear market advances rapidly. Supplier restraint (arguably largely a product of downturn in the market) could disappear. Lateral proliferation and illicit trafficking confound this problem.

These developments are likely to rekindle the nuclear supply debate of the 1970s. The demands of recipient states and divisions among suppliers will likely reappear. The Article IV problems—the loophole it offers states seeking virtual capabilities—will reemerge as central. Iran will be the poster child of this issue. The effectiveness of safeguards will come into focus again as they did after the 1981 Osirak attack, after the 1991 Gulf War, and before the 2003 coalition war with Iraq. Will safeguards remain credible? Will it be possible for safeguards to play their old confidence-building role in the new environment of noncompliance with the spirit and letter of the NPT?

On the other hand, stakes in the regime could rise with the emergence of clear, mutual interests in ensuring the benefits of the peaceful atom either for energy security or to address concerns over global warming. This may bode well for GNEP. If satisfactory institutional and economic arrangements can be reached, concerns over latent proliferation and stretching safeguards capabilities could be addressed.

At least at a high level, there may appear to be no credible alternatives to the existing regime, as any alternatives will have tremendous costs—resources and other. There may be a perceived need (a profit-reinforced motive) for effective inspections, compliance enforcement, and so on, for Europeans, Russians, Japanese, and others. Without a strong institutional element, perceived and real proliferation risks will remain relatively high and they will be corrosive to nuclear power growth, albeit not in any way the deciding factor on nuclear power decisions.

Conclusions

The pressures on, and problems with, the regime do not herald the end of the historic bargain of the 1950s. On the contrary, these challenges may be just what is required to spur the United States and the international community to take the necessary steps to repair and strengthen the regime. If existing problems are not resolved, the regime will likely fail in one or another fashion. It could go out with a bang or, more likely, a whisper.

24

A Fissile Material Cutoff Treaty

Thomas E. Shea

A fissile material cut-off treaty (FMCT) is one of the possibilities for the future under the Atoms-for-Peace umbrella, serving the nonproliferation as well as the arms control and disarmament objectives of the seminal proposal of President Dwight D. Eisenhower. Given the dangers we face today, can we design the FMCT to be vital in confronting nuclear dangers while managing the security risks of intrusive inspections?

The Dangers We Face

The greatest success of Atoms for Peace is that nuclear weapons were not used in wars during the past fifty years. Our challenge is simply to maintain that record, recognizing at the start of the second fifty years of Atoms for Peace, that rather than three nuclear powers, there are eight or nine; that while many nations have ruled out nuclear weapons, a small number of states still harbor nuclear ambitions; and that nuclear terrorism is a very real threat.

What are the prospects for success in the next fifty years? What are the chances for one or more catastrophic failures of the system? How could an FMCT make a significant difference?

The fiftieth anniversary of President Eisenhower's Atoms-for-Peace speech is also the tenth anniversary of a United Nations resolution calling for the negotiation of a treaty banning the production of fissile material for use in nuclear weapons or other nuclear explosive devices. Every year since, that resolution has been reconfirmed.

Given that history, what might an FMCT do to enhance U.S. national security and the security of other nations, how might the FMCT be put together, and how might it work? What might happen if the FMCT is not pursued?

Fissile material is essential for nuclear weapons. Controls on its production, use, and exports are the core of the international nuclear nonproliferation regime. Similar controls could serve as the foundation of future international efforts related to nuclear disarmament and an important element in the war against terrorism. An FMCT is the next step for Atoms for Peace. Its contributions will depend upon the scope of the treaty, its acceptance, and the manner in which it is implemented.

How could the idea of an FMCT be interpreted to serve the greatest security benefit, without going so far that it would be rejected out of hand? An FMCT—making modest first steps on the road to disarmament, substantial steps towards redressing existing problems in the nonproliferation regime, and substantial steps aimed at preventing nuclear terrorism—is in the best interest of all nations.

For as long as nuclear arsenals exist, nuclear war will remain a risk. We have come close, on several occasions, most recently when India and Pakistan were at odds over Kashmir several years ago. Existing nuclear arsenals also pose the risk of accidental or unauthorized use. Moreover, there is the risk that nuclear weapons might be seized, stolen, or sold and, thereby, come into the possession of another state or a terrorist organization. American nuclear weapons are safe and secure, but the security of weapons maintained by other states is less certain.

An FMCT could be the start of an international nuclear disarmament regime, providing opportunities for constructive engagement to reduce tensions and increase the security and safety of existing arsenals, for as long as they remain. A world free of nuclear weapons is a noble pursuit, and incremental steps intended to limit nuclear arsenals provide a logical way to begin what will likely be a very long-term effort. The FMCT offers a means to cap the inventory of fissile material available for weapons and a means to assure that fissile materials, once declared excess to defense requirements, could not be returned to such use at a later date. Those two steps are significant, are directly in line with the obligations of Article VI of the Treaty on the Nonproliferation of Nuclear Weapons (NPT), and respond directly to the provisions agreed for the indefinite extension of the NPT.

In addition to this nuclear disarmament role, the FMCT offers a means to extend and bolster the international nuclear nonproliferation regime. Today's nonproliferation system is remarkable in its coverage and its accomplishments. All nations except India, Israel, and Pakistan have become parties to the NPT. It is hoped that the Democratic People's Republic of Korea (DPRK) will come back into the fold. However, the NPT is notable for its failures—and its vulnerabilities—as well as for its successes. The FMCT could extend and amplify the current regime, bringing all states into a single global framework. It could provide a means to ensure that peaceful applications of nuclear energy are prudent and legitimate; that exports of technology, materials, and equipment follow uniform controls; and that all fissile material production and use are verified.

The FMCT also holds the possibility of helping to prevent nuclear terrorism. The threat of nuclear terrorism has seized attention in the United States. International progress is being made. Notably, the Convention on the Physical Protection of Nuclear Material (CPPNM)—which was limited to international shipments, had no provision for enforcement, and was not widely accepted—has been amended. An effort that began before September 11, 2001, has resulted in its being extended to all domestic peaceful nuclear facilities. This should make the CPPNM more effective, but it will remain a guideline with no reporting mechanism, no mandatory peer reviews, and no inspections.

The possibilities for nuclear terrorism include the use of nuclear weapons acquired from an existing arsenal or the manufacture of one or more nuclear explosives using bought or stolen fissile material. Nuclear terrorism might result in extensive casualties or property damage without the use of nuclear weapons or other nuclear explosives, by sabotaging a nuclear facility or transport system to release large amounts of radioactive material or by the theft of hazardous radioactive material for use in a radiological dispersal device—a "dirty bomb."

The FMCT, while not traditionally thought of in connection with nuclear terrorism, offers a means to establish a system under which the sovereign rights and responsibilities of states to protect fissile material against theft or misuse could be set out. That would allow the concerns of states about transnational nuclear terrorism to be addressed.

Scope of the FMCT

The key to the promise of the FMCT lies in "banning the production," a term in the United Nations resolution. Viewing that term in a broad sense, and without addressing the current negotiating positions of key states, the FMCT could, in principle, encompass six missions:

- Cessation of production of fissile material for nuclear weapons or other nuclear explosives in all states
- Prohibition of declared and undeclared production of fissile material for use in nuclear weapons or other nuclear explosives following the entry into force of the treaty
- Acceptance of fissile material that is determined by a state to be excess to its military needs, thereby preventing its use at a later time in nuclear weapons or other nuclear explosives
- Pre-approval of states' programs for peaceful use and nonexplosive military use of fissile material under verification, to ensure that any such applications are prudent and legitimate, and are not used as a means to mask the supply of fissile material for nuclear weapons or other nuclear explosives
- Pre-approval of exports and imports of fissile materials, technologies, and equipment for fissile material production or processing, verifying that the conditions of these pre-approvals are honored
- Requiring that fissile material permitted under the treaty is protected against theft

To provide a vital security framework, an FMCT should:

- Stop military production and verify that all production reactors and reprocessing plants, and all enrichment plants producing highly enriched uranium, are out of business, or only carry out allowed activities
- Make provisions for excess military stocks to be banned from future use in nuclear weapons, including classified forms of fissile material, to allow verification of much larger inventories much earlier[1]

1. The methods developed under the Trilateral Initiative among the United States, Russia, and the International Atomic Energy Agency (IAEA) could be used for that purpose.

- Require that all existing and future stocks of fissile material are under verification, and provide for the access needed to detect clandestine activities
- Include provisions for requiring proliferation resistant technical features and deployment arrangements, limiting the possibilities for future misuse
- Include verification and transparency measures for naval reactor fuels, to ensure that such nonexplosive military uses of fissile material do not provide a loophole for violations of the FMCT
- Require states to adhere to the CPPNM and to incorporate technical features and deployment arrangements designed to prevent peaceful nuclear activities and fissile material from misuse by terrorists

To achieve its promise, the FMCT should maximize its security benefits while minimizing its burdens. It should avoid provisions that would make it unacceptable. The FMCT should not:

- Legitimize the possession of nuclear weapons by any states or recognize the "nuclear-weapon state" designation of the NPT
- Ban peaceful nuclear activities or nonexplosive military use of fissile materials, recognizing that either might be a loophole for violations involving nuclear weapons
- Require specific disarmament steps—that would go beyond the limitations on manufacture foreseen for the FMCT, and would make it unacceptable
- Require states to divulge classified information related to nuclear-weapon design or manufacturing details, and should prohibit any verification that would reveal such information
- Require states to declare the amounts of fissile material produced prior to entry into force for military purposes, or the remaining inventories (the FMCT is about banning production and while such historical information is interesting and may later be necessary, it is not an essential part of the FMCT's scope)
- Include tritium, as tritium is not a fissile material

Achieving an FMCT

For such a treaty to succeed, it must recognize that, leaving aside for the moment, the status of the DPRK, all states except India, Israel, and Pakistan are parties to the NPT. The FMCT should not undermine that regime, but rather extend its provisions to all states in the most nondiscriminatory manner possible.

The FMCT could be designed exclusively for states possessing nuclear weapons, or for universal adoption. If it is restricted, then the treaty regime could stand alone, the verification system could be separated from the IAEA safeguards (which already bans in 183 non–nuclear-weapon states, the production of fissile material for use in nuclear weapons or other nuclear explosives, or for purposes unknown) and could be undertaken by a new organization—not the IAEA. If the FMCT were restricted to states possessing nuclear weapons, then it could be negotiated by those states rather than by the Conference on Disarmament.

However, such an arrangement would not be advisable because it would:

- Establish and perpetuate a new discriminatory arrangement
- Undermine the nonproliferation system by establishing different standards for similar facilities under the FMCT versus the NPT
- Draw off staff (and possibly financial resources) from IAEA safeguards
- Inhibit progress towards future nuclear arms reductions that would otherwise occur under a universal treaty regime

Moreover, it would deny the great majority of nations the benefits of the nonproliferation and terrorism prevention provisions, and would not meet the provisions of Article VI in the sense of "strict and effective international controls."

If the FMCT were to be a universal treaty, the most practical, most effective, and least discriminatory verification system would be to adopt the IAEA safeguards system, comprising comprehensive safeguards agreements and the full provisions of the Additional Protocol, as the foundation for the FMCT.

Recognizing that this would be a "fissile material" treaty, in those states having nuclear material that is not subject to IAEA safeguards, the verification provisions would not include natural, low-enriched, or depleted uranium or thorium. Reporting and verification would begin with production of fissile material and, thus, not include nuclear reactors unless they are fueled with fissile material (e.g., as in the use of mixed oxide fuel). As a practical matter, states with classified forms of fissile material (such as weapon-origin fissile material or submarine fuel) would have to be allowed to withhold sensitive information and the verification measures would have to be designed to respect such classification, while providing credible assurance that the fissile materials remain properly accounted for under the treaty.

This verification would be as effective as current technology allows and would provide a means to develop and implement improvements over time. IAEA safeguards need further improvement. Recall that Argentina announced that it had begun operation of a gaseous diffusion uranium enrichment plant, which was not detected by the IAEA or anyone else. Similarly, the nuclear activities in Iran—which were scattered and limited to laboratory scale—were announced by an Iranian opposition group, not by the IAEA or any other group, although suspicions had been voiced for many years. Detecting a clandestine gas centrifuge plant designed to remain hidden could be the most difficult technical challenge at present, and while a variety of methods are being pursued, this is likely to remain the weak link.

A New Type of Treaty

To carry out its disarmament, nonproliferation, and terrorism prevention roles in an effective manner, while respecting and building on the NPT framework, the FMCT should be a new type of treaty. This could be accomplished. First, a conference of states parties must be empowered with the authority to decide all matters related to funding, enforcement in cases of noncompliance, and the prudence and legitimacy of proposed peaceful and nonexplosive military applications. Within the conference, all parties should enjoy equal rights and responsibilities. The conference would have to meet frequently and regularly to carry out its tasks.

Second, the FMCT should anticipate the need to adapt as time goes by to ensure that it remains a vital security measure. The interpretation of the treaty's provisions should be reconsidered on the occasion of arms reduction treaties and at regular intervals (e.g., ten years).

Third, implementing the FMCT will cost a lot. For states with extensive nuclear applications that would become subject to inspection, operational changes and structural modifications may be needed, as well as new instruments, new and additional laboratory measurements, accounting, and reporting, radiation protection, and security escorts, among other things. Most of the expenses will be in the initial period of implementation, leveling off to operating expenses and amortization of equipment over time. Failing to provide adequate finances could prevent some states from accepting FMCT obligations or the treaty could be starved to the extent that it would not meet its objectives nor would it be verified effectively.

The new IAEA safeguards budget will run about $100 million per year for staff, equipment, travel, and technical services—expensive, but still a bargain in relation to most other options. FMCT verification would essentially double those costs.

There is a practical way to meet these financial obligations and to build the regime to meet the treaty's security objectives. In 1957, when the IAEA Statute entered into force, the only option for financing the IAEA was to adopt the United Nations arrangements under which a budget is approved and then member-states are assessed according to an agreed formula. However, today, some 440 nuclear power reactors are in operation and some experts anticipate that ten times that number may be operating by the middle of this century. In the United States, a geological repository is being constructed at great cost at Yucca Mountain in Nevada. A law passed in 1982 established a fund requiring nuclear reactor operators to pay a fee of 0.1 cents per kilowatt-hour. The cash stream from that source, together with government defense waste fees, is now about $750 million per year. If 440 reactors pay a 1-percent surcharge on all energy products, that would generate revenues of about $1 billion per year, which could finance implementation in states that would need assistance, meet all IAEA verification costs, and leave funds for projects that are consistent with the spirit of the FMCT, especially in developing countries.

Fourth, the FMCT can only be a success if it provides a mechanism for coping with allegations of noncompliance in a fair and efficient manner. Such charges might be made by the IAEA, for example, based on its inspection results, or by a state or group of states. Alleged noncompliance might involve a state attempting to acquire fissile material illicitly, or a state allowing the export of equipment that could be used to produce or process fissile material without approval by the conference of states parties.

One way to address noncompliance would be to have the conference of states parties decide to address such charges itself, to refer them to the United Nations Security Council, or to appoint a judicial panel to make a finding and define remedies when a party is found to be in violation of its obligations under the FMCT.

Fifth, if the FMCT is to serve its intended purpose, it must ultimately become universal and remain so. To accommodate such a provision, the normal practice (e.g., in the NPT) of allowing states to withdraw for reasons of supreme national interest might be allowed up to a certain point, but not thereafter. If the provision for withdrawal were to remain in effect until a certain number of states had joined the FMCT—for example, a total of 170—then it would be close enough to universality to allow the removal of that escape provision. At that point, all parties would remain party to the FMCT for as long as the FMCT would remain in force, that is, until the treaty would be amended to put it out of existence.

Conclusions

President Eisenhower deduced:

> We are learning that atomic energy is a unifying force when it is devoted to the cause of peace. It brings together nations whose scientists and engineers confer the benefits of discovery and technology on all mankind.[2]

An FMCT would help to continue this ambition.[3] A treaty banning the production of fissile material for use in nuclear weapons or other nuclear explosive devices could serve us well in the second fifty years of Atoms for Peace. It could provide a critical venue for progress towards nuclear disarmament, help to prevent further proliferation and serve to protect us from nuclear terrorism. In the end, the usefulness of such a treaty will depend on its scope, governance, and finance, and on its ability to gain universal adoption.

It is now clear that verification, among other issues, will be contentious in negotiations, but hopefully these matters can be resolved. In the end, each state should consider the FMCT through the following perspectives:

- The burdens imposed, including the intrusive inspection regime and the costs needed to facilitate inspections in the state and to support the verification system

2. "Atomic Power for Peace," an address by Dwight D. Eisenhower, President of the United States, before the General Assembly of the United Nations, December 8, 1953.
3. T. Shea, "The Fissile Material Cutoff Treaty: A Venue for Future Progress in Arms Control, Nonproliferation and the Prevention of Nuclear Terrorism," *Journal of Nuclear Materials Management* 32, no. 1 (Fall 2003): 34–49.

- The security benefit of having a cap on the ability of other states to produce nuclear weapons and the added knowledge of their programs through the inspections, export controls, and transparency measures embodied in the FMCT
- The importance of making concrete progress on the obligations of Article VI of the NPT
- The significance of applying IAEA safeguards at all enrichment and reprocessing facilities
- The importance of having a common standard for physical protection
- The benefit or damage to the international nonproliferation regime that could result from establishing or not establishing the FMCT

25

Conclusions

Joseph F. Pilat

How have the elements of the fundamental Atoms-for-Peace vision fared after fifty years? Let us consider its impacts in the areas of nonproliferation, arms control and disarmament, counterterrorism, and nuclear energy.[1]

Nonproliferation

During the last fifty years, Atoms for Peace has significantly influenced international efforts to promote nuclear nonproliferation. Atoms for Peace has been the foundation for the international nuclear nonproliferation regime centered in the Treaty on the Nonproliferation of Nuclear Weapons (NPT) and the International Atomic Energy Agency (IAEA). The regime has, over the decades since its founding, received near universal support.

1. For a discussion of the first thirty years of Atoms for Peace, from which the following benefitted, see Joseph E. Pilat, Robert E. Pendley, and Charles K. Ebinger, eds., *Atoms for Peace: An Analysis after Thirty Years* (Boulder, Colo.: Westview, 1985).

Although there have been questions about the regime for decades, it is only since the revelations of noncompliance by Iraq and North Korea in the early 1990s that the regime has been under intense and increasing pressure. Today the regime is challenged by, among other things, noncompliance and a limited consensus on enforcement; by the rising concern about non-state actors, including terrorists and black marketers; and by the rapid diffusion of, and changes in, technology.

For the last decade, there has been growing concern about increasing proliferation dangers, including those emanating from South Asia, North Korea, and Iran. The prospects of radiological and nuclear terrorism are seen to be rising; concern over a proliferation-terrorism nexus after 9/11 has never been higher. While threats have been seen as worsening, pressures on and problems with the regime have become clearer. The regime was and remains under challenge.

Beyond today's concerns, most of which have become prominent in the last decade, and in many respects underlying them, there has always been, from within the nonproliferation community, criticism of President Eisenhower's proposal and the manner in which it has developed. The most prominent critics are those who have argued that the approach to proliferation has not been sufficiently rigorous, including, perhaps especially, IAEA safeguards. There has also been a concern that the proliferation of technologies in the past, as well as the present, has increased the dangers not only of state proliferation but also that nuclear materials may be stolen or nuclear activities sabotaged by non-state actors.

Especially in recent years, there has been a debate on whether a new bargain is necessary for the survival of the nonproliferation regime and calls for "regime change"—a change in the nonproliferation regime. It seems that the temptation for regime change, which has been voiced at a level not heard before, is rational. It is certainly understandable. It is no less understandable, for example, than the idea in the early 1990s to standardize the provisions of all nonproliferation regimes targeting weapons of mass destruction to ensure that there were no weak links or loopholes. But this idea was both impracticable and potentially counterproductive to the extent it would likely result in weakening rather than strengthening the various regimes if conformity was created on the basis of the least rather than the most effective provisions of these regimes.

If there is dissatisfaction with the regime, is it possible to create something better? This is not clear. Current treaties and institutions still command significant international support and consensus, but consensus is largely limited on tough issues and on the difficult cases. This suggests there is little prospect for new institutions that would more effectively deal with the proliferation threat. This point is reinforced by the fact that such consensus as exists remains embedded in the Atoms-for-Peace bargain.

What are the alternatives to the old Atoms-for-Peace regime—or to U.S. action? Some of the proposals put forward follow:

- New Baruch Plan
- Realpolitik cartel approach to exports
- New international inspection authority

One can debate such proposals, albeit some of these ideas, notably a revised Baruch Plan, have not been developed sufficiently to judge their merits. In any event, the existing regime, with all its flaws, probably cannot be replaced without tremendous political and other costs. If we believe that nuclear energy's role in electricity generation will increase and that this growth raises the controversial issue of whether plutonium separation is needed, several reforms may be critical. Among prospective reforms to address the emerging nuclear reality and the risks it imposes are a reinterpretation of Article IV; practical steps to limit fuel cycle risks, including the international management of the fuel cycle; and more restrictive export controls. The U.S. announcement of a deal with India may also be seen as an effort to strengthen nonproliferation efforts by bringing India, which has largely acted responsibly in nuclear matters, more closely into the regime. Critics of the accord, which requires congressional action, have argued that it threatens the NPT and the regime by providing the rewards of membership, that is, access to peaceful nuclear technology, to a state that remains outside of the treaty.

These and other proposals to reform and strengthen the regime have been put forward by President George W. Bush, IAEA Director General Mohamed ElBaradei, and others. It is clear today that there has been and will be reforms to the regime, but there is little appetite for replacing it. The reforms being discussed today will have to take into account the current controversies over arms control, including differences over Article VI of the treaty. Moreover, they will have to ensure that the regime addresses the proliferation and terrorism threats that concern the entire globe.

Even if the regime is reformed, there will be a continued need to deal with difficult cases, at least in part outside of the regime. This will require far more attention than has been devoted to date to the demand side of the proliferation equation, that is, to addressing the reasons why states (and perhaps non-state actors as well) seek to acquire nuclear weapons. To the extent that this can be accomplished, and we must understand that it will be a difficult endeavor, it could help to ensure that the regime, which is based on supply-side principles—or efforts to control or cut off access to at least certain nuclear capabilities—is not further eroded. Moreover, it could help to prevent new, difficult cases from emerging out of flaws in regime. If we are ultimately to succeed in the nonproliferation project, these are paramount objectives.

Arms Control and Disarmament

Turning to the role of Atoms for Peace in furthering arms control and disarmament, it is clear that the role envisaged has not been met. There are many reasons why this occurred. Most importantly, the demands of Cold War deterrence ensured that the effort to draw down nuclear arms was, at that time, premature at best.

Since the end of the Cold War, however, considerable progress has been made in this arena. The Defense Department's 2001 Nuclear Posture Review (NPR) codified the diminished role of nuclear weapons in post-Cold War U.S. defense strategy. The NPR builds on the circumstances that ended the Cold War nuclear arms race, and reflects the fact that the United States is working to encourage a cooperative, nonadversarial relationship with Russia that sets aside Cold War hostilities and ends the outdated notion of mutually assured destruction.

The United States and Russia are progressively and systematically reducing their nuclear forces. Reflecting the new thinking about the future of nuclear weapons embodied in the NPR, the number of operationally deployed strategic nuclear warheads will be reduced under the 2002 Moscow Treaty to between 1,700 and 2,200 by the end of 2012.

Together with other states, the United States and Russia are also working to reduce the nuclear risks in the former Soviet Union and beyond. These efforts involve an unprecedented—and once unthinkable—set of initiatives and programs that encompass both traditional arms control and new, complementary measures. The U.S. program of Cooperative Threat Reduction has helped make fundamental changes in the political and strategic landscape of the former Soviet Union, including the provision of assistance to Russia to eliminate strategic offensive delivery vehicles and other capabilities. Bilateral efforts to deal with excess defense materials are also being pursued through the highly enriched uranium (HEU) deal and other initiatives. With these post–Cold War efforts, especially those for handling excess defense nuclear material, the old Atoms-for-Peace concept has had some life breathed into it.

Preventing Nuclear Terrorism

Atoms for Peace was not promulgated in an environment where the current concerns about nuclear and radiological terrorism were seriously considered. Today the situation is different.

There is a growing belief that September 11 has changed the threat of nuclear terrorism, or at least the way we perceive it. Mohamed ElBaradei, the director general of the IAEA, said explicitly:

> The willingness of terrorists to commit suicide to achieve their evil aims makes the nuclear terrorism threat far more likely than it was before September 11th.... We are not just dealing with the possibility of governments diverting nuclear materials into clandestine weapons programs. Now we have been alerted to the potential of terrorists targeting nuclear facilities or using radioactive sources to incite panic, contaminate property, or even cause injury or death among civilian populations.[2]

In the same vein, the Pugwash Council opined:

> The horrific nature of the September 11th attacks has demonstrated the ability of international terrorist networks to carry out well-planned and complex operations that can kill thousands of innocent civilians. The potential for biological, chemical, and/or nuclear terrorism has greatly increased.[3]

In practice, the potential threat of nuclear terrorism is of growing concern, even though no major act has occurred to date. Predictive capabilities are limited. However, the risk is real. It could not be ignored before 9/11, and it

---

2. Statement of the Director General, Symposium on Nuclear Safeguards, Verification and Security, Special Session on Combatting Nuclear Terrorism, November 2, 2001.

3. "The Dangers of Nuclear Terrorism," Statement of the Pugwash Council, November 12, 2001.

cannot be ignored today. The United States, the West, and the world are vulnerable to nuclear terrorism today, as on September 10, 2001. If we believe 9/11 showed that we do not know where or how terrorists will strike next, then we need to cast our nets more widely than if we believe the terrorist telegraphed their horrific actions and we did not pick up the signals. In either case, addressing vulnerabilities in this area will depend ultimately on understanding the risks of nuclear and radiological terrorism in relation to conventional, chemical, biological, and cyber terrorism and other threats in an environment of finite resources.

Calibrating the threat politically and technologically remains critical. We need to know how prevalent the terrorists who would and could commit such acts are; we need to know their motivations, and if they are really without constraints; and we need to know if and how they are influenced by realities (such as ongoing counterterrorism responses). Efforts to address this issue predate 9/11; some are now over a decade old. For example, in the early 1990s, the United States established the Material Protection, Control, and Accounting (MPC&A) program to provide nuclear security support for nuclear sites in the former Soviet Union that possess weapon-useable nuclear material. The mission of MPC&A and other programs is to reduce the threat of nuclear terrorism as well as proliferation by rapidly improving the security of such nuclear material in Russia, and other states of the former Soviet Union. Other actions had been taken as well. There was a sense, however, that further action to reduce or mitigate the threat was needed.

Post-9/11, there is an even greater sense of urgency and more resources have been devoted to addressing nuclear terrorism. After September 11, actions taken to increase security at nuclear sites, to better control nuclear material and radioactive sources, and so on, may reduce terrorist opportunities or prospects for success across the spectrum of possible threats. If these efforts are successful, it will be due in no small part to institutions created under the Atoms-for-Peace aegis, especially the IAEA, which has taken concrete, immediate steps to address this emerging threat and is putting forward new approaches for the long term.

Nuclear Energy

With respect to nuclear energy—as with nonproliferation, arms control, and terrorism—Atoms-for-Peace ideas and aspirations, however sound in principle, have not been fully realized. They will have to be adjusted if the Atoms-for-Peace vision is to serve the world in the future. If there is a growing consensus that nuclear energy will continue to offer energy benefits or opportunities to the world, this view is certainly not universally accepted. The role of Atoms-for-Peace in promoting nuclear power through regulated supply has been criticized from the beginning as advancing the proliferation of nuclear technology and capabilities around the world and thereby increasing proliferation dangers. As noted, this criticism echoes today in the charge that the NPT's Article IV is a loophole to the treaty that allows states to develop virtual nuclear-weapon capabilities without having formally to violate the NPT's strictures.

The worldwide nuclear energy industry is a direct progeny of Atoms for Peace. As elements of the Atoms-for-Peace policy were gradually institutionalized, they created a climate in which nuclear power prospered. In 1954, a major amendment of the Atomic Energy Act of 1946 provided legislative grounds for a nuclear energy and nonproliferation policy for the United States that was based on Atoms for Peace. In essence, it allowed the United States to share nuclear technology with friendly nations, providing the basis for the convocation of a series of conferences on peaceful uses of atomic energy in Geneva and the negotiation of a network of bilateral agreements of cooperation on peaceful uses of nuclear energy, the establishment of international training and exchange programs, and the support for regional nuclear cooperatives such as the European Atomic Energy Community.

From the mid-1950s to the mid-1970s, bold political leadership and domination of nuclear technology resulted in a series of U.S. initiatives that were largely responsible for global acceptance of nuclear energy under the terms set by Atoms for Peace. Since the mid-1970s, however, this view has been challenged. The 1974 Indian nuclear explosion provided a demonstration that peaceful nuclear research programs can be used for military purposes, which eroded confidence in an essential premise of Atoms for Peace. India's "peaceful nuclear explosion" also revealed the proliferation danger of near-nuclear countries outside of the nonproliferation regime. Recent proliferation developments have only reinforced this point.

Another challenge to the Atoms-for-Peace vision appeared in the 1970s, in the aftermath of the Arab oil embargo, the dramatic rise in oil prices, and the expectations of rapidly expanding nuclear energy production. With widespread commerce in nuclear material, equipment, and technology, it was feared that the world would be awash in nuclear-weapon materials and the capability to produce nuclear weapons would spread quickly. Some of these concerns are rising again with the prospect of a nuclear renaissance.

Finally, one of the challenges to nuclear energy cooperation as envisaged under Atoms for Peace during this time frame originated in the reaction of the United States and other states to the perceived growing danger of proliferation. President Gerald Ford sought and obtained voluntary agreement among nuclear suppliers to exercise greater restraint in exports of sensitive facilities in the future. The adverse internal perceptions created by the Nuclear Suppliers Group were intensified by unilateral actions by the Australian, Canadian, and American governments, which placed more restrictive conditions on, and introduced tighter controls over, nuclear cooperation and trade.

All of these actions targeted on controlling exports precipitated a crisis in international nuclear commerce that threatened to undermine the pillars of the Atoms-for-Peace regime and may have inhibited further institution building under its auspices, as was suggested, for example, by the fate of the International Nuclear Fuel Cycle Evaluation and the failure of past multilateral negotiations on international plutonium storage, spent fuel management, and assurances of supply. Although these concerns abated somewhat over the last three decades, they are once again at issue, as nuclear crises in Iran and elsewhere have once again given rise to efforts to reform the regime, particularly the elements related to Article IV. Many old interests and initiatives, including both tightening exports on sensitive nuclear technology and seeking a mechanism for assurances on supply, are being revisited today and generating increasingly intense discussion.

As the debate of decades ago and today reveals, there is continuing and evident tension over the implications of Atoms-for-Peace policies, both at present and in the future, for the spread of sensitive nuclear technologies. The dual uses of nuclear energy have long been understood to pose problems, which Atoms for Peace's realization in policies of regulated but assured supply within a consensual international regime were expected reasonably and practically to resolve. These issues require reappraisal in the emerging world, which will be unlike that of the past. The developing and expected new conditions of supply, as well as the emergence of new technologies and suppliers, especially of non-state suppliers, are of particular importance in this regard.

If the value of assured nuclear supply under safeguards is recognized, the necessity of selective denial either to certain countries or of certain sensitive technologies is not. The necessity of limiting the transfer of reprocessing and enrichment equipment, facilities, and technologies is contentious. The proliferation of these technologies exacerbates the dangers of nuclear proliferation and terrorism, but restrictions on their spread involves a more restrictive construction of Article IV of the NPT that, not surprisingly, is being challenged by some states.

These concerns are real and cannot be dismissed out of hand, but they have to be balanced against increasing interest in, and expectations for, a dramatic rise in nuclear power, due to the need to ease global warning, to produce the fuel for a prospective hydrogen economy, and to meet the growing energy needs of the world, including the developing states. The need for nuclear power is increasingly recognized. For example, as part of President Bush's Advanced Energy Initiative, the Global Nuclear Energy Partnership (GNEP) seeks to enhance energy security while promoting nonproliferation by expanding the use of nuclear energy to meet growing electricity demand. The GNEP "would achieve its goal by having nations with secure, advanced nuclear capabilities provide fuel services—fresh fuel and recovery of used fuel—to other nations who agree to employ nuclear energy for power generation purposes only. The closed fuel cycle model envisioned by this partnership requires development and deployment of technologies that enable recycling and consumption of long-lived radioactive waste. The Partnership would demonstrate the critical technologies needed to change the way used nuclear fuel is managed—to build recycling technologies that enhance energy security in a safe and environmentally responsible manner, while simultaneously promoting nonproliferation."[4]

Whatever the fate of GNEP and the predicted nuclear renaissance, nuclear production of electricity is likely to be with us as an important part of the energy mix for the foreseeable future. Moreover, the nonpower uses of nuclear energy in medicine, industry, and elsewhere are increasingly important to all the peoples of the world. This reality highlights the enduring importance of the Atoms-for-Peace bargain.

The Legacy and Future of Atoms for Peace

As we reflect on nuclear realities today—on the range of civil and military nuclear uses—it is clear that fifty years after Atoms for Peace was introduced to the world's acclaim, mixed with some Cold War–era suspicion of a major U.S. initiative, it has had a decidedly mixed legacy. It has greatly

4. "The Global Nuclear Energy Partnership: Greater Energy Security in a Cleaner, Safer World" (www.gnep.energy.gov/).

contributed to nonproliferation and the peaceful development of nuclear power, but has also created structural problems in these areas that were anticipated in the 1970s but are confronting the world today as never before. The post–Cold War arms control environment may yet allow the world to implement, to some degree, the proposal's arms control aspirations. And it has to date provided a sound, albeit limited, framework for dealing with an issue it was never designed to address—terrorism using nuclear and radiological materials.

So, mixed results and all, the legacy of Atoms for Peace profoundly influences the debate on all things nuclear. It may be expected that it will be defended or attacked, as pundits, policy analysts, and politicians put forward divergent proposals for a future in which nuclear energy remains as it was understood at the dawn of the nuclear age—a Janus-headed reality posing both extraordinary risks and benefits.

Reflecting the lessons of the last half-century, these visions will not be as naive and uncritical, or as alarmist and critical, as those from the 1950s to the 1970s and 1980s. The presentations in this volume show continuity and change. They suggest that the future will bear the imprint of the past and present, but also that we have considerable power, with bold thinking and actions, to fashion a world that meets the range of basic human needs.

If we are to maintain key elements of the Atoms-for-Peace vision in the future, the states with an interest in the existing regime—particularly the United States—must recognize regime problems and manage them. Strengthening safeguards, export controls, and compliance and enforcement are critical, as is the integration of the regime into broader thinking about national and international security. If existing problems are not resolved, the future of the regime will be at risk. A second coming of nuclear energy, if there is one, will highlight and increase pressures on the regime's weak points. But this may actually build support for efforts by the United States and others in the international community to repair and strengthen the regime.

Appendix 1

Atomic Power for Peace

An Address by Dwight D. Eisenhower, President of the United States, before the General Assembly of the United Nations

December 8, 1953

Madame President, Members of the General Assembly:

When Secretary General Hammarskjold's invitation to address this General Assembly reached me in Bermuda, I was just beginning a series of conferences with the Prime Ministers and Foreign Ministers of Great Britain and of France. Our subject was some of the problems that beset our world.

During the remainder of the Bermuda Conference, I had constantly in mind that ahead of me lay a great honor. That honor is mine today as I stand here, privileged to address the General Assembly of the United Nations.

At the same time that I appreciate the distinction of addressing you, I have a sense of exhilaration as I look upon this Assembly.

Never before in history has so much hope for so many people been gathered together in a single organization. Your deliberations and decisions during these somber years have already realized part of those hopes.

But the great test and the great accomplishments still lie ahead. And in the confident expectation of those accomplishments, I would use the office which, for the time being, I hold, to assure you that the Government of the United States will remain steadfast in its support of this body. This we shall do in the conviction that you will provide a great share of the wisdom, the courage, and the faith which can bring to this world lasting peace for all nations, and happiness and well-being for all men.

Clearly, it would not be fitting for me to take this occasion to present to you a unilateral American report on Bermuda. Nevertheless, I assure you that in our deliberations on that lovely island we sought to invoke those same great concepts of universal peace and human dignity which are so clearly etched in your Charter.

Neither would it be a measure of this great opportunity merely to recite, however hopefully, pious platitudes.

I therefore decided that this occasion warranted my saying to you some of the things that have been on the minds and hearts of my legislative and executive associates and on mine for a great many months—thoughts I had originally planned to say primarily to the American people.

I know that the American people share my deep belief that if a danger exists in the world, it is a danger shared by all—and equally, that if hope exists in the mind of one nation, that hope should be shared by all.

Finally, if there is to be advanced any proposal designed to ease even by the smallest measure the tensions of today's world, what more appropriate audience could there be than the members of the General Assembly of the United Nations?

I feel impelled to speak today in a language that in a sense is new—one which I, who have spent so much of my life in the military profession, would have preferred never to use.

That new language is the language of atomic warfare.

The atomic age has moved forward at such a pace that every citizen of the world should have some comprehension, at least in comparative terms, of the extent of this development of the utmost significance to every one of us. Clearly, if the people of the world are to conduct an intelligent search for peace, they must be armed with the significant facts of today's existence.

My recital of atomic danger and power is necessarily stated in United States terms, for these are the only in controvertible facts that I know. I need hardly point out to this Assembly, however, that this subject is global, not merely national in character.

On July 16, 1945, the United States set off the world's first atomic explosion. Since that date in 1945, the United States of America has conducted 42 test explosions.

Atomic bombs today are more than 25 times as powerful as the weapons with which the atomic age dawned, while hydrogen weapons are in the ranges of millions of tons of TNT equivalent.

Today, the United States' stockpile of atomic weapons, which, of course, increases daily, exceeds by many times the explosive equivalent of the total of all bombs and all shells that came from every plane and every gun in every theatre of war in all of the years of World War II.

A single air group, whether afloat or land-based, can now deliver to any reachable target a destructive cargo exceeding in power all the bombs that fell on Britain in all of World War II.

In size and variety, the development of atomic weapons has been no less remarkable. The development has been such that atomic weapons have virtually achieved conventional status within our armed services. In the United States, the Army, the Navy, the Air Force, and the Marine Corps are all capable of putting this weapon to military use.

But the dread secret, and the fearful engines of atomic might, are not ours alone.

In the first place, the secret is possessed by our friends and allies, Great Britain and Canada, whose scientific genius made a tremendous contribution to our original discoveries, and the designs of atomic bombs.

The secret is also known by the Soviet Union.

The Soviet Union has informed us that, over recent years, it has devoted extensive resources to atomic weapons. During this period, the Soviet Union has exploded a series of atomic devices, including at least one involving thermo-nuclear reactions.

If at one time the United States possessed what might have been called a monopoly of atomic power, that monopoly ceased to exist several years ago. Therefore, although our earlier start has permitted us to accumulate what is today a great quantitative advantage, the atomic realities of today comprehend two facts of even greater significance.

First, the knowledge now possessed by several nations will eventually be shared by others—possibly all others.

Second, even a vast superiority in numbers of weapons, and a consequent capability of devastating retaliation, is no preventive, of itself, against the fearful material damage and toll of human lives that would be inflicted by surprise aggression.

The free world, at least dimly aware of these facts, has naturally embarked on a large program of warning and defense systems. That program will be accelerated and expanded.

But let no one think that the expenditure of vast sums for weapons and systems of defense can guarantee absolute safety for the cities and citizens of any nation. The awful arithmetic of the atomic bomb does not permit any such easy solution. Even against the most powerful defense, an aggressor in possession of the effective minimum number of atomic bombs for a surprise attack could probably place a sufficient number of his bombs on the chosen targets to cause hideous damage.

Should such an atomic attack be launched against the United States, our reactions would be swift and resolute. But for me to say that the defense capabilities of the United States are such that they could inflict terrible losses upon an aggressor—for me to say that the retaliation capabilities of the United States are so great that such an aggressor's land would be laid waste—all this, while fact, is not the true expression of the purpose and the hope of the United States.

To pause there would be to confirm the hopeless finality of a belief that two atomic colossi are doomed malevolently to eye each other indefinitely across a trembling world. To stop there would be to accept helplessly the probability of civilization destroyed—the annihilation of the irreplaceable heritage of mankind handed down to us generation from generation—and the condemnation of mankind to begin all over again the age-old struggle upward from savagery toward decency, and right, and justice.

Surely no sane member of the human race could discover victory in such desolation. Could anyone wish his name to be coupled by history with such human degradation and destruction[?]

Occasional pages of history do record the faces of the "Great Destroyers" but the whole book of history reveals mankind's never-ending quest for peace, and mankind's God-given capacity to build.

It is with the book of history, and not with isolated pages, that the United States will ever wish to be identified. My country wants to be constructive, not destructive. It wants agreement, not wars, among nations. It wants itself to live in freedom, and in the confidence that the people of every other nation enjoy equally the right of choosing their own way of life.

So my country's purpose is to help us move out of the dark chamber of horrors into the light, to find a way by which the minds of men, the hopes of men, the souls of men everywhere, can move forward toward peace and happiness and well being.

In this quest, I know that we must not lack patience.

I know that in a world divided, such as our today, salvation cannot be attained by one dramatic act.

I know that many steps will have to be taken over many months before the world can look at itself one day and truly realize that a new climate of mutually peaceful confidence is abroad in the world.

But I know, above all else, that we much start to take these steps—now.

The United States and its allies, Great Britain and France, have over the past months tried to take some of these steps. Let no one say that we shun the conference table.

On the record has long stood the request of the United States, Great Britain, and France to negotiate with the Soviet Union the problems of a divided Germany.

On that record has long stood the request of the same three nations to negotiate the problems of Korea.

Most recently, we have received from the Soviet Union what is in effect an expression of willingness to hold a Four Power meeting. Along with our allies, Great Britain and France, we were pleased to see that this note did not contain the unacceptable preconditions previously put forward.

As you already know from our joint Bermuda communiqué, the United States, Great Britain, and France have agreed promptly to meet with the Soviet Union.

The Government of the United States approaches this conference with hopeful sincerity. We will bend every effort of our minds to the single purpose of emerging from that conference with tangible results toward peace—the only true way of lessening international tension.

We never have, we never will, propose or suggest that the Soviet Union surrender what is rightfully theirs.

We will never say that the people of Russia are an enemy with whom we have no desire ever to deal or mingle in friendly and fruitful relationship.

On the contrary, we hope that this coming Conference may initiate a relationship with the Soviet Union which will eventually bring about a free inter mingling of the peoples of the east and of the west—the one sure, human way of developing the understanding required for confident and peaceful relations.

Instead of the discontent which is now settling upon Eastern Germany, occupied Austria, and countries of Eastern Europe, we seek a harmonious family of free European nations, with none a threat to the other, and least of all a threat to the peoples of Russia.

Beyond the turmoil and strife and misery of Asia, we seek peaceful opportunity for these peoples to develop their natural resources and to elevate their lives.

These are not idle works or shallow visions. Behind them lies a story of nations lately come to independence, not as a result of war, but through free grant or peaceful negotiation. There is a record, already written, of assistance gladly given by nations of the west to needy peoples, and to those suffering the temporary effects of famine, drought, and natural disaster.

These are deeds of peace. They speak more loudly than promises or protestations of peaceful intent.

But I do not wish to rest either upon the reiteration of past proposals or the restatement of past deeds. The gravity of the time is such that every new avenue of peace, no matter how dimly discernible, should be explored.

There is at least one new avenue of peace which has not yet been well explored—an avenue now laid out by the General Assembly of the United Nations.

In its resolution of November 18th, 1953 this General Assembly suggested—and I quote—"that the Disarmament Commission study the desirability of establishing a sub-committee consisting of representatives of the Powers principally involved, which should seek in private an acceptable solution . . . and report on such a solution to the General Assembly and to the Security Council not later than 1 September 1954."

The United States, heeding the suggestion of the General Assembly of the United Nations, is instantly prepared to meet privately with such other countries as may be "principally involved," to seek "an acceptable solution" to the atomic armaments race which over shadows not only the peace, but the very life, of the world.

We shall carry into these private or diplomatic talks a new conception.

The United States would seek more than the mere reduction or elimination of atomic materials for military purposes.

It is not enough to take this weapon out of the hands of the soldiers. It must be put into the hands of those who will know how to strip its military casing and adapt it to the arts of peace.

The United States knows that if the fearful trend of atomic military build up can be reversed, this greatest of destructive forces can be developed into a great boon, for the benefit of all mankind.

The United States knows that peaceful power from atomic energy is no dream of the future. That capability, already proved, is here—now—today. Who can doubt, if the entire body of the world's scientists and engineers had adequate amounts of fissionable material with which to test and develop their ideas, that this capability would rapidly be transformed into universal, efficient, and economic usage.

To hasten the day when fear of the atom will begin to disappear from the minds of people, and the governments of the East and West, there are certain steps that can be taken now.

I therefore make the following proposals:

The Governments principally involved, to the extent permitted by elementary prudence, to begin now and continue to make joint contributions from their stockpiles of normal uranium and fissionable materials to an international Atomic Energy Agency. We would expect that such an agency would be set up under the aegis of the United Nations.

The ratios of contributions, the procedures and other details would properly be within the scope of the "private conversations" I have referred to earlier.

The United States is prepared to undertake these explorations in good faith. Any partner of the United States acting in the same good faith will find the United States a not unreasonable or ungenerous associate.

Undoubtedly initial and early contributions to this plan would be small in quantity. However, the proposal has the great virtue that it can be undertaken without the irritations and mutual suspicions incident to any attempt to set up a completely acceptable system of world-wide inspection and control.

The Atomic Energy Agency could be made responsible for the impounding, storage, and protection of the contributed fissionable and other materials. The ingenuity of our scientists will provide special safe conditions under which such a bank of fissionable material can be made essentially immune to surprise seizure.

The more important responsibility of this Atomic Energy Agency would be to devise methods where by this fissionable material would be allocated to serve the peaceful pursuits of mankind. Experts would be mobilized to apply atomic energy to the needs of agriculture, medicine, and other peaceful activities. A special purpose would be to provide abundant electrical energy in the power-starved areas of the world. Thus the contributing powers would be dedicating some of their strength to serve the needs rather than the fears of mankind.

The United States would be more than willing—it would be proud to take up with others "principally involved": the development of plans where by such peaceful use of atomic energy would be expedited.

Of those "principally involved" the Soviet Union must, of course, be one.

I would be prepared to submit to the Congress of the United States, and with every expectation of approval, any such plan that would:

First—encourage world-wide investigation into the most effective peacetime uses of fissionable material, and with the certainty that they had all the material needed for the conduct of all experiments that were appropriate;

Second—begin to diminish the potential destructive power of the world's atomic stockpiles;

Third—allow all peoples of all nations to see that, in this enlightened age, the great powers of the earth, both of the East and of the West, are interested in human aspirations first, rather than in building up the armaments of war;

Fourth—open up a new channel for peaceful discussion, and initiate at least a new approach to the many difficult problems that must be solved in both private and public conversations, if the world is to shake off the inertia imposed by fear, and is to make positive progress toward peace.

Against the dark background of the atomic bomb, the United States does not wish merely to present strength, but also the desire and the hope for peace.

The coming months will be fraught with fateful decisions. In this Assembly; in the capitals and military headquarters of the world; in the hearts of men everywhere, be they governors, or governed, may they be decisions which will lead this work out of fear and into peace.

To the making of these fateful decisions, the United States pledges before you—and therefore before the world—its determination to help solve the fearful atomic dilemma—to devote its entire heart and mind to find the way by which the miraculous inventiveness of man shall not be dedicated to his death, but consecrated to his life.

I again thank the delegates for the great honor they have done me, in inviting me to appear before them, and in listening to me so courteously. Thank you.

Appendix 2

Statute of the International Atomic Energy Agency

The Statute was approved on 23 October 1956 by the Conference on the Statute of the International Atomic Energy Agency, which was held at the Headquarters of the United Nations. It came into force on 29 July 1957.

The Statute has been amended three times, by application of the procedure laid down in paragraphs A and C of Article XVIII. On 31 January 1963 some amendments to the first sentence of the then paragraph A.3 of Article VI came into force; the Statute as thus amended was further amended on I June 1973 by the coming into force of a number of amendments to paragraphs A to D of the same Article (involving a renumbering of sub-paragraphs in paragraph A); and on 28 December 1989 an amendment in the introductory part of paragraph A.1 came into force. All these amendments have been incorporated in the text of the Statute reproduced in this booklet, which consequently supersedes all earlier editions.

ARTICLE I: Establishment of the Agency
The Parties hereto establish an International Atomic Energy Agency (hereinafter referred to as "the Agency") upon the terms and conditions hereinafter set forth.

ARTICLE II: Objectives

The Agency shall seek to accelerate and enlarge the contribution of atomic energy to peace, health and prosperity throughout the world. It shall ensure, so far as it is able, that assistance provided by it or at its request or under its supervision or control is not used in such a way as to further any military purpose.

ARTICLE III: Functions

A. The Agency is authorized:

1. To encourage and assist research on, and development and practical application of, atomic energy for peaceful uses throughout the world; and, if requested to do so, to act as an intermediary for the purposes of securing the performance of services or the supplying of materials, equipment, or facilities by one member of the Agency for another; and to perform any operation or service useful in research on, or development or practical application of, atomic energy for peaceful purposes;

2. To make provision, in accordance with this Statute, for materials, services, equipment, and facilities to meet the needs of research on, and development and practical application of, atomic energy for peaceful purposes, including the production of electric power, with due consideration for the needs of the under-developed areas of the world;

3. To foster the exchange of scientific and technical information on peaceful uses of atomic energy;

4. To encourage the exchange of training of scientists and experts in the field of peaceful uses of atomic energy;

5. To establish and administer safeguards designed to ensure that special fissionable and other materials, services, equipment, facilities, and information made available by the Agency or at its request or under its supervision or control are not used in such a way as to further any military purpose; and to apply safeguards, at the request of the parties, to any bilateral or multilateral arrangement, or at the request of a State, to any of that State's activities in the field of atomic energy;

6. To establish or adopt, in consultation and, where appropriate, in collaboration with the competent organs of the United Nations and with the specialized agencies concerned, standards of safety for protection of health and minimization of danger to life and property (including such standards for labour conditions), and to provide for

the application of these standards to its own operation as well as to the operations making use of materials, services, equipment, facilities, and information made available by the Agency or at its request or under its control or supervision; and to provide for the application of these standards, at the request of the parties, to operations under any bilateral or multilateral arrangements, or, at the request of a State, to any of that State's activities in the field of atomic energy;

7. To acquire or establish any facilities, plant and equipment useful in carrying out its authorized functions, whenever the facilities, plant, and equipment otherwise available to it in the area concerned are inadequate or available only on terms it deems unsatisfactory.

B. In carrying out its functions, the Agency shall:

1. Conduct its activities in accordance with the purposes and principles of the United Nations to promote peace and international cooperation, and in conformity with policies of the United Nations furthering the establishment of safeguarded worldwide disarmament and in conformity with any international agreements entered into pursuant to such policies;

2. Establish control over the use of special fissionable materials received by the Agency, in order to ensure that these materials are used only for peaceful purposes;

3. Allocate its resources in such a manner as to secure efficient utilization and the greatest possible general benefit in all areas of the world, bearing in mind the special needs of the under-developed areas of the world;

4. Submit reports on its activities annually to the General Assembly of the United Nations and, when appropriate, to the Security Council: if in connection with the activities of the Agency there should arise questions that are within the competence of the Security Council, the Agency shall notify the Security Council, as the organ bearing the main responsibility for the maintenance of international peace and security, and may also take the measures open to it under this Statute, including those provided in paragraph C of Article XII;

5. Submit reports to the Economic and Social Council and other organs of the United Nations on matters within the competence of these organs.

C. In carrying out its functions, the Agency shall not make assistance to members subject to any political, economic, military, or other conditions incompatible with the provisions of this Statute.

D. Subject to the provisions of this Statute and to the terms of agreements concluded between a State or a group of States and the Agency which shall be in accordance with the provisions of the Statute, the activities of the Agency shall be carried out with due observance of the sovereign rights of States.

ARTICLE IV: Membership

A. The initial members of the Agency shall be those States Members of the United Nations or of any of the specialized agencies which shall have signed this Statute within ninety days after it is opened for signature and shall have deposited an instrument of ratification.

B. Other members of the Agency shall be those States, whether or not Members of the United Nations or of any of the specialized agencies, which deposit an instrument of acceptance of this Statute after their membership has been approved by the General Conference upon the recommendation of the Board of Governors. In recommending and approving a State for membership, the Board of Governors and the General Conference shall determine that the State is able and willing to carry out the obligations of membership in the Agency, giving due consideration to its ability and willingness to act in accordance with the purposes and principles of the Charter of the United Nations.

C. The Agency is based on the principle of the sovereign equality of all its members, and all members, in order to ensure to all of them the rights and benefits resulting from membership, shall fulfill in good faith the obligation assumed by them in accordance with this Statute.

ARTICLE V: General Conference

A. A General Conference consisting of representatives of all members shall meet in regular annual session and in such special sessions as shall be convened by the Director General at the request of the Board of Governors or of a majority of members. The sessions shall take place at the headquarters of the Agency unless otherwise determined by the General Conference.

B. At such sessions, each member shall be represented by one delegate who may be accompanied by alternates and by advisers. The cost of attendance of any delegation shall be borne by the member concerned.

C. The General Conference shall elect a President and such other officers as may be required at the beginning of each session. They shall hold office for the duration of the session. The General Conference, subject to the provisions of this Statute, shall adopt its own rules of procedure. Each member shall have one vote. Decisions pursuant to paragraph H of article

XIV, paragraph C of article XVIII and paragraph B of article XIX shall be made by a two-thirds majority of the members present and voting. Decisions on other questions, including the determination of additional questions or categories of questions to be decided by a two-thirds majority, shall be made by a majority of the members present and voting. A majority of members shall constitute a quorum.

D. The General Conference may discuss any questions or any matters within the scope of this Statute or relating to the powers and functions of any organs provided for in this Statute, and may make recommendations to the membership of the Agency or to the Board of Governors or to both on any such questions or matters.

E. The General Conference shall:

1. Elect members of the Board of Governors in accordance with article VI;
2. Approve States for membership in accordance with article IV;
3. Suspend a member from the privileges and rights of membership in accordance with article XIX;
4. Consider the annual report of the Board;
5. In accordance with article XIV, approve the budget of the Agency recommended by the Board or return it with recommendations as to its entirety or parts to the Board, for resubmission to the General Conference;
6. Approve reports to be submitted to the United Nations as required by the relationship agreement between the Agency and the United Nations, except reports referred to in paragraph C of article XII, or return them to the Board with its recommendations;
7. Approve any agreement or agreements between the Agency and the United Nations and other organizations as provided in article XVI or return such agreements with its recommendations to the Board, for resubmission to the General Conference;
8. Approve rules and limitations regarding the exercise of borrowing powers by the Board, in accordance with paragraph G of article XIV; approve rules regarding the acceptance of voluntary contributions to the Agency; and approve, in accordance with paragraph F of article XIV, the manner in which the general fund referred to in that paragraph may be used;
9. Approve amendments to this Statute in accordance with paragraph C of article XVIII;
10. Approve the appointment of the Director General in accordance with paragraph A of article VII.

F. The General Conference shall have the authority:
1. To take decisions on any matter specifically referred to the General Conference for this purpose by the Board;
2. To propose matters for consideration by the Board and request from the Board reports on any matter relating to the functions of the Agency.

ARTICLE VI: Board of Governors
A. The Board of Governors shall be composed as follows:
1. The outgoing Board of Governors shall designate for membership on the Board the ten members most advanced in the technology of atomic energy including the production of source materials, and the member most advanced in the technology of atomic energy including the production of source materials in each of the following areas in which none of the aforesaid ten is located:
North America
Latin America
Western Europe
Eastern Europe
Africa
Middle East and South Asia
South East Asia and the Pacific
Far East
2. The General Conference shall elect to membership of the Board of Governors:

a) Twenty members, with due regard to equitable representation on the Board as a whole of the members in the areas listed in subparagraph A. 1 of this article, so that the Board shall at all times include in this category five representatives of the area of Latin America, four representatives of the area of Western Europe, three representatives of the area of Eastern Europe, four representatives of the area of Africa, two representatives of the area of the Middle East and South Asia, one representative of the area of South East Asia and the Pacific, and one representative of the area of the Far East. No member in this category in any one term of office will be eligible for re-election in the same category for the following term of office; and

b) One further member from among the members in the following areas: Middle East and South Asia, South East Asia and the Pacific, Far East;

c) One further member from among the members in the following areas: Africa, Middle East and South Asia, South East Asia and the Pacific.

B. The designations provided for in sub-paragraph A-l of this article shall take place not less than sixty days before each regular annual session of the General Conference. The elections provided for in sub-paragraph A-2 of this article shall take place at regular annual sessions of the General Conference.

C. Members represented on the Board of Governors in accordance with sub-paragraph A-l of this article shall hold office from the end of the next regular annual session of the General Conference after their designation until the end of the following regular annual session of the General Conference.

D. Members represented on the Board of Governors in accordance with sub-paragraph A-2 of this article shall hold office from the end of the regular annual session of the General Conference at which they are elected until the end of the second regular annual session of the General Conference thereafter.

E. Each member of the Board of Governors shall have one vote. Decisions on the amount of the Agency's budget shall be made by a two-thirds majority of those present and voting, as provided in paragraph H of article XIV. Decisions on other questions, including the determination of additional questions or categories of questions to be decided by a two thirds majority, shall be made by a majority of those present and voting. Two-thirds of all members of the Board shall constitute a quorum.

F. The Board of Governors shall have authority to carry out the functions of the Agency in accordance with this Statute, subject to its responsibilities to the General Conference as provided in this Statute.

G. The Board of Governors shall meet at such times as it may determine. The meetings shall take place at the headquarters of the Agency unless otherwise determined by the Board.

H. The Board of Governors shall elect a Chairman and other officers from among its members and, subject to the provisions of this Statute, shall adopt its own rules of procedure.

I. The Board of Governors may establish such committees as it deems advisable. The Board may appoint persons to represent it in its relations with other organizations.

J. The Board of Governors shall prepare an annual report to the General Conference concerning the affairs of the Agency and any projects approved by the Agency. The Board shall also prepare for submission to the General

Conference such reports as the Agency is or may be required to make to the United Nations or to any other organization the work of which is related to that of the Agency. These reports, along with the annual reports, shall be submitted to members of the Agency at least one month before the regular annual session of the General Conference.

ARTICLE VII: Staff

A. The staff of the Agency shall be headed by a Director General. The Director General shall be appointed by the Board of Governors with the approval of the General Conference for a term of four years. He shall be the chief administrative officer of the Agency.

B. The Director General shall be responsible for the appointment, organization, and functioning of the staff and shall be under the authority of and subject to the control of the Board of Governors. He shall perform his duties in accordance with regulations adopted by the Board.

C. The staff shall include such qualified scientific and technical and other personnel as may be required to fulfill the objectives and functions of the Agency. The Agency shall be guided by the principle that its permanent staff shall be kept to a minimum.

D. The paramount consideration in the recruitment and employment of the staff and in the determination of the conditions of service shall be to secure employees of the highest standards of efficiency, technical competence, and integrity. Subject to this consideration, due regard shall be paid to the contributions of members to the Agency and to the importance of recruiting the staff on as wide a geographical basis as possible.

E. The terms and conditions on which the staff shall be appointed, remunerated, and dismissed shall be in accordance with regulations made by the Board of Governors, subject to the provisions of this Statute and to general rules approved by the General Conference on the recommendation of the Board.

F. In the performance of their duties, the Director General and the staff shall not seek or receive instructions from any source external to the Agency. They shall refrain from any action which might reflect on their position as officials of the Agency; subject to their responsibilities to the Agency, they shall not disclose any industrial secret or other confidential information coming to their knowledge by reason of their official duties for the Agency. Each member undertakes to respect the international character of the responsibilities of the Director General and the staff and shall not seek to influence them in the discharge of their duties.

G. In this article the term "staff" includes guards.

ARTICLE VIII: Exchange of information

A. Each member should make available such information as would, in the judgement of the member, be helpful to the Agency.

B. Each member shall make available to the Agency all scientific information developed as a result of assistance extended by the Agency pursuant to article XI.

C. The Agency shall assemble and make available in an accessible form the information made available to it under paragraphs A and B of this article. It shall take positive steps to encourage the exchange among its members of information relating to the nature and peaceful uses of atomic energy and shall serve as an intermediary among its members for this purpose.

ARTICLE IX: Supplying of materials

A. Members may make available to the Agency such quantities of special fissionable materials as they deem advisable and on such terms as shall be agreed with the Agency. The materials made available to the Agency may, at the discretion of the member making them available, be stored either by the member concerned or, with the agreement of the Agency, in the Agency's depots.

B. Members may also make available to the Agency source materials as defined in article XX and other materials. The Board of Governors shall determine the quantities of such materials which the Agency will accept under agreements provided for in article XIII.

C. Each member shall notify the Agency of the quantities, form, and composition of special fissionable materials, source materials, and other materials which that member is prepared, in conformity with its laws, to make available immediately or during a period specified by the Board of Governors.

D. On request of the Agency a member shall, from the materials which it has made available, without delay deliver to another member or group of members such quantities of such materials as the Agency may specify, and shall without delay deliver to the Agency itself such quantities of such materials as are really necessary for operations and scientific research in the facilities of the Agency.

E. The quantities, form and composition of materials made available by any member may be changed at any time by the member with the approval of the Board of Governors.

F. An initial notification in accordance with paragraph C of this article shall be made within three months of the entry into force of this Statute with respect to the member concerned. In the absence of a contrary decision of the Board of Governors, the materials initially made available shall be for the period of the calendar year succeeding the year when this Statute takes effect with respect to the member concerned. Subsequent notifications shall likewise, in the absence of a contrary action by the Board, relate to the period of the calendar year following the notification and shall be made no later than the first day of November of each year.

G. The Agency shall specify the place and method of delivery and, where appropriate, the form and composition, of materials which it has requested a member to deliver from the amounts which that member has notified the Agency it is prepared to make available. The Agency shall also verify the quantities of materials delivered and shall report those quantities periodically to the members.

H. The Agency shall be responsible for storing and protecting materials in its possession. The Agency shall ensure that these materials shall be safeguarded against:

> hazards of the weather,
> unauthorized removal or diversion,
> damage or destruction, including sabotage, and
> forcible seizure. In storing special fissionable materials in its possession, the Agency shall ensure the geographical distribution of these materials in such a way as not to allow concentration of large amounts of such materials in any one country or region of the world.

I. The Agency shall as soon as practicable establish or acquire such of the following as may be necessary:

> Plant, equipment, and facilities for the receipt, storage, and issue of materials;
> Physical safeguards;
> Adequate health and safety measures;
> Control laboratories for the analysis and verification of materials received;
> Housing and administrative facilities for any staff required for the foregoing.

J. The materials made available pursuant to this article shall be used as determined by the Board of Governors in accordance with the provisions of this Statute. No member shall have the right to require that the materials it makes available to the Agency be kept separately by the Agency or to designate the specific project in which they must be used.

ARTICLE X: Services, equipment, and facilities

Members may make available to the Agency services, equipment, and facilities which may be of assistance in fulfilling the Agency's objectives and functions.

ARTICLE XI: Agency projects

A. Any member or group of members of the Agency desiring to set up any project for research on, or development or practical application of, atomic energy for peaceful purposes may request the assistance of the Agency in securing special fissionable and other materials, services, equipment, and facilities necessary for this purpose. Any such request shall be accompanied by an explanation of the purpose and extent of the project and shall be considered by the Board of Governors.

B. Upon request, the Agency may also assist any member or group of members to make arrangements to secure necessary financing from outside sources to carry out such projects. In extending this assistance, the Agency will not be required to provide any guarantees or to assume any financial responsibility for the project.

C. The Agency may arrange for the supplying of any materials, services, equipment, and facilities necessary for the project by one or more members or may itself undertake to provide any or all of these directly, taking into consideration the wishes of the member or members making the request.

D. For the purpose of considering the request, the Agency may send into the territory of the member or group of members making the request a person or persons qualified to examine the project. For this purpose the Agency may, with the approval of the member or group of members making the request, use members of its own staff or employ suitably qualified nationals of any member.

E. Before approving a project under this article, the Board of Governors shall give due consideration to:

    1. The usefulness of the project, including its scientific and technical feasibility;

    2. The adequacy of plans, funds, and technical personnel to assure the effective execution of the project;

    3. The adequacy of proposed health and safety standards for handling and storing materials and for operating facilities;

    4. The inability of the member or group of members making the request to secure the necessary finances, materials, facilities, equipment, and services;

5. The equitable distribution of materials and other resources available to the Agency;

6. The special needs of the under-developed areas of the world; and

7. Such other matters as may be relevant.

F. Upon approving a project, the Agency shall enter into an agreement with the member or group of members submitting the project, which agreement shall:

1. Provide for allocation to the project of any required special fissionable or other materials;

2. Provide for transfer of special fissionable materials from their then place of custody, whether the materials be in the custody of the Agency or of the member making them available for use in Agency projects, to the member or group of members submitting the project, under conditions which ensure the safety of any shipment required and meet applicable health and safety standards;

3. Set forth the terms and conditions, including charges, on which any materials, services, equipment, and facilities are to be provided by the Agency itself, and, if any such materials, services, equipment, and facilities are to be provided by a member, the terms and conditions as arranged for by the member or group of members submitting the project and the supplying member;

4. Include undertakings by the member or group of members submitting the project: (a) that the assistance provided shall not be used in such a way as to further any military purpose; and (b) that the project shall be subject to the safeguards provided for in article XII, the relevant safeguards being specified in the agreement;

5. Make appropriate provision regarding the rights and interests of the Agency and the member or members concerned in any inventions or discoveries, or any patents therein, arising from the project;

6. Make appropriate provision regarding settlement of disputes;

7. Include such other provisions as may be appropriate.

G. The provisions of this article shall also apply where appropriate to a request for materials, services, facilities, or equipment in connection with an existing project.

ARTICLE XII: Agency safeguards

A. With respect to any Agency project, or other arrangement where the Agency is requested by the parties concerned to apply safeguards, the Agency shall have the following rights and responsibilities to the extent relevant to the project or arrangement:

1. To examine the design of specialized equipment and facilities, including nuclear reactors, and to approve it only from the view-point of assuring that it will not further any military purpose, that it complies with applicable health and safety standards, and that it will permit effective application of the safeguards provided for in this article;
2. To require the observance of any health and safety measures prescribed by the Agency;
3. To require the maintenance and production of operating records to assist in ensuring accountability for source and special fissionable materials used or produced in the project or arrangement;
4. To call for and receive progress reports;
5. To approve the means to be used for the chemical processing of irradiated materials solely to ensure that this chemical processing will not lend itself to diversion of materials for military purposes and will comply with applicable health and safety standards; to require that special fissionable materials recovered or produced as a by-product be used for peaceful purposes under continuing Agency safeguards for research or in reactors, existing or under construction, specified by the member or members concerned; and to require deposit with the Agency of any excess of any special fissionable materials recovered or produced as a by-product over what is needed for the above-stated uses in order to prevent stockpiling of these materials, provided that thereafter at the request of the member or members concerned special fissionable materials so deposited with the Agency shall be returned promptly to the member or members concerned for use under the same provisions as stated above.
6. To send into the territory of the recipient State or States inspectors, designated by the Agency after consultation with the State or States concerned, who shall have access at all times to all places and data and to any person who by reason of his occupation deals with materials, equipment, or facilities which are required by this Statute to be safeguarded, as necessary to account for source and special fissionable materials supplied and fissionable products and to determine whether there is compliance with the undertaking against use in furtherance of any military purpose referred to in sub-paragraph F-4 of article Xl, with the health and safety measures referred to in sub-paragraph A-2 of this article, and with any other conditions prescribed in the agreement between the Agency and the State or States concerned. Inspectors designated by the Agency shall be accompanied by representatives of the authorities of the State concerned, if

that State so requests, provided that the inspectors shall not thereby be delayed or otherwise impeded in the exercise of their functions;

7. In the event of non-compliance and failure by the recipient State or States to take requested corrective steps within a reasonable time, to suspend or terminate assistance and withdraw any materials and equipment made available by the Agency or a member in furtherance of the project.

B. The Agency shall, as necessary, establish a staff of inspectors. The Staff of inspectors shall have the responsibility of examining all operations conducted by the Agency itself to determine whether the Agency is complying with the health and safety measures prescribed by it for application to projects subject to its approval, supervision or control, and whether the Agency is taking adequate measures to prevent the source and special fissionable materials in its custody or used or produced in its own operations from being used in furtherance of any military purpose. The Agency shall take remedial action forthwith to correct any non-compliance or failure to take adequate measures.

C. The staff of inspectors shall also have the responsibility of obtaining and verifying the accounting referred to in sub paragraph A-6 of this article and of determining whether there is compliance with the undertaking referred to in sub paragraph F-4 of article XI, with the measures referred to in sub-paragraph A-2 of this article, and with all other conditions of the project prescribed in the agreement between the Agency and the State or States concerned. The inspectors shall report any non-compliance to the Director General who shall thereupon transmit the report to the Board of Governors. The Board shall call upon the recipient State or States to remedy forthwith any non-compliance which it finds to have occurred. The Board shall report the non-compliance to all members and to the Security Council and General Assembly of the United Nations. In the event of failure of the recipient State or States to take fully corrective action within a reasonable time, the Board may take one or both of the following measures: direct curtailment or suspension of assistance being provided by the Agency or by a member, and call for the return of materials and equipment made available to the recipient member or group of members. The Agency may also, in accordance with article XIX, suspend any non-complying member from the exercise of the privileges and rights of membership.

ARTICLE XIII: Reimbursement of members

Unless otherwise agreed upon between the Board of Governors and the member furnishing to the Agency materials, services, equipment, or facilities, the Board shall enter into an agreement with such member providing for reimbursement for the items furnished.

ARTICLE XIV: Finance

A. The Board of Governors shall submit to the General Conference the annual budget estimates for the expenses of the Agency. To facilitate the work of the Board in this regard, the Director General shall initially prepare the budget estimates. If the General Conference does not approve the estimates, it shall return them together with its recommendations to the Board. The Board shall then submit further estimates to the General Conference for its approval.

B. Expenditures of the Agency shall be classified under the following categories:

   1. Administrative expenses: these shall include:

      a) Costs of the staff of the Agency other than the staff employed in connection with materials, services, equipment, and facilities referred to in sub paragraph B-2 below; costs of meetings; and expenditures required for the preparation of Agency projects and for the distribution of information;

      b) Costs of implementing the safeguards referred to in article XII in relation to Agency projects or, under sub-paragraph A-5 of article III, in relation to any bilateral or multilateral arrangement, together with the costs of handling and storage of special fissionable material by the Agency other than the storage and handling charges referred to in paragraph E below;

   2. Expenses, other than those included in sub-paragraph 1 of this paragraph, in connection with any materials, facilities, plant, and equipment acquired or established by the Agency in carrying out its authorized functions, and the costs of materials, services, equipment, and facilities provided by it under agreements with one or more members.

C. In fixing the expenditures under sub-paragraph B-l (b) above, the Board of Governors shall deduct such amounts as are recoverable under agreements regarding the application of safeguards between the Agency and parties to bilateral or multilateral arrangements.

D. The Board of Governors shall apportion the expenses referred to in sub-paragraph B-1 above, among members in accordance with a scale to be fixed by the General Conference. In fixing the scale the General Conference shall be guided by the principles adopted by the United Nations in assessing contributions of Member States to the regular budget of the United Nations.

E. The Board of Governors shall establish periodically a scale of charges, including reasonable uniform storage and handling charges, for materials, services, equipment, and facilities furnished to members by the Agency. The scale shall be designed to produce revenues for the Agency adequate to meet the expenses and costs referred to in sub paragraph B-2 above, less any voluntary contributions which the Board of Governors may, in accordance with paragraph F, apply for this purpose. The proceeds of such charges shall be placed in a separate fund which shall be used to pay members for any materials, services, equipment, or facilities furnished by them and to meet other expenses referred to in sub-paragraph B-2 above which may be incurred by the Agency itself.

F. Any excess of revenues referred to in paragraph E over the expenses and costs there referred to, and any voluntary contributions to the Agency, shall be placed in a general fund which may be used as the Board of Governors, with the approval of the General Conference, may determine.

G. Subject to rules and limitations approved by the General Conference, the Board of Governors shall have the authority to exercise borrowing powers on behalf of the Agency without, however, imposing on members of the Agency any liability in respect of loans entered into pursuant to this authority, and to accept voluntary contributions made to the Agency.

H. Decisions of the General Conference on financial questions and of the Board of Governors on the amount of the Agency's budget shall require a two-thirds majority of those present and voting.

ARTICLE XV: Privileges and immunities

A. The Agency shall enjoy in the territory of each member such legal capacity and such privileges and immunities as are necessary for the exercise of its functions.

B. Delegates of members together with their alternates and advisers, Governors appointed to the Board together with their alternates and advisers, and the Director General and the staff of the Agency, shall enjoy such privileges and immunities as are necessary in the independent exercise of their functions in connection with the Agency.

C. The legal capacity, privileges, and immunities referred to in this article shall be defined in a separate agreement or agreements between the Agency, represented for this purpose by the Director General acting under instructions of the Board of Governors and the members.

ARTICLE XVI: Relationship with other organizations

A. The Board of Governors, with the approval of the General Conference, is authorized to enter into an agreement or agreements establishing an appropriate relationship between the Agency and the United Nations and any other organizations the work of which is related to that of the Agency.

B. The agreement or agreements establishing the relationship of the Agency and the United Nations shall provide for:

1. Submission by the Agency of reports as provided for in sub-paragraphs B-4 and B-5 of article III;
2. Consideration by the Agency of resolutions relating to it adopted by the General Assembly or any of the Councils of the United Nations and the submission of reports, when requested, to the appropriate organ of the United Nations on the action taken by the Agency or by its members in accordance with this Statute as a result of such consideration.

ARTICLE XVII: Settlement of disputes

A. Any question or dispute concerning the interpretation or application of this Statute which is not settled by negotiation shall be referred to the International Court of Justice in conformity with the Statute of the Court, unless the parties concerned agree on another mode of settlement.

B. The General Conference and the Board of Governors are separately empowered, subject to authorization from the General Assembly of the United Nations, to request the International Court of Justice to give an advisory opinion on any legal question arising within the scope of the Agency's activities.

ARTICLE XVIII: Amendments and withdrawals

A. Amendments to this Statute may be proposed by any member. Certified copies of the text of any amendment proposed shall be prepared by the Director General and communicated by him to all members at least ninety days in advance of its consideration by the General Conference.

B. At the fifth annual session of the General Conference following the coming into force of this Statute, the question of a general review of the provisions of this Statute shall be placed on the agenda of that session. On approval by a majority of the members present and voting, the review will take place at the following General Conference. Thereafter, proposals on the question of a general review of this Statute may be submitted for decision by the General Conference under the same procedure.

C. Amendments shall come into force for all members when:

1. Approved by the General Conference by a two-thirds majority of those present and voting after consideration of observations submitted by the Board of Governors on each proposed amendment, and

2. Accepted by two-thirds of all the members in accordance with their respective constitutional processes. Acceptance by a member shall be effected by the deposit of an instrument of acceptance with the depositary Government referred to in paragraph C of article XXI.

D. At any time after five years from the date when this Statute shall take effect in accordance with paragraph E of article XXI or whenever a member is unwilling to accept an amendment to this Statute, it may withdraw from the Agency by notice in writing to that effect given to the depositary Government referred to in paragraph C of article XXI, which shall promptly inform the Board of Governors and all members.

E. Withdrawal by a member from the Agency shall not affect its contractual obligations entered into pursuant to article XI or its budgetary obligations for the year in which it withdraws.

ARTICLE XIX: Suspension of privileges

A. A member of the Agency which is in arrears in the payment of its financial contributions to the Agency shall have no vote in the Agency if the amount of its arrears equals or exceeds the amount of the contributions due from it for the preceding two years. The General Conference may, nevertheless, permit such a member to vote if it is satisfied that the failure to pay is due to conditions beyond the control of the member.

B. A member which has persistently violated the provisions of this Statute or of any agreement entered into by it pursuant to this Statute may be suspended from the exercise of the privileges and rights of membership by the General Conference acting by a two-thirds majority of the members present and voting upon recommendation by the Board of Governors.

ARTICLE XX: Definitions

As used in this Statute:

1. The term "special fissionable material" means plutonium-239; uranium-233; uranium enriched in the isotopes 235 or 233; any material containing one or more of the foregoing; and such other fissionable material as the Board of Governors shall from time to time deter mine; but the term "special fissionable material" does not include source material.

2. The term "uranium enriched in the isotopes 235 or 233" means uranium containing the isotopes 235 or 233 or both in an amount such that the abundance ratio of the sum of these isotopes to the isotope 238 is greater than the ratio of the isotope 235 to the isotope 238 occurring in nature.

3. The term "source material" means uranium containing the mixture of isotopes occurring in nature; uranium depleted in the isotope 235; thorium; any of the foregoing in the form of metal, alloy, chemical compound, or concentrate; any other material containing one or more of the foregoing in such concentration as the Board of Governors shall from time to time determine; and such other material as the Board of Governors shall from time to time determine.

ARTICLE XXI: Signature, acceptance, and entry into force

A. This Statute shall be open for signature on 26 October 1956 by all States Members of the United Nations or of any of the specialized agencies and shall remain open for signature by those States for a period of ninety days.

B. The signatory States shall become parties to this Statute by deposit of an instrument of ratification.

C. Instruments of ratification by signatory States and instruments of acceptance by States whose membership has been approved under paragraph B of article IV of this Statute shall be deposited with the Government of the United States of America, hereby designated as depositary Government.

D. Ratification or acceptance of this Statute shall be effected by States in accordance with their respective constitutional processes.

E. This Statute, apart from the Annex, shall come into force when eighteen States have deposited instruments of ratification in accordance with paragraph B of this article, provided that such eighteen States shall include at least three of the following States: Canada, France, the Union of Soviet Socialist Republics, the United Kingdom of Great Britain and Northern Ireland, and the United States of America. Instruments of ratification and instruments of acceptance deposited thereafter shall take effect on the date of their receipt.

F. The depositary Government shall promptly inform all States signatory to this Statute of the date of each deposit of ratification and the date of entry into force of the Statute. The depositary Government shall promptly inform all signatories and members of the dates on which States subsequently become parties thereto.

G. The Annex to this Statute shall come into force on the first day this Statute is open for signature.

ARTICLE XXII: Registration with the United Nations

A. This Statute shall be registered by the depositary Government pursuant to Article 102 of the Charter of the United Nations.

B. Agreements between the Agency and any member or members, agreements between the Agency and any other organization or organizations, and agreements between members subject to approval of the Agency, shall be registered with the Agency. Such agreements shall be registered by the Agency with the United Nations if registration is required under Article 102 of the Charter of the United Nations.

ARTICLE XXIII: Authentic texts and certified copies
This Statute, done in the Chinese, English, French, Russian and Spanish languages, each being equally authentic, shall be deposited in the archives of the depositary Government. Duly certified copies of this Statute shall be transmitted by the depositary Government to the Governments of the other signatory States and to the Governments of States admitted to membership under paragraph B of article IV.

In witness whereof the undersigned, duly authorized, have signed this Statute.

DONE at the Headquarters of the United Nations, this twenty-sixth day of October, one thousand nine hundred and fifty-six.

ANNEX: PREPARATORY COMMISSION

A. A Preparatory Commission shall come into existence on the first day this Statute is open for signature. It shall be composed of one representative each of Australia, Belgium, Brazil, Canada, Czechoslovakia, France, India, Portugal, Union of South Africa, Union of Soviet Socialist Republics, United Kingdom of Great Britain and Northern Ireland, and United States of America, and one representative each of six other States to be chosen by the International Conference on the Statute of the International Atomic Energy Agency. The Preparatory Commission shall remain in existence until this Statute comes into force and thereafter until the General Conference has convened and a Board of Governors has been selected in accordance with article VI.

B. The expenses of the Preparatory Commission may be met by a loan provided by the United Nations and for this purpose the Preparatory Commission shall make the necessary arrangements with the appropriate authorities of the United Nations, including arrangements for repayment of the loan by the Agency. Should these—funds be insufficient, the Preparatory Commission may accept advances from Governments. Such advances may be set off against the contributions of the Governments concerned to the Agency.

C. The Preparatory Commission shall:

1. Elect its own officers, adopt its own rules of procedure, meet as often as necessary, determine its own place of meeting and establish such committees as it deems necessary;

2. Appoint an executive secretary and staff as shall be necessary, who shall exercise such powers and perform such duties as the Commission may determine;

3. Make arrangements for the first session of the General Conference, including the preparation of a provisional agenda and draft rules of procedure, such session to be held as soon as possible after the entry into force of this Statute;

4. Make designations for membership on the first Board of Governors in accordance with sub-paragraphs A-1 and A-2 and paragraph B of article VI;

5. Make studies, reports, and recommendations for the first session of the General Conference and for the first meeting of the Board of Governors on subjects of concern to the Agency requiring immediate attention, including (a) the financing of the Agency; (b) the programmes and budget for the first year of the Agency; (c) technical problems relevant to advance planning of Agency operations; (d) the establishment of a permanent Agency staff; and (e) the location of the permanent headquarters of the Agency;

6. Make recommendations for the first meeting of the Board of Governors concerning the provisions of a headquarters agreement defining the status of the Agency and the rights and obligations which will exist in the relationship between the Agency and the host Government;

7. (a) Enter into negotiations with the United Nations with a view to the preparation of a draft agreement in accordance with article XVI of this Statute, such draft agreement to be submitted to the first session of the General Conference and to the first meeting of the Board of Governors; and

7. (b) make recommendations to the first session of the Conference and to the first meeting of the Board of Governors concerning the relationship of the Agency to other international organizations as contemplated in article XVI of this Statute.

Appendix 3

Treaty on the Non-Proliferation of Nuclear Weapons

The States concluding this Treaty, hereinafter referred to as the "Parties to the Treaty,"

Considering the devastation that would be visited upon all mankind by a nuclear war and the consequent need to make every effort to avert the danger of such a war and to take measures to safeguard the security of peoples,

Believing that the proliferation of nuclear weapons would seriously enhance the danger of nuclear war,

In conformity with resolutions of the United Nations General Assembly calling for the conclusion of an agreement on the prevention of wider dissemination of nuclear weapons,

Undertaking to cooperate in facilitating the application of International Atomic Energy Agency safeguards on peaceful nuclear activities,

Expressing their support for research, development and other efforts to further the application, within the framework of the International Atomic Energy Agency safeguards system, of the principle of safeguarding effectively the flow of source and special fissionable materials by use of instruments and other techniques at certain strategic points,

Affirming the principle that the benefits of peaceful applications of nuclear technology, including any technological by-products which may be derived by nuclear-weapon States from the development of nuclear explosive devices, should be available for peaceful purposes to all Parties of the Treaty, whether nuclear-weapon or non–nuclear-weapon States,

Convinced that, in furtherance of this principle, all Parties to the Treaty are entitled to participate in the fullest possible exchange of scientific information for, and to contribute alone or in cooperation with other States to, the further development of the applications of atomic energy for peaceful purposes,

Declaring their intention to achieve at the earliest possible date the cessation of the nuclear arms race and to undertake effective measures in the direction of nuclear disarmament,

Urging the cooperation of all States in the attainment of this objective,

Recalling the determination expressed by the Parties to the 1963 Treaty banning nuclear weapon tests in the atmosphere, in outer space and under water in its Preamble to seek to achieve the discontinuance of all test explosions of nuclear weapons for all time and to continue negotiations to this end,

Desiring to further the easing of international tension and the strengthening of trust between States in order to facilitate the cessation of the manufacture of nuclear weapons, the liquidation of all their existing stockpiles, and the elimination from national arsenals of nuclear weapons and the means of their delivery pursuant to a Treaty on general and complete disarmament under strict and effective international control,

Recalling that, in accordance with the Charter of the United Nations, States must refrain in their international relations from the threat or use of force against the territorial integrity or political independence of any State, or in any other manner inconsistent with the Purposes of the United Nations, and that the establishment and maintenance of international peace and security are to be promoted with the least diversion for armaments of the worlds human and economic resources,

Have agreed as follows:

Article I

Each nuclear-weapon State Party to the Treaty undertakes not to transfer to any recipient whatsoever nuclear weapons or other nuclear explosive devices or control over such weapons or explosive devices directly, or indirectly; and not in any way to assist, encourage, or induce any non–nuclear-weapon State to manufacture or otherwise acquire nuclear weapons or other nuclear explosive devices, or control over such weapons or explosive devices.

Article II

Each non–nuclear-weapon State Party to the Treaty undertakes not to receive the transfer from any transferor whatsoever of nuclear weapons or other nuclear explosive devices or of control over such weapons or explosive devices directly, or indirectly; not to manufacture or otherwise acquire nuclear weapons or other nuclear explosive devices; and not to seek or receive any assistance in the manufacture of nuclear weapons or other nuclear explosive devices.

Article III

Each non–nuclear-weapon State Party to the Treaty undertakes to accept safeguards, as set forth in an agreement to be negotiated and concluded with the International Atomic Energy Agency in accordance with the Statute of the International Atomic Energy Agency and the Agency's safeguards system, for the exclusive purpose of verification of the fulfillment of its obligations assumed under this Treaty with a view to preventing diversion of nuclear energy from peaceful uses to nuclear weapons or other nuclear explosive devices. Procedures for the safeguards required by this article shall be followed with respect to source or special fissionable material whether it is being produced, processed or used in any principal nuclear facility or is outside any such facility. The safeguards required by this article shall be applied to all source or special fissionable material in all peaceful nuclear activities within the territory of such State, under its jurisdiction, or carried out under its control anywhere.

Each State Party to the Treaty undertakes not to provide: (a) source or special fissionable material, or (b) equipment or material especially designed or prepared for the processing, use or production of special fissionable material, to any non–nuclear-weapon State for peaceful purposes, unless the source or special fissionable material shall be subject to the safeguards required by this article.

The safeguards required by this article shall be implemented in a manner designed to comply with article IV of this Treaty, and to avoid hampering the economic or technological development of the Parties or international cooperation in the field of peaceful nuclear activities, including the international exchange of nuclear material and equipment for the processing, use or production of nuclear material for peaceful purposes in accordance with the provisions of this article and the principle of safeguarding set forth in the Preamble of the Treaty.

Non–nuclear-weapon States Party to the Treaty shall conclude agreements with the International Atomic Energy Agency to meet the requirements of this article either individually or together with other States in accordance with the Statute of the International Atomic Energy Agency. Negotiation of such agreements shall commence within 180 days from the original entry into force of this Treaty. For States depositing their instruments of ratification or accession after the 180-day period, negotiation of such agreements shall commence not later than the date of such deposit. Such agreements shall enter into force not later than eighteen months after the date of initiation of negotiations.

Article IV

Nothing in this Treaty shall be interpreted as affecting the inalienable right of all the Parties to the Treaty to develop research, production and use of nuclear energy for peaceful purposes without discrimination and in conformity with articles I and II of this Treaty.

All the Parties to the Treaty undertake to facilitate, and have the right to participate in, the fullest possible exchange of equipment, materials and scientific and technological information for the peaceful uses of nuclear energy. Parties to the Treaty in a position to do so shall also cooperate in contributing alone or together with other States or international organizations to the further development of the applications of nuclear energy for peaceful purposes, especially in the territories of non–nuclear-weapon States Party to the Treaty, with due consideration for the needs of the developing areas of the world.

Article V

Each party to the Treaty undertakes to take appropriate measures to ensure that, in accordance with this Treaty, under appropriate international observation and through appropriate international procedures, potential benefits from any peaceful applications of nuclear explosions will be made available to non–nuclear-weapon States Party to the Treaty on a nondiscriminatory basis and that the charge to such Parties for the explosive devices used will be as low as possible and exclude any charge for research and development. Non–nuclear-weapon States Party to the Treaty shall be able to obtain such benefits, pursuant to a special international agreement or agreements, through an appropriate international body with adequate representation of non–nuclear-weapon States. Negotiations on this subject shall commence as soon as possible after the Treaty enters into force. Non–nuclear-weapon States Party to the Treaty so desiring may also obtain such benefits pursuant to bilateral agreements.

Article VI

Each of the Parties to the Treaty undertakes to pursue negotiations in good faith on effective measures relating to cessation of the nuclear arms race at an early date and to nuclear disarmament, and on a Treaty on general and complete disarmament under strict and effective international control.

Article VII

Nothing in this Treaty affects the right of any group of States to conclude regional treaties in order to assure the total absence of nuclear weapons in their respective territories.

Article VIII

Any Party to the Treaty may propose amendments to this Treaty. The text of any proposed amendment shall be submitted to the Depositary Governments which shall circulate it to all Parties to the Treaty. Thereupon, if requested to do so by one-third or more of the Parties to the Treaty, the Depositary Governments shall convene a conference, to which they shall invite all the Parties to the Treaty, to consider such an amendment.

Any amendment to this Treaty must be approved by a majority of the votes of all the Parties to the Treaty, including the votes of all nuclear-weapon States Party to the Treaty and all other Parties which, on the date the amendment is circulated, are members of the Board of Governors of the International Atomic Energy Agency. The amendment shall enter into force for each Party that deposits its instrument of ratification of the amendment upon the deposit of such instruments of ratification by a majority of all the Parties, including the instruments of ratification of all nuclear-weapon States Party to the Treaty and all other Parties which, on the date the amendment is circulated, are members of the Board of Governors of the International Atomic Energy Agency. Thereafter, it shall enter into force for any other Party upon the deposit of its instrument of ratification of the amendment.

Five years after the entry into force of this Treaty, a conference of Parties to the Treaty shall be held in Geneva, Switzerland, in order to review the operation of this Treaty with a view to assuring that the purposes of the Preamble and the provisions of the Treaty are being realized. At intervals of five years thereafter, a majority of the Parties to the Treaty may obtain, by submitting a proposal to this effect to the Depositary Governments, the convening of further conferences with the same objective of reviewing the operation of the Treaty.

Article IX

This Treaty shall be open to all States for signature. Any State which does not sign the Treaty before its entry into force in accordance with paragraph 3 of this article may accede to it at any time.

This Treaty shall be subject to ratification by signatory States. Instruments of ratification and instruments of accession shall be deposited with the Governments of the United States of America, the United Kingdom of Great Britain and Northern Ireland and the Union of Soviet Socialist Republics, which are hereby designated the Depositary Governments.

This Treaty shall enter into force after its ratification by the States, the Governments of which are designated Depositaries of the Treaty, and forty other States signatory to this Treaty and the deposit of their instruments of ratification. For the purposes of this Treaty, a nuclear-weapon State is one which has manufactured and exploded a nuclear weapon or other nuclear explosive device prior to January 1, 1967.

For States whose instruments of ratification or accession are deposited subsequent to the entry into force of this Treaty, it shall enter into force on the date of the deposit of their instruments of ratification or accession.

The Depositary Governments shall promptly inform all signatory and acceding States of the date of each signature, the date of deposit of each instrument of ratification or of accession, the date of the entry into force of this Treaty, and the date of receipt of any requests for convening a conference or other notices.

This Treaty shall be registered by the Depositary Governments pursuant to article 102 of the Charter of the United Nations.

Article X

Each Party shall in exercising its national sovereignty have the right to withdraw from the Treaty if it decides that extraordinary events, related to the subject matter of this Treaty, have jeopardized the supreme interests of its country. It shall give notice of such withdrawal to all other Parties to the Treaty and to the United Nations Security Council three months in advance. Such notice shall include a statement of the extraordinary events it regards as having jeopardized its supreme interests.

Twenty-five years after the entry into force of the Treaty, a conference shall be convened to decide whether the Treaty shall continue in force indefinitely, or shall be extended for an additional fixed period or periods. This decision shall be taken by a majority of the Parties to the Treaty.

Article XI

This Treaty, the English, Russian, French, Spanish and Chinese texts of which are equally authentic, shall be deposited in the archives of the Depositary Governments. Duly certified copies of this Treaty shall be transmitted by the Depositary Governments to the Governments of the signatory and acceding States.

IN WITNESS WHEREOF the undersigned, duly authorized, have signed this Treaty.

DONE in triplicate, at the cities of Washington, London and Moscow, this first day of July one thousand nine hundred sixty-eight.

Signed at Washington, London, and Moscow July 1, 1968
Ratification advised by U.S. Senate March 13, 1969
Ratified by U.S. President November 24, 1969
U.S. ratification deposited at Washington, London, and Moscow March 5, 1970
Proclaimed by U.S. President March 5, 1970
Entered into force March 5, 1970

Appendix 4

Proliferation Security Initiative: Statement of Interdiction Principles

The Proliferation Security Initiative (PSI) is a response to the growing challenge posed by the proliferation of weapons of mass destruction (WMD), their delivery systems, and related materials worldwide. The PSI builds on efforts by the international community to prevent proliferation of such items, including existing treaties and regimes. It is consistent with and a step in the implementation of the UN Security Council Presidential Statement of January 1992, which states that the proliferation of all WMD constitutes a threat to international peace and security, and underlines the need for member states of the UN to prevent proliferation. The PSI is also consistent with recent statements of the G8 and the European Union, establishing that more coherent and concerted efforts are needed to prevent the proliferation of WMD, their delivery systems, and related materials. PSI participants are deeply concerned about this threat and of the danger that these items could fall into the hands of terrorists, and are committed to working together to stop the flow of these items to and from states and non-state actors of proliferation concern.

The PSI seeks to involve in some capacity all states that have a stake in nonproliferation and the ability and willingness to take steps to stop the flow of such items at sea, in the air, or on land. The PSI also seeks cooperation from any state whose vessels, flags, ports, territorial waters, airspace, or land might be used for proliferation purposes by states and non-state actors of proliferation concern. The increasingly aggressive efforts by proliferators to stand outside or to circumvent existing nonproliferation norms, and to profit from such trade, require new and stronger actions by the international community. We look forward to working with all concerned states on measures they are able and willing to take in support of the PSI, as outlined in the following set of "Interdiction Principles."

Interdiction Principles for the Proliferation Security Initiative

PSI participants are committed to the following interdiction principles to establish a more coordinated and effective basis through which to impede and stop shipments of WMD, delivery systems, and related materials flowing to and from states and non-state actors of proliferation concern, consistent with national legal authorities and relevant international law and frameworks, including the UN Security Council. They call on all states concerned with this threat to international peace and security to join in similarly committing to:

1. Undertake effective measures, either alone or in concert with other states, for interdicting the transfer or transport of WMD, their delivery systems, and related materials to and from states and non-state actors of proliferation concern. "States or non-state actors of proliferation concern" generally refers to those countries or entities that the PSI participants involved establish should be subject to interdiction activities because they are engaged in proliferation through: (1) efforts to develop or acquire chemical, biological, or nuclear weapons and associated delivery systems; or (2) transfers (either selling, receiving, or facilitating) of WMD, their delivery systems, or related materials.

2. Adopt streamlined procedures for rapid exchange of relevant information concerning suspected proliferation activity, protecting the confidential character of classified information provided by other states as part of this initiative, dedicate appropriate resources and efforts to interdiction

operations and capabilities, and maximize coordination among participants in interdiction efforts.

3. Review and work to strengthen their relevant national legal authorities where necessary to accomplish these objectives, and work to strengthen when necessary relevant international law and frameworks in appropriate ways to support these commitments.

4. Take specific actions in support of interdiction efforts regarding cargoes of WMD, their delivery systems, or related materials, to the extent their national legal authorities permit and consistent with their obligations under international law and frameworks, to include:

a) Not to transport or assist in the transport of any such cargoes to or from states or non-state actors of proliferation concern, and not to allow any persons subject to their jurisdiction to do so.

b) At their own initiative, or at the request and good cause shown by another state, to take action to board and search any vessel flying their flag in their internal waters or territorial seas, or areas beyond the territorial seas of any other state, that is reasonably suspected of transporting such cargoes to or from states or non-state actors of proliferation concern, and to seize such cargoes that are identified.

c) To seriously consider providing consent under the appropriate circumstances to the boarding and searching of its own flag vessels by other states, and to the seizure of such WMD-related cargoes in such vessels that may be identified by such states.

d) To take appropriate actions to (1) stop and/or search in their internal waters, territorial seas, or contiguous zones (when declared) vessels that are reasonably suspected of carrying such cargoes to or from states or non-state actors of proliferation concern and to seize such cargoes that are identified; and (2) to enforce conditions on vessels entering or leaving their ports, internal waters or territorial seas that are reasonably suspected of carrying such cargoes, such as requiring that such vessels be subject to boarding, search, and seizure of such cargoes prior to entry.

e) At their own initiative or upon the request and good cause shown by another state, to (a) require aircraft that are reasonably suspected of carrying such cargoes to or from states or non-state actors of proliferation concern and that are transiting their airspace to land for inspection and seize any such cargoes that are identified; and/or (b) deny aircraft reasonably suspected of carrying such cargoes transit rights through their airspace in advance of such flights.

f) If their ports, airfields, or other facilities are used as transshipment points for shipment of such cargoes to or from states or non-state actors of proliferation concern, to inspect vessels, aircraft, or other modes of transport reasonably suspected of carrying such cargoes, and to seize such cargoes that are identified.

Appendix 5

Towards a Safer World
Mohamed ElBaradei

The shortcomings of the present nuclear nonproliferation regime are becoming evident. Mohamed ElBaradei offers his views on how it could be improved. This article was published in The Economist, *October 18, 2003, and is reproduced here with permission.*

The very existence of nuclear weapons gives rise to the pursuit of them. They are seen as a source of global influence, and are valued for their perceived deterrent effect. And as long as some countries possess them (or are protected by them in alliances) and others do not, this asymmetry breeds chronic global insecurity.

The present nuclear-arms–control regime is looking battered. But any reform of that regime must begin by conceiving a framework of collective security that does not rely on nuclear deterrence. The rise of terrorist groups makes this essential. A nuclear deterrent is clearly ineffective against such groups; they have no cities that can be bombed in reply, nor are they focused on self-preservation. Moreover, their constantly shifting targets and modes of attack demand a more co-operative and flexible international response. The "war on terror" should provide an impetus to work towards a global security culture that will serve the interests of all countries equally, and will make reliance on nuclear weapons obsolete.

Revisiting the NPT regime

In hindsight, a number of the premises of the 1970 Treaty on the Non-Proliferation of Nuclear Weapons (NPT) seem less than optimal. In a nod to "the early bird gets the nuke," it temporarily legitimised the arsenals of the five countries that had already developed nuclear weapons. It forbade other signatories to develop such weapons, but included no strategy for persuading countries that refused to sign—a loophole which India, Pakistan and, presumably, Israel have used, raising the number of nuclear-armed states to at least eight. And it relied on the promise of the signatories to use nuclear materials for peaceful purposes only. They could use them for health care, agriculture or energy production, but could not divert them to non-peaceful purposes. In fact, however, they have been able to operate very close to a nuclear-weapons capability.

In the climate of the mid-to-late-1960s in which the NPT negotiations took place, this bargain was the best that could be achieved. But the asymmetry it endorsed was never intended to be permanent. The nuclear-weapon states agreed to move towards full disarmament—a commitment renewed "unequivocally" by all five states as recently as 2000—although without a timetable. Some progress on disarmament was made in the late 1980s and early 1990s, but it had nearly ground to a halt by the end of the century, with nearly 30,000 warheads still in existence. The Comprehensive Nuclear Test-Ban Treaty, sought for over four decades as the jewel in the crown of the arms-control regime, was finally concluded in 1996; but seven years after being opened for signature, it still languishes unimplemented. The recent "Moscow Treaty" between the Russian Federation and the United States is encouraging; however, it is not permanent, and it does not address non-operational warheads. And despite volumes of rhetoric on the topic, no progress has been made on persuading India, Israel and Pakistan to abandon their nuclear-weapons programmes.

Similarly, on the non-proliferation front, many countries that have signed the NPT have never brought into force the required safeguards agreement with the International Atomic Energy Agency (IAEA). Fewer than 20% have finalised an additional protocol—endorsed in 1997 after the discovery of Iraq's clandestine nuclear programme—which gives the IAEA the authority to inspect countries more broadly, particularly for undeclared nuclear material and activities.

This sluggish performance on all fronts signals the need for a different approach. Reluctance by one party to fulfil its obligations breeds reluctance in others. Each discovery of a clandestine programme makes us question whether more exist. While I in no way wish to undercut the importance of states' adherence to their NPT obligations, I believe it is time to begin designing a framework more suited to the threats and realities of the 21st century.

In too many hands

Countries with nuclear industries have set up elaborate accounting and protection measures to ensure strong national oversight of their nuclear material. The IAEA inspects regularly to verify the accuracy of what countries report. Export controls restrict the transfer of sensitive technologies that could be misused for nuclear-weapons production.

But controlling access to nuclear-weapons technology has grown increasingly difficult. The technical barriers to designing weapons and to mastering the processing steps have eroded with time. Much of the hardware in question is "dual-use"; for example, it is hard to justify restrictions on exporting "hot cell" technology that could be used for plutonium separation when the same equipment is vital for producing radioisotopes used in modern medicine. Changes in political fortunes or economic downturns have at times found nuclear scientists without jobs and reportedly willing to offer their knowledge and services elsewhere. And with the passage of time, the sheer diversity of technology has made it harder to control both procurement and sales. In pre-1992 Iraq, for example, scientists were simultaneously pursuing no fewer than six different technologies to enrich uranium for eventual weapons use, shopping for essential equipment and specialised materials in more than ten countries.

Uranium enrichment is sophisticated and expensive, but it is not proscribed under the NPT. Most designs for civilian nuclear-power reactors require fuel that has been "low-enriched," and many research reactors operate with "high-enriched" uranium. It is not uncommon, therefore, for non-nuclear-weapon states with developed nuclear infrastructures to seek enrichment capabilities and to possess sizeable amounts of uranium that could, if desired, be enriched to weapons-grade.

While high-enriched uranium is easier to use in nuclear weapons, most advanced nuclear arsenals favour plutonium, which can be tailored for use in smaller, lighter weapons more suited for missile warheads. Plutonium is a by-product of nuclear-reactor operation, and separation technology ("reprocessing"), also not proscribed under the NPT, can be applied to extract the plutonium from spent fuel for re-use in electricity production.

Under the current regime, therefore, there is nothing illicit in a non-nuclear-weapon state having enrichment or reprocessing technology, or possessing weapon-grade nuclear material. And certain types of bomb-making expertise, unfortunately, are readily available in the open literature. Should a state with a fully developed fuel-cycle capability decide, for whatever reason, to break away from its non-proliferation commitments, most experts believe it could produce a nuclear weapon within a matter of months.

In 1970, it was assumed that relatively few countries knew how to acquire nuclear weapons. Now, with 35–40 countries in the know by some estimates, the margin of security under the current non-proliferation regime is becoming too slim for comfort.

We need a new approach

My proposal has three parts:

- First, it is time to limit the processing of weapon-usable material (separated plutonium and high-enriched uranium) in civilian nuclear programmes, as well as the production of new material through reprocessing and enrichment, by agreeing to restrict these operations exclusively to facilities under multinational control. These limitations would need to be accompanied by proper rules of transparency and, above all, by an assurance that legitimate would-be users could get their supplies.
- Second, nuclear-energy systems should be deployed that, by design, avoid the use of materials that may be applied directly to making nuclear weapons. These systems should have built-in features that would prevent countries diverting material to weapons production;

prevent the misuse of the facilities and equipment for clandestine manufacture of such materials; and facilitate efficient oversight to ensure continued peaceful use. This is not a futuristic dream; much of the technology for proliferation-resistant nuclear-energy systems has already been developed or is actively being researched. In addition, existing facilities around the world that use high-enriched uranium applications—for example, to produce medical radioisotopes—should continue, gradually but irreversibly, to be converted to low-enriched processes.

- Third, we should consider multinational approaches to the management and disposal of spent fuel and radioactive waste. More than 50 countries have spent fuel stored in temporary sites, awaiting re-processing or disposal. Not all countries have the right geology to store waste underground and, for many countries with small nuclear programmes for electricity generation or for research, the costs of such a facility are prohibitive.

Considerable advantages—in cost, safety, security and non-proliferation—would be gained from international co-operation in these stages of the nuclear fuel cycle. These initiatives would not simply add more non-proliferation controls, to limit access to weapon-usable nuclear material; they would also provide access to the benefits of nuclear technology for more people in more countries.

The new framework should also "turn off the tap," for all countries, on the production of new material for nuclear weapons. This year marks the tenth anniversary of an historic United Nations resolution calling for a ban on the production of fissile material for weapons use—the so-called Fissile Material Cut-off Treaty—on which little recent progress has been made. This treaty could cap and make public all inventories of fissile material still available, and serve as a starting point for future arms reductions.

I do not have all the answers on what this framework should look like. But it should be inclusive; nuclear-weapon states, non-nuclear-weapon states, and those outside the current non-proliferation regime should all have a seat at the table. The security concerns of all parties should be heard and weighed, and the aim should be to achieve full parity among them under a new security structure that does not depend on nuclear weapons or nuclear deterrence. This naturally should include agreement on a concrete programme for nuclear disarmament, complete with a timetable.

And lastly, once in force, this new framework should be regarded as a "peremptory norm" of international law—not vulnerable to any nation subsequently withdrawing, based on the whim of a new government or a vote of the latest parliament. In short, it should be enduring.

A call for leadership

In all of human history, no civilisation has ever voluntarily laid down its most powerful weapons. It remains to be seen whether ours can be the first.

We have not yet reached the mid-1960s' prediction of a world of 15 or more nuclear-weapon states, but we are over halfway there. And the trends indicated by recent events should have us all worried.

I worry that, in our collective memories, the horrors of Hiroshima and Nagasaki have begun to fade. I worry about nuclear weapons falling into the hands of terrorists or ruthless dictators. I worry about nuclear weapons already in the arsenals of democracies—because as long as these weapons exist, there is no absolute guarantee against the disastrous consequences of their theft, sabotage or accidental launch, and even democracies are not immune to radical shifts in their security anxieties and nuclear policies.

I worry, but I also hope. I hope that a side-effect of globalisation will be an enduring realisation that there is only one human race, to which we all belong. I hope that dynamic leaders within national governments, international institutions and civil society will step forward with the vision, the integrity and the will to reverse the inertia of fear and insecurity. I hope we can all agree to sit down together, and to start anew.

Appendix 6

President Announces New Measures to Counter the Threat of WMD

President George W. Bush
Fort Lesley J. McNair—National Defense University
Washington, D.C.
February 11, 2004
2:30 P.M. EST

Thanks for the warm welcome. I'm honored to visit the National Defense University. For nearly a century, the scholars and students here have helped to prepare America for the changing threats to our national security. Today, the men and women of our National Defense University are helping to frame the strategies through which we are fighting and winning the war on terror. Your Center for Counterproliferation Research and your other institutes and colleges are providing vital insight into the dangers of a new era. I want to thank each one of you for devoting your talents and your energy to the service of our great nation.

I want to thank General Michael Dunn for inviting me here. I used to jog by this facility on a regular basis. Then my age kicked in. (Laughter.) I appreciate Ambassador Wolfgang Ischinger, from Germany. Mr. Ambassador, thank you for being here today. I see my friend, George Shultz, a distinguished public servant and true patriot, with us. George, thank you for coming; and Charlotte, it's good to see you. I'm so honored that Dick Lugar is here with us today. Senator, I appreciate you taking time and thanks for bringing Senator Saxby Chambliss with you, as well. I appreciate the veterans who are here and those on active duty. Thanks for letting me come by.

On September the 11th, 2001, America and the world witnessed a new kind of war. We saw the great harm that a stateless network could inflict upon our country, killers armed with box cutters, mace, and 19 airline tickets. Those attacks also raised the prospect of even worse dangers—of other weapons in the hands of other men. The greatest threat before humanity today is the possibility of secret and sudden attack with chemical or biological or radiological or nuclear weapons.

In the past, enemies of America required massed armies, and great navies, powerful air forces to put our nation, our people, our friends and allies at risk. In the Cold War, Americans lived under the threat of weapons of mass destruction, but believed that deterrents made those weapons a last resort. What has changed in the 21st century is that, in the hands of terrorists, weapons of mass destruction would be a first resort—the preferred means to further their ideology of suicide and random murder. These terrible weapons are becoming easier to acquire, build, hide, and transport. Armed with a single vial of a biological agent or a single nuclear weapon, small groups of fanatics, or failing states, could gain the power to threaten great nations, threaten the world peace.

America, and the entire civilized world, will face this threat for decades to come. We must confront the danger with open eyes, and unbending purpose. I have made clear to all the policy of this nation: America will not permit terrorists and dangerous regimes to threaten us with the world's most deadly weapons. (Applause.)

Meeting this duty has required changes in thinking and strategy. Doctrines designed to contain empires, deter aggressive states, and defeat massed armies cannot fully protect us from this new threat. America faces the possibility of catastrophic attack from ballistic missiles armed with weapons of mass destruction. So that is why we are developing and deploying missile defenses to guard our people. The best intelligence is necessary to win the war on terror and to stop proliferation. So that is why I have established a commission that will examine our intelligence capabilities and recommend ways to improve and adapt them to detect new and emerging threats.

We're determined to confront those threats at the source. We will stop these weapons from being acquired or built. We'll block them from being transferred. We'll prevent them from ever being used. One source of these weapons is dangerous and secretive regimes that build weapons of mass destruction to intimidate their neighbors and force their influence upon the world. These nations pose different challenges; they require different strategies.

The former dictator of Iraq possessed and used weapons of mass destruction against his own people. For 12 years, he defied the will of the international community. He refused to disarm or account for his illegal weapons and programs. He doubted our resolve to enforce our word—and now he sits in a prison cell, while his country moves toward a democratic future. (Applause.)

To Iraq's east, the government of Iran is unwilling to abandon a uranium enrichment program capable of producing material for nuclear weapons. The United States is working with our allies and the International Atomic Energy Agency to ensure that Iran meets its commitments and does not develop nuclear weapons. (Applause.)

In the Pacific, North Korea has defied the world, has tested long-range ballistic missiles, admitted its possession of nuclear weapons, and now threatens to build more. Together with our partners in Asia, America is insisting that North Korea completely, verifiably, and irreversibly dismantle its nuclear programs.

America has consistently brought these threats to the attention of international organizations. We're using every means of diplomacy to answer them. As for my part, I will continue to speak clearly on these threats. I will continue to call upon the world to confront these dangers, and to end them. (Applause.)

In recent years, another path of proliferation has become clear, as well. America and other nations are learning more about black-market operatives who deal in equipment and expertise related to weapons of mass destruction. These dealers are motivated by greed, or fanaticism, or both. They find eager customers in outlaw regimes, which pay millions for the parts and plans they need to speed up their weapons programs. And with deadly technology and expertise going on the market, there's the terrible possibility that terrorists groups could obtain the ultimate weapons they desire most.

The extent and sophistication of such networks can be seen in the case of a man named Abdul Qadeer Khan. This is the story as we know it so far.

A. Q. Khan is known throughout the world as the father of Pakistan's nuclear weapons program. What was not publicly known, until recently, is that he also led an extensive international network for the proliferation of nuclear technology and know-how.

For decades, Mr. Khan remained on the Pakistani government payroll, earning a modest salary. Yet, he and his associates financed lavish lifestyles through the sale of nuclear technologies and equipment to outlaw regimes stretching from North Africa to the Korean Peninsula.

A. Q. Khan, himself, operated mostly out of Pakistan. He served as director of the network, its leading scientific mind, as well as its primary salesman. Over the past decade, he made frequent trips to consult with his clients and to sell his expertise. He and his associates sold the blueprints for centrifuges to enrich uranium, as well as a nuclear design stolen from the Pakistani government. The network sold uranium hexafluoride, the gas that the centrifuge process can transform into enriched uranium for nuclear bombs. Khan and his associates provided Iran and Libya and North Korea with designs for Pakistan's older centrifuges, as well as designs for more advanced and efficient models. The network also provided these countries with components, and in some cases, with complete centrifuges.

To increase their profits, Khan and his associates used a factory in Malaysia to manufacture key parts for centrifuges. Other necessary parts were purchased through network operatives based in Europe, the Middle East, and Africa. These procurement agents saw the trade in nuclear technologies as a shortcut to personal wealth, and they set up front companies to deceive legitimate firms into selling them tightly controlled materials.

Khan's deputy—a man named B.S.A. Tahir—ran SMB computers, a business in Dubai. Tahir used that computer company as a front for the proliferation activities of the A. Q. Khan network. Tahir acted as both the network's chief financial officer and money launderer. He was also its shipping agent, using his computer firm as cover for the movement of centrifuge parts to various clients. Tahir directed the Malaysia facility to produce these parts based on Pakistani designs, and then ordered the facility to ship the components to Dubai. Tahir also arranged for parts acquired by other European procurement agents to transit through Dubai for shipment to other customers.

This picture of the Khan network was pieced together over several years by American and British intelligence officers. Our intelligence services gradually uncovered this network's reach, and identified its key experts and agents and money men. Operatives followed its transactions, mapped the extent of its operations. They monitored the travel of A. Q. Khan and senior associates. They shadowed members of the network around the world, they recorded their conversations, they penetrated their operations, we've uncovered their secrets. This work involved high risk, and all Americans can be grateful for the hard work and the dedication of our fine intelligence professionals. (Applause.)

Governments around the world worked closely with us to unravel the Khan network, and to put an end to his criminal enterprise. A. Q. Khan has confessed his crimes, and his top associates are out of business. The government of Pakistan is interrogating the network's members, learning critical details that will help them prevent it from ever operating again. President Musharraf has promised to share all the information he learns about the Khan network, and has assured us that his country will never again be a source of proliferation.

Mr. Tahir is in Malaysia, where authorities are investigating his activities. Malaysian authorities have assured us that the factory the network used is no longer producing centrifuge parts. Other members of the network remain at large. One by one, they will be found, and their careers in the weapons trade will be ended.

As a result of our penetration of the network, American and the British intelligence identified a shipment of advanced centrifuge parts manufactured at the Malaysia facility. We followed the shipment of these parts to Dubai, and watched as they were transferred to the BBC China, a German-owned ship. After the ship passed through the Suez Canal, bound for Libya, it was stopped by German and Italian authorities. They found several containers, each forty feet in length, listed on the ship's manifest as full of "used machine parts." In fact, these containers were filled with parts of sophisticated centrifuges.

The interception of the BBC China came as Libyan and British and American officials were discussing the possibility of Libya ending its WMD programs. The United States and Britain confronted Libyan officials with this evidence of an active and illegal nuclear program. About two months ago, Libya's leader voluntarily agreed to end his nuclear and chemical weapons programs, not to pursue biological weapons, and to permit thorough inspections by the International Atomic Energy Agency and the Organization for the Prohibition of Chemical Weapons. We're now working in partnership with these organizations and with the United Kingdom to help the government of Libya dismantle those programs and eliminate all dangerous materials.

Colonel Ghadafi made the right decision, and the world will be safer once his commitment is fulfilled. We expect other regimes to follow his example. Abandoning the pursuit of illegal weapons can lead to better relations with the United States, and other free nations. Continuing to seek those weapons will not bring security or international prestige, but only political isolation, economic hardship, and other unwelcome consequences. (Applause.)

We know that Libya was not the only customer of the Khan network. Other countries expressed great interest in their services. These regimes and other proliferators like Khan should know: We and our friends are determined to protect our people and the world from proliferation. (Applause.)

Breaking this network is one major success in a broad-based effort to stop the spread of terrible weapons. We're adjusting our strategies to the threats of a new era. America and the nations of Australia, France and Germany, Italy and Japan, the Netherlands, Poland, Portugal, Spain and the United Kingdom have launched the Proliferation Security Initiative to interdict lethal materials in transit. Our nations are sharing intelligence information, tracking suspect international cargo, conducting joint military exercises. We're prepared to search planes and ships, to seize weapons and missiles and equipment that raise proliferation concerns, just as we did in stopping the dangerous cargo on the BBC China before it reached Libya. Three more governments—Canada and Singapore and Norway—will be participating in this initiative. We'll continue to expand the core group of PSI countries. And as PSI grows, proliferators will find it harder than ever to trade in illicit weapons.

There is a consensus among nations that proliferation cannot be tolerated. Yet this consensus means little unless it is translated into action. Every civilized nation has a stake in preventing the spread of weapons of mass destruction. These materials and technologies, and the people who traffic in them, cross many borders. To stop this trade, the nations of the world must be strong and determined. We must work together, we must act effectively. Today, I announce seven proposals to strengthen the world's efforts to stop the spread of deadly weapons.

First, I propose that the work of the Proliferation Security Initiative be expanded to address more than shipments and transfers. Building on the tools we've developed to fight terrorists, we can take direct action against proliferation networks. We need greater cooperation not just among intelligence and military services, but in law enforcement, as well. PSI participants and other willing nations should use the Interpol and all other means to bring to justice those who traffic in deadly weapons, to shut down their labs, to seize their materials, to freeze their assets. We must act on every lead. We will find the middlemen, the suppliers and the buyers. Our message to proliferators must be consistent and it must be clear: We will find you, and we're not going to rest until you are stopped. (Applause.)

Second, I call on all nations to strengthen the laws and international controls that govern proliferation. At the U.N. last fall, I proposed a new Security Council resolution requiring all states to criminalize proliferation, enact strict export controls, and secure all sensitive materials within their borders. The Security Council should pass this proposal quickly. And when they do, America stands ready to help other governments to draft and enforce the new laws that will help us deal with proliferation.

Third, I propose to expand our efforts to keep weapons from the Cold War and other dangerous materials out of the wrong hands. In 1991, Congress passed the Nunn-Lugar legislation. Senator Lugar had a clear vision, along with Senator Nunn, about what to do with the old Soviet Union. Under this program, we're helping former Soviet states find productive employment for former weapons scientists. We're dismantling, destroying and securing weapons and materials left over from the Soviet WMD arsenal. We have more work to do there.

And as a result of the G-8 Summit in 2002, we agreed to provide $20 billion over 10 years—half of it from the United States—to support such programs. We should expand this cooperation elsewhere in the world. We will retain [sic] WMD scientists and technicians in countries like Iraq and Libya. We will help nations end the use of weapons-grade uranium in research reactors. I urge more nations to contribute to these efforts. The nations of the world must do all we can to secure and eliminate nuclear and chemical and biological and radiological materials.

As we track and destroy these networks, we must also prevent governments from developing nuclear weapons under false pretenses. The Nuclear Non-Proliferation Treaty was designed more than 30 years ago to prevent the spread of nuclear weapons beyond those states which already possessed them. Under this treaty, nuclear states agreed to help non-nuclear states develop peaceful atomic energy if they renounced the pursuit of nuclear weapons. But the treaty has a loophole which has been exploited by nations such as North Korea and Iran. These regimes are allowed to produce nuclear material that can be used to build bombs under the cover of civilian nuclear programs.

So today, as a fourth step, I propose a way to close the loophole. The world must create a safe, orderly system to field civilian nuclear plants without adding to the danger of weapons proliferation. The world's leading nuclear exporters should ensure that states have reliable access at reasonable cost to fuel for civilian reactors, so long as those states renounce enrichment and reprocessing. Enrichment and reprocessing are not necessary for nations seeking to harness nuclear energy for peaceful purposes.

The 40 nations of the Nuclear Suppliers Group should refuse to sell enrichment and reprocessing equipment and technologies to any state that does not already possess full-scale, functioning enrichment and reprocessing plants. (Applause.) This step will prevent new states from developing the means to produce fissile material for nuclear bombs. Proliferators must not be allowed to cynically manipulate the NPT to acquire the material and infrastructure necessary for manufacturing illegal weapons.

For international norms to be effective, they must be enforced. It is the charge of the International Atomic Energy Agency to uncover banned nuclear activity around the world and report those violations to the U.N. Security Council. We must ensure that the IAEA has all the tools it needs to fulfill its essential mandate. America and other nations support what is called the Additional Protocol, which requires states to declare a broad range of nuclear activities and facilities, and allow the IAEA to inspect those facilities.

As a fifth step, I propose that by next year, only states that have signed the Additional Protocol be allowed to import equipment for their civilian nuclear programs. Nations that are serious about fighting proliferation will approve and implement the Additional Protocol. I've submitted the Additional Protocol to the Senate. I urge the Senate to consent immediately to its ratification.

We must also ensure that IAEA is organized to take action when action is required. So, a sixth step, I propose the creation of a special committee of the IAEA Board which will focus intensively on safeguards and verification. This committee, made up of governments in good standing with the IAEA, will strengthen the capability of the IAEA to ensure that nations comply with their international obligations.

And, finally, countries under investigation for violating nuclear nonproliferation obligations are currently allowed to serve on the IAEA Board of Governors. For instance, Iran—a country suspected of maintaining an extensive nuclear weapons program—recently completed a two-year term on the Board. Allowing potential violators to serve on the Board creates an unacceptable barrier to effective action. No state under investigation for proliferation violations should be allowed to serve on the IAEA Board of Governors—or on the new special committee. And any state currently on the Board that comes under investigation should be suspended from the Board. The integrity and mission of the IAEA depends on this simple principle: Those actively breaking the rules should not be entrusted with enforcing the rules. (Applause.)

As we move forward to address these challenges we will consult with our friends and allies on all these new measures. We will listen to their ideas. Together we will defend the safety of all nations and preserve the peace of the world.

Over the last two years, a great coalition has come together to defeat terrorism and to oppose the spread of weapons of mass destruction—the inseparable commitments of the war on terror. We've shown that proliferators can be discovered and can be stopped. We've shown that for regimes that choose defiance, there are serious consequences. The way ahead is not easy, but it is clear. We will proceed as if the lives of our citizens depend on our vigilance, because they do. Terrorists and terror states are in a race for weapons of mass murder, a race they must lose. (Applause.) Terrorists are resourceful; we're more resourceful. They're determined; we must be more determined. We will never lose focus or resolve. We'll be unrelenting in the defense of free nations, and rise to the hard demands of dangerous times.

May God bless you all. (Applause.)

END 3:07 P.M. EST

Appendix 7

Global Threat Reduction Initiative

Remarks by Energy Secretary Spencer Abraham on the Global Threat Reduction Initiative, International Atomic Energy Agency, Vienna, Austria, May 26, 2004.

Thank you, Director General ElBaradei.

Today, I have a special message for the men and women on your staff, many of whom are in the room today, and for the delegates and representatives to this body.

Your efforts are crucial to international safety and security in a world that grows ever more dangerous each day. I know that it often may seem like thankless work—certainly it is often anonymous work.

But believe me when I say that you labor on the frontlines of the twenty-first century's greatest conflict—a conflict between the civilized nations of the earth, and the terrorists and terrorist states that would use devastating technologies to destroy them.

Tens of millions of people in New York, Rome, Geneva, Tokyo, Sydney,

London, and other spots all over the globe will sleep soundly tonight because people like you and others who work on these challenges are tireless in their efforts. They rest assured that very capable men and women are on the job, thwarting the malignant designs of very bad people.

My government takes your mission very seriously. It is our mission as well. We thank you, and we pledge our determination and resources to help you go about the business of making the world a safer place.

Saying you want to make the world a safer place is simple. The challenge of actually doing that is the hard part. And that challenge is growing increasingly complicated in a world where technology and science make constant advances . . . and where terrorists and rogue states look to the use these advances for nefarious purposes.

Where one hundred years ago, authorities had to worry about the anarchist placing a bomb in the downtown square, . . . now we must worry about the terrorist who places that bomb in the square, but packed with radiological material.

Whereas once we had to worry about the madman whose ambition, within the realm of possibility, was to assassinate a world leader, . . . now we must worry about the madmen whose ambition is to destroy a world capital.

The recent revelations of the complex network established by A.Q. Khan give startling scope to the nonproliferation challenge we collectively face. Coupled with the horrific attacks of September 11, 2001, Bali, and, most recently, Madrid, we are forced to assume that rogue states and terrorists, in concert with for-profit proliferators, will act vigorously to achieve their ends.

The large quantities of uncontrolled or lightly controlled nuclear and radiological material of potential use in nuclear weapons or radiological dispersion devices have added an entirely new dimension to this worldwide threat. Over two hundred of the world's research reactors are nearing the end of their life spans. Four hundred reactors have already shut down or been decommissioned, creating large quantities of spent fuel and radiological sources that must be secured and/or disposed of.

Our challenge could not be more clear: As the 21st century takes shape, the stakes are higher. The dangers are increased. The worries are graver. Our challenge is more pronounced.

Commensurately, our resolve must be greater.

The United States already plays a prominent role in responding to these myriad proliferation threats.

Over the course of the last decade, we have developed a number of programs to support the global effort to remove and/or secure vulnerable nuclear and radiological materials:

To reduce stockpiles and available quantities of nuclear materials, we have been working closely with Russia to irreversibly blend-down at least 500 metric tons of surplus high enriched uranium (HEU). At the end of 2003, over 200 metric tons had been eliminated. We have accelerated our efforts to secure 600 metric tons of weapons-usable material in Russia. To date, we have upgraded security on over 40 percent of this material.

We are working to further reduce quantities of weapons-usable HEU by converting research reactors in the United States and abroad to use low-enriched uranium (LEU), and we are working to eliminate 174 metric tons of HEU in the United States.

We are also working proactively and cooperatively with Libya, the IAEA, and international partners to dismantle Libya's weapons of mass destruction infrastructure.

We are coordinating with our counterparts in Moscow to return Russian-origin HEU fuel to Russia. In 2003, in cooperation with the IAEA and with Minatom, we removed 17 kilograms of Russian-origin fresh HEU from Bulgaria and returned it to Russia for safe storage.

We also returned approximately 14 kilograms of fresh Russian-origin HEU from Romania to Russia to be down-blended and used for civil nuclear purposes. And most recently, working with the IAEA, we returned 17 kilograms of HEU from Libya's research reactor to Russia.

Under the U.S.-origin spent fuel return program, we have returned approximately 1,100 kilograms of HEU spent fuel to the United States for final disposition.

We are cooperating with approximately 40 countries to improve the security and controls of high-risk radiological materials that could be used in a radiological dispersal device, or "dirty bomb."

And, we have recovered and secured approximately 10,000 high-risk radiological sources in the United States, a figure that exceeds our congressionally mandated target for recovering and securing our domestic sources.

In addition, last year the United States and the Russian Federation co-hosted an international conference with the IAEA to address the threat posed by dirty bombs, and to come up with a joint course of action.

It was a very successful conference. More than 120 nations participated, and it produced action on a variety of fronts, including:

Identifying high risk radioactive sources that were not under secure and regulated control, including "orphan" sources.

Launching an international initiative to facilitate the location, recovery, and securing of such sources.

And, calling on all IAEA member-states to enhance their own national regulatory bodies to address safety and security of radioactive sources in their countries.

I am proud of our action to deal with RDDs [radiological dispersal devices], just as I am proud of all of the efforts I mentioned. The work my Department has done in conjunction with the IAEA and the international community has, to a large degree, been very effective.

But we would be fooling ourselves—and endangering our citizens—to think that these past efforts are enough. The continually shifting nature of geopolitics[,] . . . the ever-forward advancement of science and technology[,] . . . the hardened determination of terrorists to sow death and destruction—all of these demand that we continually reassess the situation, that we constantly revisit the topic at hand, and that we incessantly update our defenses and our plans to combat proliferation threats.

That is why I have come to Vienna this week.

As the global proliferation threat continues to evolve, it has become clear that an even more comprehensive and urgently focused effort is needed to respond to emerging and evolving threats.

Although we are accomplishing much, there is more we can do.

So this morning I am announcing that, in order to respond to this evolving proliferation threat, the United States is establishing a new initiative to secure, remove, or dispose of an even broader range of nuclear and radiological materials around the world that are vulnerable to theft.

We are calling this new initiate the Global Threat Reduction Initiative—or GTRI.

This Global Threat Reduction Initiative is an attempt to present a workable strategy for addressing the threat posed by the entire spectrum of nuclear materials. It reflects the realities of the twenty-first century that were so startlingly made clear on a September morning three years ago.

We have developed this initiative with the expectation it can comprehensively and more thoroughly address the challenges posed by nuclear and radiological materials and related equipment that require attention, anywhere in the world, by ensuring they will not fall into the hands of those with evil intentions.

We will do this by the securing, removing, relocating, or disposing of these materials and equipment—whatever the most appropriate circumstance may be—as quickly and expeditiously as possible.

Specifically, under the Initiative:

We will first work in partnership with Russia to repatriate all Russian-origin fresh HEU fuel by the end of next year.

We will also work with Russia to accelerate and complete the repatriation of all Russian-origin spent fuel by 2010.

We will do this on a priority basis according to security threat, so that we remove or secure the most dangerous materials first.

Likewise, we will take all steps necessary to accelerate and complete the repatriation of all U.S.-origin research reactor spent fuel under our existing program from locations around the world within a decade. Again, we will undertake these efforts in an order dictated by the need to handle the most dangerous, least secure materials first.

Third, we will work to convert the cores of civilian research reactors that use HEU to use low enriched uranium fuel instead. We will do this not just in the United States—where we are scheduled to complete core conversion by 2013—but throughout the entire world. And we will target those reactors first where the threats and vulnerabilities are highest.

Fourth, we will work to identify other nuclear and radiological materials and related equipment that are not yet covered by existing threat reduction efforts, and we will rapidly address the most vulnerable facilities first to ensure that there are not any gaps that would enable a terrorist to acquire these materials for evil purposes.

To help do all this, we will establish a single organization within the Department of Energy's National Nuclear Security Administration to focus exclusively on these efforts.

Moreover, we are prepared to spend the resources necessary to guarantee success. The United States plans to dedicate more than $450 million to this effort, which should be more than sufficient to complete the U.S. Foreign Research Reactor Spent Fuel Return, the Russian Research Reactor Fuel Return efforts, and to also fund the conversion of all targeted U.S.- and Russian-supplied research reactor cores under the Reduced Enrichment for Test Research and Test Reactors (RERTR) program. But we will need more funds—and heightened international cooperation—to finish the job.

Dedicated as we are to this effort, it is also clear to me that a truly effective nonproliferation regime is made up of the collaboration of efforts by all of us, not just a few. This is particularly the case regarding the collection of materials that are not of Russian or American origin, or that may be located in places where cooperation requires a broader international effort, and that pose certain challenges that the United States and Russian cannot address alone.

So today I am also proposing that the IAEA and international community join us in holding a Global Threat Reduction Initiative Partners' Conference later this fall. This conference would examine how to address material collection and security in places where—as mentioned before—a broader international effort is required. It would also focus on material collection and security of other proliferation-attractive materials, not of U.S. or Russian origin, such as those located at conversion facilities, reprocessing plants, and industrial sites, as well as the funding of such work.

In the coming weeks, we will be discussing this event in more detail with Director General ElBaradei and the IAEA, and I expect we will be issuing invitations very soon.

Consolidating current programs[,] . . . speeding the return of Russian and U.S. origin fuel[,] . . . securing the most dangerous materials worldwide to reduce the most perilous threats[, and] . . . working together on an international basis. That is the agenda before us.

We will take these steps because we must. The circumstances of a dangerous world have thrust this responsibility on the shoulders of the civilized world. We don't have the luxury of sitting back and not taking actions.

As President Bush said in a speech at the National Defense University in February: "The greatest threat before humanity today is the possibility of secret and sudden attack with chemical or biological or radiological or nuclear weapons. . . . America, and the entire civilized world, will face this threat for decades to come."

He is right: We will face this threat for years to come.

Not only will we. . . . We must.

The responsibility falls to us . . . to take necessary action to prevent the horrors of 9/11 being replayed, but on a nuclear scale. That is why the President has increased attention on this evolving threat and as a result of his February speech we have undertaken this new Initiative.

The responsibility falls to us . . . to ensure that the civilized world continues to enjoy the peaceful uses of the atom—in medicine, electricity generation, and beyond—while minimizing or eliminating any dangers.

I am optimistic that we can do this.

And because of the resolve shown by President Bush, Director General ElBaradei, member-nations, and the dedicated men and women of the IAEA, I am confident that we will.

Appendix 8

Multilateral Approaches to the Nuclear Fuel Cycle: Expert Group Report Submitted to the Director General of the International Atomic Energy Agency— Executive Summary

Information Circular
INFCIRC/640
Date: 22 February 2005
General Distribution
Original: English

Multilateral Nuclear Approaches (MNAs)
Executive Summary
22 February 2005

1. The global nuclear non-proliferation regime has been successful in limiting, albeit not entirely preventing, the further spread of nuclear weapons. The vast majority of States have legally pledged to forego the manufacture and acquisition of nuclear weapons and have abided by that commitment. Nonetheless, the past few years have been a tumultuous and difficult period.

2. The decades long nuclear non-proliferation effort is under threat: from regional arms races; from actions by non–nuclear-weapon States

(NNWS) that have been found to be in fundamental breach of, or in non-compliance with their safeguards agreement, and which have not taken full corrective measures; from the incomplete manner in which export controls required by the Treaty on the Non-Proliferation of Nuclear Weapons (NPT) have been applied; from burgeoning and alarmingly well organized nuclear supply networks; and from the increasing risk of acquisition of nuclear or other radioactive materials by terrorist and other non-State entities.

3. A different significant factor is that the civilian nuclear industry appears to be poised for worldwide expansion. Rapidly growing global demand for electricity, the uncertainty of supply and price of natural gas, soaring prices for oil, concerns about air pollution and the immense challenge of lowering greenhouse gas emissions, are all forcing a fresh look at nuclear power. As the technical and organizational foundations of nuclear safety improve, there is increasing confidence in the safety of nuclear power plants. In light of existing, new, and reawakened interest in many regions of the world, the prospect of new nuclear power stations on a large scale is therefore real. A greater number of States will consider developing their own fuel cycle facilities and nuclear know-how, and will seek assurances of supply in materials, services, and technologies.

4. In response to the growing emphasis being placed on international cooperation to cope with non-proliferation and security concerns, the Director General of the International Atomic Energy Agency (IAEA), Mohamed ElBaradei, appointed in June 2004 an international group of experts (participating in their personal capacity) to consider possible multilateral approaches to the civilian nuclear fuel cycle.

5. The mandate of the Expert Group was three-fold:

> To identify and provide an analysis of issues and options relevant to multilateral approaches to the front and back ends of the nuclear fuel cycle;
>
> To provide an overview of the policy, legal, security, economic, institutional and technological incentives and disincentives for cooperation in multilateral arrangements for the front and back ends of the nuclear fuel cycle; and
>
> To provide a brief review of the historical and current experiences and analyses relating to multilateral fuel cycle arrangements relevant to the work of the expert group.

6. Two primary deciding factors dominate all assessments of multilateral nuclear approaches, namely "Assurance of non-proliferation" and

"Assurance of supply and services." Both are recognized overall objectives for governments and for the NPT community. In practice, each of these two objectives can seldom be achieved fully on its own. History has shown that it is even more difficult to find an optimum arrangement that will satisfy both objectives at the same time. As a matter of fact, multilateral approaches could be a way to satisfy both objectives.

7. The non-proliferation value of a multilateral arrangement is measured by the various proliferation risks associated with a nuclear facility, whether national or multilateral. These risks include the diversion of materials from an MNA (reduced through the presence of a multinational team), the theft of fissile materials, the diffusion of proscribed or sensitive technologies from MNAs to unauthorized entities, the development of clandestine parallel programs, and the breakout scenario. The latter refers to the case of the host country "breaking out," for example, by expelling multinational staff, withdrawing from the NPT (and thereby terminating its safeguards agreement), and operating the multilateral facility without international control.

8. The "Assurance of supply" value of a multilateral arrangement is measured by the associated incentives, such as the guarantees provided by suppliers, governments and international organizations; the economic benefits that would be gained by countries participating in multilateral arrangements, and the better political and public acceptance for such nuclear projects. One of the most critical steps is to devise effective mechanisms for assurances of supply of material and services, which are commercially competitive, free of monopolies, and free of political constraints. Effective assurances of supply would have to include back-up sources of supply in the event that an MNA supplier is unable to provide the required material or services.

Overview of Options

9. Whether for uranium enrichment, spent fuel reprocessing, or spent fuel disposal and storage, multilateral options span the entire field between existing market mechanisms and a complete co-ownership of fuel cycle facilities. The following pattern reflects this diversity:

Type I: Assurances of services not involving ownership of facilities.
   a) Suppliers provide additional assurances of supply;
   b) International consortia of governments broaden the assurances;
   c) IAEA-related arrangements provide even broader assurances.

Type II: Conversion of existing national facilities to multinational facilities.
Type III: Construction of new joint facilities.

10. On the basis of this pattern, the Group has reviewed the pros and cons associated with each type and option. Pros and cons were defined relative to a "non-MNA choice," namely that of a national facility under current safeguards.

Uranium Enrichment

11. A healthy market exists at the front end of the fuel cycle. In the course of only two years, a nuclear power plant operating in Finland has bought uranium originating from mines in seven different countries. For example, conversion has been done in three different countries. Enrichment services have been bought from three different companies. Therefore, the legitimate objective of assurances of supply can be fulfilled to a large extent by the market. Nevertheless, this assessment may not be valid for all countries that have concerns about assurances of supply. Mechanisms or measures, under which existing suppliers or international consortia of governments or IAEA-related arrangements may be appropriate in such cases.

12. At first, suppliers could provide additional assurances of supply. This would correspond to enrichment plant operators, individually or collectively, guaranteeing to provide enrichment capacity to a State whose government had in turn agreed to forego building its own capacity, but which then found itself denied service by its intended enrichment provider for unspecified reasons. The pros include the avoidance of know-how dissemination, the reliance on a well-functioning market and the ease of implementation. The cons refer for example to the cost of maintaining idle capacity on reserve, and the lack of perceived diversity on the supplier side.

13. At a second level, international consortia of governments could step in, that is they would guarantee access to enrichment services, the suppliers being simply executive agents. The arrangement would be a kind of "intergovernmental fuel bank," e.g., a contract under which a government would buy guaranteed capacity under specified circumstances. Different States might use different mechanisms. Most pros and cons are shared with the preceding case.

14. Then, there are *IAEA-related arrangements,* a variation of the preceding option, with the IAEA acting as the anchor of the arrangement.

Essentially, the Agency would function as a kind of "guarantor" of supply to States in good standing and that were willing to accept the requisite conditionality (which would need to be defined, but would likely need to include foreswearing a parallel path to enrichment/reprocessing plus acceptance of the Additional Protocol for NNWS). The IAEA might either hold title to the material to be supplied or, more likely, act as facilitator, with back-up agreements between the IAEA and supplier countries to fulfill commitments made by the IAEA effectively on their behalf. In effect, the IAEA would be establishing a default mechanism, only to be activated in instances where a normal supply contract had broken down for reasons other than commercial reasons. The suggested pros and cons are therefore similar, with the added value of broad international assurances. Several questions can be raised with respect to the IAEA and its special status as an international organization subject to the control of its Member-States. Any guarantee provided by the IAEA would in fact require approval by its Board of Governors.

15. Where an MNA would take the form of a joint facility, there are two ready-made precedents, the Anglo-Dutch-German company Urenco and the French EURODIF. The experience of Urenco, with its commercial/industrial management on the one hand and the governmental Joint Committee on the other hand, has shown that the multinational concept can be made to work successfully. Under this model, strong oversight of technology and staffing, as well as effective safeguards and proper international division of expertise can reduce the risk of proliferation and even make a unilateral breakout extremely difficult. EURODIF on the other hand has a successful multinational record as well, by enriching uranium only in one country, while providing enriched uranium to its co-financing international partners, hence restricting all proliferation risks, diversion, clandestine parallel program, breakout, and the spread of technology.

Reprocessing of Nuclear Spent Fuel

16. Taking into account present capacities to reprocess spent fuel for light water reactors and those under construction, there will be sufficient reprocessing capacity globally for all expected demands in plutonium-recycled fuel during some two decades. Therefore, objectives of assurances of supply can be fulfilled to a large extent without new reprocessing facilities involving ownerships (Types II and III).

17. Currently all reprocessing plants are essentially State-owned. By the very nature of the nuclear business worldwide, any guarantee from a supplier would have the implicit or explicit agreement of the corresponding government. As to *IAEA-brokered arrangements,* these could mean an IAEA participation in the supervision of an international consortium for reprocessing services.

18. *Converting a national facility* to international ownership and management would involve the creation of a new international entity that would operate as a new competitor in the reprocessing market. The pros reflect the advantages of bringing together international expertise, while the cons include non-proliferation disadvantages related to know-how dissemination and to the return of the separated plutonium. Other cons deal with the fact that, of the existing facilities, all except two Japanese facilities are in NWS or in non-NPT States. In many of those cases, appropriate safeguards will have to be introduced if they had not been applied before.

19. As noted above, the *construction of new joint facilities* will not be needed for a long time. Therefore, a prerequisite for the construction of new facilities is the demand for additional reprocessing and for recycled-plutonium fabrication. In the future, such reprocessing and fabrication would be done on the same location.

Spent Fuel Disposal

20. At present, there is no international market for spent fuel disposal services, as all undertakings are strictly national. The final disposal of spent fuel is thus a candidate for multilateral approaches. It offers major economic benefits and substantial nonproliferation benefits, although it presents legal, political, and public acceptance challenges in many countries. The Agency should continue its efforts in that direction by working on all the underlying factors, and by assuming political leadership to encourage such undertakings.

21. The final disposal of spent fuel (and radioactive waste as well) in shared repositories must be looked at as only one element of a broader strategy of parallel options. National solutions will remain a first priority in many countries. This is the only approach for States with many nuclear power plants in operation or in past operation. For others with smaller civilian nuclear programs, a dual-track approach is needed in which both national and international solutions are pursued. Small countries should

keep options open (national, regional or international), be it only to maintain a minimum national technical competence necessary to act in an international context.

Spent Fuel Storage

22. Storage facilities for spent fuel are in operation and are being built in several countries. There is no international market for services in this area, except for the readiness of the Russian Federation to receive Russian-supplied fuel, and with a possible offer to do so for other spent fuel. The storage of spent fuel is also a candidate for multilateral approaches, primarily at the regional level. Storage of special nuclear materials in a few safe and secure facilities would enhance safeguards and physical protection. The IAEA should continue investigations in that field and encourage such undertakings. Various countries with state-of-the-art storage facilities in operation should step forward and accept spent fuel from others for interim storage.

Combined Option: Fuel-Leasing/Fuel Take-Back

23. In this model, the leasing State provides the fuel through an arrangement with its own nuclear fuel "vendors." At the time the government of the leasing State issues an export license to its fuel "vendor" corporation to send fresh fuel to a client reactor, that government would also announce its plan for the management of that fuel once discharged. Without a specific spent fuel management scheme by the leasing State, the lease deal will of course not take place. The leased fuel once removed from the reactor and cooled down, could either be returned to its country of origin which owns title to it, or, through an IAEA-brokered deal could be sent to a third party State or to a multinational or a regional fuel cycle centre located elsewhere for storage and ultimate disposal.

24. The weak part in the arrangement outlined above is the willingness, indeed the political capability, of the leasing State to take-back the spent fuel it has provided under the lease contract. It could well be politically difficult for any State to accept spent fuel not coming from its own reactors (that is, reactors producing electricity for the direct benefit of its own citizens). Yet, to make any lease-take-back deal credible, an ironclad guar-

antee of spent fuel removal from the country where it was used must be provided, otherwise the entire arrangement is moot. In this respect, States with suitable disposal sites, and with grave concerns about proliferation risks, ought to be proactive in putting forward solutions. Of course, commitment of client States to forego enrichment and reprocessing would make such undertakings politically more tolerable.

25. As an alternative, the IAEA could broker the creation of multinational or regional spent fuel storage facilities, where spent fuel owned by leasing States and burned elsewhere could be sent. The IAEA could thus become an active participant in regional spent fuel storage facilities, or third party spent fuel disposal schemes, thereby making lease-take-back fuel supply arrangements more credible propositions.

Overarching Issues

26. Apart from the cross-cutting factors related to the implementation of MNAs, such as the technical, legal and safeguards ones, there are a number of overarching issues, primarily of a broad political nature, which may have a bearing upon perceptions of the feasibility and desirability of MNAs. These issues may be decisive in any future endeavor to develop, assess, and implement such approaches at the national and international level.

Relevant Articles of the NPT

27. The NPT incorporates a political bargain with respect to peaceful uses and nuclear disarmament without which the Treaty would not have been adopted nor received the widespread adherence it obtained afterwards. The promise by all States parties to cooperate in the further development of nuclear energy and for the NWS to work towards disarmament provided the basis for NNWS to abstain from acquiring nuclear weapons.

28. Cooperation in the peaceful uses of nuclear energy, which had earlier provided the basis for the foundation of the IAEA, is embodied in Article IV, which stipulates that nothing shall be interpreted as affecting the *"inalienable right of all Parties to develop research, production and use of nuclear energy for peaceful purposes without discrimination and in conformity with Articles I and II"* (that specify the nonproliferation objectives of the Treaty). Furthermore, that same article specifies that all Parties to the

NPT shall undertake to *"facilitate, and have the right to participate in, the fullest possible exchange of equipment, materials and scientific and technological information for the peaceful uses of nuclear energy,"* and moreover to *"cooperate in contributing alone or together with other States or international organizations to the further development of the applications of nuclear energy for peaceful purposes. . ."* Article IV was specifically crafted to preclude any attempt to reinterpret the NPT so as to inhibit a country's right to nuclear technologies—so long as the technology is used for peaceful purposes.

29. NNWS have expressed dissatisfaction about what they increasingly view as a growing imbalance in the NPT: that, through the imposition of restrictions on the supply of materials and equipment of the nuclear fuel cycle by the NWS and the advanced industrial NNWS, those States have backed away from their original guarantee to facilitate the fullest possible exchange referred to in Article IV and to assist all NNWS in the development of the applications of nuclear energy. There are also concerns that additional constraints on Article IV might be imposed.

30. Article VI of the Treaty obliges NWS Parties "to pursue negotiations in good faith on effective measures relating to cessation of the nuclear arms race at an early date and to nuclear disarmament." Many NNWS deem the implementation of Article VI of the NPT by NWS as unsatisfactory, as are the non-entry into force of the Comprehensive Nuclear-Test-Ban Treaty (CTBT) and the stalemate in the negotiations on a verifiable Fissile Material (Cut-off) Treaty (FM(C)T). Such concerns have fostered a conviction among many NNWS that the NPT bargain is being corroded.

Safeguards and Export Controls

31. Some States have argued that, if the objective of MNAs is merely to strengthen the nuclear non-proliferation regime then, rather than focusing on MNAs, it may be better to concentrate instead on the existing elements of the regime itself, for example, by seeking the universality of the Additional Protocol (AP) to IAEA safeguards agreements and by the universalization of safeguards agreements and multilateral export controls.

32. The risks involved in the spread of sensitive nuclear technologies should primarily be addressed by an efficient and cost-effective safeguards system. The IAEA and regional safeguards systems have done an outstanding job in these matters. Safeguards, rationally and well applied, have been

the most efficient way to detect and deter further proliferation and to provide States Parties with an opportunity to assure others that they are in conformity with their safeguards commitments. Of course, advances in technologies require safeguards to be strengthened and updated, while protecting commercial, technological, and industrial secrets. The adoption of the Additional Protocol, and its judicious implementation based on State-level analysis, are essential steps against further nuclear proliferation. The Additional Protocol has proven to provide additional, necessary and effective verification tools, while protecting legitimate national interests in security and confidentiality. Sustained application of the Additional Protocol in a State can provide credible assurance of the absence of undeclared materials and activities in that State. Together with a comprehensive safeguards agreement, the Additional Protocol should become the de facto safeguards standard.

33. The above notwithstanding, the IAEA should endeavor to further strengthen the implementation of safeguards. For example, it should revisit three facets of its verification system:

    a) The technical annexes of the Additional Protocol, which should be regularly updated to reflect the continuing development of nuclear techniques and technologies.

    b) The implementation of the AP, which requires adequate resources and a firm commitment to apply it decisively. It should be recalled that the Model Additional Protocol commits the IAEA not to apply the AP in a mechanistic or systematic way. Therefore, the IAEA should allocate its resources on problematic areas rather than on States using the largest amounts of nuclear material.

    c) The enforcement mechanisms in case of fundamental breach of, or in case of non-compliance with, the safeguards agreement. Are these mechanisms progressive enough to act as an effective deterrent? Further consideration should be given by the IAEA to appropriate measures to handle various degrees of violations.

34. Export guidelines and their implementation are an important line of defense for preventing proliferation. Recent events have shown that criminal networks can find ways around existing controls to supply clandestine activities. Yet, one should remember that all States party to the NPT are obliged, pursuant to Article III.2 thereof, to implement export controls. This obligation was reinforced by United Nations Security Council Resolution 1540 (2004) that requires all States to enact and implement export controls to prevent the spread of weapons of mass destruction and related

materials to non-State actors. The participation in the development and implementation of export controls should be broadened, and multilaterally-agreed export controls should be developed in a transparent manner, engaging all States.

35. In fact, the primary technical barriers against proliferation remain the effective and universal implementation of IAEA safeguards under comprehensive safeguards agreements and additional protocols, and effective export controls. Both must be as strong as possible on their own merits. MNAs will be complementary mechanisms for strengthening the existing non-proliferation regime.

Voluntary Participation in MNAs versus a Binding Norm

36. The present legal framework does not oblige countries to participate in MNAs, as the political environment makes it unlikely that such a norm can be established any time soon. Establishing MNAs resting on **voluntary** participation is thus the more promising way to proceed. In a voluntary arrangement covering assurances of supply, recipient countries would, at least for the duration of the respective supply contract, renounce the construction and operation of sensitive fuel cycle facilities and accept safeguards of the highest current standards including comprehensive safeguards and the Additional Protocol. Where the demarcation line between permitted R&D activities and renounced development and construction activities has to be drawn is a matter for further consideration. In voluntary MNAs involving facilities, the participating countries would presumably commit to carry out the related activities solely under the common MNA framework.

37. In reality, countries will enter into such multilateral arrangements according to the economic and political incentives and disincentives offered by these arrangements. A political environment of mutual trust and consensus among the partners—based on full compliance with the agreed nuclear non-proliferation obligations of the partners—will be necessary to the successful negotiation, creation, and operation of an MNA.

38. Beyond this, a new **binding** international norm stipulating that sensitive fuel cycle activities are to be conducted exclusively in the context of MNAs and no longer as a national undertaking would amount to a change in the scope of Article IV of the NPT. The wording and negotiation history of this article emphasize the right of each party in good standing to choose

its national fuel cycle on the basis of its sovereign consideration. This right is not independent of the faithful abiding by the undertakings under Articles I and II. But if this condition is met, no legal barrier stands in the way of each State party to pursue all fuel cycle activities on a national basis. Waiving this right would thus change the "bargain" of the NPT.

39. Such a fundamental change is not impossible if the parties were to agree on it in a broader negotiating frame. For NNWS, such a new bargain can probably only be realized through universal principles applying to all States and after additional steps by the NWS regarding nuclear disarmament. In addition, a verifiable FM(C)T might also be one of the preconditions for binding multilateral obligations; such a treaty would terminate the right of any participating nuclear weapon States and non-NPT parties to run reprocessing and enrichment facilities for nuclear explosive purposes and it would bring them to the same level—with regard to such activities—as nonnuclear weapon States. The new restrictions would apply to all States and facilities related to the technologies involved, without exception. At that time, multilateral arrangements could become a universal, binding principle. The question may also be raised as to what might be the conditions required by NWS and non-NPT States to commit to binding MNAs involving them.

Nuclear-Weapon States and Non-NPT States

40. Weapon-usable material (stocks and flows) and sensitive facilities that are capable of producing such material are located predominantly in the NWS and non-NPT States. The concerns raised previously for MNAs in NNWS do not all apply when an MNA would involve NWS or non-NPT States. Yet, one of the questions here relates to the possibility that the nuclear material produced in an MNA could contribute to such a State's nuclear non-peaceful program. This shows again the relevance of a FM(C)T.

41. The feasibility of bringing NWS and non-NPT States into MNAs should indeed be considered at an early stage. As long as MNAs remain voluntary, nothing would preclude such States from participating in an MNA. In fact, France (in connection with the EURODIF arrangement) and the United Kingdom (in connection with Urenco) are examples of such participation. In transforming existing civilian facilities into MNAs subject to safeguards and security requirements, such States would demonstrate their support for non-proliferation and for peaceful international nuclear collaboration.

Enforcement

42. Eventually, the success of all efforts to improve the nuclear non-proliferation regime depends upon the effectiveness of compliance and enforcement mechanisms. Enforcement measures in case of non-compliance can be partially improved by MNAs' legal provisions, which will carefully specify a definition of what constitutes a violation, by whom such violations will be ruled on, and enforcement measures that could be directly applied by the partners in addition to broader political tools.

43. Nevertheless, enhanced safeguards, MNAs, or new undertakings by States will not serve their full purpose if the international community does not respond with determination to serious cases of non-compliance, be it diversion, clandestine activities or breakout. Responses are needed at four levels, depending upon the specific case: the MNA partners of the non-compliant State; the IAEA; the States Parties to the NPT; and the UN Security Council. Where these do not currently exist, appropriate procedures and measures must be available and must be made use of at all four levels to cope with breaches and non-compliance instances, in order to unequivocally make clear that States violating treaties and arrangements should not be permitted to do so unimpeded.

Multilateral Nuclear Approaches: The Future

44. Past initiatives for multilateral nuclear cooperation did not result in any tangible results. Proliferation concerns were perceived as not serious enough. Economic incentives were seldom strong enough. Concerns about assurances of supply were paramount. National pride also played a role, alongside expectations about the technological and economic spin-offs to be derived from nuclear activities. Many of those considerations may still be pertinent. However, the result of balancing those considerations today, in the face of a latent multiplication of nuclear facilities over the next decades and the possible increase in proliferation dangers may well produce a political environment more conducive to MNAs in the 21st century.

45. The potential benefits of MNAs for the non-proliferation regime are both symbolic and practical. As a confidence-building measure, multilateral approaches can provide enhanced assurance to the partners and to the international community that the most sensitive parts of the civilian nuclear fuel cycle are less vulnerable to misuse for weapon purposes. Joint facilities with multinational staff put all MNA participants under a greater degree of

scrutiny from peers and partners and may also constitute an obstacle against a breakout by the host partner. They also reduce the number of sites where sensitive facilities are operated, thereby curbing proliferation risks, and diminishing the number of locations subject to potential thefts of sensitive material. Moreover, these approaches can even help in creating a better acceptance for the continued use of nuclear power and for nuclear applications, and enhance the prospects for the safe and environmentally sound storage and disposal of spent nuclear fuel and radioactive waste.

46. As far as assurances of supply are concerned, multilateral approaches could also provide the benefits of cost-effectiveness and economies of scale for whole regions, for smaller countries or for those with limited resources. Similar benefits have been derived in the context of other technology sectors, such as aviation and aerospace. However, the case to be made in favor of MNAs is not entirely straightforward. States with differing levels of technology, different degrees of institutionalization, economic development and resources and competing political considerations may not all reach the same conclusions as to the benefits, convenience and desirability of MNAs. Some might argue that multilateral approaches point to the loss or limitation of State sovereignty and independent ownership and control of a key technology sector, leaving unfairly the commercial benefits of these technologies to just a few countries. Others might argue that multilateral approaches could lead to further dissemination of, or loss of control over, sensitive nuclear technologies, and result in higher proliferation risks.

47. In summary, the Expert Group on Multilateral Approaches for the Nuclear Fuel Cycle has reviewed the various aspects of the fuel cycle, identified a number of options for MNAs deserving further consideration, and noted a number of pros and cons for each of the options. It is hoped that the report of the Expert Group will serve as a building block, or as a milestone. It is not intended to mark the end of the road. MNAs offer a potentially useful contribution to meeting prevailing concerns about assurances of supply and non-proliferation.

48. The Group recommends that steps be taken to strengthen overall controls on the nuclear fuel cycle and the transfer of technology, including safeguards and export controls: the former by promoting universal adherence to Additional Protocols, the latter through a more stringent implementation of guidelines and a universal participation in their development.

49. In order to maintain momentum, the Group recommends that attention be given—by the IAEA Member States, by the IAEA itself, by the

nuclear industry and by other nuclear organizations—to multilateral nuclear approaches in general and to the five approaches suggested below.

Five Suggested Approaches

The objective of increasing non-proliferation assurances associated with the civilian nuclear fuel cycle, while preserving assurances of supply and services around the world could be achieved through a set of gradually introduced multilateral nuclear approaches (MNA):

1) Reinforcing **existing commercial market mechanisms** on a case-by-case basis through long-term contracts and transparent suppliers' arrangements with government backing. Examples would be: fuel leasing and fuel take-back offers, commercial offers to store and dispose of spent fuel, as well as commercial fuel banks.

2) Developing and implementing **international supply guarantees** with IAEA participation. Different models should be investigated, notably with **the IAEA as guarantor** of service supplies, e.g., as administrator of a fuel bank.

3) Promoting voluntary conversion of **existing facilities to MNAs,** and pursuing them as **confidence-building measures,** with the participation of NPT non-nuclear weapon States and nuclear-weapon States, and non-NPT States.

4) Creating, through voluntary agreements and contracts, **multinational, and in particular regional, MNAs for new facilities** based on joint ownership, drawing rights or co-management for front-end and back-end nuclear facilities, such as uranium enrichment; fuel reprocessing; disposal and storage of spent fuel (and combinations thereof). Integrated nuclear power parks would also serve this objective.

5) The scenario of a further expansion of nuclear energy around the world might call for the development of a **nuclear fuel cycle with stronger multilateral arrangements** – by region or by continent—and for broader cooperation, involving the IAEA and the international community.

Appendix 9

Global Nuclear Energy Partnership

Announcement by Secretary of Energy Samuel Bodman and Press Briefing by Deputy Secretary of Energy Clay Sell, March 2006, U.S. Department of Energy, Office of Public Affairs, Washington, D.C.

(*Note:* For more information on the Global Nuclear Energy Partnership, including a copy of Deputy Secretary Sell's slide presentation, see http://www.gnep.energy.gov/.)

SEC. BODMAN: Hello again. Thank you all for being here as we will be discussing the Global Nuclear Energy Partnership that we alluded to in the other room.

GNEP is part of the President's Advanced Energy Initiative, the one that he announced last Tuesday evening in the State of the Union. If we are successful in implementing GNEP, we will be able to increase energy security, both here in the United States and abroad; we'll be able to encourage clean economic development around the world; and we'll be able to improve the environment.

The idea is that GNEP will leverage new technology to effectively and safely recycle spent nuclear fuel without producing separated plutonium. That's the whole idea behind it. By doing so we will extract more energy from nuclear fuel, reduce the amount of waste that requires permanent disposal, and greatly reduce the risk of nuclear proliferation. If we can make GNEP a reality, we can make the world a better, cleaner and safer place to live.

We're very pleased with the President's request of $250 million, which is an initial investment in what we believe will be a very ambitious plan to accelerate the development of nuclear technologies. GNEP, like other aspects of the President's Advanced Energy Initiative and the American Competitiveness Initiative, is based on the idea that scientific discovery will ultimately hold the answers to the questions that the world is facing today, and in particular, the questions that we in the energy department are facing today.

Deputy Secretary Sell is going to walk you through the details of the GNEP policy, but before he does, I want to thank the many people here at this department who have worked so hard on this initiative, both here in the headquarters building as well as in our laboratories. These include the Deputy Secretary himself, who I asked to undertake the leadership in this area of looking at the questions related to the development of a nuclear initiative when he came on board about 10 months ago, 11 months ago.

They also include Under Secretary Dave Garman and Linton Brooks, both of them, and I want to thank them for their participation in this; Ray Orbach, who is here, who is the Director of the Office Science; and the Acting Director of the Office of Nuclear Energy, Shane Johnson; as well as the Acting Assistant Secretary of the Civilian Radioactive Waste Management Program, Paul Golan. These people and their teams have provided quite extraordinary insight and direction, and they have worked really day and night to develop a program that we all believe has the potential to change the world—we believe that.

I would also say, before introducing the Deputy—and that the Deputy Secretary, by tradition in the government is—looks after the day-to-day operations and is in effect the chief operating officer of the department. And I have chosen to associate with that job the person who is the chief budgeting officer that makes the tough decisions, and he has worked very closely with Susan Grant and her folks in the CFO's office, and in my judgment, he's done a first-class job. Clay?

CLAY SELL: Thank you very much, Mr. Secretary, for your opening remarks and your very kind remarks.

I'm pleased today to finally gather together today with you and discuss the Global Nuclear Energy Partnership. And the Global Nuclear Energy Partnership at its core is a way that we anticipate dramatically expanding nuclear power here in the United States, but also in the world in a way which effectively addressed two of the great concerns that have historically been associated with nuclear power here in the United States, but also in the world, in a way which effectively addresses two of the great concerns that have historically been associated with nuclear power. Those are what do you do with the waste and what about the proliferation of technologies that can lead to the bomb. We think the Global Nuclear Energy Partnership effectively addressees both of those great questions in a way which will enhance the expansion of nuclear power worldwide. Those are the policy goals.

I want to spend a little time on this next chart and step back and really focus on the problem that we are contemplating. In the next 50 years, world energy demand is expected to double, and not only is it expected to double, it is our great desire that it double. Large segments of the world today are still coming up the development curve, and those countries need great increases in the amount of power in order to come up the curve, and we're going to have a lot more people in 2050.

Now if we try to manage that increased energy growth on the backs of fossil fuels, we will have a very significant greenhouse gas concern and a very significant pollution concern, and it is our view here in the Department of Energy that we need all alternatives to address this. We need a great expansion of renewables, we need a great expansion of biomass, we need a great expansion of clean coal technology, but we must—anyone that fairly looks at this question whether you're from the energy side of the debate or the environmental side of the debate concludes that nuclear power must play a significant role in meeting this dramatic growth in energy demand.

I'd like to make a point about nuclear. The world has recognized that nuclear power must play a significant role in meeting this demand. There are over 130 nuclear power reactors either under construction, in the planning stage or under consideration around the globe. Now when I started briefing this slide a few months ago, the United States was nowhere on this list. Now, fortunately, due to the provisions that the president signed into law in the Energy Policy Act last summer, there is now talk and consideration of new nuclear power plants, even here in the United States.

But the point of this slide is nuclear power is going to go on without us. We can either be a part of it or we can observe, and it's our view that from a nonproliferation standpoint, from an economic—U.S. economic standpoint, we are in a much stronger position to shape the future if we are part of it and if we are building it.

MR.: (Off mike.)

MR. SELL: Yes, the green bar—on the bottom this is 5, 10, 15, 20. The green bars are reactors under construction. The blue bar is reactors planned or approved for construction, and the yellow bar is reactors formally under consideration in each of these various countries.

And so really the initiative began with us thinking forward to the year 2050, a world with perhaps 1,000 nuclear reactors in it, and thinking about what are the technologies, what are the policies, what are the international regimes we would want to have in place when we get there, and that is the origin, and that's what we seek to address in the Global Nuclear Energy Partnership.

The provisions of GNEP are consistent, quite frankly, with the policies that were laid out in the President's National Energy Policy five years ago. It was a—I recall—I was working on the Hill at the time. I recall what a dramatic thing it was when the President called for an expansion of nuclear power five years ago, and that he advocated developing advanced reprocessing/recycling technologies. Now it is accepted, really, that the world must have a great expansion of nuclear power, and the United States must have an expansion of nuclear power. And as that realization has set in, our thinking as to what policies and technologies we need have also evolved.

As the Secretary indicated, GNEP is going to start with $250 million budget in fiscal year '07. We do have some monies in fiscal year '06 that we think we can dedicate towards it to get moving on it, and this budget is expected to increase dramatically in the coming years, and most notably in the three years remaining in this administration.

The benefits of—if we can in fact expand nuclear power in concert with the way we think about the Global Nuclear Energy Partnership, we think the benefits are substantial. It will allow us in the United States to dramatically reduce America's dependence on fossil fuels: certainly coal; certainly natural gas, which we are increasing our imports of and plan to dramatically increase our imports of, but in the future as we think about a transportation sector more dependent on the electricity sector, through hybrid vehicles or through hydrogen fuel cells, nuclear power and the electricity power generation sector will have a growing impact on the transportation side as well.

And I would also add, to the extent we dramatically expand nuclear power worldwide, that can significantly reduce world demand for oil. Many countries around the world generate a significant amount of their electricity with fuel oil and, in fact, much of the increased demand and growth out of China over the last few years has been driven by their greater use of diesel generation in that country. So to the extent we can replace diesel and fuel oil generation for electricity with nuclear power, that can significantly affect and reduce the growth in demand for oil worldwide.

The impact—the second point, the impact of nuclear power on greenhouse gases, is not questioned. It is the only large, mature technology capable of baseload generation of electricity that does not emit any greenhouse gases.

To the extent—on the third point, to the extent we can recycle used nuclear fuel, the secretary indicated in the earlier press conference it dramatically minimizes the amount of waste that we ultimately have to dispose of.

On the fourth point, we think there are significant nonproliferation benefits to the Global Nuclear Energy Partnership, which I will elaborate on later in the presentation.

The fifth point—through recycling and utilization of the actinide fuel and fast reactors, we are able to get much greater efficiency from nuclear fuel. Today in our policy we burn spent nuclear—we burn nuclear fuel once and then it goes for ultimate disposition, and when it goes—under current policy, when it goes in Yucca Mountain, it will still have over 90 percent of its energy value to it.

Under the Global Nuclear Energy Partnership and advance recycling technologies, we can utilize a great—much greater percentage of the energy value in fuel. And then if we are able to do that, we will dramatically reduce the volume and radiotoxicity of the material that ultimately has to be disposed of, and instead of having to build many Yucca Mountain-like facilities over the course of this century, we think we can dramatically grow nuclear power and dispose of all of the waste that would be generated in one Yucca Mountain facility, and we would not have to face the prospect of building a second, third, fourth, fifth, or sixth throughout the century.

I want to focus on one of the key—the benefits of GNEP here and the key program elements are in developing the technology and in facilitating a regime of the future that allows for fuel leasing. And there's really—there's a key nonproliferation benefit that I want to focus on, that is today much of the world has gone on. The other major nuclear economies have continued with reprocessing. The United States stopped reprocessing in 1970. We stopped reprocessing because the technology of that day separated plutonium, and that presents a significant proliferation concern, but the rest of the world—France, Japan, Russia, the United Kingdom—went on and continued to develop these reprocessing technologies, and we now have over 200 metric tons of separated civil plutonium around the globe today.

It is our goal to develop, in partnership with these other nations, technologies that will allow for the recycling of spent fuel but not separate plutonium, and in the process of developing those technologies and coupling them with fast reactors that can burn down the spent fuel. We hope to develop an international regime that will allow for fuel leasing so that fuel can be leased to a county interested in building a reactor and taking fuel, but then the fuel can be taken back to the fuel cycle country.

I'm going to tick through a number of the key elements here, kind of stepping back and going through the seven elements of GNEP. Certainly the first part of it is to expand the use of nuclear power, consistent with the provisions in the Energy Policy Act, Nuclear Power 2010, and the other provisions that have been passed. We're confident that a number of current-generation or next-generation reactors will be built in the United States. I've talked about the goal—the importance of minimizing the nuclear waste. I've talked about the advanced recycling demonstration. That's a key part of what we're going to try to accomplish in the next few years. The technologies on this will be—there are two key technologies that we're looking at—one called UREX Plus—which, instead of separating out pure plutonium combines the plutonium with other actinides and some portion or uranium so that it is not attractive or usable as weapons material. And the other technology is dry reprocessing, or pyroprocessing, which uses a slightly different technology.

And of course, in addition to the recycling piece we will couple that with fast reactors. We've built a number of fast reactors in this country over the years. Japan, France, Russia have also developed fast reactors. The key will be developing a fast reactor which can burn the actinide-based fuel and reduce that down, and we hope to demonstrate that technology over the course of the next ten years. Once again, that will allow a system of reliable fuel services, which is elaborated—I can elaborate somewhat on with this chart.

It is our hope to develop this technology in partnership with a number—with the other great nuclear economies of the world. Two weeks ago the Undersecretary of State for Nonproliferation Bob Joseph and I visited the other capitals of the leading nuclear economies. We went to London, Paris, Moscow, Beijing, Tokyo. We also stopped to see Dr. ElBaradei in Vienna to lay out our vision of reordering the global nuclear enterprise. And it would be our hope to work in partnership with these other countries to develop these advanced recycling technologies to a state where they could be deployed in the existing countries that have the full elements of the fuel cycle. And once those advanced technologies are deployed, that will lead us to a situation where we can sell reactors to other countries that are interested in the benefits of nuclear power, lease that fuel to those countries, and then take it back for recycling and for waste disposition.

Now, the value in that—we have found that it is unproductive often to talk in terms of rights, and what rights do the countries have to develop the fuel cycle? Well, what we're hoping to do is develop commercially attractive incentives so that a country interested in bringing the benefits of nuclear power to their economy can purchase a reactor and then lease fuel and not have to worry about making their own investments in the fuel cycle. So the goal here and the reason we think this can work from a nonproliferation standpoint is that we are seeking to provide commercially attractive incentives for countries to lease fuel rather than make investments in their own fuel cycle.

It is also a key element of this initiative that we would cooperate with existing fuel cycle states or any other country in the development of small-scale reactors. And we think there is a great opportunity here to enhance our nuclear cooperation with many countries on developing reactors of a size and with the nonproliferation benefits that would be appropriate for the developing world. It would be of a smaller scale appropriate for smaller grids.

Another key aspect of the initiative is enhanced nuclear safeguards and ensuring that we install best practices on handling nuclear material and in building the advanced fuel cycle of facilities. And so what are the next steps? We're going to continue to work to expand nuclear power here in the United States by implementing the provisions in the Energy Policy Act and making progress on Yucca Mountain as quickly as possible. It is our goal, with the GNEP initiative, to raise the level of debate and to make progress more quickly on Yucca Mountain than we have in the past. And as part of this we will be sending for a legislative package in the coming weeks that will make a number of legislative changes to the Nuclear Waste Policy Act that will allow us to make progress much more quickly on Yucca Mountain. We hope to join in partnership and broaden our consultation with other countries to develop the advanced recycling technologies and we hope to continue to build on the—build the global consensus for this GNEP vision, and that is that we need a world with a dramatic expansion of nuclear power. We must recycle in order to manage the waste. We should recycle in a way that does not separate plutonium, and we should develop a fuel-leasing regime that ensures we do not see a greater proliferation of the key aspects of the fuel cycle which worry us the most, which are the enrichment technology and the reprocessing technology.

So in conclusion, we think the U.S. and the world are faced with a set of challenges related to energy supply, nuclear proliferation and global climate change. And the global nuclear energy partnership, we think, uniquely addresses these challenges to meet the rapidly growing energy demand, reduce carbon emissions, enable the clean development of the world, and avoid proliferation. And so with that I'll take your questions.

Q: Andrei Sitov from TASS, the Russian News Agency. You mentioned you went to Moscow. Could you tell us what the response was from the Russian side? Generally speaking, how does this initiative correlate with the recent proposal from President Putin for basically the same thing?

MR. SELL: We think it's consistent. In our meetings in Moscow, as well as our meetings elsewhere, the vision, the goals, were all very well received—in some cases enthusiastically received. But as is the case between partners, there are different perspectives and different angles and there are many details to be worked out, and quite frankly, many more consultations to occur with those countries that we've been to as well as other countries. But the ideas were very well received in all of the capitals.

Q: One of the details that you probably mean is this reprocessing thing. Do you mean to take back nuclear waste for reprocessing in this country?

MR. SELL: What we mean to do is develop the technologies that allow us to effectively deal with waste on the backend. If we can do that—and, sir, it's our view that those technologies should be in existing fuel cycle states. If we can do that there is certainly—you know, if you look at the existing fuel cycle states, that's almost 70 percent of the nuclear reactors in the world. And so certainly those countries have a significant incentive and economic reasons to make investments in the full elements of the fuel cycle, including in ultimate repository.

But what we really want to do is develop the technologies that allow us to deal with the waste. And whether the final waste is ultimately disposed of in a repository in a fuel cycle country, or whether it is ultimately disposed of in a repository elsewhere, the nonproliferation goals have been met.

Q: (Inaudible.) My question is aimed at what you're going to be doing with this waste. From what I understand, when you separate it, over 90 percent is depleted uranium. Is this then going to be put back into a fast reactor or re-enriched and then put into a fast reactor to create more energy, or does it need to be disposed of?

MR. SELL: Either way. It could be re-enriched or it could be disposed of, but if it's disposed of I believe that it would be disposed of as low-level waste. And so the cost of doing something—the cost of that is substantially less, but it certainly—we contemplate that it could be re-enriched, and the market may drive it to be re-enriched in the future.

Q: Just one quick follow-up. So would this depleted uranium—if you're not going to dispose of it, it would need to be put somewhere as a temporary basis. Is that right? I mean, how would we set up some—would there have to be a new sort of schematic to deal with that?

MR. SELL: To deal with the depleted uranium?

Q: With the depleted uranium, the storage of it.

MR. SELL: Yes.

Q: Dan Whitten with *Inside Energy*. Looking at the legislation, would it expand the capacity of Yucca Mountain—would your legislative proposal expand the capacity of Yucca Mountain, and do you envision retrieving the waste from Yucca Mountain for reprocessing, or would it be stored somehow above ground? And then finally, is there anything related to GNEP authorization in the legislation, or is that separate?

MR. SELL: That was several questions. I'll try to get them all.

Q: Sorry about that.

MR. SELL: As far as what we intend to do over the next few years, specifically as it relates to GNEP, we will work with the Congress on that, but it is our view that we have sufficient authority under the Atomic Energy Act to proceed. As to Yucca Mountain, it is our great desire, and it is in the nation's interest, and it is the interest in facilitating a nuclear renaissance, which we greatly need, that we get Yucca Mountain licensed and that we get it opened. And once we get it opened, then we can start moving spent fuel there. And we would certainly contemplate it as possible that fuel could move there and then be recycled, or it is possible that we would build recycling centers—and I think there will be significant interest from various states in building these centers in which spent fuel would be staged there temporarily while it is in the process to be recycled and before it ultimately goes to Yucca Mountain for disposition.

Q: Matt Wald, *New York Times*. Do you have a target price in mind for uranium and a target year at which point it makes sense to use something besides virgin newly enriched uranium—would make sense to use actinides or something else instead, or are you putting some dollar value on the kilos of waste that don't go into Yucca?

MR. SELL: We think, from a—the scale of what we are proposing to undertake is massive, and this is still a technology development and demonstration program. And so there is significant uncertainty about the cost of it. But a few things we are confident in. One, the cost of disposing of once-through spent fuel in Yucca Mountain is significant. It is very significant when you contemplate what we will do in order to license a facility for a million years, which is what is contemplated. The spent fuel going into Yucca Mountain will not have its peak dose until approximately year 1 million. And so, in order to license a facility with material like that in it, we are going to have to spend a tremendous amount of money and build massive packaging materials in order to ensure that that is possible.

So one of the benefits of disposing of recycled waste is that it's much more stable, it has a much lower radiotoxicity, and therefore it is a simpler and more straightforward proposition to ultimately dispose of it, and that will result in significant cost savings on Yucca Mountain, or the multiple Yucca Mountains that would have to be built over the coming years.

Secondly, there are significant, we believe, nonproliferation benefits in recycling and burning down spent fuel. And we start from the view that economics, the environment, clean development, and concerns about greenhouse gases are going to drive the world to many, many more nuclear power plants, and that is going to present a significant proliferation challenge if we have not thought through and presented a well organized way to address it, and the way we think is appropriate to address it is by recycling that spent fuel in a way that does not separate plutonium, and building an international regime that allows for fuel leasing and take back to eliminate concerns about proliferation.

So the nonproliferation benefit of what we are talking about is quite substantial, and it's also quite difficult to quantify, but we are seeking to develop these technologies, we are seeking to lessen the amount of uncertainty as to what it would cost to build these facilities on a commercial scale, and ultimately we hope to be in a position to make a judgment about the commercial viability of this approach in the coming years.

Q: Very quick follow-up. You are implying that the 1 mil per kilowatt hour won't pay for Yucca. Is that right? I mean, you have the money in hand from commercial sources to pay for waste disposal.

MR. SELL: Each year under the Nuclear Waste Policy Act the Secretary is called upon to make a judgment as to whether the 1 mil fee is sufficient. And certainly it is my view that in the coming years, if we do not develop a better way, we may come to the conclusion that it's not sufficient.

Q: Thank you. Just a brief clarification. I am—(unintelligible)—from Kyoto News Japanese Wire Service. You mentioned that you have visited United Kingdom, France and Russia, China and Japan to discuss this partnership. Are these all the countries you plan to working on this partnership?

MR. SELL: No. This was just the initial round of consultations, and we expect to have many more consultations and with many other countries, but the countries that we've been to certainly today represent the most advanced—the countries that have mad the most significant investments in the commercial fuel cycle.

Q: Sorry, just a brief—would you name one or two other countries you are going to work on?

MR. SELL: We would contemplate in the future that once India has met the nonproliferation commitments that it has made and that were memorialized in the joint statement between our two heads of state last summer, that they would be a great candidate for participation as well. But we also anticipate that there are many countries that have significant technologies, particularly as far as reactors, that we would look forward to participating with. In part this is voluntary. We're going to see who's interested.

Q: I'm John Fialka with the *Wall Street Journal.* Could you describe to me what this separated fuel does to the problem of making a nuclear weapon? You have now mixed up the actinides with the fuel. Does that make it impossible to make a nuclear weapon?

MR. SELL: It makes it dramatically more difficult because the radiotoxicity of the material and the quantity of the material, and we believe if we—we only contemplate deploying these technologies on a commercial scale in existing fuel cycle countries. And we contemplate doing that with the most sophisticated of safeguard arrangements. And it is the ability to have these advanced recycling technologies, and most importantly the ability to dispose of the actinides, which offer the great nonproliferation benefit over the coming decades.

Q: Tom Doggett with Reuters. To be clear, so when you recycle this fuel and you're going to loan it to other countries for fuel for their reactors, if they give it back, if we had it working today, this program, would we have these worries we do now about Iran, if indeed they wanted to have a nuclear program for electricity production? Would we loan this to future countries like Iran to make sure they don't develop a nuclear weapon? Will this avoid that?

MR. SELL: All countries that are signators to the Nonproliferation Treaty, like Iran, have the right to develop the fuel cycle for commercial nuclear purposes. It is our concern that that right—and we've seen it in history—

has been used as a cover to develop a clandestine weapons program. As far as GNEP we have found the discussion of rights to be unhelpful. But what we hope to do is provide commercial, attractive—or commercially attractive opportunities for countries that are genuinely interested in bringing the benefits of nuclear power to their country, to buy a reactor, build it, and then lease fuel and return that fuel to a fuel-cycle state for ultimate recycling, and we think we can offer that on terms that would be very attractive commercially, and in exchange that country would agree to suspend any investments in the fuel cycle, and we think that can be a very workable framework going forward to greatly discourage the proliferation of the fuel cycle.

Q: I am Suzanne Struglinski with the *Deseret Morning News,* serves Salt Lake City. In December, several companies dropped out of the private fuel storage program. I was wondering if the administration presented this plan to them at that point and if you could talk a little bit more about what the industry and how they are involved at this point and what their opinions are on the waste storage ideas that you are talking about.

MR. SELL: We did not present this plan to industry, but certainly last year we saw a significant uptick under the leadership of Chairman Hobson in the House. I had discussion of advanced recycling. And so certainly that prospect has been out there, but I don't know of any direct link between our initiative and what has transpired with PFS. It is our view I would say that Yucca Mountain is the right answer and PFS is not.

Q: You have talked about this program as a technology development effort at this point. What about the implementation? And do you have any target dates for when GNEP would be a viable program for implementation or is it something that could be done in stages with other countries with the technologies such as (inaudible) or reprocessing or what not to begin implementing right away.

MR. SELL: As far as the technologies it is our goal to work in partnership with our nations to develop these technologies and to demonstrate them on an engineering scale. The reprocessing technologies, the recycling technologies that we have talked about have only been demonstrated at a laboratory scale, and so we need to demonstrate those on an engineering scale, and make judgments, and understand them better so that each of the involved countries can make a judgment on commercialization. We would hope to demonstrate those technologies over the next five to 10 years and then be in a position to make judgments on the next round of investments thereafter.

Q: To follow up on that, is it too soon—is it too soon at this point to be talking about whether the United States is contemplating the building of new nuclear power plants or are these recycling facilities that you talked about in certain states, where those would go, how you would negotiate with states to build them. Is all that too far down the road?

MR. SELL: As far as new nuclear power plants, that is an issue that is before us now, and there are a number of states that are interested; there are a number of potential applications to the nuclear regulatory commission for new plants, and that is something that is quite exciting and quite encouraging. As far as the recycling and fast reactor piece, we are still in the mode of demonstrating the technology and future decisions on siting will be exactly that, decisions of the future.

Q: Martin Schneider with *Weapons Complex Monitor.* You mentioned about plans for a significant increase in the investment in GNEP. Do you have plans money wise at least what the requests are going to be in this administration going forward in the out years, '08, '09.

MR. SELL: We have an understanding and one of the—the scale of what we are proposing is substantial, and the level of R&D and demonstration funding that would be required of this country is significant. That was discussed at length on an interagency basis as we developed this proposal with OMB and they are aware and committed to a level of investment, which will get us where we need to be. We hope to do this and we seek to do this on a partnership basis with significant foreign contributions as well but we would contemplate that the budget would increase substantially or could increase substantially over the next few years, and there is agreement within the administration to do that.

Q: Is that more or less a billion dollars?

MR. SELL: I am going to go with my answer the way I said a while ago.

Q: (Off mike)—*Financial Times.* Has any thought been given to who would decide what countries could be eligible for the renting on this fuel? For example, Beijing might be more interested in working out something with a place like North Korea than Washington might feel more comfortable with that? Would it be determined by the United States? Would it be something that would be done in conjunction with other partners of the IAEA play into this at all? How would it work out?

MR. SELL: We expect that that IAEA will play some role in this. Certainly the proposal is attractive to user nations only if they can have some sense of energy security, and energy security comes from a diversity of potential suppliers. And so certainly that is a key element of this, and that is why we contemplated early on developing these technologies in the existing major nuclear economies including China, including Russia, so that there would be a diversity of potential fuel cycle nations that could supply on a commercial basis to user nations.

Q: Steve Tetreault, *Las Vegas Review Journal.* I want to make sure I understood. Does this plan envision that GNEP fuel at the end would be disposed at Yucca Mountain, and if so, does that necessitate any further design changes or legislative changes to accept this type of fuel?

MR. SELL: You did understand correctly that we contemplate disposing of the ultimate disposition, the ultimate waste in Yucca Mountain. We think it is absolutely the right place and it is the place that we should do it. Certainly the design requirements for disposing of once through spent nuclear fuel are dramatically different than the design requirements for the product that would ultimately be disposed because the product after recycling is a substantially lower radio toxicity. It is in a stable glass form. And so the packaging that would be association with it and the design requirements associated with disposing of it would change. Paul, would you like to elaborate on that? This is Paul Golan from our Office of Civilian Radioactive Waste Management.

PAUL GOLAN: Sure. And today we contemplate putting reprocessed waste in Yucca Mountain, the glass that was manufactured at Savannah River at West Valley and the glass that will be manufactured at Hanford. So it is already contemplated as part of our waste acceptance criteria—also the spent nuclear fuel from the Navy and from the commercial sites are and our designed case right now is to accommodate all of that fuel certainly as this moves forward. We are just going to keep our eye on that but we are going forward with all of the things that currently Yucca Mountain is envisioned to accept today.

Q: This is one of the current designs?

MR. GOLAN: This would fall under the umbrella of the current design.

Q: How about fuel that has been foreign and back?

MR. GOLAN: The only fuel that we have in our current inventory today is university fuel that went out in the '50s and '60s that the United States is accepting today, and it's U.S.-origin fuel, and so that is included in our waste acceptance criteria, but it's a very small fraction of the total fuel that is envisioned at Yucca.

Q: What about fuel that has been used overseas and that is coming back for disposal? Is that getting ahead?

MR. SELL: I think it is an open question in my mind when we think about the vision, and this is still—this is a vision as to how the world we would like to see in 50 years and it is dependent on a number of things, the development of the technology, international agreements, and other things, and it is an open question in that vision as to where the ultimate waste material would go. It is certainly possible that it could stay in a country where it is recycled and burned down, but it is also possible that it could go back to the user nation as well. But once that material has been recycled and burned down, it does not present the proliferation risk that spent fuel does today.

Q: Dan Horner from McGraw-Hill Nuclear Publications. A couple points of clarification: Since you're talking about fuel supply in the context of this initiative I gather you are talking about supplying mixed oxide fuel rather than low enriched uranium fuel, and if you could talk about that a little bit and all of that. And secondly, the $250 million for this year, how much of that is new money and how much of that is existing programs that are now just being grouped for better cohesion under the rubric of GNEP? Thanks.

MR. SELL: Let me address your first question. We did not contemplate a MOX fuel cycle as part of GNEP and I want to be clear on that. This issue came up when we were in Paris. The French have moved forward with commercial reprocessing using the PUREX, which separates plutonium and then burning that plutonium in light water reactors in a MOX fuel cycle. We do not concur in their—(audio break, tape change)—use of an actinide-based fuel so plutonium and other actinides to be burned in a fast reactor, what we call the advanced burner reactor. That is the GNEP vision that will allow for a significant burn down in reduction of the world actinide inventory.

Q: I'm sorry, if I could just clarify that. So what we're talking about—having the separation facilities and the fast reactors only in a limited number of countries, not to the countries that are being supplied or are you envisioning fast reactors in the recipient countries of the fuel supply as well?

MR. SELL: We would anticipate—I mean, certainly there are some small reactor technologies that may involve fast spectrum technology. But as it relates to the recycling facilities and the burn down of the actinide-based, plutonium-based fuel in fast reactors, we contemplate that all occurring within fuel cycle nations, not the user nations. We anticipate the sale of many, many more light-water reactors all around the globe to user nations as well as to fuel cycle states in the decades to come.

Q: (Off mike)—question about the $250 million?

MR. SELL: Oh, how much of that is new? Shane, can you address that?

MR. JOHNSON: Yes, in our current fiscal year 2006 we have an appropriation of 80 million for advanced real cycle initiative. The GNEP program, which is an acceleration of our advanced real cycle is the 250. So do the math here—about $170 million of due money.

Q: I'm Ben Grove, *Las Vegas Sun.* Can you outline what Yucca Mountain-related items there are in the legislation, the DOE is proposing?

MR. SELL: The legislation that we're working to send forward would address a number of issues associated with the project including providing a secure funding stream for the project; it would—what are the other key elements of it, Paul? Do you want to talk about that?

MR. GOLAN: There are a couple of things. First is the funding stream. The second large aspect of that is land withdrawal, and we have to permanently withdraw 147,000 acres of land as a condition for getting a license to receive and possess on the nuclear regulatory commission. I think that is what I am prepared to talk about today on that as we have to get clearance from our office and management and budget before we can talk much more.

Q: (Off mike.)

MR. GOLAN: It is the 147,000 acres that surround the Yucca Mountain repository area. So part of that is BLM land; part of that is Department of Energy land today, and part of that is Air Force land. So it would be the area surrounding the Yucca Mountain repository.

Q: (Off mike.)

MR. GOLAN: No, we don't.

ANNE KOLTON: One more question.

Q: I don't know—have you had any discussions with Congress yet as of the—Jeff Thompson of CQ. Had you had any discussions with Congress yet? I mean, as of last week there had no official briefings and there are already some eyebrows raising about the appropriations moving forward.

MR. SELL: We have had a number of discussions with key congressional leaders and others.

MS. KOLTON: Okay, one more question.

Q: David Kestenbaum, National, . . . Public Radio. It is my understanding that reprocessed fuel can be used in a bomb, that it is not the best stuff to work with but you can still make a nice kiloton explosive. So to be clear, you're saying that reprocessed fuel will not be sent to other countries to be used as fuels in reactors there?

MR. SELL: Let me—the premise of your question, which is reprocessed fuel can be used in a bomb—using existing technology, PUREX-based technology, it results in separated plutonium.

Q: But even the stuff that comes out of UREX (sp) Plus?

MR. SELL: The stuff that comes out of UREX Plus provides significant nonproliferation benefits from the—from its radiotoxicity, its handleability, as well as the quantity that would have to be utilized. And all of these advanced recycling facilities would only be built as we contemplate in existing fuel cycle states. The most important thing from a nonproliferation standpoint is the burn down of that material to your question would occur in these burner reactors in the fuel cycle states and that would not be exported or we would not contemplate that that would be exported to other what we call user nations.

Q: What was wrong with GNEI as a name for this as I understand was the original working title? G-N-E-I.

MR. SELL: We have working titles, then the communicators take over. (Laughter.)

Q: Not something that should be kept in a bottle? Is that one of the advantages of GNEP?

MR. SELL: I guess. We do not intend to keep GNEP in a bottle. (Laughter.)

Q: Thank you very much.

MS. KOLTON: Great. Thank you very much, everybody.

Select Bibliography

Acheson, Dean. *Present at the Creation: My Years in the State Department.* New York: Norton, 1969.
Bird, Kai, and Martin J. Sherwin. *American Prometheus: The Triumph and Tragedy of J. Robert Oppenheimer.* New York: Vintage, 2006.
Bowie, Robert R., and Richard H. Immerman. *Waging Peace: How Eisenhower Shaped an Enduring Cold War Strategy.* New York: Oxford University Press, 1998.
Branyan, Robert L., and Lawrence H. Larsen. *The Eisenhower Administration, 1953–1961: A Documentary History.* 2 vols. New York: Random House, 1971.
Brodie, Bernard, ed. *The Absolute Weapon: Atomic Power and World Order.* New York: Harcourt, Brace, and Company, 1946.
Bundy, McGeorge. *Danger and Survival: Choices about the Bomb in the First Fifty Years.* New York: Random House, 1988.
———. "Early Thought on Controlling the Nuclear Arms Race: A Report to the Secretary of State, January 1953." *International Security* 7 (Fall 1982): 3–27.
Cantelon, Philip L., Richard G. Hewlett, and Robert C. Williams, eds. *The American Atom: A Documentary History of Nuclear Policies from the Discovery of Fission to the Present, 1939–1984.* Philadelphia: University of Pennsylvania Press, 1984.
Center for Global Security Research. *Atoms for Peace after 50 Years: The New Challenges and Opportunities.* Livermore, Calif.: Lawrence Livermore National Laboratory, December 2003.

Deutch, John, Arnold Kanter, Ernest Moniz, and Daniel Poneman. "Making the World Safe for Nuclear Energy." *Survival* 46, no. 4 (Winter 2004–2005): 65–80.
Divine, Robert A. *Eisenhower and the Cold War.* New York: Oxford University Press, 1981.
Eisenhower, Dwight D. *Mandate for Change, 1953–1956: The White House Years.* Garden City, N.Y.: Doubleday, 1963.
Fermi, Laura. *Atoms for the World: United States Participation in the Conference on the Peaceful Uses of Atomic Energy.* Chicago: University of Chicago Press, 1957.
Fischer, David. *History of the International Atomic Energy Agency: The First Forty Years.* Vienna: International Atomic Energy Agency, 1997.
Gaddis, John Lewis. *Strategies of Containment: A Critical Appraisal of Postwar American National Security Policy.* New York: Oxford University Press, 1982.
———. *We Now Know: Rethinking the Cold War.* Oxford: Clarendon Press, 1997.
Goldschmidt, Bertrand. *The Atomic Complex: A Worldwide Political History of Nuclear Energy.* La Grange Park, Ill.: American Nuclear Society, 1982.
Herken, Gregg. *Counsels of War.* New York: Knopf, 1985.
Hershberg, James G. *James B. Conant: Harvard to Hiroshima and the Making of the Nuclear Age.* New York: Alfred A. Knopf, 1993.
Hewlett, Richard G., and Oscar E. Anderson, Jr. *The New World: A History of the United States Atomic Energy Commission,* Vol. 1, 1939–1946. Berkeley: University of California Press, 1962.
Hewlett, Richard G., and Francis Duncan. *Atomic Shield: A History of the United States Atomic Energy Commission,* Vol. 2, 1947–1952. Berkeley: University of California Press, 1962.
Hewlett, Richard G., and Jack M. Holl. *Atoms for Peace and War, 1953–1961: Eisenhower and the Atomic Energy Commission.* Berkeley: University of California Press, 1989.
Hogerton, John F., ed. *Atoms for Peace: U.S.A. 1958.* Cambridge, Mass.: Arthur D. Little, Inc., 1958.
Institute for Foreign Policy Analysis. *Nuclear Energy and Science for the 21st Century: Atoms for Peace Plus 50.* Final report from a conference organized by the Institute for Foreign Policy Analysis and the International Security Studies Program of the Fletcher School, Tufts University, Medford, Mass., 2004.
Kistiakowsky, George B. *A Scientist at the White House: The Private Diary of President Eisenhower's Special Assistant for Science and Technology.* Cambridge, Mass.: Harvard University Press, 1976.
Kramish, Arnold. *The Peaceful Atom in Foreign Policy.* Published for the Council on Foreign Relations. New York and Evanston: Harper & Row, 1963.
Lavoy, Peter R. "The Enduring Effects of Atoms for Peace." *Arms Control Today* 33, no. 10 (December 2003): 26–30.
Lilienthal, David E. *Change, Hope and the Bomb.* Princeton, N.J.: Princeton University Press, 1963.
———. *The Journals of David E. Lilienthal.* 7 vols. New York: Harper & Row, 1964–1983.
Newhouse, John. *War and Peace in the Nuclear Age.* New York: Knopf, 1989.
Nogee, Joseph L. *Soviet Policy Towards International Control of Atomic Energy.* Notre Dame, Ind.: University of Notre Dame Press, 1961.

Oppenheimer, J. Robert. "Atomic Weapons and American Policy." *Foreign Affairs* 31 (July 1953): 525–535.

Pilat, Joseph F., Robert E. Pendley, and Charles K. Ebinger, eds. *Atoms for Peace: An Analysis after Thirty Years.* Boulder, Colo.: Westview Press, 1985.

Seaborg, Glenn T. *A Chemist in the White House: From the Manhattan Project to the End of the Cold War.* Washington, D.C.: American Chemical Society, 1998.

———, and William R. Corliss. *Man and Atom: Building a New World through Nuclear Technology.* New York: E. P. Dutton, 1971.

Smith, Alice Kimball, and Charles Weiner. *Robert Oppenheimer: Letters and Recollections.* Stanford, Calif.: Stanford University Press, 1980.

Smyth, Henry DeWolf. *Atomic Energy for Military Purposes: The Official Report on the Development of the Atomic Bomb under the Auspices of the United States Government, 1940–1945.* Princeton, N.J.: Princeton University Press, 1945.

Snyder, Glenn. "The 'New Look' of 1953." In *Strategy, Politics, and Defense Budgets,* edited by Warner R. Schilling, Paul Y. Hammond, and Glenn Snyder, 379–524. New York: Columbia University Press, 1962.

Strauss, Lewis L. *Men and Decisions.* Garden City, N.Y.: Doubleday, 1962.

U.S. Atomic Energy Commission. *Nuclear Milestones: A Collection of Speeches by Glenn T. Seaborg.* Vol. 1, Builders and Discoverers. Washington, D.C.: Atomic Energy Commission, 1971.

———. *Uranium, Plutonium, and Industry: A Summary of the U.S. Atomic Energy Program.* Washington, D.C.: U.S. Atomic Energy Commission, 1953.

U.S. Department of State. *A Report on the International Control of Atomic Energy.* Washington, D.C.: Government Printing Office, 1946.

Walker, Martin. *The Cold War: A History.* New York: Henry Holt and Company, 1993.

Weiss, Leonard. "Atoms for Peace." *Bulletin of the Atomic Scientists* 59, no. 6 (November/December 2003): 34–41, 44.

York, Herbert F. *Making Weapons, Talking Peace: A Physicist's Odyssey from Hiroshima to Geneva.* New York: Basic Books, Inc., 1987.

Zuckerman, Solly. *Nuclear Illusion and Reality.* New York: Random House, 1983.

Contributors

JACQUES BOUCHARD has headed the Commissariat à l'Énergie Atomique's (CEA's) nuclear energy division since November 2000. Dr. Bouchard joined the CEA as an engineer in 1964. He became head of the experimental physics unit in 1973, and then head of the nuclear engineering department in 1975. In that capacity, he conducted work in support of pressurized water reactor technology. He also led studies in physics for fuel-cycle applications. In 1982, Dr. Bouchard became head of the fast neutron reactor department in Cadarache. In 1990, he was appointed head of the CEA's nuclear reactor department and, in 1994, head of the CEA's defense applications department.

AMBASSADOR LINTON F. BROOKS was sworn in as undersecretary of energy for nuclear security/administrator of the National Nuclear Security Administration (NNSA) in 2003. He had been acting in this position since 2002. Immediately prior to his appointment, he served as the NNSA's deputy administrator for defense nuclear nonproliferation, a post he assumed in 2001. Ambassador Brooks previously served as a vice president at the Center for Naval Analyses and as an adviser to Sandia National Laboratories. During the George H.W. Bush administration, he served as assistant director for strategic and nuclear affairs at the U.S. Arms Control and Disarmament Agency, and in the State Department as head of the U.S. delegation on nuclear and space talks and chief strategic arms reductions negotiator.

KORY W. BUDLONG SYLVESTER has been a technical staff member at Los Alamos National Laboratory (LANL) in the Nuclear Nonproliferation Division since 1998. At LANL he has worked on a variety of projects related to nonproliferation, international safeguards, and arms control. In August 2005, he began an appointment to the U.S. House of Representative's Committee on Homeland Security to provide technical advice on nuclear affairs to the Subcommittee on the Prevention of Nuclear and Biological Attack. He has lectured at the Massachusetts Institute of Technology and the University of California, and his work has appeared in *Science and Global Security* and *The Nonproliferation Review,* as well as in numerous conference proceedings. The views expressed in his contribution are his own, and not those of LANL or of any other organization.

AMBASSADOR CHOI YOUNG-JIN assumed the role of permanent representative of the Republic of Korea to the United Nations in June 2005. Prior to his present appointment, Dr. Choi served as vice foreign minister of the Republic of Korea from 2004 to 2005 and chancellor of the Institute of Foreign Affairs and National Security of the Ministry of Foreign Affairs and Trade from 2003 to 2004. Dr. Choi has also served as ambassador to Austria and the International Atomic Energy Agency (IAEA) in Vienna in 2002; deputy minister of foreign affairs for policy planning and multilateral cooperation in 2000–2001; assistant secretary-general in the United Nations Secretariat for Peacekeeping Operations in 1998–1999; deputy executive director of the Korean Peninsula Energy Development Organization (KEDO) in 1995–1997; and director-general for international economic cooperation in 1993–1994.

CHRISTOPHER F. CHYBA is a professor of astrophysics and international affairs at Princeton University, where he also co-directs the Program on Science and Global Security at the Woodrow Wilson School of Public and International Affairs. Previously he was the co-director of the Center for International Security and Cooperation at the Stanford Institute for International Studies, and associate professor (research) in the Department of Geological and Environmental Sciences at Stanford University. Dr. Chyba served on the National Security Council staff, then on the national security and international affairs staff of the White House Office of Science and Technology Policy from 1993 to 1995, entering the Clinton administration as a White House Fellow.

AMBASSADOR JAYANTHA DHANAPALA is the former UN undersecretary general for disarmament. He entered the Sri Lanka Foreign Service in 1965. Between 1965 and 1983, he held diplomatic appointments in London, Beijing, Washington, D.C., and New Delhi, in addition to being director of the Non-Aligned Movement (NAM) Division of the Foreign Ministry during Sri Lanka's chairmanship of the NAM. Dhanapala was appointed undersecretary general for disarmament affairs in the United Nations, and functioned in that capacity from February 1998 until May 2003. In addition, the secretary-general appointed Dhanapala as a commissioner in the United Nations Special Commission on Iraq and the head of the Special Group visiting the presidential sites in Iraq in 1998.

SENATOR PETE V. DOMENICI is the senior U.S. senator for the State of New Mexico. As chair of the Senate Energy and Water Appropriations Subcommittee, which funds the Department of Energy, he has worked to bolster the evolving mission of the national laboratories from weapon research and production to stewardship over the nation's existing nuclear-weapon stockpile. He is also chair of the Senate Energy and Natural Resources Committee and serves on the Appropriations Committee, Budget Committee, Homeland Security and Governmental Affairs Committee, and Indian Affairs Committee.

MOHAMED ELBARADEI has been the director general of the International Atomic Energy Agency (IAEA) since December 1, 1997. He and the Agency were awarded the Nobel Peace Prize in 2005. He was a senior member of the IAEA Secretariat from 1984, holding a number of high-level policy positions, including that of the Agency's legal adviser and, beginning in 1993, assistant director general for external relations. He began his career in the Egyptian Diplomatic Service in 1964, serving on two occasions in the permanent missions of Egypt to the United Nations in New

York and Geneva, in charge of political, legal, and arms control issues. From 1974 to 1978, he was a special assistant to the Egyptian foreign minister. In 1980, he left the Diplomatic Service and became a senior fellow in charge of the International Law Program at the United Nations Institute for Training and Research. From 1981 to 1987, he was also an adjunct professor of international law at the New York University School of Law.

LAURA S.H. HOLGATE is vice president for the Russia/New Independent States Program at the Nuclear Threat Initiative (NTI). Holgate joined the NTI after serving in a number of senior positions in the federal government. She managed the Cooperative Threat Reduction program at the U.S. Department of Defense, which provides assistance to Russia and the new independent states in securing and destroying excess nuclear, chemical, and biological weapons and materials. She also served as director of the Office of Fissile Materials Disposition at the U.S. Department of Energy.

BRIGADIER GENERAL (RETIRED) FEROZ KHAN is a visiting professor of national security affairs at the Naval Postgraduate School. General Khan served with the Pakistani Army for 30 years with numerous assignments in the United States, Europe, and South Asia. He has experienced combat action and command on active fronts on the line of control in Siachin Glacier and Kashmir. Most recently, he held the post of director, Arms Control and Disarmament Affairs, within the Strategic Plans Division, Joint Services Headquarters. General Khan has held a series of visiting fellowships at Stanford University's Center for International Studies and Arms Control, the Woodrow Wilson International Center for Scholars, the Brookings Institution, the Center for Nonproliferation Studies at the Monterey Institute of International Studies, and the Cooperative Monitoring Center at Sandia National Laboratory.

RICHARD K. LESTER is a professor of nuclear engineering at the Massachusetts Institute of Technology (MIT) and the founding director of the MIT Industrial Performance Center. In 1977–78, Dr. Lester was a visiting research fellow in international relations at the Rockefeller Foundation. He has been a member of the MIT faculty since 1979. As director of the Center, which he founded in 1992, he works with faculty and students from all five of MIT's schools on a broad range of interdisciplinary research projects concerning the uses of science and technology in industry and the implications of these developments for productivity and society. Dr. Lester served as a member of the MIT Study Group on the Future of Nuclear Power.

ARIEL LEVITE has been the principal deputy director general (policy) of the Israeli Atomic Energy Commission since September 2002. In 2000–2002, he was a visiting fellow at the Center for International Security and Cooperation (CISAC), and co-leader of the CISAC Discriminate Force project, at Stanford University. In 1999–2000, he was deputy national security adviser (defense policy) and before that, head of the Bureau of International Security at the Israeli Ministry of Defense. Before joining the Ministry, Levite was a senior research associate and head of the Project on Israeli Security at the Jaffee Center for Strategic Studies, Tel-Aviv University.

ROBERT S. LITWAK is director of the Division of International Security Studies at the Woodrow Wilson International Center for Scholars, and adjunct professor in the School of Foreign Service at Georgetown University. Dr. Litwak served as director for nonproliferation on the National Security Council staff. He is the author of *Rogue States and U.S. Foreign Policy* (2000) and *Regime Change: U.S. Strategy through the Prism of 9/11* (2007).

PER F. PETERSON is a professor of nuclear engineering at the University of California, Berkeley. Promoted to full professor at Berkeley in 1998, he chaired the Energy and Resources graduate group from 1998 to 2000. Since 2000, Peterson has been chair of nuclear engineering. He was a National Science Foundation Presidential Young Investigator from 1990 to 1995. His research focuses on fundamental problems in heat and mass transfer and fluid mechanics, with applications in reactor safety, inertial fusion, and radioactive waste management.

JOSEPH F. PILAT is with the director's office at the Los Alamos National Laboratory. Dr. Pilat served as representative of the secretary of defense to the Fourth NPT (Treaty of the Nonproliferation of Nuclear Weapons) Review Conference and as an adviser to the U.S. delegation at the 1995 NPT Review and Extension Conference. He also served as representative of the secretary of defense to the Open Skies negotiations, special assistant to the principal director and assistant for nonproliferation policy in the Office of the Deputy Assistant Secretary of Defense for Negotiations Policy, senior research associate in the Congressional Research Service, and research associate at the International Institute for Strategic Studies. Dr. Pilat has taught at Georgetown University, Cornell University, and the College of William and Mary. He has been a senior associate member of St. Antony's College, University of Oxford, a visiting fellow at Cornell's Peace Studies Program, and a Philip E. Mosely Fellow at the Center for Strategic and International Studies. The views expressed in his contributions are his own and not those of LANL or any other organization.

DANIEL B. PONEMAN is a senior fellow of the Forum for International Policy. From 1993 through 1996, Mr. Poneman served as special assistant to the president and senior director for nonproliferation and export controls at the National Security Council, with responsibilities for the development and implementation of U.S. policy in such areas as peaceful nuclear cooperation, missile technology and space-launch activities, sanctions determinations, chemical and biological arms control efforts, and conventional arms transfer policy.

STEPHEN G. RADEMAKER is policy director for national security affairs and senior counsel, Office of the Majority Leader, U.S. Senate. Previously he served as acting assistant secretary, Bureau of International Security and Nonproliferation in 2005–2006 and as assistant secretary of state for arms control from 2002 to 2005. In February 2005 he was also named as head of the Bureau of Nonproliferation. Immediately prior to joining the State Department, Mr. Rademaker was chief counsel to the Select Committee on Homeland Security of the U.S. House of Representatives, where he had lead responsibility for drafting the legislation that created the Department of Homeland Security. For most of the previous decade, he held positions on the staff of the Committee on International Relations of the House of Representatives, including deputy staff director and chief counsel (2001–2002), chief counsel (1995–2001), and minority chief counsel (1993–1995).

TARIQ RAUF is the head of verification and security policy coordination in the Office of External Relations and Policy Coordination at the International Atomic Energy Agency. Dr. Rauf was scientific secretary for the IAEA Expert Group on Multinational Approaches to the Nuclear Fuel Cycle (2004–2005). The views expressed in his contribution do not necessarily represent those of the IAEA or any other organization.

MITCHELL B. REISS is the vice-provost for international affairs at the College of William and Mary. Previously he served as the director of the Office of Policy Planning at the U.S. Department of State. Prior to his appointment at the State Department, Dr. Reiss was dean of international affairs, director of the Reves Center for International Studies, professor of law at the Marshall-Wythe Law School, and professor of government in the Department of Government at the College of William and Mary. Earlier, Dr. Reiss helped establish KEDO, a multinational organization created to address nuclear-weapon proliferation concerns in North Korea. His responsibilities there included serving as chief negotiator and as general counsel. His government service includes positions in the National Security Council and as a consultant to the U.S. Arms Control & Disarmament Agency, the State Department, the Congressional Research Service, and the Lawrence Livermore and Los Alamos National Laboratories. Dr. Reiss has also been a guest scholar at the Woodrow Wilson International Center for Scholars and worked as an attorney at Covington & Burling.

LAWRENCE SCHEINMAN is a distinguished professor, Center for Nonproliferation Studies, Monterey Institute for International Studies. During the Clinton administration, he was the assistant director of the United States Arms Control and Disarmament Agency for Nonproliferation and Regional Arms Control. Prior government service included counselor for nonproliferation in the Department of Energy, principal deputy to the deputy under-secretary of state for security assistance (Carter administration), head of international policy planning, Energy Research and Development Administration (Ford administration), and senior adviser to the director general of the International Atomic Energy Agency—all while on leave from his position as professor of government (international law and relations) and associate director of the Peace Studies Program at Cornell University. Dr. Scheinman also has been a tenured member of the faculties of political science at the University of California–Los Angeles and of the University of Michigan.

JAMES SCHLESINGER is senior adviser to the investment banking firm of Lehman Brothers and chairman of the MITRE Corporation board of trustees. He also serves as counselor to the Center for Strategic and International Studies. From 1955 to 1963, Dr. Schlesinger served as assistant and associate professor of economics at the University of Virginia. Subsequently, he was associated with the RAND Corporation as a senior staff member (1963–1967) and director of strategic studies (1967–1969). During this period, he also served as consultant to the Federal Reserve System Board of Governors and to the U.S. Bureau of the Budget. In March 1969, Dr. Schlesinger began his government service as assistant director of the Bureau of the Budget (later the Office of Management and Budget) and served for a period as acting director. He left in August 1971 when President Nixon selected him to become chair of the Atomic Energy Commission. He held that post until February 1973 when he was named director of the Central Intelligence Agency. He served in the latter position until July 1973 when he was appointed secretary of defense. He remained at the Defense Department until November 1975. In 1976, President-elect Carter asked him to become assistant to the president, charged with the responsibility of drafting a plan for the establishment of the Department of Energy and a national energy policy. On August 5, 1977, Mr. Schlesinger became the nation's first secretary of energy. He held that post until August 1979.

AMBASSADOR MOHAMED I. SHAKER is vice chair of the board for the Egyptian Council for Foreign Affairs. Ambassador Shaker previously served as ambassador of the Arab Republic of Egypt to the United Kingdom. He served as president of the 1987 UN Conference to Promote International Cooperation in the Peaceful Uses of Nuclear Energy and of the 1985 Third Review Conference of the Parties to the NPT. He has also served as representative of the director general of the IAEA to the United Nations in New York. He is the author of *The Nuclear Non-Proliferation Treaty: Origin and Implementation, 1957–1979* (Oceana Publications, 1980).

THOMAS E. SHEA is director of defense nuclear nonproliferation programs at the Pacific Northwest National Laboratory. He had previously been with the International Atomic Energy Agency. An IAEA safeguards expert, he headed technical work on the Trilateral Initiative and IAEA studies in support of a fissile material cut-off treaty and on proliferation resistance and physical protection in future nuclear energy systems. He is a fellow of the Institute of Nuclear Materials Management.

FIONA SIMPSON is currently with the Center for International Cooperation at New York University. She was an external relations and policy coordination officer in the Office of External Relations and Policy Coordination at the International Atomic Energy Agency, and the principal staff writer for the IAEA Expert Group on Multinational Approaches to the Nuclear Fuel Cycle (2004–5). The views expressed in her contribution do not necessarily represent those of the IAEA or any other organization.

ATSUYUKI SUZUKI is commissioner of the Nuclear Safety Commission of Japan and holds the title of professor emeritus, Department of Quantum Engineering and Systems Science, University of Tokyo. He has also been a member of the Board of Radioactive Waste Management at the U.S. National Academy of Sciences since 2001 and, in that capacity, has been involved with a number of committee activities at the U.S. National Academy of Sciences, particularly in connection with high-level radioactive management. In addition to his thirty-year career as a faculty member at the University of Tokyo, he has had extensive experiences in advising the Japanese government on nuclear issues, including serving as chair of the Nuclear Regulatory Standard Committee, task force chair of the JCO Accident Investigation Committee at the Nuclear Safety Commission, chair of the Fast Reactor Development Subcommittee of the Long-Term Nuclear Energy Planning Committee at the Atomic Energy Commission, and chair of the Project Team on Reforming the Power Reactor and Nuclear Fuel Development Corporation at the Science and Technology Agency.

DAVID B. WALLER has been the IAEA deputy director general since January 1993. Previously Mr. Waller served, from 1986–1989, as U.S. assistant secretary of energy for international affairs and, from 1981–1986, at the White House as a legal counsel to President Reagan. Mr. Waller began his professional career in 1974 as a lawyer, first working under the Attorney General's Honor Program at the U.S. Department of Justice in Washington, D.C., and thereafter at the Washington-based private law firm, Hogan and Hartson.

Index

Abraham, Spencer, 48, 173, 294–300
ABM Treaty. *See* Anti-Ballistic Missile Treaty
ABWR. *See* Advanced Boiling Water Reactors
Acheson-Lilienthal report, 12, 57, 186, 207, 208, 209. *See also* Baruch Plan
actinides, 152–54, 161, 321, 325, 327, 332
ADA. *See* Atomic Development Authority
Additional Protocol (AP): adoption and coverage of, 28, 107; as condition for peaceful nuclear trade, 109, 190, 216, 292, 305, 309–10, 311, 314; and demand-side of deterrence, 126; and FMCT, 224; and IAEA, 173, 179, 187, 211, 213; and Iran, 35, 36, 77–78, 182; and Iraq, 76, 211; and Libya, 75; limitations on, 65, 88; mandatory accession to, 61; Model, 28, 43, 54, 59, 61, 310; and non–nuclear-weapon states, 120; progress with, 64–65; safeguard agreements, 64, 120*n*, 185; and U.S., 292; and verification, 64, 310
Administrative Procedures Act, 18
Advanced Boiling Water Reactors (ABWR), 158, 159, 161
Advanced Energy Initiative, 237, 316, 317. *See also* Global Nuclear Energy Partnership (GNEP)
advanced fuel cycle. *See* fuel cycle
Advanced Fuel Cycle Initiative, 180

AEC. *See* U.S. Atomic Energy Commission
Agreed Framework for North Korea, 28, 29, 34, 79, 81, 211
Ahmadinejad, Mahmoud, 79
Albright, Madeline, 73
Al-Qaeda, 40
Anglo-Saxon law, 18, 19
Annan, Kofi, 62, 101
Anti-Ballistic Missile (ABM) Treaty, 58, 122n
AP. *See* Additional Protocol
Arab oil embargo, 235
Argentina, 39, 67, 210, 225
Argentine-Brazilian Agency for the Accounting and Control of Nuclear Materials (ABAAC), 39, 67
Arms Control and Regional Security (ACRS), 67
Article IV of NPT: and George W. Bush, 122; challenges to, 120–23, 179; conflict over, 199–200; cooperation under, 36, 126; and CTR, 215; and ElBaradei, 44; and fuel cycle, 30–31, 188; "fullest possible exchange" requirement of, 188–89; future of, 123–24; "grand bargain" of, 43–44, 213; implementation of, 37–38, 46, 221, 228; and India, 44, 212; and Iran, 4, 44, 184, 212, 217, 236; and Japan, 90; "loophole" in, 4, 12, 17, 78, 81, 84, 85, 109, 188, 216, 235, 309–10; and Moscow Treaty, 37, 122n, 215; and North Korea, 44; and nuclear renaissance, 217; and prevention of terrorism, 237; reform of, 186, 231, 236; and Russia, 199
Article VI of NPT: thirteen steps related to, 56, 58, 65–66, 199; and U.S., 36–37, 44–45, 103, 122, 190
Asia. *See* Northeast Asia; South Asia; *specific countries*

Atomic Development Authority (ADA), 207, 208, 210. *See also* Acheson-Lilienthal report
Atomic Energy Act of 1946, 2, 235
Atomic Energy Act of 1954, 5–6, 18
atomic testing. *See specific countries and treaties*
Atoms for Peace. *See* Eisenhower's Atoms-for-Peace program
Aum Shinrikyo, 40
Australia, 24, 49, 90, 97
"axis of evil," 54, 74, 82

ballistic missiles, 40, 74n, 75, 86, 216, 286, 287. *See also* Anti-Ballistic Missile (ABM) Treaty
Baruch, Bernard, 194
Baruch Plan, 2, 57, 186, 194, 231
Belarus, 39, 111
bin Laden, Osama, 112
Biological and Toxin Weapons Convention (BWC), 33, 45, 57
biotechnological proliferation, 10, 117–18
black market, 4, 107, 119, 214, 230, 301. *See also* suppliers; terrorism
Blix, Hans, 23–24, 27, 31, 62, 64
Bouchard, Jacques, 10, 11, 146–55, 339
Boucher, Richard, 73
Bratislava Summit, 106, 114, 115
Brazil, 39, 67, 90, 210, 212
Britain. *See* United Kingdom
Brooks, Linton F., 9–10, 104–10, 339–40
B-61 Mod 11 weapon system, 37
Budlong Sylvester, Kory W., 11, 12, 206–18, 340
Bundy, McGeorge, 100
Bush, George W.: and Article IV of NPT, 122; and energy needs, 231; and enrichment and processing technology, 200, 210; and fuel leasing, 180–81; and Libyan policy, 76; non-

proliferation initiatives of, 105–9, 110, 216, 231, 299; and North Korea, 79; and PSI, 125; and rogue states policy, 72, 74–75, 82; on terrorist threat, 50; and WMD countermeasures, 42, 49, 114, 119*n*, 285–293. *See also* Global Nuclear Energy Partnership (GNEP)
Bushehr, Russia nuclear reactor, 34
BWC. *See* Biological and Toxin Weapons Convention

Calvert Cliffs nuclear plant decision, 18
Canada, 57, 90
carbon dioxide emissions, 150–51, 167. *See also* fossil fuels; greenhouse gases
carbon tax, 11, 169. *See also* fossil fuels
Carter, Jimmy, 178
CAS (Committee on Assurances of Supply). *See* International Atomic Energy Agency (IAEA)
CCGT. *See* combined cycle gas turbine
CD. *See* Conference on Disarmament
Central America, 24
centrifuge enrichment activity, 187
Chemical Weapons Convention (CWC), 33, 45, 57, 59, 75, 87
Chernobyl, 8, 25–26, 54, 139, 149, 156, 180
China: biotech in, 124; crops disease eradication in, 24; and Indian cooperative agreement, 213; and Iran, 90; and nonproliferation, 83; and North Korea, 75, 79, 80, 92; and NSG, 125; and nuclear power, 213, 320; nuclear power in, 134, 150, 168; and Taiwan strait crisis, 101*n;* and U.S. policy, 77
Choi Young-jin, 9, 91–94, 340
Churchill, Winston, 16, 35
Chyba, Christopher, 9, 10, 117–27, 340–41
CIRUS, 178

Clinton, Bill, 37, 72–74, 77, 156, 157
closed fuel cycle. *See* fuel cycle
Code Napoleon, 19
Code of Conduct on the Safety and Security of Radioactive Sources, 48, 109
Cold War: arms control goals in, 5, 7, 232; and Atoms for Peace, 3, 17, 40, 53, 131; end of, 36–37, 62, 114, 143, 232–33; legacy weapons from, 114, 181; and superpowers, 15, 40, 95, 232, 237–38; weapons in, 54
College of William and Mary, 7
combined cycle gas turbine, 147, 148, 158
Committee on Assurances of Supply (CAS). *See* International Atomic Energy Agency (IAEA)
Comprehensive Nuclear Test Ban Treaty (CTBT), 8, 58–59, 66, 212, 215, 309
Conference on Disarmament (CD), 56, 58, 59, 68, 86, 224
"Confronting Backlash States" (Lake in *Foreign Affairs*), 72–73
conscientious objection, 59
Convention on the Physical Protection of Nuclear Material (CPPNM), 10, 26, 55, 109, 213, 221, 223
Cooperative Threat Reduction (CTR) Program: and Article IV, 215; effect of, 216, 232; expansion of, 61, 125; and Nunn-Lugar, 132, 291; role of, 55, 58, 125, 211
CPPNM. *See* Convention on the Physical Protection of Nuclear Material
crops, disease eradication in, 24
CTBT. *See* Comprehensive Nuclear Test Ban Treaty
CTR. *See* Cooperative Threat Reduction (CTR) Program
Cuba, 72
Cuban missile crisis, 53

cultivars, 24
CWC. *See* Chemical Weapons Convention
Czech Republic, 106

Department of Energy Waste Fund Fee Adequacy Report, 164
Dhanapala, Jayantha, 8–9, 52–62, 341
Diablo Canyon, 159
direct-cycle electricity conversion, 161–62
dirty bombs, 26, 47–48, 109, 133, 221, 296
Disarmament Commission (DC), 56–57, 63–68
disease eradication, 23–24, 121
Domenici, Pete, 10, 131–36, 341
DPRK (Democratic People's Republic of Korea). *See* North Korea
dual-use facilities, 40–41, 192, 207, 281

Economic and Social Council (ECOSOC), 57
Economic Cooperation and Development/Nuclear Energy Agency (OECD/NEA) report, 147
economic deprivation, 61, 136
Economic Simplified Boiling Water Reactor (ESBWR), 160, 161
Economist article by ElBaradei. *See* ElBaradei, Mohamed
Egypt, 67
Einstein, Albert, 110, 138
EIS (Environmental Impact Statement), 18
Eisenhower, Susan, 17, 136
Eisenhower's Atoms-for-Peace program: accomplishments of, 15–17, 20; and ambiguity, 100–101; and arms control, 5, 232–33; challenge of, 140; conference on, xv–xvi, 7; evaluation of, 1–12; future of, 52–62, 237–38; goals of, 17, 51, 83–84, 85, 95–96; model of, 33–34; and nonproliferation, 93, 98, 229–32; and nuclear power, 134, 234–37; origins and development of, 3, 15, 63; and prevention of terrorism, 6, 7, 9, 17, 233–34, 238; and proliferation, 99–100; relevance and legacy of, xiii–xiv, xv, 237–38; and rogue states, 80–81; text of, 1–2, 239–46; themes of, 53–56, 206; and UN, 56–60; verification under, 2, 59, 71, 192; vision of, 39, 50, 131–32, 136, 192–95, 227. *See also* International Atomic Energy Agency (IAEA); Nonproliferation Treaty (NPT)
ElBaradei, Mohamed: and Article IV of NPT, 44; biography of, 341–42; *The Economist* article of, 30–31, 44, 62, 186, 293–98; leadership of, 31; on mission of IAEA, xiii–xiv; and multilateral approach to fuel cycle, 11–12, 30–31, 65, 86, 89, 197–98, 201, 279–84, 302; and non–nuclear weapon states, 54; and nonproliferation, 65, 186, 231; on political debates, 21–22; on reappraisal of NPT, 62; on relevancy of Atoms-for-Peace proposal, xiii–xiv; on security, 23; on terrorism, 233. *See also* Multilateral Approaches to the Nuclear Fuel Cycle (MNA)
Energy Department, U.S., 48
Energy Policy Act of 2005, 133–36
Environmental Impact Statement (EIS), 18
environmental protection, 18. *See also* fossil fuels; global warming; greenhouse gases
environmental sampling techniques, 27, 30, 187
ESBWR. *See* Economic Simplified Boiling Water Reactor

ethics, code of, 59
EURATOM, 235
Europe, 147, 151, 169
European Energy Independence Rate, 150
European pressurized water reactors, 148–49
European Union (EU), 34, 75, 90, 92
"European utilities requirements," 149
export controls: and Article I, 119, 125; and Article III, 125; effect of, 55, 200–201, 217, 281, 302; erosion of, 211; and FMCT, 28; measures for, 179, 196; and multilateral approach to nuclear cycle, 309–311; and plutonium, 187; and prevention of terrorism, 105, 125; proposals for, 231; and Resolution 1540, 125; tightening of, 8, 216, 238, 291, 314. *See also* Zangger Committee

Finland, 48, 168
first-tier suppliers, 117*n,* 119
Fissile Material Cut-Off Treaty (FMCT), 8–9, 12, 56, 58, 103, 212, 219–28
Ford, Gerald, 236
Foreign Affairs Lake article (1994), 72–73
former Soviet Union. *See* Soviet Union and former Soviet Union
fossil fuels: dependence on, 51, 319; depletion of, 19, 146; environmental costs of, 11, 18, 84, 146, 167, 200, 332; and nuclear power compared, 143, 146–48, 169–70. *See also* global warming; greenhouse gases
France, 19, 34, 49, 97, 147, 151, 159; radioactive waste management Research and Development Act of 1991, 152
fuel cost comparisons, 143, 146–48, 169–70

fuel cycle: advanced, 152, 153, 164, 180; and Article IV, 188; and ban on new states, 216; challenges of, 173; closed, 11, 151, 153–55, 163, 170, 171; and construction of facilities, 89; and current nonproliferation predicament, 83–84, 85; dual nature of, 84; front end of the cycle, proposal for, 30–31; inducements, 6; and INFCE, 236; and INPRO, 25; and Iran, 34, 183–84; and leasing, 181; MIT report on, 174; new sources of supply for, 86; once-through, 170, 171–72; and proliferation resistance, 207–10; and regional centers, 186, 190; safeguards and security for, 23, 31, 44, 113, 114, 170–73, 186, 206, 231, 283; technology for, 17, 81, 86, 109, 120; and terrorism, 113, 114. *See also* Article IV of NPT; Multilateral Approaches to the Nuclear Fuel Cycle (MNA)
fuel leasing: development of, 126, 190, 315, 321; model of, 321–22; and nuclear proliferation, 180–81, 323, 326
Future of Nuclear Power study. *See* Massachusetts Institute of Technology (MIT) study on Future of Nuclear Power

gas turbine modular helium reactor (GTMHR), 162–63
G-8: and Bush's nonproliferation initiatives, 105, 109; and CTR program, 61; "Global Partnership against the Spread of Weapons and Materials of Destruction," 48–49, 113, 115, 291; and Proliferation Security Initiative (PSI), 49; and Radioactive Source Initiative, 47–48
Generation II reactors, 148–49
Generation III reactors, 149

Generation IV reactors (Gen IV), 25, 148–55, 158, 162, 180
Generation-IV International Forum (GIF), 150
Germany: and Atoms for Peace, 243; inspections and Weimar government in, 35; law in, 19; as non-nuclear state, 60; and non-state suppliers, 289; nuclear power in, 138, 149; and PSI, 49, 290
Ghadafi, Mohamed, 76, 77. *See also* Libya
Glenn, John, 178
Global Nuclear Energy Partnership (GNEP), 6, 210, 217, 237, 316–34
Global Threat Reduction Initiative (GTRI), 8–9, 48, 106, 115, 294–300
global warming, 19, 144, 146, 217. *See also* greenhouse gases
Gorbachev, Mikhail, 98
grand bargain. *See* Article IV of NPT; Article VI of NPT
Greater Middle East Initiative, 76
greenhouse gases, 19, 140, 146–47, 167–69, 302, 318, 320, 326. *See also* carbon dioxide emissions; fossil fuels
Group of 8. *See* G-8
GTMHR (gas turbine modular helium reactor), 162–63
Gulf War. *See* Iraq

HEU. *See* highly enriched uranium
high-level, long-lived radioactive waste (HLLLW), 152
highly enriched uranium (HEU), 10, 40, 47, 106, 113, 180, 181, 187, 222. *See also* Radioactive Source Initiative
high-temperature ceramic fuels, 162
Holgate, Laura S.H., 9, 10, 111–16, 342
Hussein, Saddam, 212

IAEA. *See* International Atomic Energy Agency

ICC (International Criminal Court), 59
ICJ (International Court of Justice), 54, 56
India: and Article IV of NPT, 44, 212; atomic testing by, 28, 177, 178, 196, 211, 235; and export control, 187–88; and international relations, 96–98, 99n; and nonproliferation regime, 67; and NPT, 4, 6–67, 114, 183, 221, 224, 294; and NSG, 213–14; and nuclear-free zones, 66–67; and nuclear power, 134, 168, 213, 235; nuclear-weapon program in, 91, 97, 113, 115, 178, 183, 195; plutonium in, 196; U.S. policy toward, 178; and war risk, 220. *See also* U.S.-Indian Civil Nuclear Cooperation Initiative of 2005
INFCE. *See* International Nuclear Fuel Cycle Evaluation (INFCE) study
INFCIRC/153, 184–85, 224
INFCIRC/540. *See* Additional Protocol (AP)
INFCIRC/640, 203
INPRO (International Project on Innovative Nuclear Reactors and Fuel Cells), 25
inspections. *See* verification; *specific countries*
International Atomic Energy Agency (IAEA), 21–32; budget of, 126; certification of good standing by, 61; challenges for, 31–32, 212; Code of Conduct on the Safety and Security of Radioactive Sources, 48, 109; Committee on Assurances of Supply (CAS), 64, 67, 197; and duality, 22–23, 31; ElBaradei on mission of, xiii–xiv; establishment of, xiii, 2, 3, 42, 53–59, 84, 163, 195; Expert Group on International Plutonium Storage (IPS), 197; Expert Group on Multilateral

Approaches to the Nuclear Fuel Cycle (MNA), 203–5, 301–315; and FMCT, 222n; framework for, 3; and NPT, 45; and nuclear technology applications, 23–25; and prevention of terrorism, 8, 106, 108, 109, 112, 115, 184, 213, 234; reform of, 191–92; role of, 3, 8, 11, 16, 86–89, 178–79, 183, 229; safeguard regime of, 184–93, 210, 225, 226, 228, 230; September 2003 resolution of, 77; statute of, 57, 247–67; strengthening of, 42–43, 59–60, 173, 211; and supplies, 204; toward universal nonproliferation and disarmament, 63–68; and Trilateral Initiative, 56; and UN, 252; U.S. and Soviet collaboration on, 17. *See also* Additional Protocol (AP); verification; *specific countries*

International Commission on WMD, 62

International Conference on Multilateral Approaches for the Nuclear Fuel Cycle, July 2005, 204–5

International Court of Justice (ICJ), 54, 56

International Criminal Court (ICC), 59

International Monitoring System (IMS), 59

International Nuclear Fuel Cycle Evaluation (INFCE), 197, 236

International Plutonium Storage (IPS), 197

International Project on Innovative Nuclear Reactors and Fuel Cells (INPRO), 25

Iran: and Additional Protocol (AP), 35, 36, 77–78, 182; and Article IV of NPT, 4, 44, 184, 212, 217, 236; clandestine network use by, 195, 201, 211, 288; dual containment in, 72; environmental sampling techniques in, 30; and fuel cycle technology, 34, 183–84; and IAEA, 34, 36, 54, 65, 67, 77–78, 81, 84–88, 185, 192, 195, 213, 225, 293; inspection and verification in, 30, 71; and international nuclear nonproliferation regime, 41; and Japan, 92; and A.Q. Khan, 201; "megatons to megawatts" model in, 11; Natanz enrichment facility in, 77, 182, 185; non-state suppliers in, 86; and North Korea, 86; and NPT, 36, 38, 40, 59, 65, 84, 85, 91, 108, 185, 212, 292; nuclear facilities in, 8, 34–35, 36, 84; nuclear weapons program in, 9, 34, 38, 45, 78–82, 84, 90–93, 214, 217, 230, 288, 293; and PSI, 90; reprocessing technology in, 109; and Russia, 34, 90, 182; and spent fuel management, 183; as supplier, 120; and terrorism, 50; transparency in, 30; and UN, 35, 59, 77–78, 86, 108, 213, 214; and uranium enrichment technology, 81, 192, 195, 287; and U.S., 34, 72–75, 82

Iraq: and Additional Protocol, 76, 211; disarmament of, 65; dual containment in, 72; employment of scientists from, 108; environmental sampling techniques in, 30; Gulf and Second Gulf Wars in, 64, 74–75, 88, 119n, 126, 212, 217; and IAEA, 88; inspection and verification in, 27, 28–29, 30, 35, 64, 65, 185; and NPT, 27; nuclear-weapon program in, 27, 29, 54, 64, 183, 185, 211, 229, 281, 287; supply networks for, 201; and UN, 27, 29, 108, 211, 214; U.S. policy in, 72, 74–75; violations by, 4, 8; WMDs in, 119n, 287, 291

Iraq Nuclear Verification Office, 28–29

isotope hydrology, 24

Israel: and NPT, 4, 40, 66, 91, 114, 183, 195, 221, 224; and nuclear-free zone,

Israel (*continued*)
67; nuclear-weapon program in, 66, 91, 97, 98, 113, 115, 183, 280
Italy, 49

Japan: and Article IV, 90; crops disease eradication in, 24; and GNEP, 218; and international nuclear nonproliferation regime, 41; and Iran, 92; and North Korea, 75, 92; and NPT, 90, 169; nuclear power in, 20, 139, 143, 158, 306, 321; nuclear weapons in, 60, 92, 97; and PSI, 49, 290; reprocessing technology in, 321
Joint Committee on Atomic Energy (JCAE), 3, 18
Joint Statement on Nuclear Security Cooperation, 106

Kananaskis Summit, 48
Kashmir, 220
Kazakhstan, 39, 111
Kemeny Commission, 19
Kennedy, John F., 16, 39, 53
Khan, Abdul Qadeer (A.Q.): and combatting nuclear terrorism, 105; and Iran, Iraq, and North Korea, 211; and Libya, 107; media attention on, 201; role of, 86, 195, 288–89; and second-tier relationships, 119; and uranium enrichment technology, 209; use of suppliers by, 124
Khan, Feroz, 9, 95–103, 342
Khan, Munir Ahmad, 23
Kim Jong Il, 79, 80
Korea. *See* North Korea; South Korea
Kuwait, 64
Kyoto Treaty, 180

Lake, Anthony, 72–73
Law of the Sea, 60
leasing. *See* fuel leasing; nuclear power

Lester, Richard K., 10, 11, 165–74, 342–43
LEU. *See* low-enriched uranium
Levite, Ariel, 9, 83–90, 343
Libya: disarmament of, 9, 75–77, 81, 192, 195; disease eradication in, 24; employment of scientists from, 108; and IAEA, 75; illicit acquisition of technology by, 109; inspection and verification in, 30*n*, 71, 87, 88; and A.Q. Khan, 86, 107, 195, 211, 288–89; and NPT, 75, 108; transparency of, 76; U.S. policy toward, 72; WMDs in, 310
licensing. *See* nuclear power
Litwak, Robert S., 9, 71–82, 343
"loophole" in Article IV of NPT. *See* Article IV of NPT
Lorenz, Konrad, 93
Los Alamos National Laboratory, 7
low-enriched uranium (LEU), 47, 187
Lugar, Richard, 112, 132, 291

Madrid peace process, 67
Major, John, 189
Malaysia, 107, 124, 289
Mandelbaum, Michael, 97, 98
Massachusetts Institute of Technology (MIT) study on Future of Nuclear Power, 11, 19, 153, 157, 167–74
Materials Protection, Control and Accounting (MPC&A) Program, 132, 211, 234
Mexico, 24
Middle East, 66–67, 76, 189–90. *See also* nuclear-weapon-free zones; *specific countries*
military expenditures, global, 61
military industrial complex, 55
Missile Technology Control Regime (MTCR), 119

MIT. *See* Massachusetts Institute of Technology (MIT) study on Future of Nuclear Power
mixed oxide (MOX) fuel, 24, 152
MNA. *See* International Atomic Energy Agency (IAEA)
Model Additional Protocol. *See* Additional Protocol (AP)
Moscow Theater terrorist attack (2002), 112
Moscow Treaty: and arms control, 179; and Article VI of NPT, 37, 215; critique of, 215–16, 280; effect of, 36, 44–45, 58, 232, 280
MOX (mixed oxide) fuel, 24, 152
MPC&A. *See* Materials Protection, Control and Accounting (MPC&A) Program
MTCR (Missile Technology Control Regime), 119
Mubarek, Hosni, 67
Mujaheddin-e Khalq, 78
Multilateral Approaches to the Nuclear Fuel Cycle (MNA): and Article IV, 30–31; Export Group Report on, 301–15; and NPT Review Conference, 67; proposal for, 11–12, 89, 141, 186, 190, 194–205, 210; and reform, 4, 31–32. *See also* ElBaradei, Mohamed; International Atomic Energy Agency (IAEA)
multilateralism, 53–54, 58–59, 95, 98–99
multinational control of fuel cycle. *See* Multilateral Approaches to the Nuclear Fuel Cycle (MNA)

NASA (National Aeronautics and Space Administration), 123
Natanz enrichment facility, 77, 182, 185. *See also* Iran
National Defense University, 200

National Environmental Policy Act, 18
National Strategy to Combat Weapons of Mass Destruction, 42
National Technical Means (NTM), 59
NATO (North Atlantic Treaty Organization), 41
Netherlands, 48, 49
New Framework for the Utilization of Nuclear Energy in the 21st Century, 205
New Mexico, 163
Next Generation Nuclear Plant (NGNP), 161–62
93 + 2 program. *See* Program 93 + 2
Nixon, Richard M., 77, 100–101
nonproliferation: and ambiguity, 100–102; assessment of, 7; and cooperative security, 102–3; Eisenhower in perspective on, 98–99; and fuel cycle inducements, 6; future of, 39–51, 95–103; and IAEA and NPT, 3; and inevitability of spread, 99–100; intangible, 100; and international nuclear nonproliferation regime, 41; motives for proliferation and nonproliferation, 96–98; tangible, 100; toward universal nonproliferation and disarmament, 63–68
Nonproliferation and Preparatory Meeting (2003), 122
Nonproliferation Treaty (NPT): adoption of, 187; Article I, 38, 84, 118–19, 120, 125, 188, 199; Article II, 38, 43, 84, 119–21, 126, 188, 199; Article III, 38, 43, 120–21, 125, 199; Article V, 121; Article VI, 37, 44–46, 56, 65, 103, 120, 122, 215, 231; Article X, 46, 184, 188, 212; challenges to, 118–23, 179, 183, 212–13; creation of, 16, 53–54, 84, 195, 229; and disarmament, 244; and duality, 22; escape clause of, 46; Executive

Nonproliferation Treaty (NPT) (*continued*) Council or Board for, 61; extension of, 58; and FMCT, 224; and former-Soviet republics, 111; framework for, 3, 17; and IAEA safeguards, 45; "jury" for violations of, 61; new weapon designs under, 37; and non–nuclear-weapon states, 61; nonsignatories to, 40; and other initiatives, 46–47; parties under, 38; pressure on regime of, 7; reform of, 8, 41–42, 64–67, 173, 190, 195–205; Review Conference of 1990, 27; Review Conference of 2000, 31, 54, 56, 58, 65–66, 199; Review Conference of 2005, 58, 66, 67, 203; and safeguard agreements, 4–5, 107; status of, 210–11; support to, 43, 59–60; text of, 268–74; and transparency, 59. *See also* Article IV of NPT; Article VI of NPT; *specific countries*

North America, 24, 92, 229. *See also specific countries*

North Atlantic Treaty Organization (NATO), 41

Northeast Asia, 9, 91–94. *See also specific countries*

North Korea: and Article IV of NPT, 44; and IAEA, 40, 54, 67; inspection and verification in, 27–28, 29, 40, 71, 190; and international nuclear nonproliferation regime, 41; and Iran, 86; and Japan, 75, 92; and A.Q. Khan, 302; "megatons to megawatts" model in, 11; multilateral approach to, 59; noncompliance by, 65, 109, 229; and NPT, 17, 28, 33–34, 38, 40, 46, 84–86, 91, 108, 195, 212, 292; nuclear power in, 81, 141, 182; nuclear-weapon program in, 33–34, 38, 79–82, 91–93, 113, 120, 183, 211, 217, 230, 287, 288; physical deterrent in, 45; and Program 93 + 2, 27–28; as rogue state, 9, 79–80; September 2005 agreement with, 29, 79, 81; and terrorism, 50; and UN, 28, 86, 108, 195*n;* and U.S., 79, 81, 82, 92; violations by, 4, 8. *See also* Agreed Framework for North Korea

Norway, 49

Notification and Assistance Conventions, 25

NPR. *See* Nuclear Posture Review

NPT. *See* Nonproliferation Treaty

NRC. *See* Nuclear Regulatory Commission

NSG. *See* Nuclear Suppliers Group

NTM (national technical means), 59

nuclear energy. *See* nuclear power

Nuclear Exporters Committee. *See* Zangger Committee

Nuclear Posture Review (NPR), 37, 66, 212, 215–16, 232

nuclear power, 131–74; and Atoms-for-Peace legacy, 234–37; and developing countries, 61; development of, 5–6, 10, 24–25; disappointment of, 10, 18–19; future of, 6, 146–74; and leasing of reactors, 126; and legacy warheads, 181; legislation for, 5–6, 185–86; and plutonium, 208; and reactor construction and operation, 18, 34, 138, 147–55, 159–63, 170; safety and security of, 6, 19–20, 25–26, 139–40; siting and licensing of, 8, 18, 19, 159–60; and soft power, 10–11, 139–45; and transparency, 139, 140, 144–45. *See also* nuclear renaissance; spent fuel management; *specific countries*

nuclear reactors. *See* nuclear power; *specific types of reactors*

Nuclear Regulatory Commission (NRC), 19, 160

nuclear renaissance, xv, 6, 12, 25, 206–18, 235, 237, 238, 325
Nuclear Security Fund, 26
Nuclear Suppliers Group (NSG), 200, 201, 213–14; action on license applications by, 192; countries outside of, 125; and export control, 63, 179, 196, 200–201, 236; and new sources of supply, 86; reprocessing requirement for sales by, 200, 292; and second-tier suppliers distinguished, 117n; and transfer restrictions, 109
nuclear terrorism. *See* terrorism
nuclear testing. *See specific countries and treaties*
nuclear waste management. *See* waste management
Nuclear Weapon Convention, 59
nuclear weapon–free zones, 58, 65, 66–67, 189–90
nuclear-weapon programs. *See* warheads; *specific countries, agreements, initiatives, and treaties*
Nunn, Sam, 132
Nunn-Lugar Cooperative Threat Reduction, 132, 291. *See also* Cooperative Threat Reduction (CTR) Program
Nuremberg Principles, 59
nutrition, improvement of, 24
Nye, Joseph, 10, 137–40, 142–43

oil embargo, 235
Organization for Economic Cooperation and Development/Nuclear Energy Agency (OECD/NEA) report, 147
Organization for the Prohibition of Chemical Weapons (OPCW), 75, 87, 108, 303
Osirak, Iraq reactor attack (1981), 217

Pakistan: atomic testing by, 28, 211; and NPT, 4, 40, 76, 114, 183, 195, 221, 224, 280; nuclear power in, 84, 213; nuclear-weapon program in, 40, 66, 84, 91, 97–98, 99n, 101, 113, 115, 120, 178, 183, 217; as supplier, 120; supplier network in, 86; technology profusion and brain drain in, 211, 217; and terrorism, 115; U.S. policy toward, 178; and war risk, 220. *See also* Khan, Abdul Qadeer (A.Q.)
The Paradox of American Power: Why the World's Only Superpower Can't Go It Alone (Nye), 10, 137–40, 142–43
Partial Test Ban Treaty (PTBT) of 1963, 58
partitioning and transmutation (P&T), 152, 153, 170, 171
peaceful development of nuclear energy. *See* Article IV of NPT
pesticides, 24
Peterson, Per F., 10, 11, 156–64, 343
Pilat, Joseph, xv–xvi, 1–12, 206–18, 229–38, 343–44
Piqua, Ohio nuclear plant, 18
plutonium: and advanced nuclear arsenals, 282; and CIRUS, 178; and dangerous activities, 207; denatured, 208; disposal and storage of, 197, 209, 236; "economy," 197; and export control, 187; and fuel cycle evaluation, 197; and fuel-leasing, 181; in India, 196; and IPS, 197; in Iran, 34; in Korea, 28, 79; and MOX fuel, 332; and nuclear power, 208; and PUREX, 332, 334; recycling of, 151–52, 171, 305, 306, 317, 332; reprocessing of, 40, 171, 188, 190n; safeguards for, 106, 113; separated, 281, 321, 323, 326, 332, 334; separation technology for, 190n, 196, 198, 231, 320; and spent fuel, 144; and uranium extraction plus (UREX+), 190n; and weapons, 100, 113, 151, 171, 282

Plutonium Management and Disposition Agreement,, 58, 132, 133
Poland, 49
Poneman, Daniel, 11, 177–82, 344
Portugal, 49
Powell, Colin, 122
preemption, 60, 64, 80–82, 101, 211, 212, 215
Price-Anderson statute, 134
production tax credit, 172
Program 93 + 2, 27–28, 64
proliferation: and Atoms-for-Peace model, 33–38; and current proliferation predicament, 83–90; and prevention of nuclear terrorism, 104–16; and prospects for nonproliferation and arms control, 95–103; and rogue states, 71–82; and second-tier suppliers, 117–27; spread of, 4; toward integrative approach to nuclear terrorism, 104–10. *See also* proliferation resistance
"Proliferation Chernobyl," 180
proliferation resistance, 11, 121, 151, 155, 173, 207–10, 223, 283
Proliferation Security Initiative (PSI): and cooperative security regime, 102; described, 49; and existing law, 60; role of, 8, 90, 107, 191, 211; as supply-side measure, 125; text of Statement of Interdiction Principles, 289–98; and U.S. policy, 216
prudency hearings, 19
public hearings, 18
Pugwash Council, 233
PUREX, 332, 334
Putin, Vladimir, 106, 114

Quinlan, Michael, 101

Rabi, Isador, 100
Rademaker, Stephen G., 8, 33–38, 344

Radioactive Source Initiative, 47–48
radiotherapy, 24
RAND Corporation, 16
Rauf, Tariq, 11–12, 194–205, 344–45
reactors. *See* nuclear power
Reagan, Ronald, 98
Reduced Enrichment for Test Research and Test Reactors (RERTR), 299
reduction of nuclear weapons, 36. *See also* Moscow Treaty
regime change, 9, 74–76, 78, 79–80, 81, 230
Regional Nuclear Fuel Cycle Centers (RFCC) study, 196–97
Reiss, Mitchell B., 8, 39–51, 345
Resolution 687 (UN Security Council), 41
Resolution 1540 (UN Security Council), 107, 125, 188, 214–15
Review Conferences of NPT. *See* Nonproliferation Treaty (NPT)
RFCC (Regional Nuclear Fuel Cycle Centers) study, 196–97
Rice, Condoleezza, 74
rogue states, 9, 40, 51, 71–82, 295
Rumsfeld, Donald, 74, 79
Russia: and Article IV of NPT, 199; disposal of fissile material from, 44, 58, 106, 132–33, 181, 216, 234; and G-8, 48; highly enriched uranium minimization in, 47, 106, 131–32, 180; and IAEA, 213; and Iran, 34, 90, 182; and nonproliferation, 83, 106, 218; and North Korea, 75, 92; and NSG, 213; nuclear weapons in, 115, 180; and Soviet Union and former Soviet Union, 16, 17, 20; and terrorist threat, 106, 114, 115; and Trilateral Initiative, 56; and U.S., 36, 114, 115, 232; warheads in, 115, 180; and WMDs, 184. *See also* Soviet Union and former Soviet Union; *specific agreements, initiatives, and treaties*

Russian Research Reactor Fuel Return, 298–99

Scheinman, Lawrence, 11, 21, 183–93, 345
Schlesinger, James, 7–8, 15–20, 345–46
Scomi Precision Engineering, 124
Sea Island Summit, 49, 109
second coming of nuclear power. *See* nuclear renaissance
Second Gulf War. *See* Iraq
second-tier suppliers, 9, 10, 117–27
September 11 terrorist attacks: IAEA response to, 26; and proliferation, 211; and risk of nuclear terrorism, 9–10, 54, 104, 112, 178, 233–34; and rogue states, 74. *See also* terrorism
Shaker, Mohamed I., 8, 63–68, 346
Shea, Thomas E., 11, 12, 219–28, 346
Shinrikyo, Aum, 40
Simpson, Fiona, 11–12, 194–205, 347
SIT. *See* sterile insect technique, 23–24
sleeping sickness, 24
Smith, Gerard, 100
Snow, C.P., 16–17
soft power, 10–11, 139–45
Sokolski, Henry, 101
SORT (U.S.-Russian Treaty on Strategic Offensive Reductions). *See* Moscow Treaty
South Africa, 29, 30*n*, 39, 83, 210
South America, 39
South Asia, 9, 45, 97, 211, 216, 217, 230. *See also specific countries*
South Korea, 75, 80, 92, 97, 168, 169
sovereignty. *See* state sovereignty
Soviet Union and former Soviet Union: atomic testing by, 15; and Atoms-for-Peace proposal, 239–46; break up of, 39, 111, 210, 211, 232; and cooperation with U.S., 16, 17, 20; employment of scientists in, 108; and highly enriched uranium minimization, 47; and mutual deterrence, 56; and NPT, 111; nuclear power in, 180; nuclear weapons in, 5, 39, 131, 181, 234; and spread of technology, 100; technology profusion and brain drain in, 211. *See also* Russia
Spain, 49
Special Committee on Safeguards and Verification (IAEA), 186
spent fuel management: and advanced fuel cycle, 152; and closed fuel cycle, 154; and fuel leasing, 180–81; and GNEP, 210; of highly enriched uranium, 106; and IAEA, 26, 197; and Iran, 183; and multilateral approaches to nuclear fuel cycle, 31, 62, 65, 145, 196, 198, 202, 203–4, 236, 283; and nuclear-waste policy, 135, 141, 144, 312–13; and plutonium, 40, 144, 151–52, 282; and recycling, 141; and reprocessing waste volume, 152–53, 163; and Russia, 181, 182; standard for, 209; storage options for, 141, 172. *See also* U.S.-Russia Highly Enriched Uranium (HEU) Purchase Agreement; Yucca Mountain project
Stade, German nuclear power plant, 138
Stassen, Howard, 100
Statement of Interdiction Principles of PSI, 49, 275–84
State of the Union Address (1993), 156
state sovereignty, 27, 64, 87, 120*n*, 141, 202, 274, 314
sterile insect technique (SIT), 23–24
Stockholm Peace Research Institute, 61
Strategic Arms Reduction Treaty (START II), 58
Strategic Offensive Reductions Treaty (SORT) of 2002. *See* Moscow Treaty
strategic warheads. *See* warheads
Straw, Jack, 200

suppliers, 86, 196. *See also* first-tier suppliers; Khan, Abdul Qadeer (A.Q.); second-tier suppliers
supreme national interests, 46, 227
Suzuki, Atsuyuki, 10–11, 137–45, 347
Sweden, 62, 97
Switzerland, 49
Syria, 50
Szilard, Leo, 16

Taiwan, 92, 97, 158, 169
take-back agreements, 190, 307–8, 315. *See also* fuel leasing
Tehran, 74, 77–78
"10 plus 10 over 10" initiative, 58
terrorism: and Atoms-for-Peace policies, 6, 7, 9, 17, 238; and CNEP, 6; and economic depravation, 61, 136; and FMCT, 12, 220–25, 227; IAEA response to, 8, 31, 184, 213; integrative approach to, 104–10; and Moscow Theater terrorist attack (2002), 112; and non-state actors, 17; and NPT, 92; and nuclear power, 206; prevention of, 9–10, 104–16, 138, 214, 231, 233–34, 321; state sponsors of, 50, 72, 74, 76; and technology, 236–37; threat of, xiii, xv, 4–5, 10, 45–46, 50, 91, 211, 219, 230; and warheads, 125. *See also* September 11 terrorist attacks; weapons of mass destruction (WMDs)
Texas A&M University, 157
Thailand, 24, 62
Three Mile Island power station accident, 19, 149, 158
Tokyo Electric Power Company, 140
"Toward a Safer World" (ElBaradei *Economist* article), 279–84. *See also* ElBaradei, Mohamed
transparency: and Atoms-for-Peace proposal, 54; and FMCT, 223, 228; importance of, 190, 192; and Iran, 30; and Libya, 76; and multilateral approaches, 197, 201; and NPT conferences, 59; and processing of weapon-usable material, 282; and use of nuclear power, 139, 140, 144–45; on warhead numbers, 55
transportation sector, 150–51
Treaty on the Nonproliferation of Nuclear Weapons. *See* Nonproliferation Treaty (NPT)
Trilateral Initiative, 56, 222*n*
Turner, Ted, 116

Ukraine, 39, 97, 111
U.N. Secretary General's High Level Panel on Threats, Challenges and Change, 214
United Kingdom, 15, 34, 49, 75, 125
United Nations: and Atoms-for-Peace program, 2, 5; George W. Bush at, 50; Charter of, 60; Conference on Disarmament, 67–68; Department of Disarmament Affairs, 61; Eisenhower and disarmament dialogue of, 56–60; and fissile material ban, 220, 222; fluctuations in support for, 53; General Assembly actions, 52, 56, 59; and IAEA, 226; Millennium Development Goals, 61; Monitoring, Verification, and Inspection Commission (UNMOVIC), 211; and multilateralism, 98; and NPT, 61; Special Session on Disarmament, 67–68; and UNCPIC-PUNE, 197. *See also* United Nations Security Council (UNSC)
United Nations Security Council (UNSC): challenges for, 214–15; conferences of, 66–67; disarmament dialogue of, 57; enforcement by, 126, 179, 189, 212, 226; and IAEA, 27, 213; and Iran, 35, 59, 77–78, 86, 108,

213, 214; and Iraq, 27, 29, 108; and nonproliferation regime, 41, 91, 126, 214–15; and North Korea, 28, 86, 108, 195n; and preemption, 60; and WMDs, 191, 214–15. *See also specific resolutions*
United Nations Special Commission on Iraq (UNSCOM), 211
United States: and AP, 107, 292; arsenal reduction by, 36, 40, 44–45, 114, 132, 232; and Article IV of NPT, 36, 44–45, 122, 190; chemical and biological weapons in, 45; and CIRUS reactor, 178; and cooperation with Soviet Union, 16, 17, 20; and disarmament initiatives, 57; disease eradication in, 24; and employment of former weapon scientists, 108; and FMCT, 58, 221; fuel disposal in, 144; and G-8, 47–48; and highly enriched uranium minimization, 47, 180; and IAEA, 42, 192; impact of polices of, 215–16; and India, 178; and international nuclear nonproliferation regime, 41, 83, 101, 105–9; and Iran, 34, 72–75, 82; and Libya, 75–76; and management of regime problems, 238; and multilateralism, 98, 99–100; and nonproliferation initiatives, 47–50, 125, 178, 236; and North Korea, 79, 81, 82, 92; and NPR, 232; and nuclear fuel leasing, 181; nuclear power in, 5–6, 10, 20, 136, 149, 156, 157, 160, 163, 169, 170, 235; nuclear weapons in, 36–38, 44–45, 123; and Pakistan, 40, 178; and preemption, 101, 212, 215; rogue state policy of, 72–74; role of, xvi, 6, 10; and Russia, 36, 114, 115, 232; and soft power, 10–11, 139–45; and terrorist threat, 106–7, 114, 115, 234; and Trilateral Initiative, 56. *See also* Yucca Mountain project; *specific agreements, initiatives, and treaties*
University of California at Berkeley, 157
University of Illinois at Urbana–Champaign, 157
University of Michigan, 157
UNMOVIC (United Nations Monitoring, Verification, and Inspection Commission), 211
UNSC. *See* United Nations Security Council
UREX+ (uranium extraction plus), 190n, 321, 334
U.S. Atomic Energy Commission (AEC), 3, 18, 100
U.S. Department of Defense Nuclear Posture Review. *See* Nuclear Posture Review (NPR)
U.S. Department of Energy, 48
U.S. Foreign Research Reactor Spent Fuel Return, 312
U.S.-Indian Civil Nuclear Cooperation Initiative of 2005, 213–14, 231
U.S. National Academy of Sciences, 141–42
U.S.-Russia Highly Enriched Uranium (HEU) Purchase Agreement, 11, 132, 180, 296, 298
U.S. Senate Energy and Natural Resources Committee, 133
Uzbekistan, 106

verification: and Additional Protocol, 64, 310; ancillary arrangements for, 189; and arms control goals, 5; and Atomic Energy Act of 1954, 6; evasion of, 35, 71; under FMCT, 222–27; IAEA role in, 3–4, 23, 26–31, 64, 66, 71, 87, 108–9, 184–87, 196, 202, 256, 292, 310; limitations of, 35, 87–88; and multinational ownership of

verification (*continued*)
  fuel cycle, 89; by non–nuclear weapon states, 54; and NPT, 120, 185–86, 270; and nuclear power, 6; as policy under Atoms for Peace, 2, 59, 71, 192; proposal for, 231; and strengthening nonproliferation, 202; technology for, 59, 202. *See also specific countries*
Versailles, Treaty of, 35
virtual weapon capability, 4, 7, 41, 212, 217

Waller, David B., 8, 21–32, 347
warheads: in advanced nuclear arsenals, 282; dismantling, 36, 45; inspection and monitoring of, 122*n;* new class of, 122, 123; non-operational, 280; and nuclear power, 181; numbers of, 55, 280; reduction of, 45, 232; Russian, 115, 180; strategic, 36, 45, 66; and terrorists, 125. *See also* Moscow Treaty
Waste Isolation Power Plant, 163
waste management, 141–42, 152, 163–64, 170–71, 172. *See also* spent fuel management
weapons of mass destruction (WMDs): acquisition of, 40, 50, 112, 114, 184; conference on, 67–68; countermeasures to, 35, 42, 57–58, 60, 104, 191, 214–15, 285–93, 310–11; criminalization of, 61; defined, 119*n;* growing threat of, 41, 50, 51, 189; International Commission on, 62; and international nuclear nonproliferation regime, 41; in Iraq, 199*n,* 287; and Libya, 296; and nonproliferation talks, 230; and NPT philosophy, 33; and prevention of nuclear terrorism, 105, 107, 108, 112, 114; proliferation of, 119, 189; and rogue states, 72; and treaty compliance, 45; and UN, 67; zone free of, 66–67. *See also* Biological and Toxin Weapons Convention (BWC); Chemical Weapons Convention (CWC); Proliferation Security Initiative (PSI)
weapon programs. *See* warheads; *specific countries, agreements, initiatives, and treaties*
Weimar government, 35
whistleblowing, 59
WMDs. *See* weapons of mass destruction
Wohlstetter, Albert, 16
Woodrow Wilson International Center for Scholars, 7
World Association of Nuclear Operators (WANO), 19–20

Yucca Mountain project, 141, 163–64, 172, 226, 320, 322–23

Zangger Committee, 117, 179, 196, 201
Zanzibar, 24, 121